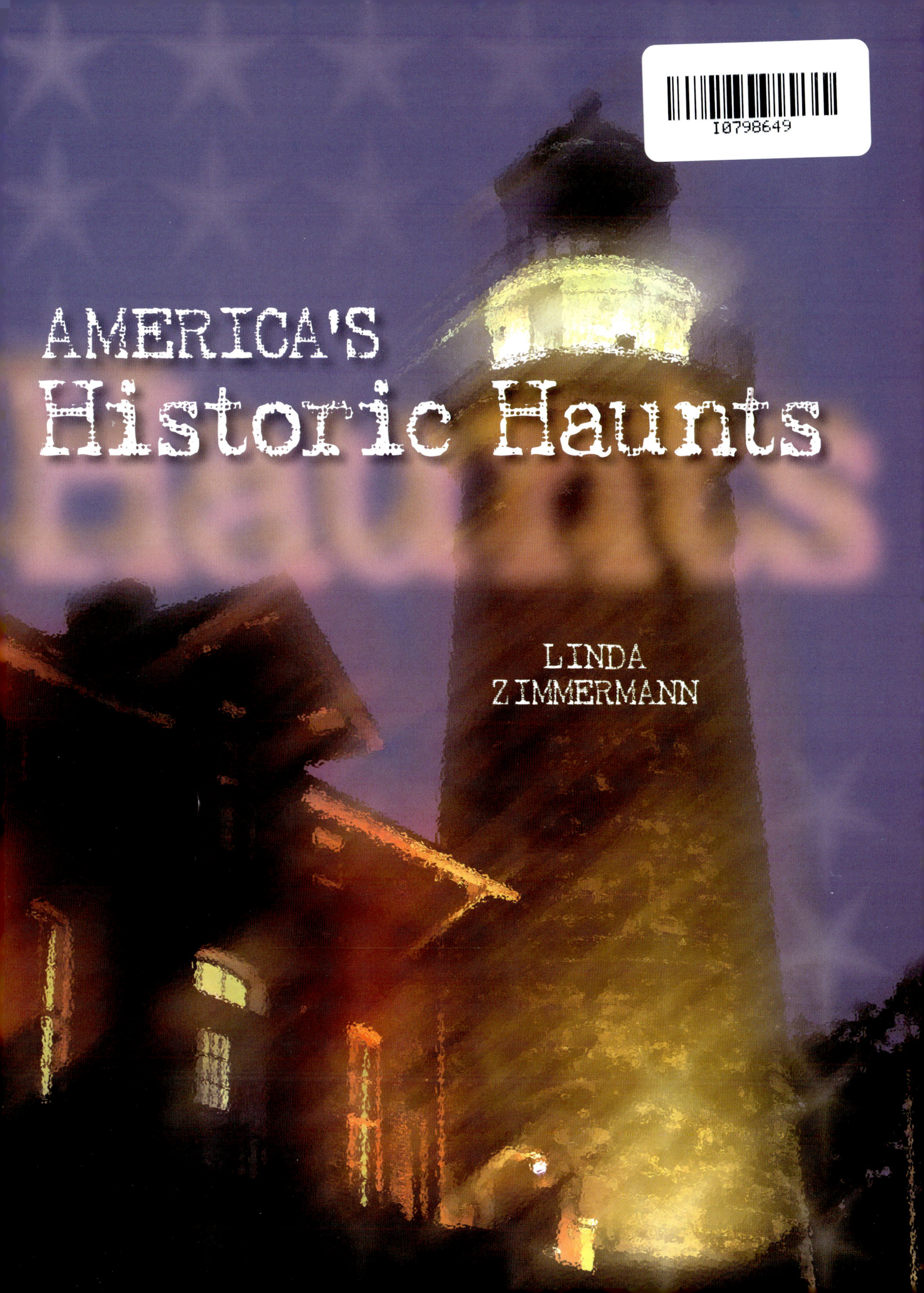

# AMERICA'S Historic Haunts

LINDA ZIMMERMANN

*Text and photos by author unless otherwise noted in courtesy lines*



*Visitor Information is subject to change, so it is best to call ahead or research prior to visiting sites.*

Library of Congress Control Number: 2011921545



Designed by Danielle D. Farmer
Cover Design by Bruce Waters
Type set in Batik Regular/Arial

ISBN: 978-0-7643-3700-0

Printed in China

Schiffer Books are available at special discounts for bulk purchases for sales promotions or premiums. Special editions, including personalized covers, corporate imprints, and excerpts can be created in large quantities for special needs. For more information contact the publisher:

Published by Schiffer Publishing Ltd.
4880 Lower Valley Road
Atglen, PA 19310
Phone: (610) 593-1777; Fax: (610) 593-2002
E-mail: Info@schifferbooks.com

For the largest selection of fine reference books on this and related subjects, please visit our website at
**www.schifferbooks.com**

We are always looking for people to write books on new and related subjects. If you have an idea for a book please contact us at the above address.

This book may be purchased from the publisher.
Include $5.00 for shipping.
Please try your bookstore first.
You may write for a free catalog.

In Europe, Schiffer books are distributed by
Bushwood Books
6 Marksbury Ave.
Kew Gardens
Surrey TW9 4JF England
Phone: 44 (0) 20 8392-8585; Fax: 44 (0) 20 8392-9876
E-mail: info@bushwoodbooks.co.uk
Website: www.bushwoodbooks.co.uk

# Dedication

In Loving Memory of
Katrina Knapp Pitman
A woman who was all heart
1954-2010

# Contents

# Acknowledgments

Many thanks to all the wonderful people across the country who shared their knowledge and experiences. As for Barbara Roth Bleitzhofer, who made countless phone calls, kept detailed records and notes, and was a tireless cheerleader for this project, what can I say? You're the best, Barb! And special thanks to my editor, Dinah Roseberry, who asked that fateful question, "Have you thought about writing a national tour book?"

# Introduction

Starting a new book project is always an adventure, for better or for worse. There's the excitement of discovering new places, people, and stories, but there's also an unsettling dose of what-have-I-gotten-myself-into? This project has provided plenty of both kinds of experiences, but in the end, it's always worth the ride when you get to hold that new book in your hand.

I was particularly excited about this book as it is my first to have a national scope. I wondered how different ghost stories would be across the country, but found that regardless of whether it was a remote village in Alaska, an ancient Native American settlement in the southwest, an old Spanish town in Florida, or a bustling metropolitan area in the northeast, the settings may change, but the characters and plots remain the same. To put it simply, human nature is human nature, and ghosts are ghosts, no matter where you are.

The same type of passion, violence, or strong emotions and attachments that keeps the spirit of the proprietor of a western saloon haunting his place of business that he built and fought for with his own sweat and blood, is the exact same type of thing that keeps the spirit of the young girl looking out the window of her southern mansion, still awaiting the return of her fiancé from the war.

This inability to "let go" of whatever set of cards life has dealt you is what keeps those 1940s murder victims in that former hotel in St. Augustine, the 1860s fallen soldiers on the fields of Gettysburg and Cold Harbor, as well as the countless souls from the 1600s to the twenty-first century who still inhabit their former homes in all fifty states, because they simply can't accept that this life is over and they need to move on.

Another constant in the haunted realm is something I have been saying for many years: Death does not improve one's personality! If you were mean-spirited in life, you will be a mean spirit after death—and heaven help the homeowner that "inherits" you. The kind-hearted spirit may still be unnerving as they walk about or make an occasional appearance, but at least they mean no harm.

Which all leads to the inescapable conclusions that are reached through extensive research into the paranormal world: How you live your life dictates how you will exist in death—and make no mistake, as these stories prove, there is much more to come after you've taken your last breath!

Starting a new phase in life, or death, is always an adventure, for better or for worse. There's the excitement of discovering new places and people, but there's also an unsettling dose of what-have-I-gotten-myself-into? But in the end, it's always worth the ride when you get to step back, examine what you've done, and be satisfied that you did the best with the cards you were dealt.

The following stories may send a shiver up your spine or bring a tear to your eye, or they may even make you laugh at the endless follies of man. Whatever your reaction, I hope that they inspire you to get out and experience the historic haunted treasures of this great, vast country.

~ Linda Zimmermann ~

# Alabama

OLD CAHAWBA

USS ALABAMA

ST. JAMES HOTEL

The Chrocheron Mansion in decay.

# Old Cahawba

There are ghost towns where nature has reclaimed abandoned buildings. Then there are ghost towns where nature may have reclaimed the buildings, but not the souls of the people who lived and died there.

Native Americans called this land home for at least 4,000 years before the Europeans arrived. The earliest European to the area may have been Spanish explorer Hernando de Soto in 1540. In 1819, the new state of Alabama needed a capital and Cahawba was chosen. This was not a popular choice amongst the rich and powerful, and claiming the flood-prone region had an unhealthy atmosphere, they were able to use their influence to move the capital to Tuscaloosa in 1826. Within weeks of the move, Cahawba was all but abandoned.

All that's left of the columns of the mansion. *Courtesy of Old Cahawba.*

However, this was a town that would die hard, and Cahawba was revitalized by commerce, becoming a busy port for transporting cotton down the Alabama River to Mobile. With the arrival of the train in 1859, things were really looking up and the town enjoyed a building boom. Unfortunately, booms do have a habit of going bust.

During the Civil War, the Confederate government ordered the removal of the train tracks to be used on a military line. A cotton warehouse in the center of town was transformed into Castle Morgan, a prison that held 3,000 Union soldiers. (After surviving the horrors of prison, many of these soldiers died tragically after their release in the explosion of the riverboat *Sultana*.) The town suffered a major flood in 1865, adding a final insult to all the injury. In 1866, the county seat was moved from Cahawba to Selma and much of the population soon followed. By the mid-1870s, even many of the homes were gone, having been taken apart and moved to other towns.

The old town had one gasp left, when former slaves created a new community, but even that wasn't to last. By 1900 almost all of the buildings had either been moved, burned, or had succumbed to neglect. The abandoned former state capital had played its last card, and Cahawba was officially unincorporated in 1989.

Today, the town may be mostly gone, but certainly not forgotten. The Old Cahawba Archaeological Park maintains the cemeteries and the few remaining buildings, as well as the memories. They are also, by default, the caretakers of the ghostly legends of this true ghost town. Stories date back over a century, and the number of encounters and experiences grows every year.

## The Pegues' House

The first recorded sighting was in 1862, when a couple walking in the gardens behind Colonel Pegues' house encountered a white ball of light that moved as though it had some intelligent direction—going left when they went left, right when they moved right. Finally summoning the courage to confront this mysterious light, the man tried to grab it, but it simply vanished. Many others have seen what came to be called Pegues' Ghost.

In contrast to this ethereal light, there were numerous encounters with a very real and solid figure. A young boy used to play in the ruins and by the cemetery and river, and a concerned caretaker named Gat urged him to be very careful. He saw Gat just about every day and never thought there was anything strange about him. It wasn't until many years later that he discovered that Gat had died long before he was even born!

On a regular basis, visitors report to staff that they've heard children playing in the cemetery near closing time, and they are concerned that they would get locked in for the night. No children have ever been found. Many other voices have been heard and recorded in the cemeteries. In particular, several grounds keepers have quit after hearing a deep male voice ask, "Who...are...you?"

Old Cahawba offers a very unique opportunity—an expansive site steeped in history and hauntings along its spooky abandoned streets hanging with moss, in the ruins of its buildings, in its cemeteries, and its buildings. It is a ghost town in every sense of the word, and the sites, sounds, and feelings will challenge all six of your senses.

## Recommendations

**Old Cahawba is closed at night, except for one night a year in October when you can take part in a group ghost hunt. Any other time of the year you are free to roam the grounds from 9am – 5pm. Be sure to keep your audio recorders going as voices can be heard any time of day. Be sure to check out the Bell grave, where a father and son killed in a shoot-out in town are buried. No criminal charges were ever filed in their deaths, and Bell's widow added an inscription to the monument about the murders. St. Luke's Church is undergoing restoration, and old slave quarters are still standing. Guided tours help bring this town back to life with stories of the people and events.**

## Visitor Information

**Old Cahawba Archaeological Park**
**9518 Cahaba Road**
**Orrville, AL 36767**
**(334) 872-8058**
**www.cahawba.com**

**Hours:**
**The park is open daily from 9am – 5pm, the visitors center from Noon – 5pm.**

**Admission:**
**Adults $5, Seniors $4, Children 7-18 $3, Children 6 and under Free, Families $12, Grounds and Gardens Only Free.**

**Directions:**
**From their website—The site of Old Cahawba lies at the confluence of the Alabama and Cahaba Rivers. From downtown Selma, take Highway 22 west 8.6 miles. Turn onto Country Road 9 and follow this quiet country road another 5 miles to Cahawba.**

## The Bottom Line

**The History:** Cahawba is the first state capital of Alabama, 1820-1826, inhabited and abandoned three times. Site of a Civil War prison.

**The Haunting:** A white ball of light was first seen in 1862, a former caretaker didn't let death stop him from doing his job, and many voices are heard and recorded, especially in the cemeteries.

The U.S.S. *Alabama* in 1942.

# USS Alabama

The battleship *Alabama*, affectionately called the "*Mighty A*" by her crew, was launched and commissioned in 1942 and was to see service on both sides of the globe during WWII. She began her distinguished career on the "Murmansk Run," guarding convoys bringing vital supplies from England through the North Sea to Russia. The Alabama was transferred from the icy waters of the north to the tropics in August 1943. As part of the Pacific fleet, her guns provided support for amphibious assaults. At the Battle of the Philippine Sea, it was the *Alabama's* radar that was able to detect enemy bombers at a distance of 190 miles, which was unprecedented at the time. The advanced warning helped the U.S. forces to destroy over 400 Japanese planes.

Despite the many months of combat, the ship was never damaged and no one was killed from enemy fire, earning the *Alabama* the additional nickname of the "*Lucky A.*" Unfortunately, not everyone was so lucky, however, as two men died during her construction, and there was a tragic friendly-fire incident. During enemy air attacks in the Mariana Islands, *Alabama's* gun mount No. 9 accidentally fired into gun mount No. 5. There were supposed to be precautions in place to prevent such accidents, and the bloody result of the mistake was that five men were literally blown to bits, and eleven others were wounded.

As with so many of the country's mighty fighting ships, the *Alabama* was decommissioned after the war and was "mothballed" in Bremerton, Washington. The citizens of Alabama didn't want to see their namesake rot away or be cut up for scrap, so they raised almost $1 million to bring her home and have her restored. Almost $100,000 of those donations came from school children giving their nickels and dimes. In 1964, the *Lucky A* was towed from Seattle to Mobile Bay, and in January of 1965 she was opened to the public as a museum.

Life should have been peaceful and quiet for the old battleship, but in an ironic twist of fate, the ship that had literally dodged so many bullets was damaged by Hurricane Katrina in 2005. Aircraft on exhibit were destroyed, the ship listed eight degrees to port, and the total damage exceeded four million dollars. It seems that Mother Nature's wrath accomplished what the Japanese fleet and their aircraft could not!

Today, the *Alabama*, which was fully repaired, welcomes visitors from all walks of life by day, and hosts youth groups who stay overnight. During all of these decades with all of these visitors and staff, has anyone ever encountered anything unusual anything that has gone bump in the night? According to a park official, no one has ever seen or heard anything out of the ordinary. Not one member of the staff, none of the

13 million visitors, which includes over 160,000 people who have spent the night. Never. Ever.

That's the official stance, but the unofficial story is quite different. Footsteps, apparitions of sailors, voices, doors opening and closing on their own, intense feelings of being watched, and even physical contact have all been reported by people who only came to see a battleship, and found there was much more to experience.

Where does the truth lie? Is the *Lucky A* still lucky in that not a single wandering spirit is on board, or do old sailors make themselves known to a precious few who are reluctant to voice their experiences for fear of ridicule? The only way to know for sure is to keep an open mind, step aboard the USS *Alabama,* and discover the truth for yourself.

## The Bottom Line

**The History:** This is a World War II battleship that saw thirty-seven months of active service in the North Sea and the Pacific. The ship never sustained any damage or casualties from enemy fire, but there was a tragic friendly-fire incident, and damage from Hurricane Katrina.

**The Haunting:** The official stance is that there isn't any haunted activity, but visitors have reported seeing apparitions, hearing all sorts of inexplicable sounds, feeling an intense presence, and at least one instance of physical contact.

## Recommendations

**In addition to the battleship *Alabama*, the park also has the submarine *Drum*, tanks, artillery, and aircraft from World War II to Iraqi Freedom. Look for the bunk of Major League Baseball Hall of Famer Bob Feller who served on the *Alabama* during World War II. Take a "flight" in the simulator. Tours are self-guided so you go at your own pace, but allow about two hours to see both ships and the Aircraft Pavilion. A bit of trivia: the *Alabama* was used for most of the battleship scenes in Steven Seagal's 1992 film *Under Siege*.**

## Visitor Information

**Battleship Memorial Park**
2703 Battleship Parkway (Highway 90/98)
**Mobile, AL 36602**
**(251) 433-2703**
**www.ussalabama.com**

**Hours:**
**Open everyday except Christmas Day**
**Opens 8am, Closes 4pm October-March, 6pm April-September**

**Admission:**
**Age 12 and up: $12, Ages 6-11: $6, under age 6: Free; $2 Park Use, Fee per vehicle $25, Fee for Semi-Trucks (includes one admission)**

**Directions:**
**In Mobile take Interstate 10 headed west, and get off at either Exit 27 or 30.**

# St. James Hotel

A dock on the Alabama River was bringing businessmen and visitors to Selma, and in 1837, the Brantly Hotel was built to accommodate them. All manner of people—famous and infamous—passed through its doors, and for a time the place was run by a rather unique individual.

The hotel's owner inherited a slave, Benjamin Turner, who was educated and had shown a talent for management. Turner was made manager of the Brantly, and was given a share of the profits. Apparently, Turner's skills went beyond mere hotel management, and in 1871, he became the first African-American to serve in the U.S. Congress.

During the Civil War, Selma saw its share of devastation, with over two-thirds of the town being burned to the ground. The only reason the hotel escaped the torch was because Union troops were occupying it. As a result, it is the only surviving antebellum hotel in Selma.

The post-war years saw a return to prosperity as the town was rebuilt. In 1871, the hotel was renamed the St. James, and it eventually became a long-term residence. Two of those residents in the 1880s are believed to have been outlaws Frank and Jesse James. Jesse's mistress, Lucinda, was also said to live there, and her portrait hangs in the hotel today.

Unfortunately, by the early 1890s the hotel was showing its age and couldn't compete with newer places in town. Around 1892, the St. James closed its doors. For a time the guest rooms served as offices, and the first floor was converted to a feed store, then a tire recapping factory. Eventually, the rear wings were demolished and then the building was abandoned all together. For almost a century the former grand hotel stood empty and appeared to be destined for the wrecking ball.

Then in 1997, a combination of public and private funding saved the structure and it was restored to its former glory. Guests can once again experience the charm and hospitality of this Selma landmark, and imagine what the past was like back in the days of hoop-skirted southern belles and dangerous outlaws. But perhaps you don't need all that much imagination—perhaps the past is still very much alive in the old hotel?

Witnesses have seen a man dressed like a cowboy from the 1880s walking the halls. He has also been seen in rooms 214, 314, and 315, as well as sitting at a table to the left of the bar. It is believed that this is the spirit of none other than Jesse James, but why would James return to the hotel? Well, if you saw the beautiful Lucinda's portrait, and considered the fact that her tall, lavender-scented spirit has also been seen in the hotel, it makes a lot more sense. If you have a good thing going, why let something trivial like death get in the way!

In addition to Jesse and Lucinda, a black dog has been seen and heard throughout the hotel and in the courtyard. Again, this dog has been connected to Jesse James, so it seems he is doing quite well in the other world, where he has his faithful dog, his lovely girlfriend, and very comfortable accommodations!

Anyone interested in the paranormal would be thrilled to know that this hotel may have these three ghosts, but psychics and investigators feel there could be many, many more. The courtyard could be a gathering spot for souls from the 1800s who still appear to be going about their business, unaware that time, and life, have passed them by. Strange sounds are heard throughout the original sections of the hotel, objects move, and other figures have been seen in both the rooms and public areas.

Just remember, if you do spend the night at the historic St. James Hotel and a lovely lavender-scented apparition manifests in your room, don't get too friendly with her. She might just tell her boyfriend...

*Courtesy of the St. James Hotel.*

## The Bottom Line

**The History:** Built in 1837, it is the only surviving antebellum hotel in Selma as it escaped being burned during the Civil War because Union troops were occupying it. Jesse and Frank James were said to have been guests here. Saved from the wrecking ball and restored in 1997.

**The Haunting:** Jesse James is thought to be the cowboy that has been seen on numerous occasions. His girlfriend and dog are also thought to be behind the other apparitions.

## Recommendations

**Take a close look at the beautiful and ornate iron railings which are original. The hotel has a fine view of the river and the Edmund Pettus Bridge, which is famous for the civil rights march from Selma to Montgomery in 1965. For your best chance at a paranormal experience, request room 214, 314, or 315.**

## Visitor Information

**St. James Hotel**
**1200 Water Avenue**
**Selma, AL, 36701**
**(334) 872-3234**
**Toll-free reservations (800) 678-8946**
**www.historichotels.org/hotel/St_James_Hotel_Selma**

**Directions:**
**From Montgomery: Take I-65 South to the Selma/Highway 80 exit. Travel west on Highway 80 for 45 miles, cross the Edmund Pettus Bridge.**

# Alaska

GAKONA LODGE & TRADING POST

EKLUTNA VILLAGE HISTORICAL PARK

HISTORIC ANCHORAGE HOTEL

*Courtesy of Gakona Lodge.*

# Gakona Lodge and Trading Post

When roadhouses were being established in Alaska in the early 1900s, they were placed about every 20 miles, as it was considered to be a reasonable distance for a person to travel in one day—but we aren't talking about cars here, strictly by foot or horse. Apparently, Alaskan living requires different standards of "reasonable!"

When Jim Doyle built his roadhouse in 1904 in Gakona, there wasn't even a bridge, so travelers had to cross the river by boat. However, this location was selected as it was at the junction of two trails—the Valdez-Eagle and Valdez-Fairbanks. Weary travelers to the roadhouse could get a bed, a hot meal, stock up on supplies, send telegrams, and get work done at the blacksmith, before heading back into the wilderness between Gakona and the next roadhouse.

In 1910, Doyle's Roadhouse became the primary stop for the Orr Stage Company. In 1912, Doyle sold the property, and subsequent owners included a mining company. In 1929, the Alaska Road Commission widened the Eagle Trail, so miners had an easier route to gold mines to the east.

The owner at that time was Arne Sundt, and he capitalized on the opportunity by building the larger Gakona Lodge, which is the one still in operation today. The expanded facility included nine private rooms, a bunkhouse (attic), two bathrooms, a general store, a post office, a wagon repair shop, two cabins, and several other buildings.

The last period of construction came during WWII, when the Army Corps of Engineers added a garage, which was later turned into a store. In 1942, they also built a shower house, which was eventually converted into the present-day Trapper's Den Tavern. Many famous figures in Alaskan history stayed at the lodge, and all of the buildings on the property have been placed on the National Register of Historic Sites, including the original 1904 roadhouse which is still standing, but no longer in use.

Gakona Lodge and Trading Post is currently owned (2011) by Valori and Greg Marshall, and they strive to maintain the character of the old roadhouse, while still providing modern amenities, such as WiFi. Visitors come for the spectacular scenery, river rafting, and salmon and trout fishing, but occasionally get something extra—an encounter with the resident ghost.

While this gentleman spirit seems to prefer room #5 and the lobby, his presence and pipe smoke have been experienced throughout the lodge. And far from being menacing, this ghost enjoys playing tricks, such as locking doors from the inside. Other activity includes footsteps, voices, doors opening and closing, and electronic devices turning themselves on. While the spirit has not been positively identified, some speculate that it's the congenial spirit of John Paulsen, a former customer and business partner.

Could any other former residents, miners, or travelers be behind some of the activity here, or perhaps a few wandering spirits of the Ahtna Indians who inhabited this area for many thousands of years? If you are up for a true Alaskan adventure, journey to the Gakona Lodge to explore both the natural and supernatural worlds and find out for yourself.

Note: If the name Gakona rings a bell, it may be due to the controversial HAARP project, the High-frequency Active Auroral Research Program that the government has established here. The official stance is that this twenty-three-acre facility with its massive array of antennae is for harmless atmospheric research, but conspiracy theorists have placed it on something of a "Top 10 Most Wanted" list. All manner of sinister applications have been attributed to HAARP including a death ray, a means of changing the weather, producing earthquakes, and causing a tear in the fabric of space. How can you beat a town with history, ghost stories, and one of the world's top conspiracy theories? Go to www.haarp.alaska.edu/ for more information and web cams of the site.

## The Bottom Line

**The History:** One of the only remaining original roadhouses in Alaska, first built in 1904.

**The Haunting:** At least one mischievous spirit makes his presence known in the lodge in a variety of ways, most often in room #5 and the lobby.

## Recommendation

If you want to experience Alaska beyond the cities and cruise ship stops, this is an excellent place to stay. Ask for room #5 for the best chance to encounter the resident ghost. Allow plenty of time to enjoy the rivers, parks, wildlife, and scenery. (And if you are curious about HAARP and want to knock on their gate and ask to see your tax dollars at work, don't expect to get in. They have one Open House Day during the summer. Check their website for dates and times.)

## Visitor Information

**Gakona Lodge and Trading Post**
Mile 2 – Tok Cutoff Road
Gakona, AK 99586-9800
(907) 822-3482
www.gakonalodge.com/

**Hours:**

The lodge, Trappers Den Tavern, and Carriage House Restaurant are open 7 days a week from May to September.

**Directions:**

From their website—The lodge is at MILE 2 on the TOK CUTOFF approximately 198 miles northeast of Anchorage and 250 miles south of Fairbanks. If traveling from Anchorage, go north on the Glenn Highway. Location is 15 miles north of Glennallen and borders Wrangell-St. Elias National Park. If driving through Canada, turn south at TOK on the Tok Cutoff as though you're going to Anchorage.

The Cemetery at Eklutna. *Courtesy of Land Design North.*

### Recommendations

**In addition to possibly glimpsing wandering spirits, a hike through the park offers scenic views of a glacier, and wildlife such as foxes, eagles, and black bears. The Heritage House Museum has photographs and craft displays portraying the native lifestyle and Russian influence. A gift shop offers Native Alaskan baskets and jewelry.**



### Visitor Information

**Eklutna Village Historical Park**
Glenn Highway
Eagle River, AK 99577
(907) 696-2828

**Hours:**
Mid-May to mid-September: 8am – 6pm daily.

**Admission:**
$3.50 per person. Children under 6 free. Group discounts available.

**Directions:**
From Anchorage, go northeast on the Glenn Highway to mile 26.5, and turn onto Eklutna Lake Road.

# Eklutna Village Historical Park

Native Americans have inhabited this site for over 800 years, making it the oldest continually inhabited place in the Anchorage area. This particular Dena'ina Athabascan village dates back to 1650 and may now appear rather odd to someone who isn't expecting to see a Russian Orthodox Church there.

When Russian settlers first arrived in 1741, they created an interesting blend of cultures and religions. St. Nicholas Church, originally built in the 1830s and the oldest standing building in the greater Anchorage area, overlooks a most unique Native American cemetery. The unusual combination of beliefs held that after a person died, their spirit remained on earth for forty days. These spirits wandered in search of their possessions, and to prevent them from going beyond the confines of their graves, "spirit houses" were erected.

These small wooden structures were built over the graves of the recently deceased, painted in bright family colors, and filled with everyday items such as cups and plates, as well as personal items such as a camera and rifle. It was hoped that the spirits would be content with these items and remain in their spirit house for those forty days, and especially during those long forty nights! However, many believe that the spirits still wander through the cemetery to this day, still looking for the things they held dear in life.

### The Bottom Line

**The History:** The park is the oldest continually inhabited place in the Anchorage area, and a unique blend of Native American and Russian Orthodox beliefs.

**The Haunting:** The spirit houses in the Native American cemetery were built to contain the wandering spirits, but they didn't seem to work.

*Courtesy of the Historic Anchorage Hotel.*

# Historic Anchorage Hotel

In 1916, the entire population of Alaska was estimated to be only 58,000. Few of those residents lived in the town that was to become Anchorage, but that would rapidly change. In that year, President Woodrow Wilson authorized funds for the construction of the Alaska Railroad, and Anchorage would be the site of its headquarters. The population of the town jumped to over 2,000, and a "Tent City" was erected to accommodate this rapid growth.

Amidst these challenging living conditions, a hotel was built at the corner of 3rd Avenue and E Street. To illustrate how the hotel represented a small slice of civilization in the expanding town, for many years, it was the only place in Anchorage where visitors could dine on fine china with linens and silver. Celebrities, politicians, and famous people of all sorts stayed at the Anchorage Hotel, including wilderness activist and explorer Bob Marshall and landscape artist Sydney Laurence, who had a studio in the hotel lobby. Humorist Will Rogers and pioneering pilot Wiley Post stayed at the hotel only two days before they were killed in a plane crash.

As Anchorage continued to grow, the hotel was not big enough to meet the demands, so an annex was constructed across the alleyway in 1936, with a sky bridge to connect the two buildings. Hard times eventually hit the hotel and the original building was sold and demolished, while the annex deteriorated due to neglect. Fortunately for this Alaskan landmark, new owners purchased the property in 1989, and by 1994, the Historic Anchorage Hotel had been restored to its former glory.

Today, the hotel stands as a reminder of the town's past, but it also may contain several souls that long ago passed. In fact, there have been so many sightings of these departed souls that the hotel began keeping a ghost logbook in December of 2004 to record the experiences of the staff and guests. One of the recognizable spirits is believed to be Anchorage's first police chief, John J. Sturgus. In February of 1921, Sturgus was found in the rear stairwell of a drugstore in the alley by the original hotel. He had been shot in the chest and died before he could reveal his murderer. The case was never solved. The current hotel was built on the site of the homicide, and many people have witnessed a figure they believe to be the slain cop.

There may be another tragedy involving a female spirit who is seen wandering the halls in a wedding dress. There are at least two versions of her story: One in which she is about to be wed, but receives the erroneous news that her soldier fiancé has been killed, the other that her fiancé struck it rich with a gold mine and abandoned her. However, there is one detail upon which both stories agree—in her terrible grief she hung herself in the hotel, and her troubled soul remains to this day.

The second floor appears to be the most active, with rooms 215 and 217 having the most reports of unexplained occurrences. Curtains move when there is no breeze, and televisions, radios, and faucets turn themselves on and off. Guests have also complained about children running up and down the halls at night, but the staff can never find these children and none were registered at the hotel. There is a shadowy figure seen by a staircase, and footsteps can often be heard on the staircase when no one is there.

While Alaskan towns may not have centuries of history like some other states, it still does have an impressive haunted history—just ask the chief of police or the bride-to-be when you stay at the Historic Anchorage Hotel.

## The Bottom Line

**The History:** The Hotel was originally constructed in 1916 when the town of Anchorage was beginning to grow due to the railroad. An oasis of civilization in the rugged town, many famous people stayed here over the decades.

**The Haunting:** The police chief was shot and killed on the site in 1921. A bride who committed suicide is seen in her wedding dress. Various sights and sounds, including a shadowy figure and children running up and down the halls.



## Recommendations

**Every year the hotel has special events for the Halloween season, so be sure to book a room far in advance as they are very popular. Ask for rooms 215 or 217 for a good chance at experiencing the paranormal. And if you do experience something, don't forget to add it to the ghost logbook.**

## Visitor Information

**Historic Anchorage Hotel**
**330 E. Street**
**Anchorage, AK 99501**
Reservations: **(907) 272-4553**
Toll Free: **(800) 544-0988**
**anchoragehotel@alaska.com**
**www.historicanchoragehotel.com**

**Directions:**

**From their website**—The Historic Anchorage Hotel is centrally located in the heart of the downtown area, just 6 miles from the airport.

**From Ted Stevens International Airport:** Head east on International Airport Road to Minnesota Drive. Turn north on Minnesota Drive. Minnesota Drive will become I Street. Follow I Street to 4th Avenue and turn right on 4th Avenue. Turn left on E. Street. The Historic Anchorage Hotel will be immediately to your left, next to Grizzly's Gifts.

# Arizona Haunts

CASA GRANDE RUINS NATIONAL PARK

BIRD CAGE THEATER

BIG NOSE KATE'S SALOON

EL TOVAR HOTEL

The ruins of Casa Grande. *Courtesy of the National Park Service.*

# Casa Grande Ruins National Park

There are great mysteries surrounding Casa Grande. Who built it? What was it used for? Why was it abandoned?

When Padre Eusebio Francisco Kino came across the site in 1694, he found a large building that had been abandoned for many years, and he named it Casa Grande, or Great House. The 3-story structure is 60 feet long and 40 feet wide, and was built on a 7-foot-high platform, giving it a total height of 35 feet. Archaeological evidence points to a construction date of around 1300, and the site was abandoned around 1450.

Some of the more unique features are holes in the floors of the Casa Grande, in which poles may have been inserted to determine such things as the equinoxes and solstices. As the region has evidence of over a thousand years of farms and irrigation ditches prior to the building of Casa Grande, it would have been important for these people to know when the planting seasons were beginning. Perhaps other astronomical events were of ceremonial importance to the builders, but as they left no written records, it is only speculation.

Another interesting structure on the site proves that the builders of Casa Grande were not all work and no play. There are the remains of an oval ball court, and the games that may have been played on them could have come from Mesoamerican cultures, where two teams competed using a rubber ball.

So, who were these farmers who kept track of the sky and enjoyed an occasional ball game? No one knows what they called themselves, but they are known today as the Hohokam, which is an O'odham word meaning "Those Who are Gone." Which brings up the mystery of where the Hohokam went, and why they left.

Unfortunately, there is no definitive answer to either question. Some tribes in the region claim to have been descended from the Hohokam, but there is no proof. There is speculation that Casa Grande was deserted due to the weather, or disease, or some type of conflict—in other words, no one knows. What *is* known is that they had a developed farming and trading culture, they made beautiful pottery and shell jewelry, and they constructed a three-storey building that obviously had great significance to them.

But are the ruins of Casa Grande all that is left of Hohokam here? Perhaps not, if you believe the reports of witnesses seeing the figure of an old Indian chief who appears by the visitor center. Others claim to have seen a group of Indians conducting some sort of ceremony by Casa Grande, but when they go to investigate, the Indians have vanished. Are these simply ancient imprints, snapshots of the past that only certain sensitive individuals can see? Or are there active energies here from over a thousand years of habitation by the Hohokam in the region? We must add these appearances to the list of the mysteries of Casa Grande.

AZ

## The Bottom Line

**The History:** An ancient Hohokam Indian site with a structure built in 1300, abandoned in 1450. No one knows what Casa Grande was used for, where the Hohokam went, or why they left.

**The Haunting:** The figure of an Indian chief is seen by the visitor center, and a group of Indians has been seen conducting ceremonies.

## Recommendations

Whatever your beliefs, just remember that this place still has significance to Native Americans, so treat it with respect. This is one of those unique ancient sites in America where you get to stretch your imagination and try to picture what this place was like 700 years ago. The site of the ball court can be viewed from a platform by the picnic area. Check the website for details on special events, such as the American Indian Music Fest which is held each January.

## Visitor Information

**Casa Grande Ruins National Monument**
1100 Ruins Drive
Coolidge, AZ 85128-3200
(520) 723-3172
www.nps.gov/cagr

**Hours:**

Open every day from 9am – 5pm, except Thanksgiving Day and December 25th.

**Admission:**

Entrance Fee for Casa Grande Ruins National Monument is charged per person and is valid for 7 days from date of purchase. Each adult (16 years or older) will be charged $5. Children 15 and younger are free.

**Directions:**

Casa Grande is about an hour from both Phoenix and Tucson.

**From their website**—From Phoenix: Take I-10 East toward Tucson to AZ-387 at Exit 185, approximately 36 miles from Sky Harbor International Airport. Turn left at the end of the off-ramp onto AZ-187/AZ-387. Go over the I-10 overpass and then make a right turn onto AZ-387. Proceed east 7 miles to AZ-87. At the stop sign, make a right turn onto AZ-87. Continue towards Coolidge for 7 miles to the traffic light at the intersection of AZ-87 and AZ-287. Turn right (south) onto Arizona Boulevard. Look for the entrance to the monument about 1/2 mile on your right. Proceed for 3/4 mile down the entrance road to the visitor center.

**From Tucson:** Take I-10 West (toward Phoenix) approximately 47 miles to AZ-87 at exit 211b. Continue straight onto Frontage Road for 1/2 mile. Stay in the right lane to go North on AZ-87 for 19 miles to Coolidge. Continue through Coolidge about 3 miles and look for the entrance to the monument on your left directly across from Safeway Plaza shopping area on your right. Proceed for 3/4 mile down the entrance road to the parking lot.

The Bird Cage Theater in 1940.

# Bird Cage Theater

There are so many hokey recreations of the Old West that it's almost impossible to know where Hollywood ends and reality begins. If only there was some sort of a time capsule, somewhere you could step back over a century to see the era as it really was.

Well actually, there is one place, the Bird Cage Theater in Tombstone. The Bird Cage opened its doors on Christmas Day in 1881, just two years after the town was founded. Silver mines may have given birth to the town, but its life blood was booze, women, and gambling, and the Bird Cage had all of them in abundance. In fact, the *New York Times* reported that "the Bird Cage Theatre is the wildest, wickedest night spot between Basin Street and the Barbary Coast."

There was a high stakes poker game in the basement—which cost $1,000 to buy in—which ran continuously 24 hours a day for 8 years, 5 months, and 3 days, which is a record that will most likely never be broken. And let us not forget the 14 "bird cages" suspended from the ceiling. These were small rooms where for $25 a man could roost for the night with lady of his choice. This unique arrangement was immortalized in the popular song, "She's Only a Bird in a Gilded Cage," which was written about the women of the Bird Cage Theater.

Wherever there are women, drinking, gambling, and guns, there are bound to be gunfights, and the Bird Cage had plenty of them, as well. In fact, in the eight years the place was open, there were sixteen gunfights, and 140 bullet holes can still be seen in the walls, ceilings, and furniture. Including the gunfight deaths, two suicides, and a couple of stabbings, there were a total of twenty-six deaths in the building.

So, apart from the history and the bullet holes, what makes this place so authentic? When the silver mines closed, the Bird Cage Theater "temporarily" closed in 1889. Everything was left inside and covered with canvas tarps as they expected to reopen in about six weeks. Well, those six weeks stretched into forty-five years as the doors were not opened again until 1934! People realized they were looking at exactly what western legends like Wyatt Earp and Doc Holliday had seen. It was a time capsule of the Old West, and wisely the decision was made to preserve the place just as it was, down to the position of the chairs at the high stakes poker game the day the last hand was dealt, the liquor in the bottles, and the beds in the bird cages.

The Bird Cage Theater Museum is without question the most authentic western experience you can find. In

AZ

addition to all of the original furnishings, gambling tables, piano, wallpaper, and chandeliers, there are many other amazing artifacts on display:

**Black Moriah: The hearse that carried the dead to the Boot Hill Cemetery. It is estimated to be worth in excess of $1 million.**

**Doc Holliday's dentist chair.**

**Original owner "Dutch Annie" Smith's 1881 business license for the Bird Cage, listing it as a "House of Ill Fame."**

**The blood-stained pool table Morgan Earp was playing on when he was shot and killed.**

**The stiletto one of the brothel girls used to stab another in the heart.**

**The Tombstone Merman, a P.T. Barnum-like concoction of skeletons of a fish and an animal.**

Then there are all the unusual things that can't always be seen, namely the ghosts. Some researchers believe The Bird Cage is the most haunted place in America. Of course, there's no way to prove that, but to even be considered for such a title is an indication of just how many ghosts still cling to the place where so many laughed, loved, fought, and died.

One of the most common occurrences is the sound of voices and music, as if a party was taking place. Then there's the smell of cigar smoke and whiskey. Many people have described a man dressed in black wearing a visor, perhaps a former employee at one of the gaming tables who was caught in the crossfire of a gunfight? There are also the figures of various men in cowboy hats, men playing poker, and women dressed in the risqué costumes of their profession. So essentially, it is still business as usual at The Bird Cage Theater!

## Recommendations

**Do you want to go to a place that has a modern recreation of the Old West, or do you want to see the real thing? For the full experience, you need to come here twice—once during the day to tour the building and view all of the original artifacts, then again at night to take part in one of their ghost hunts. Does it get any better than this for a historical haunted site?**

## Visitor Information

**Bird Cage Theater Museum**
Corner of 6th and Allen Streets
Tombstone, AZ 85638
(520) 457-3421
http://tombstonebirdcage.com/

**Hours:**
Daily 8am – 6pm (Call to verify), every day but Christmas.

**Admission:**
$10 for adults, teens are $8, seniors $9, and $28 for a family. You must be at least 16 for The Bird Cage Theatre Ghost Tour, which is a guided tour held Wednesday, Thursday, Friday, and Saturday nights, starting at 8pm, and costing $20. If they fill up the first tour and have additional guests they will offer a 9:30pm tour, and if the first two tours fill up they can offer an 11pm tour. On three-day holiday weekends they also offer tours on Sunday night.

**Directions:**
I-10 exits 303, 304, or 306, then south on Highway 80 for 23 miles. One block to the right, on Allen Street, at the corner of Sixth Street, south side.

## The Bottom Line

**The History:** A time capsule of the Old West. The doors to this saloon/brothel/gambling hall closed in 1889 and everything was left exactly as it was, including the 140 bullet holes from all the gunfights. Everything is all original and unrestored.

**The Haunting:** The party has never stopped here as there are the sounds of voices and music, and the sights of men and women in 1880s clothing.

Big Nose Kate (Mary Katharine Horony) at age 40 in 1890.

## Big Nose Kate's Saloon

Could a haunted western saloon have a better address than Tombstone? In a town made famous by the shoot out at the OK Corral, is it any wonder that the turbulent past has left its mark on the present? Do spirits return here because of some regrets, or simply to relive the good times?

Good times certainly were to be had in Tombstone in the 1880s, when thousands of silver miners spent their hard-earned cash on gambling, drinking, and women (but not necessarily in that order). In fact, for a town of only 5,000 people, there were an astounding 110 saloons and 14 gambling halls willing to take your money 24 hours a day. The bordellos also did a remarkable amount of business, with some of the most talented ladies making as much as $150 a week, at a time when a miner would work 12 back-breaking hours in dangerous conditions for a mere $3.

Big Nose Kate, who was born Mary Katherine Horony, is believed to have been one of those enterprising women, but it is for her relationship with only one man for whom she is famous. Kate's boyfriend was none other than Doc Holliday, and she was staying with him in Tombstone when the famous gunfight occurred.

Today, Big Nose Kate's Saloon is a living tribute to those legendary days of western history. The building was first constructed in 1880 as the elegant Grand Hotel, and it was the place to stay in Tombstone. In fact, the night before the shoot out at the OK Corral, Ike Clanton and the two McLaurys (who were killed in the gunfight) spent the night at the Grand Hotel.

Other than the clientele, a very unique feature of the hotel was the bar in the basement. Tombstone is built over a series of mine shafts, and a tunnel was dug from the basement of the hotel so miners could travel underground straight to the basement bar, have a few drinks and go right back to work!

Unfortunately, the good times at the Grand Hotel were short-lived, as a fire devastated the place in May of 1882. The second and first floors collapsed into the basement, and all that was left were the arches in the front of the building. The place was rebuilt, but without the second floor.

In the 1970s, Big Nose Kate's Saloon opened as a restaurant and bar. In fact, they have the original long bar from the Grand Hotel, so you can bend an elbow at the very same bar as Wyatt and Virgil Earp, Doc Holliday, the Clantons, and McLaurys. And if you are sensitive to such things, you might actually see one of them, as several men in 1880s clothing have appeared at the bar. Guests and staff have also seen a woman in an 1880s-style dress carrying a parasol. There are the sounds of disembodied footsteps of boots and jingling spurs, women get pinched, and objects move and fly through the air. In short, spirits of more than one variety can be had at Big Nose Kate's!

Perhaps the most mysterious spirit of all is known only by his nickname, The Swamper. He had been a janitor at the Grand Hotel, doing just about any menial job that was required. However, despite his lowly position, The Swamper was determined to elevate his status in a unique way—by digging down.

The Swamper stayed in a small room in the basement, and slowly but surely he dug a secret tunnel that connected to one of the silver mine shafts. He would then sneak through the tunnel and steal the precious metal from the unsuspecting mine owner. Perhaps he made his fortune this way and ran off in the night, or maybe the owner found out who was depleting his valuable veins of silver and dealt with him with some western justice, but the fact remains that The Swamper simply disappeared without a trace. There is some speculation that he had hidden his silver somewhere in the Grand Hotel, that he was indeed murdered, and today the ghost of The Swamper still searches the building for his lost treasure—which could very well still be hidden somewhere on the property!

With a history of gunfighters, fire, and secret tunnels, Big Nose Kate's Saloon is a fascinating place to visit for some western food, live music, and drinks. Add to that The Swamper and various other spirits dressed in 1880s clothing, and you have a wonderful opportunity to truly experience the past firsthand. So put on your boots, belly up to the bar, hang onto your silver, and look very carefully at the people around you—especially the ones who may have died a hundred years ago…

### The Bottom Line

**The History:** The building was originally the Grand Hotel, built in 1880, and frequented by the gunfighters from the famous OK Corral shoot out. Burned in 1882, and rebuilt without the second floor.

**The Haunting:** The Swamper still searches for his silver. Various men and women in 1880s clothing are seen. Objects move and people are touched.

### Recommendations

**Have a drink at the original long bar where famous gunfighters once drank. The tunnel in the basement is sealed, but still visible. Note the arches in the front of the building that were part of the original Grand Hotel. You can dress up in old-fashioned clothing and have your picture taken by the bar. A very unique feature is that you can request a "hanging" for a friend or spouse. Costumed reenactors put on a skit with the "accused," but as of the publication of this book, no one has actually been hung as they have all received last minute reprieves!**

### Visitor Information

**Big Nose Kate's Saloon**
**417 E. Allen Street**
**Tombstone, AZ 85638**
**(520) 457-3107**
**www.bignosekates.info/**

**Hours:**
**Open daily, 10am – Midnight**

**Directions:**
**Big Nose Kate's is about a block away from the OK Corral. From Route 80 in Tombstone, turn south on 4th Street, go one block and turn left onto East Allen Street to #417 on the right.**

**From Tuscon, take I-10E. Take exit 303 for I-10 Bus Loop/AZ-80 toward Benson/Douglas. Merge onto West 4th Street/AZ-80. Slight right at AZ-80. Turn right at 4th Street. Take the 1st left onto East Allen Street to Big Nose Kate's Saloon on the right.**

## El Tovar Hotel

The Grand Canyon is one of the most magnificent places on earth, offering ever-changing vistas as the blazing Arizona sun paints an endless variety of colors and shadows. In the early 1900s, wealthy tourists making the long railroad journey to the canyon began demanding a grand place to stay, and thus the Atchison, Topeka, and Santa Fe Railroad spent the princely sum of $250,000 to build the El Tovar Hotel, which sits just twenty feet from the canyon's South Rim. It opened in 1905 and was managed by the Fred Harvey Company, and their famous Harvey Girls.

Tourists flocked to the elegant hotel, and many famous people were guests, including Presidents Theodore Roosevelt and William Howard Taft, Albert Einstein, western novelist Zane Grey, playwright George Bernard Shaw, and inventor Guglielmo Marconi.

While the El Tovar has seen countless people come and go, there are a few souls who apparently never left. Before the ghost stories, however, a misconception must be cleared up. There is a legend of a grave of one Piri Ward said to be located in the hotel parking lot. The story claims that Piri was a Harvey girl, and the mistress of Fred Harvey. Despite this romantic tale, the truth is that this is simply a marker dedicated to a man, Pirl A. Ward, 1879-1934, for his role in building the El Tovar. Ward is actually buried in California.

The El Tovar in the early 1900s.

However, it's understandable that this marker has been mistaken for a grave, because one of the El Tovar's most popular ghosts is regularly seen there. The figure is described as wearing a black cape and it walks along the path by the hotel to this marker and then continues on.

While the identity of this caped figure is unknown, some believe that the ghost of Fred Harvey frequents the hotel, although he died four years before the place was even built. He seems to inhabit the third floor of the hotel, which along with the kitchen appear to be the most active areas. Mr. Harvey, or whoever he is, has not allowed death to interfere with his commitment to providing hospitality, as there have been reports that during the Christmas season he invites guests to a party!

The Grand Canyon is a place of beauty and power, and if some spirits linger in and around the El Tovar, one can't blame them. The view here is so heavenly, perhaps the departed are simply a little confused...

## The Bottom Line

**The History:** A first-class hotel built by the railroad in 1905 to accommodate wealthy tourists, including many famous people. It stands just twenty feet from the South Rim of the Grand Canyon.

**The Haunting:** A caped figure is seen walking along the path, and a hospitable man on the third floor invites guests to a Christmas party.

## Recommendations

**The Grand Canyon is spectacular every season of the year, and the El Tovar is the best place to stay on the South Rim. Be sure to make reservations far in advance, especially during the summer.**



## Visitor Information

**El Tovar Hotel**
Apache Street and Center Road South Rim
Grand Canyon National Park, AZ 86023
Reservations: (888) 297-2757 or (303) 297-2757
Main Switchboard: (928) 638-2631

**Admission:**
National Park Service entrance fees apply for the park.

**Directions:**
From their website—From Flagstaff, Arizona: Take Interstate 40 West to Williams. At the Arizona Highway 64 junction turn North. Proceed to the South entrance of Grand Canyon National Park.

From Las Vegas, Nevada: Go south on US Highway 93 (over the Hoover Dam) to Kingman, AZ. Go East on Interstate 40 to Williams. At the Arizona Highway 64 junction, turn left (north) and proceed to the south entrance of Grand Canyon National Park.

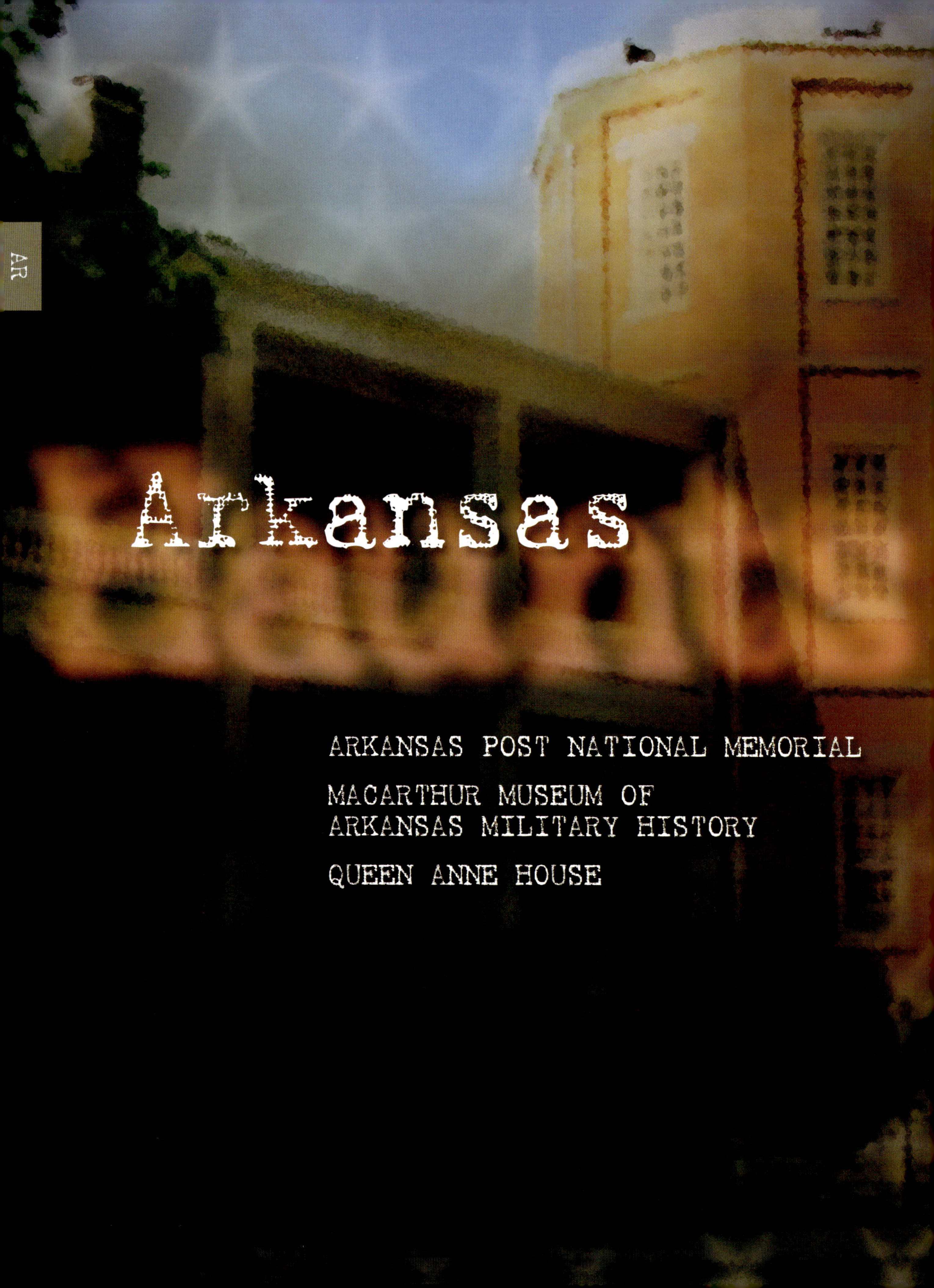

# Arkansas

ARKANSAS POST NATIONAL MEMORIAL

MACARTHUR MUSEUM OF ARKANSAS MILITARY HISTORY

QUEEN ANNE HOUSE

"Bombardment and capture of Fort Hindman, Arkansas Post, Arkansas. January 11, 1863," by Currier & Ives.

# Arkansas Post National Memorial

The first European settlement in the lower Mississippi Valley was established in 1686 by Henri de Tonti, and was known as Poste de Arkansea. As French settlers so often did, the handful of men running the trading post married local Quapaw women. While peaceful coexistence with the Native Americans was a positive sign for the settlement, over the following century, France, Spain, and England would all fight for control of the Mississippi River Valley and its lucrative fur trade.

In 1762, the land fell under Spanish control and they proceeded to build Fort St. Charles III to protect their interests in the region. In 1783, during the Revolutionary War, they were attacked by the British, who were led by Colonel James Colbert. The Colbert Raid was the only action in Arkansas during the war, and it was ultimately a Spanish victory.

The area was finally to come into American hands in 1803 as a result of the Louisiana Purchase. In 1819, the post became the first capital of the new Arkansas Territory and grew in population, becoming a busy port city. Unfortunately, the prosperity was brief as the capital moved to Little Rock just two years later, and the post began a steady decline.

During the Civil War, Confederate troops built a large earthen fort at the post, called Fort Hindman. In January of 1863, the fort came under fire from Federal gunboats in the river and troops on the ground. The Confederates, outnumbered at least five to one, surrendered the fort after two days of fighting, and victorious Union troops burned everything that was still standing. Total losses for the battle were 6,547—with 1,047 for the Union, with 134 killed; Confederate losses were 5,500, with most of that number the result of the surrendered troops.

In the early twentieth century, it seemed as though even Mother Nature was against the post. Over the years, the course of the Arkansas River changed, with the water shifting away from the riverboat landing. The railroads had already caused a significant decrease in steamboat traffic in the last decades of the nineteenth century, and now the shifting river rendered the landing useless. The old settlement appeared destined to be forgotten, until its historic significance was recognized and efforts were made to establish a park. In 1929, the former site of Arkansas Post became a state park, and in 1960, it was designated a National Memorial and a National Historic Landmark.

While the remarkable history of this site is being preserved with exhibits and trails, is there anything else from the past that can be experienced? Yes, if you believe the accounts of the sound of a galloping phantom horse, which some believe is connected with the Colbert Raid. Then there is the smell of gunpowder and the sound of an explosion or cannon fire, which may be some form of residual impressions from the battle fought during the Civil War.

Too, there are the mysterious Fort Hindman Lights, which witnesses describe as eerie lights dancing through the trees. While legend has it that they are the souls of soldiers trying to find their way home, they are more likely caused by frogs—not the glowing souls of frogs, but rather the lights of people on airboats in the river trying to catch frogs at night!



Could there be shades and impressions of the past at the old Arkansas Post? If human habitation and conflict are ingredients for a haunting, then over three centuries of trials and tribulations at this site would make it a prime candidate for such things. So pack a picnic lunch, walk the trails, visit the exhibits, and try to imagine what this place was like hundreds of years ago, and the many cultures that called it home. And if you hear a galloping horse or the sharp report of an artillery piece, consider yourself lucky to have experienced a very unique piece of Arkansas history!

## The Bottom Line

**The History:** The oldest European settlement in the lower Mississippi Valley, contested by the French, Spanish, and British, before becoming American land in the Louisiana Purchase. It was the capital of the Arkansas Territory from 1819-21. The site of the Colbert Raid of 1783 and the Battle of Fort Hindman in 1863. Became a park in 1929.

**The Haunting:** Over three centuries of history can provide plenty of fodder for hauntings. Activity includes the sound of a galloping horse, the smell of gunpowder and the sound of a cannon firing.

## Recommendations

**There are some wonderful trails through the park, both paved and unpaved, such as the nature/historic Point Trail which starts at the visitor's center, goes to the river, and loops back. There are special events throughout the year, so call or check their website for the latest information. The park encompasses 1,000 acres, so allow plenty of time to explore.**

## Visitor Information

**Arkansas Post National Memorial**
1741 Old Post Road
Gillett, AR 72055
(870) 548-2207
www.nps.gov/ARPO/index.htm

**Hours:**

The park grounds are open daily: 8am to dark. The visitor center is open daily from 8am – 5pm. The visitor center is closed Thanksgiving Day, Christmas Day, and New Year's Day.

**Admission:**

There is no entrance fee to visit the park. Individuals or groups seeking to utilize the park for commercial or special event purposes must contact the park at least thirty days prior to the event to obtain a Special Use Permit. There may be a cost associated with Special Use Permits.

**Reservations:**

Groups planning a visit to the park should contact the park and make a reservation at least one week prior to their scheduled visit.

**Directions:**

From their website—Arkansas Post National Memorial is located in southeastern Arkansas. The entrance to the park is on AR169, nine miles south of Gillett, via US165 (The Great River Road), and about 20 miles northeast of Dumas, via US165.

From Little Rock, AR: From I-40 merge onto I-30 south. South of Little Rock, exit onto I-530 and continue to Pine Bluff. When I-530 ends, exit to US65. Follow US65 to Gould, AR and turn left onto AR212. When 212 ends, turn left onto US165, and cross over the Arkansas River. Continue on US165 for five miles, and turn right on AR169. Follow it two miles into the park.

From Memphis: From the Airport travel west on I-240 to the interchange with I-55. Exit onto I-55 South (toward Jackson) and follow it 10 miles south to I-69. Then take I-69 south and west to US61. Turn left on US61 and travel south approximately 20 miles to US49. Turn right on US49 and cross the Mississippi River to Helena. Follow US49 through or take the bypass around Helena to US49 West. Then follow the directions below from Helena to the park.

From the South: (Lake Village, AR / Greenville, MS / Monroe, LA) Follow US65 or US165 north to Dumas, AR. In Dumas, turn right at the second stoplight onto US165, and continue north for about 18 miles. Turn right onto AR169 and follow it two miles into the park.

From the East (Helena, AR): Head west on US49. Turn onto AR1 at Marvell, and continue on to DeWitt. On the south edge of DeWitt, AR1 joins US165. From DeWitt, continue on US165 about 20 miles. Turn left onto AR169 and follow it two miles into the park.

*Courtesy of the MacArthur Museum of Arkansas Military History.*

AR

# MacArthur Museum of Arkansas Military History

To protect against hostile Indians, a military post was needed in Little Rock when Arkansas became a state in 1836. Over thirty buildings were constructed, including the brick Arsenal Building—with its three-foot-thick walls and imposing octagonal tower—which was completed in 1840.

In May of 1861 when Arkansas joined the Confederacy, there was a peaceful transition of power at the post, but that would change dramatically two years later. In September of 1863, Union forces under Major General Frederick Steele drove Major General Sterling Price's Confederate troops out of the post and out of the Arkansas capital. The violence would not end there, however, as an execution was to take place several months later.

David Owen Dodd was just seventeen when he went to Little Rock on business for his family. Although given a pass to return home behind the Confederate lines, he returned to Union-held territory and was stopped and searched. Dodd was found to be carrying a book with pages written in Morse Code. When deciphered, it was discovered that the book contained valuable information about Union strengths and positions in Little Rock.

Dodd was convicted of being a spy and sentenced to death. However, General Steele offered to spare the boy's life if he would name the source of his information, but Dodd refused, bravely replying, "I can die, but I cannot betray the trust of a friend." Unfortunately, the execution was not swift and merciful. A rope was placed around Dodd's neck, and he had to step off the back of a wagon. Because the wagon was so low to the ground his neck did not break, and he died an agonizingly slow death by strangulation in front of 6,000 horrified onlookers.

More peaceful times followed the end of the war, and by 1873, most of the buildings were used as troop barracks until the post closed in 1890. While the arsenal had also been converted to housing during this time, there was one event of great significance that occurred there. In 1880, an officer's wife gave birth to a baby boy, and they named him Douglas MacArthur. After being born in the old Arsenal Tower Building, is it any wonder that this boy would go one to become a towering figure in military history?

In 1892, a thirty-six-acre park was established on this site. All of the buildings—except the arsenal—were torn down, and the arsenal was essentially left to rot. The Arsenal Tower Building was rescued in 1930, when renovations began. In 1942, the building was opened to the public as the Museum of Natural History and Antiquities. In 1997, more extensive renovations took place, and in 2001, the place reopened as the MacArthur Museum of Arkansas Military History.

Of course, that's just part of the story of this old arsenal building. There's also the part where sights and sounds of the past cross paths with the present. For example, a member of the staff was in her office in the basement when she heard what sounded like a party on the first floor. Hurrying upstairs to see what was going on, the voices, laughter, and music suddenly stopped. As soon as she returned to her office, the party started again. Perhaps the social affairs held here between 1873-1890 have left a happy imprint on the building?

A decidedly less than happy encounter occurred in a theater room in the tower. An employee was closing for the night, and saw a man in a dark uniform lying down across several chairs. The man looked real and solid, until someone tried to touch him to wake him up. He simply vanished into thin air!

Other more ethereal figures have been seen coming down a staircase to the ground floor. Shadows and shadowy figures have also been witnessed throughout the building, but in particular under the basement stairs where a deadly duel was said to have occurred.

Could any of these apparitions be attributed to David Dodd, whose life was cut so short at the end of a rope? Some speculate that he may at least be behind some playful activity in the old arsenal building—objects have been thrown through the air by the staircase going from the third floor down to the second.

Despite this building's long military history and the violence that occurred at the location, there doesn't appear to be any angry or vengeful spirits—just old soldiers still going about their business and occasionally enjoying some good times. A visit to the MacArthur Museum of Arkansas Military History will remind you that people and objects from our past are still with us today, perhaps in more ways than one!

## The Bottom Line

**The History:** A military post that once contained over thirty buildings, including the Arsenal Tower completed in 1840. Site of a Civil War battle, and the hanging of a Confederate spy, David Dodd. General Douglas MacArthur was born in the arsenal building in 1880.

**The Haunting:** Solid apparitions, voices, music, objects being thrown.

## Recommendations

The museum features both new and ongoing exhibits of artifacts, photographs, weapons, documents, uniforms, and other objects relating to the state's military history, and they have special events and lectures throughout the year. Check out the Dodd stained-glass memorial, which depicts him as a saintly figure with curly blond hair—even though his photograph clearly shows he had straight black hair. Keep your eyes open for figures in the theater, and look and listen carefully near the stairs.

## Visitor Information

**MacArthur Museum of Arkansas Military History**
503 East 9th Street
Little Rock, AR 72202
www.arkmilitaryheritage.com
(501) 376-4602

**Special Events:**
Every Halloween they host the Big Boo!-seum Bash, a free event for children and families. Little Rock Tours holds a Murder Mystery Dinner Theatre in the Old Arsenal Building, call (501) 868-7287 or 1-800-933-3836 or visit www.littlerocktours.com for more information. There is a gift shop with souvenirs and books related to Arkansas's military past.

**Hours:**
Tuesday-Friday 9am – 4pm, Saturday 10am – 4pm; Sunday 1pm – 4pm; Closed on Mondays and major holidays.

**Admission:**
Free

**Directions:**
From their website—The MacArthur Museum of Arkansas Military History can be found on the 36-acre park, off of East 9th, between Commerce Street and McMath Avenue, just a block or so west of I-30 W.

*Courtesy of the Queen Anne House.*

## Queen Anne House

Owner Warren White likes to say that "Everybody's Welcome" at this bed and breakfast in historic Harrison—and that goes for both guests and ghosts.

In 1850, Henry Frick laid out a section of town for a new development. It wasn't until 1893 that this home was constructed by William Duncan, and sold to Archibald John and Ella McMurray for $1,000. Unfortunately, the first owners did not realize a profit on their investment, as the widowed Ella sold the house in 1900 for only $115!

In 1903, the house was sold again, then again in 1905 when it became the parsonage for the Reverend D. Shuck of the Christian Church of Harrison, which is still active today. The reverend claimed that he found inspiration in the light shining through the beautiful windows of the Turret Room, and it was here that he wrote his Sunday sermons.

Perhaps the house should have been built with a revolving front door, as it was sold over and over again every few years. Finally in 1919, some relatively long-term residents moved in, the town Marshal, J.P. Callicott, and his wife Gertrude. Callicott may have been able to keep the peace in town, but it's doubtful he was as successful at home as he and his wife had eleven children—ten boys and one girl! That one girl, Callie, sold the house in 1943 for $100, and the buyer sold it just three days later for $1,650 to Ada Ragland, who's daughter, Walsa Castleberry, owned the house for forty-three years. The Castleberrys were both schoolteachers and gave piano lessons in the parlor of the house for two decades, and many older residents can recall getting their musical education in the Queen Anne House.

In 1986, a shipping tycoon who founded a famous freight company purchased the house, and a major restoration took place. More changes occurred with new owners in 1991, as they transformed the old home into a bed and breakfast. Fortunately, the Queen Anne elements of the house were preserved through all this reconstruction, but it's too bad they didn't install that revolving door, as several more owners were to follow. Finally, the property was sold in 2004 to Warren and Kay White, who reopened the place as a bed and breakfast.

The long and varied life of the "Duncan House," as it came to be called because of the original builder, was recognized in 2005 with a listing on the National Register of Historic Places. While the detailed history of the occupants has now become part of the official history, there is part of that history which probably wasn't included in the listing—the paranormal part.

The activity can be summed up in an unexpected addition to an email Warren received from a former owner:

"By the way, some guests have heard children playing in the front yard, (and there were none), and we had a heavy rocker in the turret room and it had been moved, and lights had been going off and on. One night I got up and asked them not to do that anymore and the lights stayed off. Yes, the house is somewhat haunted. Sometimes you get an eerie feeling upstairs that someone is up there with you. We were never afraid or anything but it makes interesting conversation. One night my wife woke up and a man was sitting on a chair by the bed. As soon as he noticed her looking at him he disappeared. Our bedroom was downstairs near the bathroom."

Yes, voices, apparitions, furniture moving, and lights going on and off certainly do make for interesting conversation!

There have been so many residents since 1893 it would be impossible to say exactly who these spirits were in life. However, perhaps we could speculate that the lights going on and off in the Turret Room could be from the reverend who had been so inspired by the light from these windows, the playful children might be residual energy from the Marshal's eleven children, and possibly the moving rocking chair and the man by the bed was the Marshal himself, who according to Callie "spent many hours smoking his pipe in a rocking chair in the living room by the wood stove."

In the final analysis, it doesn't really matter, because as Warren said, "Everybody's welcome here."

## The Bottom Line

**The History:** An original Queen Anne style house built in 1893 that was owned by a prominent local clergyman, the town marshal, and a shipping tycoon, before being converted into a bed and breakfast.

**The Haunting:** In the Turret Room, lights go on and off and a rocking chair moves. Children are heard playing in the yard. A man was seen sitting by the owner's bed.

## Recommendations

Harrison is located "in the heart of the Ozark Mountains" and has been named one of the "Top 100 Small Towns in America." The center of town has a national historic district, and there is a historic walking tour of Main Street. There are many events throughout the year, so you can plan your trip to coincide with the Bluegrass Festival in the summer, the Fiddler's Convention in early spring, the Crawdad Days Music Festival in late spring, or Harvest Homecoming in the fall. Doing nothing but relaxing is also perfectly acceptable. The Queen Anne House is within walking distance of the historic downtown, museums, and restaurants. For the full experience you can spend the night in the main house or the carriage house, but if time is limited you can also arrange a tour for yourself or a group for five dollars per person. All rooms with or without breakfast include: beverage bar with morning coffee, snacks, evening dessert, WiFi, a movie and book library, and use of the hot tub. The Queen Anne House is also available for weddings, receptions, and special events.

## Visitor Information

**Queen Anne House**
610 West Central Avenue
Harrison, AR 72601
(870) 365-0888
Toll Free 1-800-419-9907
queenanneB&B@windstream.net
www.queenannehouse.net/

**Directions:**
*From their website*—The Queen Anne House sits only blocks from the historic downtown square. Harrison is conveniently located near the Buffalo National River, Branson, Missouri, and Eureka Springs, Arkansas. Harrison prides itself as being "the Crossroads of the Ozarks." The town is easily reachable from the many highways (Highways 7, 62, and 65) that convene into Harrison, or the regional airport that is known for an oversized runway.

# California

USS HORNET

DRUM BARRACKS

1859 HISTORIC NATIONAL HOTEL AND RESTAURANT

HOTEL DEL CORONADO

The USS *Hornet* Museum. *Courtesy of the USS* Hornet *Museum.*

# USS Hornet

Unless you've stood on the flight deck of an aircraft carrier, you can't fully appreciate their enormous size. If you were never in battle, you are unable to comprehend what the men on these fighting ships went through. And unless you have witnessed the figure of a sailor disappear before your eyes, you could never truly understand how the past is intertwined with the present.

The USS *Hornet* (CV-12) is a remarkable piece of history that has many levels to explore, and in more ways than one. The ship is now a museum in Alameda that carries on a great tradition of its predecessors. The original Hornet was built in 1775 as one of the Navy's first ships. It was the aircraft carrier *Hornet* (CV-8) that launched Doolittle's B-25s on their famous raid on Tokyo in April of 1942. When that ship was lost later that year, a new carrier being built, the *Kearsarge*, had its name changed to *Hornet*.

This new carrier saw sixteen consecutive months of combat operations and racked up records for the number of planes and ships they destroyed, as well as the number of aces they produced.

The *Hornet's* 40mm guns in action on February 16, 1945.

Ten of *Hornet's* pilots achieved "Ace in a Day" status by scoring five or more aerial victories in a single day.

The ship's crew shot down 668 Japanese planes and destroyed another 747 on the ground.

The *Hornet* was credited with 73 ships sunk, 37 probable, and 413 damaged.

In total, the *Hornet* came under attack 59 times, but miraculously it was never hit by a bomb, torpedo, or Kamikaze!

While the ship somehow avoided serious damage, there were many combat deaths and accidents, with about 300 crewmen losing their lives in the 27 years of the carrier's active service. The flight deck is a dangerous place, and any time planes, ordinance, and men are in such close contact, accidents are bound to happen. Explosions, propellers, and snapping flight arrest cables all took a fatal toll. Unfortunately, the *Hornet* also had the highest suicide rate in the Navy.

The *Hornet* and most of her crew did survive World War II, and rather than fade into obscurity—or go straight to the scrap yard—like many other ships and planes, she was to play a role on the world stage once again in 1969. It was this ship that had the honor of retrieving the astronauts from both Apollo 11 and 12—from the Moon to the *Hornet*!

In 1991, the USS *Hornet* (CVS-12) was designated a National Historic Landmark, and opened to the public as an aircraft carrier museum in 1998. They offer a variety of exhibits, events, and programs, including the opportunity to spend the night aboard the ship. These very unique accommodations have occasionally presented guests with something even more special—the opportunity to hear and see crew members who long ago crossed that ocean from which no one is supposed to return, but in light of what happens here we clearly need to rethink that.

A member of the staff who had been a Navy SEAL saw a man in a khaki uniform go down a ladder to another deck. He quickly followed the man, but no one was there.

Volunteers from the Coast Guard were painting a section of the ship, and they were wearing white Tyvek suits to protect their clothing. When one of them went to get more paint, he saw a man in white go into a room. Thinking it was one of his friends, he followed the man, but no one was in the small room, and there were no other exits. Later, when he told his story to a member of the staff, he was informed that he had probably encountered their "Dress Whites Ghost."

Other overnight volunteers have heard hatches slamming shut, voices, and activity as if the crew was back on board.

Several men in officers' uniforms have been seen, and some believe one of the officers is Admiral Joseph "Jocko" Clark, even though Clark died in 1971 in New York, and is buried in Arlington. (An interesting note, Clark was a Cherokee, and the first Native American to graduate from the United States Naval Academy, in 1917.)

There have been over 200 reported sightings and experiences from staff, volunteers, veterans, and visitors.

Do old ships creak and make strange noises? Of course, so every sound that is reported is not a ghost. However, even skeptics must take note when reliable witnesses and trained military men from the Navy and Coast Guard see sailors who vanish into thin air. Many men loved the ships upon which they served, and they often sacrificed their lives in the line of duty. Would it be so surprising then, that these devoted service men returned to the *Hornet* for one more tour of duty?

If you do visit the *Hornet* and encounter someone from another time, don't be alarmed. Give him a salute and say, "Job well done, sailor!"

## Recommendations

**Allow plenty of time for your visit; this is a big ship. Wear comfortable shoes as there are ladders and a lot of walking to do. In addition to the ship itself, you can see aircraft and Apollo program items on display, as well as various special exhibits. For those with more of a sense of adventure, there is a flight simulator. And for the ultimate adventurer, you can spend the night aboard ship, sleeping in the same racks as the crew had used. Definitely one of the best opportunities for experiencing the realm of historic haunts!**

## Visitor Information

**USS Hornet Museum**
707 W. Hornet Avenue, Pier 3
Alameda CA 94501-5006
(510) 521-8448
www.uss-hornet.org

**Hours:**
Daily 10am – 5pm, every day except Thanksgiving, Christmas, and New Years Day. There is plenty of free parking available.

**Admission:**
Adults $14, Seniors, Military w/ID, Students w/ID $12, Children (5-17) $6, Children (4 and under) free with paying adult, Museum Members free. Lower rates for groups. Overnights are $60 per person, regardless of age.

**Directions:**
From their website—From San Francisco: Cross the Bay Bridge towards Oakland and follow the signs for 880 South/San Jose/Alameda. Take the Broadway/Alameda exit and turn right at the bottom of the ramp onto 5th Street. Continue on 5th Street, staying on street level. At the Broadway intersection, veer to your left; the Webster Street Tube (tunnel) to Alameda is under the freeway. After emerging from the tube, continue on Webster Street to the first stoplight (Atlantic Avenue/Ralph Appezzatto Memorial Parkway). Turn right on Atlantic Avenue and continue straight into Alameda Point (formerly Naval Air Station Alameda), crossing Main Street. Continue to the T-intersection at the water. Turn left onto Ferry Point and proceed towards the cluster of large ships.

From San Jose and 880 Northbound: Proceed toward downtown Oakland and take the Broadway exit. At the end of the ramp, follow the signs to Alameda, turning right on Broadway and then immediately turning right on 7th Street. Go two blocks to Webster Street and turn right again, entering the Webster Tube (tunnel) to Alameda. (Alternate: Turn left on Broadway and left again to enter Tube under freeway overpass.) After emerging from the tube, continue on Webster Street to the first stoplight (Atlantic Avenue/Ralph Appezzatto Memorial Parkway). Turn right on Atlantic Avenue and continue straight into Alameda Point (formerly Naval Air Station Alameda), crossing Main Street. Continue to the T-intersection at the water. Turn left onto Ferry Point and proceed towards the cluster of large ships. (See Detour instructions in the event of Tube closure.)

USS *Hornet* en route to the Apollo 11 capsule. *Courtesy of the USS* Hornet *Museum.*

## The Bottom Line

**The History:** A WWII aircraft carrier that set many battle records, then served as the recovery vessel for the Apollo 11 and 12 astronauts.

**The Haunting:** Over 200 reported sightings of officers and sailors, sounds of crew activity, and numerous other experiences.

*Courtesy of Drum Barracks Civil War Museum.*

# Drum Barracks

When discussing the Civil War, the state of California rarely arises, but consider this: How would events have played out if the Confederacy had gained control of what are now the states of California, Arizona, and New Mexico?

The Union commanders recognized the importance of maintaining control over the vast Southwest territories, and present-day Wilmington was chosen to house the headquarters for the Department of the Pacific. Camp Drum, named after Adjutant General Richard Coulter Drum, was built on sixty acres of land and became the training and supply base of operations for the region in 1861. After the war, Drum Barracks continued to house soldiers fighting the Indian wars until the camp closed in 1871, although its medical facility remained in operation for two more years.

While the land reverted back to the original owners, the buildings themselves were auctioned off in 1873, and many of the structures were picked up and moved to other locations. One of the former officer's quarters that remained became a private residence for a time. Then between 1890-1910, it served as the Wilmington Town High School. In

1963, it was the only Civil War-era structure still remaining and there were fears that it would be sold and demolished. Fortunately, a group of concerned citizens were able to raise funds and the building was saved. Restoration took place in 1976-77. Finally in 1987, it opened to the public as the Drum Barracks Civil War Museum.

Opening a museum in an old military building is always a wonderful idea as it doubles the experience by combining a historic structure with all of the items on exhibit. However, it also doubles the chances for being haunted—from the people and events of the historic site, as well as possible attachments to the weaponry, clothing, and belongings of the deceased in the museum collection.

It should come as no surprise then, that there have been many inexplicable sights, sounds, and scents at the museum, but are they from the building itself, the exhibits, or both?

A woman in a Civil War-era hoop skirt has been seen, often accompanied by the scent of lavender.

Civil War soldiers have appeared in the house and on the grounds.

A little boy has been heard and seen playing on the second floor of the house and standing in the yard.

There is often the scent of cigar or pipe smoke.

When a woman started playing Dixie on the piano, the lights flickered on and off until she stopped. Apparently, the Union soldiers did not appreciate the southern song!

Whether you come here to experience the history, the ghosts, or both, the Drum Barracks Civil War Museum represents an important period for our nation. If it hadn't been for the soldiers like those who were trained here and sent to war, we may all be whistling Dixie today.

## The Bottom Line

**The History:** A former officer's quarters and the only remaining Civil War-era building remaining on what was a 60-acre camp. After the camp closed, the building was a private residence and then a high school. Restored in the 1970s and opened as a museum in 1987.

**The Haunting:** A woman in a hoop skirt accompanied by the scent of lavender, Civil War soldiers, a little boy, tobacco smoke, and an angry reaction to the playing of Dixie.

## Recommendations

There are Civil War reenactments, special events, and roundtables throughout the year. Check out the model of the 1863 camp buildings to get a good idea of how this place looked during the war years. A Civil War veteran's artificial leg is on display, and the museum has photos and detailed information about his life. The armory has many examples of Civil War weaponry, from Springfields to a Gatling gun. There is a rare, restored, 1864 rosewood Steinway Box Grand piano that visitors are encouraged to play (although it may be prudent to pick a northern tune). Note the fireplace andirons with the eagles, they are the only original items from the building and were discovered in a box under the house during the restoration in the 1970s. There is also the remarkable autograph book of Captain Dunbar, who from 1862 to 1916 collected the signatures of 50 Union generals, 2 Presidents, Confederate generals, politicians, and celebrities, including a rare Helen Keller autograph. A computer is available to view color scans of Dunbar's entire book. Last, but certainly not least, there are the beautiful Scottish Lady Banksia roses that were planted way back in 1876 by Reverend Doag for his Scottish wife.

## Visitor Information

**Drum Barracks Civil War Museum**
1052 Banning Boulevard
Wilmington, CA 90744
(310) 548-7509
www.drumbarracks.org

**Hours:**

Guided tours of the museum are offered: Tuesday, Wednesday, Thursday 10am, 11am, 12pm, and 1pm. Saturday and Sunday 11:30am, 12:30pm, 1:30pm, and 2:30pm.

**Admission:**

A $5 donation is requested per person, children under 12 are free.

**Directions:**

**From their website**—From the 110 Freeway: Exit Pacific Coast Highway east to Avalon Boulevard. Take Avalon south (right) to "L" street. Turn left on "L" Street and go three blocks to Banning Boulevard. Turn right on Banning Boulevard. The Barracks is located about 1 block down on the left hand side. Look for the large white house with a parking lot and flag pole in front.

**From the 710 Freeway:** Exit Pacific Coast Highway, west to Avalon Boulevard. Take Avalon south (left) to "L" street. Turn left on "L" Street and go three blocks to Banning Boulevard. Turn right on Banning Boulevard. The Barracks is located about 1 block down on the left hand side. Look for the large white house with a parking lot and flag pole in front.

*Courtesy of the 1859 Historic National Hotel.*

# 1859 Historic National Hotel and Restaurant

The founding of Jamestown can be summed up in a single word—gold. In 1848, Benjamin Wood founded the first claim in Tuolumne County, and the mining camp that sprung up was at first called Woods' Diggings, then Woods' Crossing. With gold nuggets available by the handfuls, the growing town attracted many people, including many unsavory characters.

Colonel George James came into town with smiles and champagne for everyone. He became so popular they renamed the town once again to Jamestown. Unfortunately, the Colonel would end up leaving secretly in the middle of the night, because he had been swindling the local miners. Those who had lost money wanted to change the town's name yet again, but the post office had already been established, and Jamestown it remained.

When the gold ran out, the town could have become yet another ghost town, but thanks to places like the National Hotel, which offered liquor, gambling, and prostitutes, the town survived until the return of prosperity in 1897 with the arrival of the Sierra Railroad.

It was 1859 when Heinrich and Hanna Neilson opened the National Hotel. It may seem odd to even have to mention that the hotel was one of the first permanent wooden buildings in town, but gold rush settlements often consisted of nothing more than tents and temporary wooden buildings. Unfortunately, many of the structures intended to be permanent were lost in several devastating fires, but the National, though damaged, remained standing and open for business. Today, the National Hotel is among the ten oldest continuously operating hotels built since 1859.

One can only imagine what went on here during the early years, but the wild times were certainly not confined to the nineteenth century. During Prohibition, the hotel was raided on more than one occasion, and quite a stash of illegal liquor was found in 1927. A newspaper account lists what was discovered: 9 – 50 gallon barrels of wine, 1 – 100 gallon barrels of wine, 1 – demijohn of wine, 2 – 10 gallon kegs of brandy and corn whiskey. The liquor was seized and the owner was fined $500. As for the hotel's other popular vices, legal prostitution was practiced here through the 1930s, and gambling continued until 1949.

In 1974, brothers Stephen and Michel Willey purchased the hotel and began restoration projects that are on-going to this day. Arguably, the greatest improvement was in 1979 with the installation of plumbing to the guest rooms, which previously all used a single bathroom in a separate building!

The charm and character of the place has been maintained, as has another aspect of the original hotel—its resident ghost! Flo, as she is known, is most often seen and heard in the upstairs rooms at the front of the building, but has been known to float through the dining room and go right through the walls. Is there any event in the National Hotel's long history that would account for this spirit?

In fact, there is. In the 1880s, a pretty young woman from San Francisco named Flora came to the hotel. She was eloping, and she ordered a special dress to be made for the wedding. Her fiancé joined her at the hotel, but before the ceremony could take place, the man was shot dead on the hotel stairs and the culprit was never apprehended. For days the staff heard Flora sobbing uncontrollably in her room. Then on New Year's Eve, there was silence.

The door to Flora's room was opened, and inside they found her lifeless body. She was seated by an open window, wearing the dress intended for her wedding, but would now be used for her funeral. That very night, people began seeing the misty figure of a lady in white. In addition to her appearances and the sound of sobbing, much mischievous activity has been attributed to Flo, such as lights and televisions going on and off, objects being moved, and clothing being dumped out of suitcases.

Perhaps it is Flo that remains here, in denial of her fiancé's tragic death, and perhaps her own, as well. She may be clinging to the happy memories of those few precious days that were to start a life of bliss with the man she loved. Her spirit certainly seems playful enough, so if you do encounter Flo, maybe you should just congratulate her on her upcoming wedding.

## Recommendations

**Flo is most often experienced in the upstairs rooms in the front of the building. There are logbooks for the guests to write their paranormal experiences. There's an old gold mine shaft in the courtyard. A working cash register from 1881 is in the original back bar. If you aren't brave enough to spend the night, you can come to the restaurant for lunch or dinner. The town and its historic trains have appeared in over 200 movies and shows, including *High Noon, Back to the Future III*, and *Petticoat Junction*, so take a look around to see if anything is familiar. Grizzly Adams once ran a business in town.**

## Visitor Information

**1859 Historic National Hotel**
**18183 Main Street**
**Jamestown, CA 95327-9748**
**Phone: (209) 984-3446**
**Reservations: (800) 894-3446**
**www.national-hotel.com**

**Directions:**

**From I-580 E and I-205 E, take exit 461 to merge onto CA-120 E toward Manteca/Sonora. Take the exit onto CA-120 E/CA-99 N toward Sacramento/Sonora N. Take exit 242 for CA-120 E/Yosemite Avenue toward Sonora. Turn right at CA-120 E/Yosemite Avenue and continue to follow CA-120 E. Turn left at CA-108 E/East F Street. Continue to follow CA-108 E. Turn right at Main Street, the National Hotel will be on your right.**



## The Bottom Line

**The History:** One of the first permanent structures in the gold rush town of Jamestown. One of the ten oldest continuously operating hotels built since 1859. Had a legal brothel that operated into the 1930s, and gambling that continued until 1949. Was raided several times during Prohibition.

**The Haunting:** A young woman's fiancé was shot and killed in the hotel, and she died several days later of a broken heart. Her spirit, clad in her wedding dress, makes its presence known in a variety of ways.

Hotel Del Coronado circa 1900.

# Hotel del Coronado

When the Hotel del Coronado opened across from the beach on San Diego Bay in 1888, it was the largest resort hotel in the world. Built all of wood and in the Victorian style, guests must have marveled at its size during the day and its electric lights at night. In fact, this was the first hotel to have electric lighting, and today it is still one of the largest wooden structures in the country. Other firsts included the world's first oil furnace, and the first outdoor Christmas tree lit by electricity. As grand beach resorts go, the Hotel del Coronado was the grandmother of them all.

In its long history, the hotel has had many famous guests, including sixteen presidents, as well as countless movie stars, sports legends, writers, inventors, and royalty. In fact, it may have been in the Crown Room of the hotel in 1920 that Prince Edward first met Wallis Simpson, the woman for whom he would later give up the thrown of England. Another interesting bit of trivia is that L. Frank Baum wrote much of *The Wonderful Wizard of Oz* while staying at the hotel, and the vast structure may have been his inspiration for his concept of the Emerald City. Along with being the inspiration and setting for many books, there have also been at least thirteen movies filmed here.

The party temporarily ended during War World II when the Hotel del Coronado was used as housing for pilots training at the North Island Naval Station, and their families. During the post-war years the grand hotel began to show its age. In 1960, $2 million went into updating the hotel. In 1963, a new owner planned on leveling the structure, but perhaps it was the charm of the place that ultimately swayed him to instead invest $150 million into a major restoration and expansion project. Two more multi-million dollar upgrades have taken place in recent years. No one ever said it was cheap to maintain one of the largest wooden beach resorts!

No one ever said it was cheap to stay in such a place, either, but if you are looking for a unique and historic hotel, which also happens to have a mysterious death that may have produced a very active female ghost, this is the place.

It was in November of 1892 when a woman without any luggage checked into the Hotel del Coronado. She appeared to be distraught and ill, and the hotel staff was both suspicious and concerned. Registering as Lottie Bernard, the woman claimed that she was traveling with her brother and they had gotten separated, and he would join her shortly with their luggage.

Days passed, no brother arrived, and Lottie's condition appeared to be deteriorating. Several days later, her body was found outside the hotel on steps leading to the beach. However, she hadn't died of any illness. She had a gun in her hand and a bullet in her head, and her death was ruled a suicide.

Who was Lottie Bernard, and why did she kill herself? The mystery only deepened after her death, and today there are many theories and versions of the events leading up to the apparent suicide. During the official investigation, it was determined that the woman's true identity was Kate Morgan, and the man she was waiting for was actually her husband, and they were both con artists. Some say Kate claimed to have stomach cancer, but was actually trying to end a pregnancy. Then there are the theories that it was murder, because the bullet was a .38 caliber and Kate's gun used .44 caliber shells. Some believe it wasn't Kate Morgan at all, it was actually Lottie Bernard. There are theories that the maid who had befriended her and then disappeared was murdered at the same time, but that crime was covered up so as not to lose customers.

In other words, no one knows anything for certain, other than a woman died at the Hotel del Coronado of a gunshot wound to the head. Whether it was Kate who was pregnant, or Lottie who was sick, or someone else entirely, the fact remains that the spirit of a woman has made her presence known throughout the property, especially in the room where she spent her final days, which now bears the number 3327. There is also a lot of activity in room 3502, which had been the disappearing maid's room.

The ghost, which is called Kate, has been seen in the halls, standing at windows, and in the gift shop. Objects move on their own, lights and televisions turn on and off by themselves, an intense presence is felt, and people encounter icy cold spots—all the classic signs of a haunting. While Kate appears most often, she may not be spending eternity alone at the hotel, as witnesses have also reported seeing a young boy and girl, a former caretaker, and another woman in Victorian clothing.

Who was the woman found dead at the Hotel del Coronado, and was it suicide or murder? Does she still occupy her room and walk the halls trying to tell guests the truth about her death, and her life? And why do the spirits of others linger here? Do they, too, have sad tales to tell, or do they stay simply because they loved this beautiful resort?

Since 1888, this has been the playground for the rich and famous, people like Marilyn Monroe, Charles Lindbergh, presidents, and future kings. In the whole scheme of things, perhaps the spirits here aren't as restless and unfortunate as we might think. Anyone would feel lucky to spend a week at the lovely Hotel del Coronado, and some are spending eternity here. Did you ever think you would envy the dead?

## Recommendations

**If you want to stay in 3327 you will have to book it far in advance as everyone wants Kate's room. If it is booked, try for an adjoining room, or try 3502. Check out the staircase where Kate died, as strange things have also been reported there. The gift shop sells a book about Kate if you want all the theories and evidence, but don't get too wrapped up in all the ghosts, as there is a beautiful beach and dozens of things to do.**

## Visitor Information

**Hotel del Coronado**
**1500 Orange Avenue**
**Coronado, CA 92118-2918**
**800-468-3533**
**www.hoteldel.com/**

**Directions:**

**From their website—From San Diego International Airport/Lindbergh Field: Exit the airport by turning left onto North Harbor Drive. Travel approximately 1.4 miles, and then turn left onto West Grape Street. Travel approximately 1/2 mile, and look for the Interstate 5 South on-ramp, accessible from the far right lane. Merge onto Interstate 5 freeway, traveling south. Travel approximately three miles (through Downtown San Diego) until you see the California 75 – Coronado Bay Bridge exit, accessible from the far right lane. Merge onto California 75 Coronado Bay Bridge. (No toll is required.) After driving over Coronado Bay Bridge, stay to the left on Third Street. Travel approximately 0.10 mile on Third Street, and turn left onto Orange Avenue. Follow Orange Avenue approximately two miles to the Hotel del Coronado. The resort main entrance is just past R. H. Dana Place to the right.**



## The Bottom Line

**The History:** One of the largest beach-front resorts when it opened in 1888, and the first to have electric lights. Guests have included sixteen presidents, and a *Who's Who* of the rich and famous.

**The Haunting:** A woman apparently committed suicide here in 1892, or was it murder? Her ghost is seen throughout the hotel. There are also several other ghosts, and all the classic signs of a haunting.

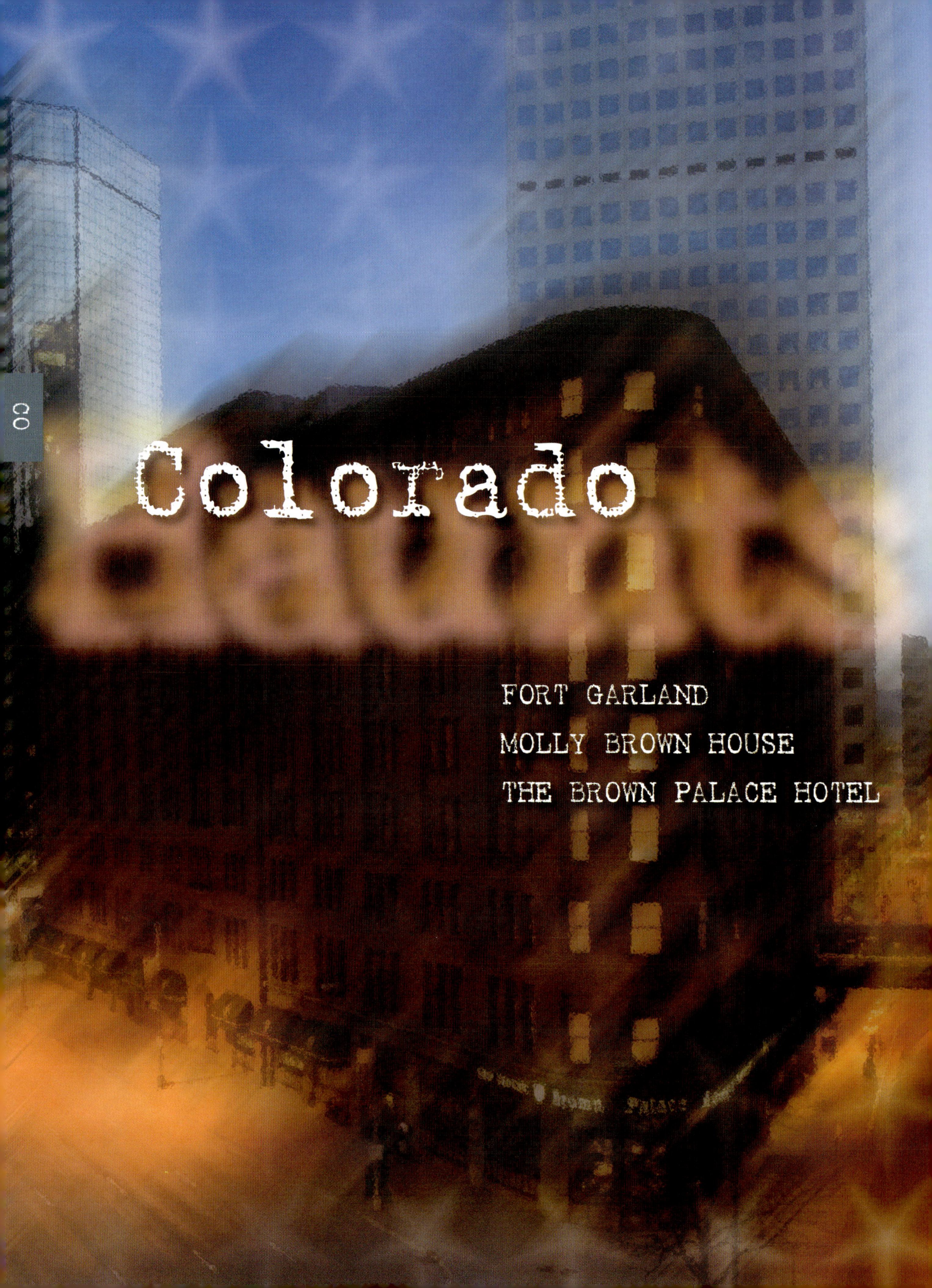

# Colorado

FORT GARLAND

MOLLY BROWN HOUSE

THE BROWN PALACE HOTEL

The isolation of Fort Garland is evident in this 1874 photo.

CO

# Fort Garland

The story was repeated far too often along America's expanding frontier in the nineteenth century—settlers encroaching on Indian lands, forts being constructed to protect the settlers, Indians eventually forced to reservations. It's a plot line you can use over and over again, just plugging in the various names of the tribes, soldiers, and the fort. What makes Fort Garland unique, however, is the name of one the commanders—the legendary frontiersman Kit Carson.

To plug in the other details, Fort Garland was constructed in 1858 to protect settlers in the San Luis Valley of southern Colorado. The Indians in this case were the Utes, who, after a thousand years of living in the region, were relocated to reservations. With the threat of attack gone, the fort was no longer needed and was abandoned in 1883.

Of course, the fact that this story was repeated in so many locations does not diminish the drama of the events that unfolded here. In a world where everyone is always electronically connected with countless handheld devices, it is difficult to imagine the harsh conditions for those sent to this remote garrison. Fortunately, since the fort was restored and reconstructed and opened as a museum in 1950, visitors can get a sense of what army life was like in the time of the Indian wars.

In addition to the museum's rotating exhibits, there are permanent exhibits on Kit Carson's adventures and his years at Fort Garland (1866-67), as well as the members of the 9th Cavalry who were stationed here in 1876-79, the famous black Buffalo Soldiers. Other highlights include the culture and folk art of the Hispanic community, military artifacts, and a soldier named Manuel Lujan.

What is a soldier still doing at the fort? Just going about his business as he did back in 1863 when he died, but perhaps this requires a little more information.

On a pay day in 1863, Manuel Lujan and another soldier had too much to drink and began fighting. The fight took a fatal turn early the next morning when the angry soldier walked up to Lujan, who was asleep on his bed, and shot him in the back of the head. In the 1980s, a former curator of the museum found that, on a regular basis, visitors came up to her and asked, "Do you know you have the ghost of a soldier here?" After listening to dozens of people tell tales of their encounters with this soldier, especially in the barracks, she decided there may be something to the stories.

While conducting some research, she uncovered the account of the murder. However, rather than being scared, the curator would start every day by greeting

Manuel, and at night asking him to watch over the place, commenting that he was the museum's "ghostly sentinel, the only guard I have that is actually in uniform."

Of course, the place may have other spirits, as well, remnants of the fort's turbulent past. When you walk the parade grounds, explore the officer's quarters and barracks, don't assume that man in a uniform or dressed in traditional Indian garb is a participant in a special event. On the other hand, it is quite a special event when figures from history walk among us…

## The Bottom Line

**The History:** A fort constructed in 1858 to protect settlers in the San Luis Valley from the Utes. Kit Carson was a commander here in 1866-67.

**The Haunting:** A murdered soldier makes his presence known.

## Recommendations

**In the past, the fort has conducted candlelight ghost hunts, so call for availability and the latest list of events and special exhibits, which include music and living history. There is a visitor center, museum, gift shop, and various buildings to explore.**

## Visitor Information

**Fort Garland**
**29477 Highway 159**
**P.O. Box 368**
**Fort Garland, CO 81133**
**(719) 379-3512**
**http://museumtrail.org/fortgarlandmuseum.asp**

**Hours:**
**April 1-October 31: open 9am – 5pm daily, November 1-March 31: 10am – 4pm Thursday-Monday; Closed Thanksgiving, Christmas Day, and New Years Day.**

**Admission:**
**Adults $4; Seniors (65+) $3.50, Age 6-16 $4; Under 6 Free, Free to CHS Members.**

**Directions:**
**The Fort Garland Museum and Visitor Center is located in Fort Garland, Colorado, 25 miles east of Alamosa on U.S. Highway 160.**

# Molly Brown House

When Molly Brown was rescued from the *Titantic* and brought to New York, reporters asked how she managed to survive the ordeal.

"Typical Brown luck," she said. "We're unsinkable."

Thus began the enduring and endearing character of the "Unsinkable Molly Brown." Some character's lives are actually larger than their fictional personas, and that can definitely be said about the daughter of Irish immigrants who rose to fame and fortune. Born Margaret Tobin in 1867 in Hannibal, Missouri, she left school at the age of 13 to work in a factory. She succumbed to the lure of the west, moved to Colorado and worked in a store. At the age of 19, Molly married a 31-year-old mining engineer, J.J. Brown. They didn't have much money, but they had that Brown luck.

While working as the superintendent of a mine, J.J. discovered gold; the owners rewarded him with shares in the lucrative company, and two new millionaires were born. Molly had gone from a poor factory worker to a wealthy woman of leisure who loved to travel—and hence her date with destiny on the *Titanic*. However, Molly never forgot the poverty and tragedy she had encountered growing up, and always lent a charitable hand to those in need. For her efforts in France during WWI, she was even awarded the French Legion of Honor.

The Molly Brown House in Denver was originally built in 1889 and contained state-of-the-art technology such as electricity, indoor plumbing, steam heat, and telephones. Unfortunately, the owners lost their mining fortune in the silver crash, and J.J. Brown bought the mansion in 1894 for $30,000. The title was transferred to Molly's name in 1898, and while she owned the house until her death in 1932, she lived there for only a short time and rented it out during most of these years. Other residents included the governor.

This once prestigious Capitol Hill neighborhood underwent many changes in the following decades—none of them good—and the former mansion of millionaires was sold for just $6,000 when Molly died. The place became a boarding house and then a home for wayward

Photo by Jeff Padrick. *Courtesy of the Molly Brown House Museum.*

girls. By 1970, historic homes were being demolished for urban renewal, and this one could easily have also met that fate. Fortunately, owner Art Leisenring and a group of concerned citizens formed Historic Denver, Inc. and saved the house from the wrecking ball. Then they raised enough money for a total restoration, and today the Molly Brown House Museum is open for visitors to enjoy. It appears as though there was just enough of that famous Brown luck left to work its magic!

It is debatable, however, whether the spirits that inhabit the old mansion are lucky to be in such a beautiful place, or unfortunate to not have moved on. One of the spirits is believed to be that of J.J. Brown, as cigar smoke has been detected in both the attic and the basement. As Molly forbid smoking in the house, perhaps he is still indulging in the guilty pleasure of sneaking the cigars he loved so much?

Among the numerous sightings are an unknown woman in Victorian clothing seen around the dining room, and a cat that some believe had been Molly's, as well as shadowy figures. Other people have claimed to see Molly herself and some of the former servants. Blinds go up and down, doors open and close, the dining room chairs often rearrange themselves, and there are cold spots. In other words, the house is still bustling with activity, just the way Molly liked it!

## The Bottom Line

**The History:** A mansion built in 1889, purchased by "Unsinkable" Molly Brown in 1894. Converted into a boarding house, saved from demolition, restored, and turned into a museum.

**The Haunting:** Cigar smoke, figures of women, a cat, cold spots, doors opening, and chairs moving.

## Recommendations

**There are rotating exhibits, workshops, and special events throughout the year. A wonderful way to experience the elegance and history of the mansion is to attend one their popular holiday high teas, which include a tour. Keep your eyes open for women in period costume, as they may not be members of the staff...**

## Visitor Information

**Molly Brown House Museum**
**1340 Pennsylvania Street**
**Denver, CO 80203**
**(303) 832-4092**
**www.mollybrown.org/**

**Hours:**

***Tuesday to Saturday:* Open at 10am, last tour starts at 3:30pm. Sunday: Open at 12pm, last tour starts at 3:30pm. Guided tours start every half hour. The Museum will be closed on New Year's Day, Easter, Memorial Day, Independence Day, Labor Day, Thanksgiving Day, Christmas Eve, Christmas Day, and New Year's Eve.**

**Limited museum parking is available in a lot at the corner of 13th Avenue and Pearl Street, one block east of the Museum. This lot opens at 9am and is locked at 5pm each day. Please note this lot may be closed on snowy days.**

**Admission:**

**$8 for adults (13-64), $6 for seniors (65+), $4 for children (6-12).**

**Directions:**

**From East Colfax Avenue (also called Routes 70/287/40), turn south on Pennsylvania Street. The Molly Brown House Museum is located just one block south of Colfax Avenue and five blocks east of Broadway at 1340 Pennsylvania Street.**

Courtesy of the Brown Palace Hotel.

CO

# The Brown Palace Hotel

Henry C. Brown was a carpenter in Ohio in the nineteenth century—not someone you would think would ever own a palace. In 1860, he moved to Colorado and eventually bought land, paying about $200 for 168 acres, a few of which he used to graze his cow. The area around that cow pasture was to become some very expensive real estate in downtown Denver, the Capitol Hill district to be specific, and the wealthy ex-carpenter wanted a palace.

Brown decided that the growing city needed a first class hotel, something that was "unprecedented" at the time. In 1892, his dream was realized on the former cow pasture land and the Brown Palace Hotel opened its doors, and hasn't closed them even for a single day since. He constructed a 400-room showpiece with an expansive 9-floor atrium, and filled it with stained glass, marble, onyx, gilding, antiques, and wrought iron. Rates were initially $1 to $4 per room and offered the best Denver had to offer, including a rooftop restaurant with views of the Rockies. Over the years the hotel has been host to many U.S. Presidents, foreign presidents and prime ministers, royalty, Nobel Prize winners, and the rich and famous from all walks of life.

Guests of particular note have included Dwight Eisenhower who ran his 1952 presidential campaign from the second-floor Brown Palace Club, and who left a golf ball dent on the fireplace of the suite that bears his name. Another popular place is the Beatles suite. When it was learned they would be staying there, the hotel received a flood of applications from female fans who suddenly wanted jobs. After their stay, fans offered to buy anything the Beatles had touched.

In such an ornate and elegant setting, one would not envision livestock, but in 1945 a future governor of Colorado, Dan Thorton, brought his prize-winning bulls to the hotel for a photo shoot for *Life* magazine, starting a tradition of cattle—and even a rodeo rider—in the lobby. The tradition continues to this day when the National Western Stock Show comes to town in January and champion steer are paraded through the hotel down a red carpet!

Several people were fortunate enough to make the Palace their permanent home, including the queen of Denver society, Louise Crawford Hill, who lived there for many years until her death in 1955. However, Louise's death may be something of a technicality as this is where the haunted side of this historic hotel begins to come into play.

It seems that while Mrs. Hill was married, she was having an affair with a much younger man. When her husband died, she planned on finally marrying her lover, but he dumped her for a much younger woman! The broken-hearted Louise became something of a recluse in the hotel's room 904, and her grief may have bound her to that room for eternity. The hotel offers historical tours, and when a group would reach her door and her story was being told, the switchboard would receive calls from the empty room 904, but no one was ever on the line. The mysterious calls only stopped when they eliminated Louise's tragic tale from the tour!

Actual sightings include what appear to be travelers in old-fashioned clothing carrying luggage. People have also seen men in railroad conductor uniforms walking through the walls of a particular room—a room which long ago used to sell train tickets and was frequented by railroad employees!

Perhaps the most bizarre encounter came one night when an employee heard music coming from the San Marco Room, which is now called Ellyngton's. This is where bands played, but none were scheduled to be there at that time. The employee entered the room and found several musicians practicing. He informed the band members that they would have to leave. They replied that they lived there, and then vanished into thin air!

Whether you are drawn to the Brown Palace Hotel for the ghosts, the history, the restaurants and high tea, the parade of cattle, or a chance to sleep in the Beatle's suite, this is truly a place where the spirit and spirits of the west can be experienced with class and distinction!

## The Bottom Line

**The History:** A former carpenter turned wealthy entrepreneur built an elegant hotel in 1892 that has been host to presidents, royalty, the Beatles, and many famous figures.

**The Haunting:** A broken-hearted society woman may still inhabit her room, phantom musicians still play, and former guests and railroad employees are seen.

## Recommendations

Of course you must ask for room 904 if you want to try to communicate with Louise Hill. If you don't have the time or money to stay overnight, at least take one of their informative tours. Look for the 2 out of 700 wrought iron panels that ring the lobby that were placed upside down, one to show that man isn't perfect, the other the work of a disgruntled employee. The Palace Arms restaurant has antiques from the Napoleonic era. Look for the profile of Henry Brown etched by the Broadway entrance, and the twenty-six carved stone medallions on the seventh floor that depict Rocky Mountain animals. There is a full-service spa if you really want to indulge and pamper yourself. And if you find the need to store large quantities of meat on your visit you won't be alone—actor Steven Seagal shot an elk on a hunting trip and stored the carcass in Palace's freezer during his stay!

## Visitor Information

**The Brown Palace Hotel and Spa**
321 17th Street, Denver, CO 80202-4003
(303) 297-3111 or (800) 321-2599
www.brownpalace.com/

**Hours:**

Public guided historical tours recounting interesting anecdotes about the general history of The Brown Palace Hotel are offered every Wednesday and Saturday at 3pm. In October, they hold the ghost tours. Children must be 10 years of age or older. Private Tour groups may request one of several themed tours of the hotel: Ghost, Architectural, Romance, Presidential, and Ladies of The Brown. Reservations are required.

**Directions:**

*From their website*—From Denver International Airport: Take Pena Boulevard 10 miles to I-70 exit (exit West). Take I-70 West to the Colorado Boulevard Exit 276B (turn left on To Colorado Boulevard). Take Colorado Boulevard 2½ miles to 17th Avenue (turn right). Continue on 17th Avenue West until you reach York Street. At York, 17th Avenue becomes 18th Avenue (slight turn left). Continue on 18th Avenue past Broadway where the street becomes Tremont. The Grand Entrance to the Brown Palace Hotel is located on Tremont Street. A Doorman will be at the entrance to assist with valet parking.

*From the foothills:* Take 1-70 East to 6th Avenue Exit. Continue on 6th Avenue Freeway East for approximately 10 Miles. Turn Left at Lincoln Street. Continue on Lincoln Street to 18th Avenue (turn Left). Take 18th to Broadway and soft Left on to Tremont Street to the Grand Entrance.

*Arrival from Colorado Springs and I-25 South:*
Take I-25 North until you reach the Lincoln Broadway Exit (exit right on Lincoln), then follow directions above.

*Arrival from Fort Collins and I-25 North:* Take I-25 South to the Park Avenue Exit (turn on to downtown exit). Take Park Avenue to Broadway (turn right). Continue on Broadway to Tremont Street (turn Right).

*Super Shuttle* provides scheduled runs from the airport every 15 minutes, beginning at 5:30am and ending at midnight. To make arrangements with Super Shuttle, call 1-800-BLUE-VAN.

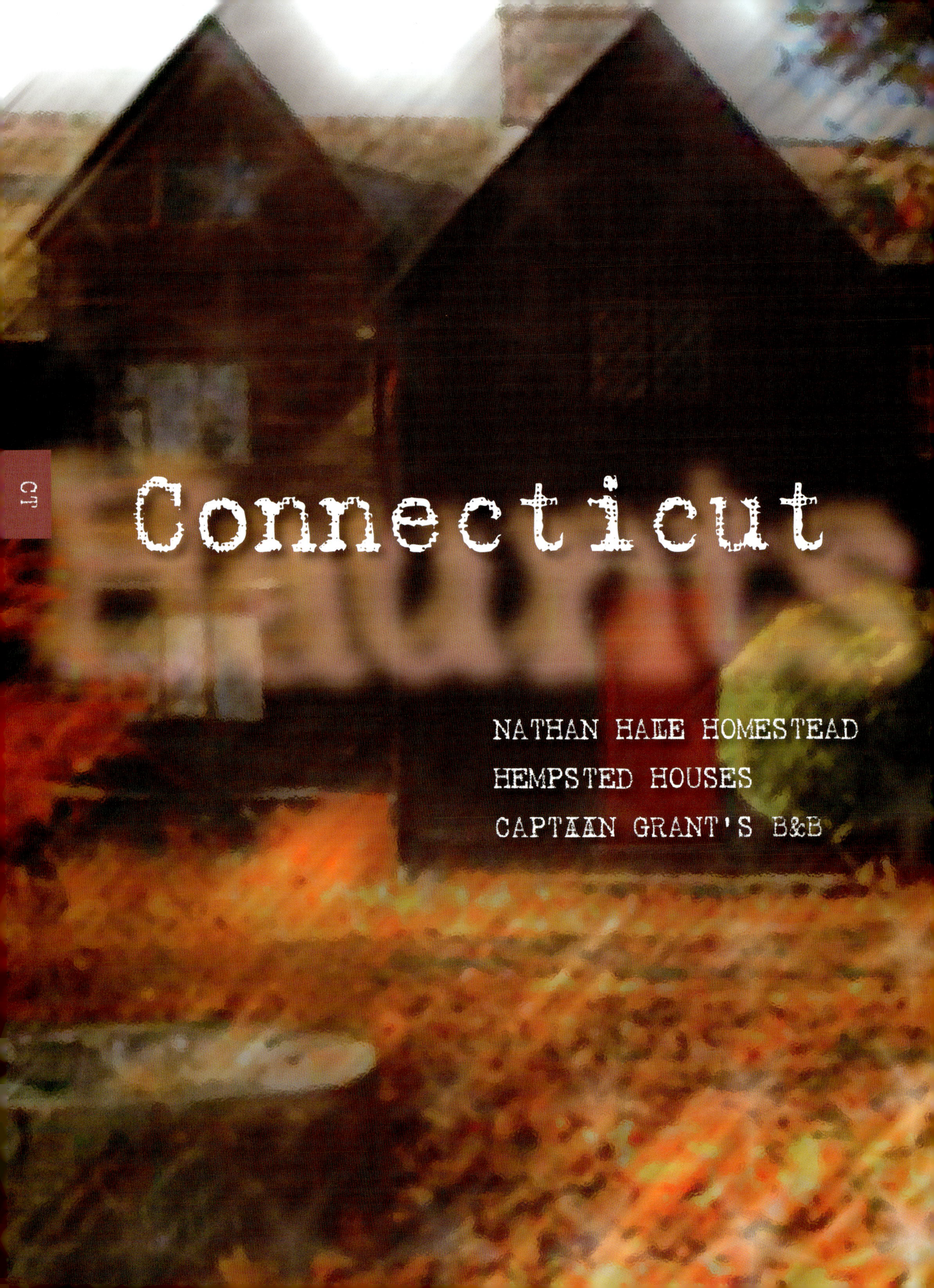

CT

# Connecticut

NATHAN HALE HOMESTEAD

HEMPSTED HOUSES

CAPTAIN GRANT'S B&B

Nathan Hale Homestead. *Courtesy of Connecticut Landmarks.*

CT

# Nathan Hale Homestead

"I regret that I have but one life to give for my country."
~ Nathan Hale ~

With those famous last words, 21-year-old Nathan Hale was hung by the British for being a spy. It was September 22, 1776, and the execution site was a tree by the current intersection of 66th Street and 3rd Avenue in Manhattan. Hale had volunteered to go behind enemy lines to gather information for the Continental Army, and had shed his Captain's uniform for civilian clothing. Captured and sentenced to death, by all accounts Hale carried himself with dignity and composure in his final moments, and gave a patriotic speech that is still often quoted today.

Nathan Hale was born in Coventry, Connecticut, in 1755. At the age of only thirteen, Nathan attended Yale College. Upon graduation, he became a teacher. Had the Revolutionary War not begun, he may have quietly lived out his days as a schoolteacher, but history had a different course for him.

The house that now stands at the Nathan Hale Homestead was built in 1776. While Nathan never lived in this house, it is on the site of the home in which he grew up, and it is believed to have been constructed using materials from the original house. His father, the widower Deacon Richard Hale, needed to build this new house, as he had twelve children and he married a widow who had seven children!

The house remained in the Hale family until the 1820s. In 1914, the property was purchased by George Dudley Seymour, a passionate historian who wanted to restore everything to how it would have appeared in 1776. He did a wonderful job, except for one little thing…

Actually, it wasn't so little—despite Seymour's insistence on making the Hale Homestead as authentic as possible, he built a massive stone pyramid as a grave marker. Now, before you say what a fine idea it was to commemorate the final resting place of an American hero, in fact, no one knows where Nathan Hale's body was buried. No, this pyramid marks the final resting place of Seymour's favorite horse! (Who, by the way, was named Thomas Hooker Bones, after the founder of Connecticut, Thomas Hooker.)

While Seymour may have been a bit on the eccentric side, he is responsible for the preservation of an important historic site. Upon his death in 1945, the property was bequeathed to Connecticut Landmarks, which has continued to care for the place and make it available to the public to appreciate and enjoy.

Seymour brought many period antiques and Hale family objects into the house, and he also brought something even more unique—he began the long history of Hale Homestead ghost stories. He claimed that after buying the place, he and a friend were taking a look around. He put his face up to a window to look inside, and there was the face of Deacon Richard Hale looking back at him!

In recent times, a young boy walked away from a tour group and the guide went to retrieve him. The boy insisted he was following a man in colonial attire and kept pointing to the room the man had entered. They checked the room, but no one was there. Was this just a boy's imagination, or was Richard Hale making another appearance?

Other activity has led some to speculate that Nathan's brother, Joseph, may inhabit the basement, and a Hale family servant, Lydia Carpenter, is still attending to chores in the house. Most of the guides have experienced footsteps, voices, laughter, lights going on and off, and doors opening and closing. One guide, who was alone in the house, was locking up for the night when she heard a woman weeping. Another guide, who was opening the place for the day, stepped inside and decided to ask if anyone was there, and a reply came from upstairs, "I'm up here." Of course, no one else was in the house.

Do Hale family members still make their presence known here? Do they regret having only one short life to live? Perhaps if you visit the Nathan Hale Homestead, you will meet them in person and find out.

## The Bottom Line

**The History:** A 1776 house built by Nathan Hale's father on the site of where Nathan grew up. Bought in 1914 and restored by George Dudley Seymour. Contains Hale family objects and many antiques.

**The Haunting:** A man in colonial clothing, possibly Hale's father, has been seen. His brother and a servant may also be in the house. The sounds of footsteps, weeping, laughing, and voices.

## Recommendations

**Nathan Hale's trunk and fowling iron (his gun) are on display in the house. Look for the profile of a man's face etched into one of the doors; it just may be the only known likeness of Nathan! Take time to enjoy the grounds, and check for special events. And, of course, check out the stone pyramid, which you can't miss.**

## Visitor Information

**Nathan Hale Homestead**
**2299 South Street**
**Coventry, CT 06238**
**(860) 742-6917**
**hale@ctlandmarks.org**

**Events:**
**In the barn visitors can watch a short video on the life of Nathan Hale and his contributions to the Revolution. Next to the house is a field where, every October, they host a haunted corn maze. Check their website for special events such as teas and cooking demonstrations.**

**Hours:**
**Open for tours Memorial Day weekend through October 31; May, Saturday and Sunday, 11am – 4pm; June-August, Wednesday, Friday, Saturday and Sunday, 11am – 4pm; September-October, Saturday and Sunday 11am – 4pm. Open on Memorial Day, Labor Day and Columbus Day, 11am – 4pm. Group tours may be scheduled by appointment.**

***Please call ahead to confirm as hours are subject to change.**

**Admission:**
**Adults: $7; Students with ID; Seniors (65+); AAA members, Teachers-$6; Children age 6-18: $4; Children under 6 and Connecticut Landmarks Members: Free; Family Price (2 adults and unlimited number of children) $15**

**Directions:**
***From their website*—From West: I-84. From I-384, turn right Route 6 From Route 6, make a left turn onto South Street (NOT South Road). Stay on South Street and follow the signs to Hale Homestead. The Homestead is 6.3 miles from I-384 .**

***From East:* I-84 Take I-84 to the Coventry exit (#67), Stay south on Route 31. Make a left onto Route 44. Make a right onto Silver Street. At end of Silver Street, turn left onto South Street. Staying on South Street, follow the signs to Hale Homestead. The Homestead is 9 miles from I-84.**

Hempsted House. *Courtesy of Connecticut Landmarks.*

CT

# Hempsted Houses

One of the two Hempsted Houses in New London was built in 1759, which makes it something of a rare structure in today's world. However, considering the other Hempsted house is eighty-two years older, you have a remarkable pair of buildings steeped in history.

The Joshua Hempsted house was built in 1678, making it one of Connecticut's oldest houses. Joshua was born in the house that same year, and he lived his entire life there. He was something of a Renaissance man, having at some point in his life been a farmer, carpenter, surveyor, Justice of the Peace, judge, gravestone carver, and shipwright. He was also quite prolific in two other areas—fatherhood and writing.

Joshua Hempsted was the father of nine children, and he kept a diary for five decades. What he left behind is an amazing view of everyday life in America from 1711 to 1758. Among those thousands of diary entries were hundreds of pages containing information about Adam Jackson—one of Hempsted's slaves. Jackson's day-to-day activities were chronicled in great detail, arguably making him the most documented slave in history. Typically, the only time a slave's name would even be written was on a bill of sale, or in a list of property in a will, so Hempsted's diaries truly offer a unique historical perspective.

The diaries also offer wonderful personal stories that enrich visitor's experiences. For example, without the diaries you could glance out a particular window in the Joshua Hempsted House and not give it another thought. However, if you had read Joshua's diary entry involving an incident with that same window and his youngest daughter, Molly, you would view it in a totally different light.

It seems that Molly was a very accident-prone little girl. Joshua wrote about how she had been trampled by cows and badly scalded by hot milk. Poor Molly had various other misadventures, including falling out of that window! Miraculously, she somehow managed to survive, and grew up to marry and have a family of her own—and we can only hope she did not pass down her uncanny ability to get into harm's way.

The 1759 house was built for Nathaniel Hempsted, Joshua's grandson whom he had raised. This place is built of stone, which is unusual for Connecticut houses. Both houses remained occupied by the Hempsted family until 1937, and were shortly after acquired by the Connecticut Antiquarian and Landmarks Society. Both homes have been restored and filled with period antiques, some of which are original to the Hempsted family. For instance, there is a chair that belonged to Sheriff Joshua Hempsted, the diarist's grandson. What is special about this chair is the size of its seat. To put it tactfully, it's obvious that the Sheriff was a larger-than-life historical figure!

There is something even more unique from the family that can be seen here—one of the Hempsted women. When a team of workmen were restoring the exterior of the Joshua Hempsted House, they all kept seeing a blond woman inside. This was unusual, because it was their understanding that the house was closed, and they never saw the woman enter or exit the house. Indeed, the house was locked up during the renovations, so no one could have entered. Was this woman keeping an eye on the workmen to make sure they did a good job on her home?

There have been other reports of unusual activity and feelings of a strong presence in the house, but as of yet there is no clear indication as to who the spirit, or spirits, are that walk the halls. It is just one of those fascinating mysteries, that along with such things as diary entries and antiques, bring the past to life in the Hempsted Houses.



## The Bottom Line

**The History:** The Joshua Hempsted House was built in 1678, making it one of Connecticut's oldest houses. The Nathaniel Hempsted House was built in 1759. Joshua kept a diary for 47 years, which brings a fascinating, in-depth view of the everyday lives of people in colonial America.

**The Haunting:** Workmen repeatedly saw a blond woman inside the Joshua Hempsted House. People have felt a strong presence.

## Recommendations

The diaries of Joshua Hempsted are available in a book, but if you don't want to read forty-seven years of diary entries, take a tour of the houses and the knowledgeable guide will fill you in on some highlights. Take a look through Molly's window, and look for the Sheriff's large chair. There is also an old gun which may be the one Joshua used "to hunt wolves in ye Great Swamp." There is a Harvest Festival held in October. Check the website for information on other special events.

## Visitor Information

**Hempsted Houses**
11 Hempstead Street
New London, CT 06320
(860) 443-7949
hempsted@ctlandmarks.org
www.ctlandmarks.org

**Hours:**

Open for tours Memorial Day weekend through Columbus Day weekend. May-June, Saturday, and Sunday 12 – 4pm; July-August, Friday, Saturday, Sunday 12 – 4pm; September-October: Saturday and Sunday 12 – 4pm. Group tours may be scheduled by appointment.

**Admission:**

Adults: $7, Students with ID; Seniors (65+); AAA members, Teachers-$6, Children age 6-18: $4, Children under 6 and Connecticut Landmarks Members: Free, Family Price (2 adults and unlimited number of children): $15

**Directions:**

*From their website*—From the East: Take I-95N. Take exit #83A off I-95. Follow Huntington Street through downtown New London, past the Old Court House. Turn right onto Jay Street. The Hempsted Houses are prominently situated a couple blocks down on the right at the corner of Jay and Hempstead Streets.

*From Hartford via Route 85:* Take route 2 South to Route 11 toward New London. Take the last exit on route 11. Turn left on Route 82. Turn right on Route 85 and follow into New London. Make a right onto Hempstead Street (there is a large stone church on the left hand side). Hempstead Street curves to the left. The museum is on the left hand side.

Courtesy of Captain Grant's Inn.



# Captain Grant's B&B

Captain William Gonzales Grant made his money by bringing shipments of mahogany back from Honduras. A life at sea was always fraught with peril, and at the age of only 32, Grant's ship hit a storm off Cape Hatteras and he was lost at sea. Actually, he wasn't lost that long, as his body was found tied to a mast, and he was only wearing one boot. Had there been foul play, or had the good captain simply been determined to go down with his ship?

Fortunately, he had provided for his wife and children at Poquetanuck Village:

"Let it be known that on this date, I, William Grant, hath built a home suitable for my wife Mercy and our sons who God wilth provide for us. God save the King."
February 13, 1754

It's fortunate he spent money on this house, as he had a bad gambling habit. (Curiously, two of the country's largest casinos are now nearby.) When he lost a lot at cards, he would leave his wife and family and take off to sea to make more money. Though left alone after her husband's death, Mercy Adelaide Grant was able to manage to raise the children, and she lived to a ripe old age in her 80s. Three generations of Grants would call this place home.

During the Revolutionary War, soldiers were stationed in the house, and there is strong evidence that George Washington himself stayed here at that time. There is a mural in the city hall depicting the event.

Many years later, the Grant home was used to house some other people—runaway slaves. Many of the homes in the village had secret tunnels running down to Poquetanuck Cove. It's believed that ships coming into the cove may have delivered or picked up the runaways as part of the Underground Railroad leading to freedom in Canada.

By the 1990s, the old house needed work, so a major restoration took place from 1994 through 1996. Today, Captain Grant's home is on the National Register of Historic Places, and is operated as a bed and breakfast by Carol and Ted Matsumoto. They also own two other properties where guests can stay, both built in 1790—the Stagecoach Inn, which has one of those tunnels, and the adjacent Avery House, which by the way, just might have a ghost or two.

However, when it comes to ghosts, Captain Grant's is the place to stay, specifically in the Adelaide Room. While Carol suspected the house was haunted, she didn't advertise the fact as she didn't want to frighten away guests. She finally had to "come clean" and admit it, though, after an early morning incident.

A New York City detective was spending the night in the Adelaide Room, and at 7am he came downstairs in quite a huff. He explained that between 4am and 5am someone was walking around in the attic above his room. This person was wearing heavy boots (or could it have been only one boot!?) and was making quite a racket. How could the owners be so rude as to stomp around like that, and what on earth were they doing in the attic at that hour?

"The house is haunted," Carol finally confessed. "And after breakfast I will prove it to you."

The detective was understandably skeptical, until he followed Carol into the attic. The area above his room was covered in piles of lumber and building materials, so it would have been impossible for anyone to walk across the floor. The detective was stunned, and his anger turned to a curiosity that has brought him back to stay in that room again.

The most often encountered spirit is that of a woman in a blue dress with puffy sleeves and a white apron. Everyone who has seen this woman has described her in the same exact manner. Could this be Mercy, still going about her business of managing the household and caring for the children?

At least two children have also been seen, a little boy and a girl. The girl made the most dramatic appearance, and to a total nonbeliever. A woman who worked there didn't believe a word about the ghost stories, and emphatically insisted that such things simply did not exist. One day when she was cleaning the Adelaide Room, she noticed that the blinds were askew for the third day in a row. When she reached up to straighten them, the little girl walked right under her arms! The skeptic became so distraught she had to go home.

Of course, even harmless spirits can be startling, but for the most part, there is no fear experienced with the ghosts here. In fact, many people who have stayed in the Adelaide Room report in the morning that they feel great, that there is "something unusual" about that room that makes them feel good.

Are there the spirits of soldiers, runaway slaves, or members of the Grant family at this place that have witnessed over 250 years of human occupation and the daily dramas of life? Those who have spent the night would say yes. Even the nonbelievers would have to admit that Captain Grant's 1754 Bed and Breakfast offers a genuine old New England experience...right down to the genuine old New Englanders themselves!



## Recommendations

**Carol strongly recommends that you bring your cameras and camcorders, as guests are always capturing strange images. There are special events at Halloween, but you can obviously have an encounter any time of year; just book well in advance if you want the Adelaide Room. While waiting for a ghost to appear, you can cozy up to the fireplace and munch on some fresh popcorn from their machine, watch a movie, or take advantage of the WiFi. And if you decide you want to practice Captain Grant's old hobby, both Foxwoods and Mohegan Sun casinos are nearby.**

## Visitor Information

**Captain Grant's Bed and Breakfast**
109-111 Route 2A
Preston, CT 06365-8539
(800) 982-1772
(860) 887-7589
www.captaingrants.com/

**Directions:**

*From N.Y./West:* North on I-95 to Exit 76 on to I-395 (North). Take Exit 79A onto Route 2A. Follow to "T" intersection (traffic light). Turn left on to Routes 2A/12. After about 500 feet, take right fork on to Route 2A. Captain Grant's is 1.6 miles on the right. Turn in driveway immediately before sign.

*From Boston/East:* South on I-95. Take Exit 92 onto Route 2 West. Approximately 12 miles (and 4 miles past Foxwoods), take a left on to Route 2A (traffic light and left hand only turn). Captain Grant's is 1.1 miles on the left. Turn in immediately after the sign.

*From the north:* Take I-395 south to Exit 79A. Follow to "T" intersection (traffic light). Turn left onto Routes 2A/12. After about 500 feet, take right fork on to Route 2A. Captain Grant's is 1.6 miles on the right. Turn in the driveway immediately before the sign.

## The Bottom Line

**The History:** A house built by a sea captain in 1754. George Washington and his soldiers stayed here during the Revolutionary War. The house sheltered runaway slaves as part of the Underground Railroad.

**The Haunting:** Staff and guests have seen a woman in a blue dress, a little girl and boy, and heard a man stomping around the attic.

# Delaware Haunts

FORT DELAWARE

WOODBURN

ADDY SEA

DE

Fort Delaware.

DE

# Fort Delaware

It may not exactly be time travel, but a short ferry ride can bring you back to 1864. You can take part in an artillery drill—but don't forget to plug your ears when the cannon is fired—get all the latest fort gossip from the laundress as you help her scrub clothes, or watch the blacksmith pound hot metal into shape. If you're lucky, you might even be able to speak to a Confederate prisoner about his plans to escape.

Okay, so perhaps these people are just living historians reenacting the roles of the men and women from Fort Delaware during the Civil War, but it certainly beats learning about the war from a book! And there is always the possibility here of coming in contact with someone who actually was in the Civil War, but more on that shortly.

As early as 1794, Pea Patch Island was recognized for its ideal defensive position by Pierre Charles L'Enfant, the designer of Washington, D.C. Construction of a fort didn't begin until 1817, and much of that original structure was damaged by fire in 1833. The remains were torn down, and plans were set in motion for a bigger and better fort—in fact, by the time a decade of construction was completed in 1859, it would be the largest fort in the country. The fortress was part of the coastal defense system during World Wars I and II, then became a state park after an extensive restoration.

While the fort's guns never fired a shot in anger, the island did play a role during the Civil War as a prison for Confederate soldiers (including those captured at Gettysburg), and southern sympathizers who were deemed to be traitors. Barracks were erected across the 178-acre island to hold these prisoners, which at one time numbered as many as 12,500. A total of over 40,000 prisoners were kept here during the course of the war, with over 2,900 of them dying due to disease and the harsh conditions. That's a lot of deaths for one tiny island!

It should come as no surprise, then, that ghosts abound at Fort Delaware. Visitors and staff have seen the figures of Confederate soldiers, both solid and transparent—some running as if trying to escape, while others stand perfectly still. There are moans and groans and the sounds of rattling chains that echo from the dungeons. A park ranger claims to have encountered a very clear figure of a pirate and was able to describe the apparition's clothing in great detail.

Even though daylight doesn't appear to inhibit the ghosts of this island, many people prefer a spookier experience by investigating at night. Thanks to the fort's popular candlelight ghost tours, held on several weekends throughout the summer, you can get a chance to meet a Civil War soldier face to face in the darkness. Just remember, be careful what you wish for, as you might just get it at Fort Delaware!

## The Bottom Line

**The History:** An island that was the site of an early nineteenth century fort that burned and was replaced in 1859 by what was then the largest fort in the country. Held over 40,000 prisoners during the Civil War, with over 2,900 dying in captivity.

**The Haunting:** Both solid and transparent figures of Confederate soldiers, moaning, groaning, and chains rattling. Considered by many to be a very haunted location.

## Recommendations

Unlike many museums where it is "look, but don't touch," Fort Delaware is an interactive experience, and the costumed staff offers visitors the opportunity to participate in many aspects of daily life. You can learn about everything from Civil War photography, to medicine, to fixing cannons, to how the heck you feed all of those soldiers and prisoners. This is one of those places where you need to plan on two trips, one during the day to soak up all the history, and one at night to delve into the paranormal. Book the ghost tours well in advance, though, as they fill up quickly.

## Visitor Information:

**Fort Delaware**
Pea Patch Island
Park Office: P.O. Box 170
Delaware City, DE 19706
(302) 834-7941
www.destateparks.com/park/fort-delaware/index.asp

**Events:**

It is a one-half-mile ferry ride from Delaware City to Pea Patch Island. A jitney provides transport from the island dock to the fort. There is a food concession stand on the island, or you can bring a picnic lunch as tables and grills are provided. There are a variety of daily programs; call for specific information. The second week of June there is an "Escape from Fort Delaware" triathlon, where competitors begin the event by "escaping" from the island and swimming back to Delaware City, in recognition of the fifty-two Confederates who made it to freedom.

**Hours:**

Closed during the winter, reopens in April. Call for exact dates.

Ferries to the island run from 10am – 4pm. Returning ferries run from 10:30am – 5:30pm.

**Admission:**

*For Ferry to the Island:* Adults (13+) $11, Children (2-12) $6, Under 2 Free, Seniors (62+) $10. For reservations, go online or call 1-877-98-PARKS.

**Directions:**

Fort Delaware State Park is located on Pea Patch Island. To reach the island, you must take a ferry from 45 Clinton Street, Delaware City, Delaware.

*From Interstate 95:* Take exit 4A for DE-7 S toward DE-1 S/Christiana Mall Road. Keep right at the fork to continue toward DE-1 S/DE-7 S and merge onto DE-1 S/DE-7 S. Continue to follow DE-1 S. Take exit 156 to merge onto South Dupont Parkway/US-13 N toward Wilmington. Turn right at Hamburg Road. Take the 1st right onto DE-9 S/Hamburg Corner River Road/River Road. Continue to follow DE-9 S/Hamburg Corner River Road. Turn left at DE-9 S. Turn left at Clinton Street; ferry will be on the right.

*Courtesy of Woodburn.*

DE

## Woodburn

In 1683, William Penn granted 3,000 acres of land to John Hillyard. Over a hundred years and several generations later, Hillyard's great-grandson, Charles, built a magnificent Georgian-style mansion on part of that land. Over two centuries after that, Charles and other former residents may still be calling Woodburn home.

Charles Hillyard III was a colonel during the Revolutionary War, and in the 1790s he needed a large house as he and his wife, Mary, were to have ten children. Charles died in 1814, but the house remained in the family with his daughter, Mary, and her husband, Martin Bates. Mr. Bates appears to have been one of those early American jack-of-all-trades, as he earned a medical degree, was admitted to the bar, served as a U.S. Senator, and ran a mercantile business. Though still owning the house, the Bates family moved out in 1820, and the Governor of Delaware, Jacob Stout, moved in. While Stout was the first governor to live here, he certainly wasn't the last, as Woodburn was purchased in 1965 to become the home to all of Delaware's governors since that time.

Several other families owned the property in the interim, including another senator, a Quaker who freed all his slaves, a judge, a dentist, and two doctors. There are rumors that Woodburn was a stop on the Underground Railroad, and that there were secret tunnels leading from the basement to the river, but that has yet to be confirmed. Legend also has it that this was the site of one of Patty Cannon's raids.

Cannon was head of a gang that captured fugitive slaves, and also kidnapped free blacks and sold them into slavery. While there wasn't much of an outcry for her to stop these violent and illegal activities, the justice system did finally draw the line at murder. After the graves of some of her victims were discovered, she was taken into custody and died in prison, some say by her own hand. And FYI, the nearby Dover Public Library has a grisly relic of this infamous criminal—her skull!

While on the subject of death, are their any ghosts of this old mansion with its colorful history? Yes, in fact, with the general consensus being that there are several distinct entities. The earliest sighting goes way back to 1815, when Lorenzo Dow, a Methodist preacher, was a guest at Woodburn. Mrs. Bates asked Dow to say grace before breakfast, and he suggested he wait until the other guest came to the table. Dow was obviously mistaken, as there were no other guests, but he insisted he passed a man on the staircase who was wearing old-fashioned knee breeches and a ruffled shirt. Mrs. Bates was stunned, as the preacher's detailed description fit that of her deceased father, Charles Hillyard!

Hillyard has been seen on numerous occasions over the years, most notably in the 1960s by Governor Charles Terry Jr., who saw an apparition in a powdered white wig. This spirit was indulging in spirits, as he was seen taking wine from a decanter in the dining room. In fact, wine appears to disappear from decanters, bottles, and glasses on a regular basis at Woodburn. Apparently, old habits are very hard to break, even after you're dead!

In 1985, guests at the inauguration party for Governor Michael Castle complained that some unseen presence had tugged on their clothing. This presence wasn't completely invisible, however, as one of the guests saw the apparition of a little girl floating in the reception room. That's one governor who really knew how to throw a party!

This little girl has been seen at least since the 1940s, and is always described as wearing a red gingham dress. While she has appeared in the house, she is most often seen outside by the reflecting pool.

There are conflicting accounts surrounding arguably the unhappiest spirit at Woodburn. There was a large tree where a man was said to have died, and his spirit can be seen there to this day, along with the sounds of moaning, and the rattle of chains. Depending upon the version being told, this man was either an unfortunate runaway slave who died while hiding in the tree, or a ruthless slave hunter who had climbed the tree to wait for his prey, then slipped and caught his head between two branches and suffocated. Whether the activity was the result of one of these scenarios, or something entirely different, the fact remains that this was one creepy tree. While Dead Man's Tree was removed in 1998, strange experiences are still to be had on this spot.

With a long line of distinguished residents and almost two hundred years of recorded ghostly activity, Woodburn embodies all the aspects of a historic haunted home. But you don't need to be governor of Delaware to walk these old halls, staircases, and grounds looking for a man in a powdered wig or a little girl. The house is open daily for tours, and for Halloween the place is transformed into a haunted house...which seems rather redundant, considering its haunted history...

## Recommendations

There are many special occasions throughout the year that give visitors a chance to enjoy this beautiful home. For a more personal experience, take one of the private tours, but don't just show up, be sure to book twenty-four hours in advance. While the architecture, furnishings, and paintings are spectacular, try to visit when the gardens are in bloom. Look for the bullet in the front door, which legend has it was fired by Charles Hillyard at his son during an argument.

## Visitor Information

**Woodburn**
151 King's Highway
Dover, DE 19901-7307
(302) 739-5656
http://woodburn.delaware.gov/

**Events:**
Annual events include an Easter Egg Hunt, Old Dover Days, Fall Festival, Halloween Haunted House, and Christmas Open House.

**Hours:**
Tours of Woodburn are open to the public Monday through Friday, 8:30am – 4pm, by appointment only, and must be scheduled twenty-four hours in advance.

Admission:
Admission is free.

**Directions:**
From Route 1: Take exit 98 for DE-8 toward Downtown Dover/Little Creek. Turn right at North Little Creek Road/State Road 8. Continue to follow State Road 8. Turn left at Kings Highway. Woodburn will be on the left.



## The Bottom Line

**The History:** A Georgian-style house built in the 1790s that has had many distinguished residents and has been the home of the governors since 1966. May have been a stop on the Underground Railroad, and the site of a raid to capture free blacks and runaway slaves.

**The Haunting:** The ghost of the original owner first appeared in 1815, and has been seen many times since. A little girl is seen, and moaning sounds come from the site of Dead Man's Tree. Wine mysteriously disappears.

# Addy Sea

Reward: Stolen bathtub.
Last seen about five years ago.
Very heavy. May have come with its own ghost.

This is not a typical newspaper ad, but then the story of the Addy Sea is far from typical. John Addy was from Pittsburgh, Pennsylvania, and earned his living as a plumbing supplier. In 1902, he built a home for his family in Bethany Beach. This made the Addys one of the earliest families in town, as it had been founded only the year before by members of the Disciples of Christ Church as a place for Christians to meet.

As plumbing was his business, the new home had something many houses at that time did not—modern indoor bathrooms. Addy also drilled through the bedrock to make sure his family would have plenty of fresh well water. Finally, the crowning glory of all this plumbing was John Addy's personal bathtub, which was a Victorian claw-foot beauty made of solid copper!

One of the ghostly stories about the inn was that this tub, which was in Room #1, would shudder violently. Some people claimed it was because all this copper and water together acted like a magnet for paranormal energy. Of course, it could simply have been the result of the plumbing, as old pipes are prone to shake, rattle, and roll, often being mistaken for something otherworldly. Unfortunately, there is no way to examine the copper tub to determine the cause of the shaking, as thieves somehow managed to carry it off. (Many websites and books urge guests to request Room #1 to experience the haunted tub, unaware that the tub is long gone.)

Something else was removed in 1927—the entire house was moved from its original foundation! After a severe storm, it was decided to move the house back away from the ocean's edge. Not only were the Addys safer, but the old foundation made a great place to have a party on the beach!

During the Depression, the house was rented to various church groups, and in 1935, it was converted into a boarding house. The children of John Addy, and then the grandchildren, continued to run the business until it was sold out of the family in 1975. Today, the Addy Sea is a bed and breakfast that offers guests the opportunity to step back into the elegance of the Victorian era. It may also offer a step back into the paranormal.

While the copper bathtub may be gone, there have still been enough reports of haunted activity to keep any ghost enthusiast happy. For example, over the years, some have heard footsteps in the second-floor hall, but even more telling, they have heard them on the roof. This had lead some to believe that these footsteps are the result of the spirit of John's son, Kurtz, a high-energy boy who fell off of the roof and died.

Other activity includes the sound of organ music in Room #6. A famous swimmer, Paul Dulaney, once worked as a handyman for the Addys, and he is said to haunt Room #11 on the third floor. If you unable to book one of the haunted rooms (there are a total of 13 rooms, a fitting number!), don't despair, as the sudden scent of an old perfume or strange music can pop up anywhere. Even the beach is said to be haunted. There have been claims of hearing a woman crying out when the tide is low, while others claim to have watched as footprints mysteriously appear in the sand on moonlit nights!

There are obviously many mysteries to explore in and around the Addy Sea. And if while you're in town someone offers to sell you a large copper tub, just remember, it may come with a ghost.

## The Bottom Line

**The History:** A home built in 1902 that had all the modern conveniences at the time. Was rented out to church groups during the Depression and became a boarding house in 1935. The house was moved back from the water's edge after a storm in 1927.

**The Haunting:** People claim to hear the footsteps of a boy who died in a fall from the roof; there's music, the scent of perfume, and phantom footsteps appear in the sand.

## Recommendations

**Summer is obviously their busiest season, so if you are looking for more than just wonderful accommodations right on the beach (does anyone really need more than that!?), try another time of year when there aren't as many people, and things will be quieter. The rooms with the most activity are #6 and #11. Room #1 had activity when the copper tub was there, but it is unknown whether or not there has been recent activity.**

## Visitor Information

**Addy Sea**
**99 Ocean View Parkway**
**Bethany Beach, DE 19930-9262**
**(302) 539-3707 or (800) 418-6764**
**www.addysea.com/**

**Directions:**

**From Dover take Route 1 south for 53 miles. Turn left onto Ocean View Parkway. The Addy Sea is at the end of the street.**

# Florida

ST. AUGUSTINE

RIPLEY'S MUSEUM

ST. FRANCIS INN

# St. Augustine

An exception will be made for this entry as it involves multiple locations. It's just that there are so many haunted places in St. Augustine that to give it fair treatment would require an entire book of its own! Three locations will be discussed here; the fort, the old city gates, and the lighthouse. Two other locations will be discussed in more detail in the entries that follow.

Founded by the Spanish in 1565, this is America's oldest continuously occupied European city, as well as being its oldest port. You will need to get out your scorecards when it comes to keeping track of the city's history and cultural influences, as it was governed by the Spanish, the British, back to the Spanish again, then the Americans, briefly the Confederacy, and finally back to the good old USA. And let us not forget the original residents of the area, the Timucua Indians, whose once-thriving population was decimated by European diseases and wars, until they became extinct in the early 1700s. People from many other cultures also came to St. Augustine, and through the centuries the inhabitants have suffered from battles and epidemics, as well as all the usual human dramas of life.

In other words, this place is ripe for haunting.

The city gates.

## The Old City Gates

But where to begin in this city of the restless dead? A logical place would be the old city gates, where a young barefoot girl in a nightgown has often been seen late at night. On a regular basis, the local police get calls from concerned residents and tourists reporting a girl who appears to be dazed and sick, just standing by the gates. The police always advise the witnesses to take another look to see if she is still there, and these people are always astonished that she has vanished. This frequently seen spirit even has a name, Elizabeth, and she is believed to be one of the many victims of the devastating yellow fever epidemic of 1821.

FL

Castillo de San Marcos.

## Castillo De San Marcos

Just across the street from the old city gates is the impressive stone fort, the Castillo De San Marcos. Construction began in 1672, giving this place more than enough time to pick up a ghost or two (or dozens) along the way. Of course, time alone doesn't create hauntings, death and suffering does, and the fort has had plenty of that, as well. The British attacked the fort and held it under siege for a period of fifty days in 1702, then for twenty-seven days of bombardment in 1740. The fortress also served as a prison, housing at various times Seminole and Plains Indians, captured Confederates, and army deserters.

It should come as no surprise then, that there have been many sightings of strange glowing lights, Spanish soldiers, American soldiers, and Indian prisoners—one of whom was killed trying to escape, and who continues to be seen still trying to jump from the wall to his freedom.

## St. Augustine Lighthouse

Speaking of lights, there is one that shines over the entire area—the powerful beacon of St. Augustine's famous lighthouse. A watchtower had been built by the Spanish in the late 1500s, and it became Florida's first lighthouse in 1824. The present lighthouse was finished in 1874 with 219 steps leading up to the beacon, giving spectacular views of the city and ocean.

As with many places, there is a lot of misinformation about the tragic events that may be responsible for the ghostly activity in and around the lighthouse. But to be sure, there have been numerous tragedies at this site. In 1859, Joseph Andreu fell from the first lighthouse and died. Other lighthouse keepers and family members died of natural causes in the keeper's house. The worst



## Recommendations

**Go in the spring, go in the summer, or in the fall or winter; just go to St. Augustine! This city is the epitome of historic haunts, and whether you are walking down one of the old streets, staying at an inn, or dining in one of their fine restaurants, you are bound to be somewhere that has ghost stories. This is a wonderful place to explore on foot, so park the car as soon as possible. The red trains are also very convenient ways to get around town. St. Augustine presents the unique opportunity to sleep in a haunted B&B, eat in a haunted restaurant, shop in haunted stores, and spend all day visiting haunted attractions.**

## Visitor Information

**Castillo de San Marcos National Monument**
1 South Castillo Drive
St. Augustine, FL 32084-3252
(904) 829-6506
www.nps.gov/casa/index.htm

**Hours:**
Open to the public from 8:45am – 5:15pm every day of the year except December 25. The Park grounds are closed from midnight until 5:30am.

**Admission:**
Adults (Age 16 and above) entrance is $6 valid for 7 days. Children (age 15 and under) are admitted free of charge but must be accompanied by an adult.

**Directions:**
*From I-95:* Take the exit for St. Augustine Historic Sites and Downtown (Route 16, Exit 318). Follow Route 16 to US 1. Turn right on US 1 for two miles to Castillo Drive. Turn left on Castillo to the traffic light. Turn right at the light. The Castillo and parking are ahead on the left.

*From US A1A:* The Castillo is located on A1A in downtown St. Augustine.

**The Old City Gates**
The old gates are located across the street from the Castillo on San Marco Avenue at the end of St. George Street.

The St. Augustine Lighthouse.

event occurred in 1873, when the superintendent of construction, Hezekiah Pittee, lost two of his daughters and one of their friends in a terrible accident.

There was a cart that was used to bring building supplies from the ocean to the lighthouse. On July 10, five children took a ride in the cart for fun, but the cart fell into the water. Two children were rescued, but the three girls drowned. It is believed that one of Pittee's daughters is the "girl in the blue dress" who is most often seen on the property. Girl's voices and laughter have also been heard in and around the lighthouse.

There is also evidence that some former employees are still in residence, as witnesses have described a man in the basement of the keeper's house, the smell of cigar smoke, footsteps echoing through the lighthouse, and locked doors opening on their own. This is definitely a place you need to visit twice—once during the day for the scenery, then again at night for one of their ghost tours. But if you can't make it at night, don't worry; the ghosts of the St. Augustine lighthouse are not shy about making their presence known in broad daylight.

There are precious few places in this country where there is such a concentration of history and hauntings, so if you want to experience something out of the ordinary—way out of the ordinary in some cases—you can't beat St. Augustine, the oldest continuously haunted city in America!

## The Bottom Line

**The History**: The area was originally the home of the Timucua Indians. The city was founded by the Spanish in 1565, and is America's oldest continuously occupied European city, as well as being its oldest port.

**The Haunting:** Ghosts are everywhere!

## Visitor Information

**St. Augustine Lighthouse**
**81 Lighthouse Avenue**
**St. Augustine, FL 32080-4650**
**(904) 829-0745**
**www.staugustinelighthouse.com/**

**Hours:**

Open daily at 9am. It's recommended that you allow at least one hour to tour the site and climb the tower. The last ticket to climb the tower is sold at 5:45pm. The site closes at 6pm. During July and many holidays they are open until 7pm, with the last ticket being sold at 6:45pm. Closed Thanksgiving Day, December 24th, and December 25th.

During inclement weather, the observation deck and/or tower may be closed for your safety. If the weather looks threatening, call 904-829-0745 to check the tower's status.

**Admission:**

Adults $9, Seniors (60 and over) $7.50, Children (11 or under and 44" or taller) $7, and includes museum, audio tour, and climb to the top.

Value Pack-Includes Admission, T-Shirt, Audio Tour, *I Climbed* Certificate, $19.95. Family Fun Pack-Includes Free Admission/Membership (1-Year), A Drink for Each Member, 2 Packages of Fudge, 20 Percent Off Museum Store Purchases, $59.95.

*Admission is not required to shop in the gift shop.*

**Directions:**

*From their website*—From the North (I-95): Take exit 318 (old exit 95) and proceed east for 5.4 miles. Turn RIGHT onto US 1 and proceed south for 1.9 miles. Turn LEFT onto King Street and proceed east for 0.8 miles. Cross the Bridge of Lions and proceed south on Anastasia Boulevard (A1A) for 1.4 miles. Turn LEFT onto Red Cox Road, proceed north for 0.2 miles. The St. Augustine Lighthouse and Museum is on the Left side of the street.

*From the South (I-95):* Take Exit 311 to SR 207, then proceed east for 3.5 miles. Turn RIGHT onto SR 312 and proceed east for 3.5 miles. Turn LEFT onto SR A1A and proceed north for 1.4 miles. Turn RIGHT onto Red Cox Road, proceed north for 0.2 miles. The St. Augustine Lighthouse and Museum is on the Left side of the street.

Castle Warden, now Ripley's Museum.

# Ripley's Museum

FL

Ghost stories and castles just seem to go together, and Castle Warden in St. Augustine truly tips the paranormal scales when it comes to spirits and supernatural energies. Of course, architecture alone doesn't produce ghosts, so what predisposed this place to a haunting?

The building was constructed as a winter home in 1887. William Warden, who made a fortune with the Standard Oil company, chose the Moorish revival style for his castle. He also chose to build next to the fort, the Castillo de San Marcos, and therefore was placing his new home on an old battlefield and burial ground.

**Strike One.**

The house remained in the family until 1925, and during the years of the Depression, the building was empty and became home to vagrants. In 1941, the property was purchased by Norton Baskin and his wife, Pulitzer prize-winning novelist, Marjorie Kinnan Rawlings, author of *The Yearling*, and the castle was transformed into an exclusive hotel.

Tragedy struck in 1944 when a fire broke out in the hotel. Damage was minimal—none of the original woodwork was harmed and the hotel reopened just a couple of days later—but two women were found dead. Instead of easily escaping through an exit or window, these women were found in bathrooms (on different floors). Both were in bathtubs with wet towels over their faces, and neither had any burns or signs of smoke inhalation. Despite the extremely suspicious nature of these deaths, both were ruled to be accidents as a result of the fire. The truth is most likely far more sinister.

One of the women, 28-year-old Betty Richeson, had just checked into the hotel ninety minutes earlier with a man known only as Mr. X (this was a place where people went when they didn't want anyone to know who they were). Chances are, Mr. X was having an affair with Betty; they quarreled, and he killed her. The other victim, Ruth Pickering, had somehow unfortunately been a witness, so she had to be disposed of, as well. Mr. X then set the fire to conceal his crimes, and the hotel was more than happy to accept two murders as accidents, therefore avoiding any scandal.

**Strike Two.**

Then we come to the Ripley era. At one time, Robert Ripley was the most popular man in America because of his *Believe It Or Not!* cartoons and newsreels. He was an artist, explorer, adventurer, and collector of all things weird and bizarre. Much of his personal collection contained objects of torture and death—such as executioners' implements, shrunken heads, and weapons and musical instruments made of human bones. When the castle became Ripley's Museum in 1950, many of these objects were placed on permanent exhibit.

### Strike Three!

You are now out of the normal world and firmly into the paranormal realm at Castle Warden.

Over the years, many members of the staff and visitors have heard a woman sobbing on the second floor, and have seen a woman standing at a window where one of the bodies was found. On several occasions, the police have been called to investigate the sighting of this woman—who appears to be crying for help—only to find that the place is empty and the window in which she appeared was boarded over. Several psychics with no prior knowledge of the place have had remarkably identical impressions of a man killing two women with 1940s hair styles, then setting a fire to conceal his crime! It seems clear that at least one of these murder victims is still bound to the scene of the crime.

In fact, so much activity occurs in what may have been the murder room, it has come to be called the Vortex Room. This room also contains several bizarre artifacts—including a Sumatran Soul Boat—so that could certainly add to the paranormal energies here. Visitors have often reported a breath on their necks or ears in this room, and the strong feeling of a presence.

Throughout the building there are also reports of a television that turns itself on even when it's unplugged, footsteps, doors slamming, the sounds of furniture being moved, and inexplicable feelings of panic that can be overwhelming.

However, as intense as this place is during the day, the creepy factor grows exponentially when the sun goes down and the lights go off. The museum hosts an excellent ghost tour of St. Augustine—the Ghost Train Adventure—and it culminates with the opportunity to investigate Ripley's at night! Participants are given K2 meters (for measuring electromagnetic fields) and cameras, and encouraged to test their ghost hunting skills, as well as their sixth senses.

## Recommendations

This is one place that is not to be missed. There is the history of the land, the murders, the grisly objects of suffering and death, and decades of haunted activity. This place truly has it all. The ghost tour is excellent, and affords you the rare opportunity to investigate this creepy building at night. Check out the Sumatran Soul Boat in the Vortex/Murder Room. The execution garrote bench has elicited feelings of being strangled. Just be prepared for a flood of energies and sensations in every inch of this building!

## Visitor Information

**Ripley's Believe It Or Not! Museum**
19 San Marco Avenue
St. Augustine, FL 32084-3278
(904) 824-1606
http://staugustine.ripleys.com/

**Hours:**
Sunday to Thursday 9am – 7pm, Friday and Saturday 9am – 8pm. There is plenty of free parking at the museum.

**Admission:**
*Museum Only:* Adults (12+) $14.99, Children (5-12) $7.99, Seniors (55+) $12.26. Combo: Adults (12+) $29.99, Children (5-12) $14.99, Seniors (55+) $29.26. Combo includes Admission to Ripley's Believe It or Not! Museum, Bayfront Mini Golf, and 3 days of unlimited on and off privileges aboard the Red Trains.

*Ghost Trains:* Adults: $26/$23 Online, *Children:* $13 (6-12)/$11 Online
www.ghosttrainadventure.com

**Directions:**
Ripley's is located next to the Castillo de San Marcos, at 19 San Marco Avenue, which is also Route A1A and a short walk to the north from the City Gates of the old town. By car, from Routes 1/5, take West Castillo Drive and the museum parking lot will be directly ahead at the light.



## The Bottom Line

**The History:** A winter home built in 1887 on a battlefield next to the old fort. Vacant during the Depression. In 1941, it was turned into an exclusive hotel where the murders of two women occurred. In 1950, it became Ripley's Museum, containing bizarre and gruesome objects from around the world.

**The Haunting:** The murdered women are seen, heard, and felt. Numerous paranormal experiences throughout the building both day and night.

The St. Francis Inn.

# St. Francis Inn

If you are going to visit America's oldest city, shouldn't you spend the night in its oldest inn? The St. Francis Inn is the oldest continuously operating inn in the country and it's been witness to enough history to fill its own book.

In 1791, while the fledging United States of America was still rejoicing in its freedom from the King of England, Florida was back under the rule of the King of Spain. Ever mindful of the threat of invasion, the King decreed that new structures in St. Augustine should be built to "serve as a defensive fortress against those who might attempt to occupy the town." This directive accounts for the inn's unique design with its front entrance and inner courtyard shielded from the street.

The first owner, Gaspar Garcia, must have felt right at home as he had been a soldier in the Spanish army and had been granted the land from the King of Spain. A sea captain, Juan Ruggiers, bought the property in 1802, and his family still occupied the house during the transition to American rule in 1821. The military tradition continued when in 1838, retired British Colonel Thomas Henry Dummett became the new owner.

Dummett may have had an honorable career with the Royal Marines, but his journey to America from his home in Barbados was somewhat less than dignified. Due to some legal issues for which British authorities wanted to detain the Colonel, it is said he was forced to sneak away from the Caribbean island by hiding aboard ship in a large sugar barrel. It was a fitting means of escape, as Dummett was to go on to prosper with his rum distillery and sugar plantation along the Tomoka River.

The next military connection was to come when Dummett's daughter, Elizabeth, married William J. Hardee, who is known for his popular book of military tactics, as well as being a famous Confederate general during the Civil War. Another daughter also married a general, but it was the daughter who never married, Anna, who arguably had the greater impact on the history of the house. In 1845, Anna converted the family home into a lodging establishment. She must have been a woman of considerable energy, as she also commanded a small army of her own—raising no less than ten nieces and nephews after three of her sisters passed away! (She also raised the funds for the Confederate memorial obelisk that stands in the town's central plaza.)

The inn underwent extensive renovations and additions after it was purchased in 1888 by philanthropist John L. Wilson. It was through Wilson's generosity that St. Augustine got its first public library. However, there was one big string attached. If the town accepted the money for the library, they had to accept Wilson's daughter, Emily, as its librarian, which was an offer they ultimately couldn't refuse.

The long military influence eventually gave way to one of a decidedly literary nature. Many noted writers and authors became residents of the inn, including Pulitzer Prize winner Van Wycks Brooks, and a Pulitzer runner-up, Mrs. Verle Pope (Edith Everett Taylor). Edith was also a close friend of the famous author, Marjorie Kinnan Rawlings, who owned the hotel that is now the haunted Ripley Museum (see page 68.)

Speaking of hauntings, with such a long history, does anything from the past linger at the St. Francis Inn? There may be at least one spirit who walks the halls in search of her lost love, and the story may be the result of a tragic romance—something of a Romeo and Juliet story, St. Augustine style.

William Hardee's nephew was living in the house in the middle of the nineteenth century, and the young man fell in love with a servant girl who worked there. Such a match would not have been socially acceptable to begin with, but throw in the fact that the girl had dark skin, and one can only imagine the future Confederate general's reaction when one day he discovered the two lovers together.

The servant girl was ordered out of the house, and the nephew was forbidden to see her again. The young man was so distraught at the loss of his love, he committed suicide—either by hanging himself in the attic, or jumping from the window, depending on the version you hear. There are also different stories regarding the servant girl's fate, some of which have her also committing suicide with the same noose. In any case, two lives were cut short, and people say the girl, now known as Lily, can still be seen as a figure dressed in white passing silently down a hallway, or searching for her lover in the room which was once the attic.

In addition to her appearances, Lily is also blamed for some mischievous activity such as moving objects, turning lights and appliances on and off, cold spots, and the sound of someone whispering when no one else is there. In Lily's Room, women have often complained that their makeup has been strewn around the floor, as if a jealous spirit did not like the idea of having another woman in the room. One day, a workman complained about the dark-skinned maid who kept glaring at him, but no one on staff or any guests fit his description of the girl.

Some witnesses have also claimed to see the figure of a man in various places throughout the inn. We can only hope that he is Lily's true love, and the two are now finding the happiness in death that they were denied in life.

Whatever spirits still occupy the oldest inn in America, they are all gentle and harmless. In a town where history is an integral part of the fabric, consider the ghosts of the St. Francis Inn to be just another fascinating piece of its rich tapestry.

## The Bottom Line

**The History:** America's oldest continuously operated inn, built in 1791 when Florida was ruled by the King of Spain. Owners and residents have included famous military men and literary figures.

**The Haunting:** A tragic and forbidden romance may have led to the spirit of a young servant girl searching for her lost love. Figures of both a man and a woman have been witnessed, along with mischievous activity throughout the inn. Be sure to ask for Lily's Room.

## Recommendations

If sites in this book were to be rated, the St. Francis Inn would definitely earn a gold star as it embodies everything the haunted history tourist is seeking. In addition to its own charm and history, it's the perfect "base of operations" for your exploration of this fascinating city. Be sure to ask for "Lily's Room" if you want prime paranormal accommodations, but book far in advance as it is the most requested room.

Owners Joe and Margaret Finnegan purchased the property in 1985. They were drawn to this inn by their love of St. Augustine and its history, and their warm hospitality will make you feel right at home.

If you've ever tried to find parking near the Historic District, you can appreciate the rare commodity of the inn's complimentary parking—it is worth its weight in Spanish gold! Their extraordinary amenities go far above and beyond your average B&B and include: Food and beverage: buffet breakfast with mimosas and make-your-own Bloody Mary bar, evening social hour with wine, beer, and hors d'oeuvres, evening desserts, and all-day coffee, tea, and goodies. Then there are the complimentary bicycles, pool, courtyard tables, high speed wireless, beach towels, chairs and showers, fitness club access, Admission to the famous haunted St. Augustine Lighthouse, and half-price Admission to the Oldest House Museum just a block away.

## Visitor Information

**St. Francis Inn Bed and Breakfast**
279 St. George Street
St. Augustine, FL 32084
(904) 824-6068, Reservations: (800) 824-6062
www.stfrancisinn.com
info@stfrancisinn.com

**Directions:**

*From the South:* Travel northbound on I-95 until Exit 311 (landmark: St. Johns County Flea Market). Turn east (right) onto State Road 207, following it approximately 6 miles to the intersection of SR 207 and US 1 (landmark: Winn Dixie on the right). Turn north (left) onto US 1 and travel approximately 1/2 mile to the intersection of US 1 and King Street. Turn east (right) onto King Street (heading into the Historic District) and travel approximately 2/3 mile to the intersection of King Street and St. George Street (the 5th traffic light – landmark: Trinity Episcopal Church). Turn south (right) onto St. George Street and travel 2 blocks. Their parking lot is on the right side of the street, identified with a sign that reads: St. Francis Inn Guest Parking. Park your vehicle and walk across the street to the Main Inn.

*From the North:* Travel southbound on I-95 until you reach St. Augustine's first exit—Exit 318 (landmark: Factory Outlet Malls). Turn east (left) onto Route 16 and travel approximately 6 miles to the intersection of S.R. 16 and US 1 (landmark: CVS Drugstore on right). Turn south (right) onto US 1 (Ponce de Leon Boulevard) and travel to the intersection of US 1 and King Street. From this point follow directions above.

# Georgia

SAVANNAH

CHICKAMAUGA AND CHATTANOOGA

ANDERSONVILLE PRISON

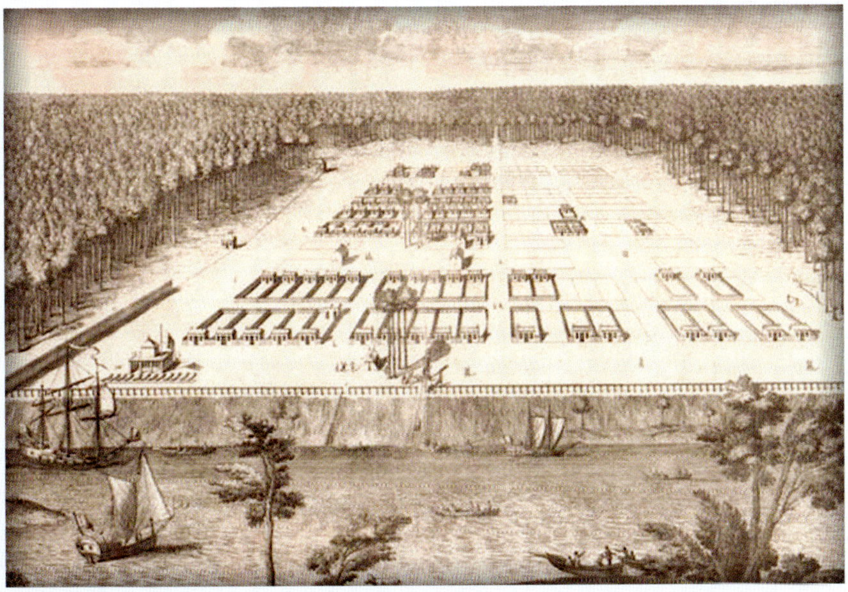

This early 1700s drawing shows Savannah's humble beginnings.

# Savannah

Savannah is one of those remarkable places so steeped in history and lore it has to be declared an occupied city—occupied by ghosts, that is. Unlike some more reticent locations, Savannah embraces its haunted history and offers so many haunted inns and restaurants and ghost trolley tours that you couldn't possibly do them all justice in the span of a single book, let a alone a single chapter in a book. Therefore, it is recommended on your first day or two in Savannah you get a room in one of the following haunted inns, dine at one of the haunted restaurants, and take one of the tours. Once you get your paranormal bearings, you can then delve more deeply into the haunts you find most compelling.

This city, and the colony of Georgia, were founded on February 12, 1733, by British General James Oglethorpe to protect the Carolinas from the Spanish in Florida and the French in Louisiana. In an attempt to make the colony profitable, an experimental farm called the Trustees' Garden grew mulberry trees which were necessary for the silk industry. Unfortunately, that business didn't succeed, but the garden wasn't a total loss—they were successful introducing cotton and that iconic Georgia fruit, the peach.

Of course, the history of Savannah was not all gardens and peaches. There were the battles of the Revolutionary War, and General Sherman taking the city during the Civil War. Mother Nature hit the city with hurricanes and two terrible yellow fever epidemics. Then there were all types of colorful characters, from pirates to voodoo practitioners, who filled the city and added a unique undercurrent to the genteel southern society. In other words, Savannah has had almost three centuries to cultivate a bumper crop of ghosts.

After a long day of walking the historic streets and cemeteries—don't forget to bring some trinket to leave at Gracie Watkin's grave at the Bonaventure Cemetery to make her spirit happy—you will need a place to eat and rest your weary head. The following are just some of the many places you can get an excellent meal, a beautiful room...and maybe a ghost or two.

*(All of these places are located in the north Historic District.)*

## The Pirates' House

The Pirates' House restaurant was built in 1753 and is adjoining the oldest house in Georgia, which was built in 1734 for the gardener of the Trustees' Garden. The Pirates' House was the inspiration for part of Robert Louis Stevenson famous book, *Treasure Island*, and was a tavern for sailors, and, of course, pirates. Unfortunately, though, not every man who walked in the front door left that way. Unsavory characters would get men drunk—or save the money and simply hit them over the head—then drag them through a secret tunnel to the river and put them aboard a ship. By the time they awoke, they were too far out to sea to escape and had no choice but to work until they returned. It is said that one Savannah policeman went into the tavern to have a drink on his way home, and woke up to find himself on a two-year voyage to the Far East!

These hard-partying pirates apparently have not yet left the building, as staff and guests hear laughter, find chairs rearranged, and see the figures of sailors throughout the building. One scarred, scurvy looking pirate has appeared so often they've named him Captain Flint.

So whether you are just looking for a great meal, or want to toss back a tankard of grog with Captain Flint and his friends, don't sail past the Pirates' House!

### Visitor Information

**The Pirates' House**
20 East Broad Street
Savannah, GA 31401-2929
(912) 233-5757
www.thepirateshouse.com

**Hours:**
Lunch Menu 11am – 4pm, Southern Style Buffet 11am – 3pm. Dinner Menu 4pm – 9:30pm Friday to Saturday 4pm – 10pm.

**Directions:**
East Broad Street is between East Bay and East Liberty Streets.

## 17Hundred90

17Hundred90 inn and restaurant also has a ghost with a name, Anna Powers. There are several versions of her story, but they all have the same tragic ending. In the early 1800s, Anna was in love with a sailor who left her, and she watched his ship leaving port from a third-floor balcony. As the sails faded from view, Anna jumped to her death, and her spirit has been seen throughout the inn ever since, particularly in Room #204.

### Visitor Information

**17Hundred90**
307 East President Street
Savannah, Georgia 31401-3808
(912) 236-7122
www.17hundred90.com

**Directions:**
The Islands Expressway becomes President Street. Cross East Broad and go around Greene Square (crossing Houston Street). Continue on President Street, cross Price Street and go around Columbia Square (crossing Habersham Street). 17Hundred90 is in between Habersham Street and Lincoln Street on the left hand side.



## The Kehoe House

The Kehoe House was built in 1892 for William Kehoe. As the owner of an ironworks foundry, Kehoe spent $25,000 on his mansion, which was, of course, suitably adorned with decorative iron everywhere. There were ten children in the Kehoe family, and there is a story that a pair of twins both died while playing in one of the chimneys. As if that wasn't sufficient to create a haunting, the house was a funeral parlor for much of the twentieth century.

Not surprisingly, the predominant paranormal activity involves the spirits of high-spirited children who can be heard laughing and running up and down the halls. Guests have complained about the boisterous children, only to be informed that there were none spending the night. (No, just spending eternity!) In Room #201, one guest in bed felt a hand on her cheek and opened her eyes to come face to face with a child, who then just disappeared. Another guest in bed in Room #203 felt someone sit on the bed next to her. There was indeed an impression on the bed as if someone was sitting there, it was just that no one was visible. The encounter certainly left an impression on the guest!

## The Marshall House

The Marshall House was Savannah's first hotel. It was built in 1851 by Mary Marshall, a business woman who saw that the city needed a proper place for visitors to stay. However, more than tired travelers stayed here, as twice the place was used as a hospital for yellow fever victims, and a third time during the Civil War as a hospital for Union troops. Think there's any chance this all has something to do with why this place is so haunted?

Staff and guests have reported seeing and hearing a variety of ghosts of men, women, and children throughout the building. There are loud crashing sounds from the fourth floor. Several people have felt an unseen hand grab their wrist, like a nurse trying to take someone's pulse. If this sounds like your idea of a good time, the Marshall House offers a special 3-day/2-night Haunted Hotel Package that includes accommodations, breakfast, one of the ghost tours of the city, and a ghost book.

### Visitor Information

**Keyhoe House**
**123 Habersham Street**
**Savannah, GA 31401-3820**
**(912) 232-1020**
**www.kehoehouse.com**

**Directions:**
**From I-95, Exit 99-A (I-16 to East Savannah Exit) I-16 East, Exit 167B (Montgomery Street). Go through stoplight. At the second Stoplight, turn right onto Oglethorpe Avenue. Turn left onto Habersham Street. The Kehoe House is on the left side of Columbia Square.**

### The Bottom Line

**The History:** Founded in 1733, Savannah has been the site of battles, epidemics, hurricanes, pirates, and voodoo practitioners.

**The Haunting:** Quite simply, one of the most haunted places in America.

### Visitor Information

**The Marshall House**
**123 East Broughton Street**
**Savannah, GA 31401-3303**
**(912) 644-7896**
**www.marshallhouse.com**

**Directions:**
**From I-95: Follow I-16 into Savannah from I-95. I-16 will dead end and merge into Montgomery Street. Follow Montgomery Street to the third light. This is Broughton Street. Turn right onto Broughton Street. Follow Broughton Street for six blocks. The Marshall House will be on your right.**



## Chickamauga and Chattanooga

Chattanooga, Tennessee was a major railroad center that was vital to the flow of soldiers and supplies for the Confederacy. In the fall of 1863, the region saw Union forces under General Rosecrans repeatedly clashing with Confederate troops commanded by General Braxton Bragg. After weeks of the two armies maneuvering and meeting in minor engagements, the full force of about 60,000 Union soldiers and 65,000 Confederates squared off on the morning of September 19, along the Chickamauga Creek, just south of Chattanooga in Georgia. The meaning of the Cherokee word *Chickamauga* has been given as *River of Death* or *Bloody Creek*. Perhaps neither translation is correct, but both terms would apply by the time the awful two-day battle was over.

The first day saw fierce fighting, often at such close quarters that the two sides struggled in hand-to-hand combat. The Union line was pushed back, but did not break. The battle began again on September 20, and still the Union forces held, until they committed a fatal mistake. In the confusion of battle, Rosecrans believed that a gap had opened up in the Union line and ordered men to shift position. In actuality, there had not been any gap, but the movement of troops created one and Confederate General Longstreet took full advantage of it and his men poured through the opening.

Rosecrans and half the Federal Army were routed and began retreating back toward Chattanooga, but Union General George Thomas staged an epic defense on Snodgrass Hill which earned him the title of "The Rock of Chickamauga." Despite the gallant opposition, the Confederate forces proved too much even for Thomas' men, and that night they, too,

The entrance to Point Park. *All Chickamauga photos courtesy of the National Parks Service.*

retreated back to Chattanooga. However, it is difficult to consider the Battle of Chickamauga a victory for anyone, considering the heavy losses.

The Confederate forces suffered over 18,000 casualties with 2,312 killed, 14,674 wounded, and 1,468 captured or missing. The Union losses were over 16,000, with 1,657 killed, 9,756 wounded, and 4,757 captured or missing. That translates into a casualty rate of one out of every four soldiers, but the fighting was far from being over.

While the Union forces occupied Chattanooga, the key terrain was occupied by the Confederates. With their artillery strategically placed on Missionary Ridge, Lookout Mountain, and in the Chattanooga Valley, Bragg's men prevented supplies from reaching the Union troops. That left three options to Rosecrans' army—starve, surrender, or have more troops come to their rescue.

The bleak situation turned brighter for the Union forces in Chattanooga in October and November due to two things: the arrival of 36,000 troops and General Grant assuming overall command. Supply lines were quickly opened and plans were made to drive the Confederate forces from Missionary Ridge and Lookout Mountain. A series of attacks on November 23, 24, and 25 culminated in one of the greatest charges of the war as union troops raced up the steep slopes of Missionary Ridge, driving back Bragg's troops and bringing the Chattanooga-Chickamauga Campaign to an end. These final battles resulted in over 10,000 additional casualties.

The Peace Memorial where the Union and Confederate soldiers are shaking hands.

With such staggering numbers of killed and wounded, it wouldn't be unusual to have legends and haunted tales arise in the years following the battles. What is unexpected, however, it that the predominant legend—that of Green Eyes—may actually have been in existence long before the Civil War. There are many versions of Green Eyes, including him being some sort of animal with light-colored hair and glowing green eyes, but he most often appeared in human form wearing a long black coat or cape. There are claims that the Native Americans spoke of Green Eyes long ago, and that soldiers during the battle of Chickamauga encountered this terrifying figure. Eyewitnesses—including at least one park ranger—claim to see him to this day, and some people who have had car accidents in the area say it was because they were distracted and scared by old Green Eyes! Try telling that story to your insurance agent...

The earliest documented ghost sighting was in 1876, when travelers saw what at first appeared to be a very tall person with a large, white head. When they got closer, they saw it was an African-American woman carrying a bundle of clothes on her head. Neither the clothes nor the woman were solid, however, and the frightened travelers hurried on, convinced that the battlefields were haunted.

Had this unfortunate woman been caught in the crossfire during one of the battles, or was she, too, from another time like Green Eyes? Most likely, the origins of these spirits will remain a mystery, unlike the many figures of Civil War soldiers which have been seen across the battlefields. Then there are the sounds of horses galloping where there aren't any horses, and eerie moaning and groaning where the wounded and dying once covered the fields. There have also been many reports of strange lights at night, and some speculate it is phantom lantern light from women who still search the battlefield for their missing husbands and relatives.

Could shades of the past still be seen along the misty heights of Missionary Ridge and Lookout Mountain, and

Wilder Brigade Monument and Observation Tower.

around the Chickamauga Creek? With so much blood spilled on this land, the region around the River of Death no doubt lives up to its name…

## The Bottom Line

**The History:** One of the pivotal campaigns of the Civil War. The bloody battle of Chickamauga in September of 1863 saw Union forces mistakenly shift troops and open a gap in their lines, costing them the battle. In November, Union troops ascended Missionary Ridge and routed the Confederates in one of the greatest charges of the war. The campaign cost thousands of lives and tens of thousands were wounded and captured.

**The Haunting:** The figure of a man (or some say a strange animal) with green glowing eyes. A woman carrying a bundle of clothes. Many sightings of Civil War soldiers. The sounds of moaning, and of horses galloping.

## Recommendations

This was the first National Military Park upon which all others have been patterned, and there are 666 markers and monuments to explore. Look for the New York Peace Memorial on the top of Lookout Mountain where the Union and Confederate soldiers are shaking hands. Climb to the top of Wilder's Brigade Monument Tower at Chickamauga for a bird's-eye view. There is a lot of ground to cover, so allow plenty of time to be able to fully appreciate the park!

## Visitor Information

**Chickamauga and Chattanooga National Military Park,**
Georgia and Tennessee
Mailing Address:
Park Superintendent, P.O. Box 2128
Fort Oglethorpe, GA 30742

**Chickamauga Visitor Center**
(706) 866-9241

**Lookout Mountain Battlefield Visitor Center**
(423) 821-7786

There is metered parking on the street, but parking is free in the lot behind the Visitor's Center.

**Hours:**

All units of the National Military Park are open between sunrise and sunset.

The Chickamauga Battlefield Visitor Center and Lookout Mountain Battlefield Visitor Center are open daily from 8:30am – 5pm. Both Visitor Centers are closed on Christmas Day.

The historic Cravens House on Lookout Mountain is open for tours weekends during the summer. Contact the Lookout Mountain Battlefield Visitor Center for hours of operation.

**Admission:**

*Chickamauga Battlefield:* **No Entrance Fee.**
Craven's House on historic Lookout Mountain: **No Fees Charged.**

*Point Park at Lookout Mountain Battlefield:* Adults (16 or older) $3, Children 15 and under are free.

**Directions:**

**Chickamauga Battlefield**
*From Interstate 75:* At Exit 350 take Battlefield Parkway (Georgia 2) west to Fort Oglethorpe. Turn left at the intersection of Battlefield Parkway and Lafayette Road. Go one mile on Lafayette Road to the park entrance and visitor center.

*From Interstate 24:* At Exit 180 take U.S. Highway 27 south (Rossville Boulevard) to Fort Oglethorpe. At the intersection of Battlefield Parkway, continue straight through the intersection onto Lafayette Road to the park entrance one mile ahead.

**Lookout Mountain Battlefield**
*From Interstate 24:* From Exit 178, turn left onto Broad Street. Broad Street will become U.S. Highway 41 (Cummings Highway). Turn left onto TN Highway 148. Continue on TN Highway 148 to the top of Lookout Mountain. At the top, turn right onto East Brow Road. The Lookout Mountain Battlefield Visitor Center is located at the end of East Brow Road, across the street from the Point Park Entrance Gate.

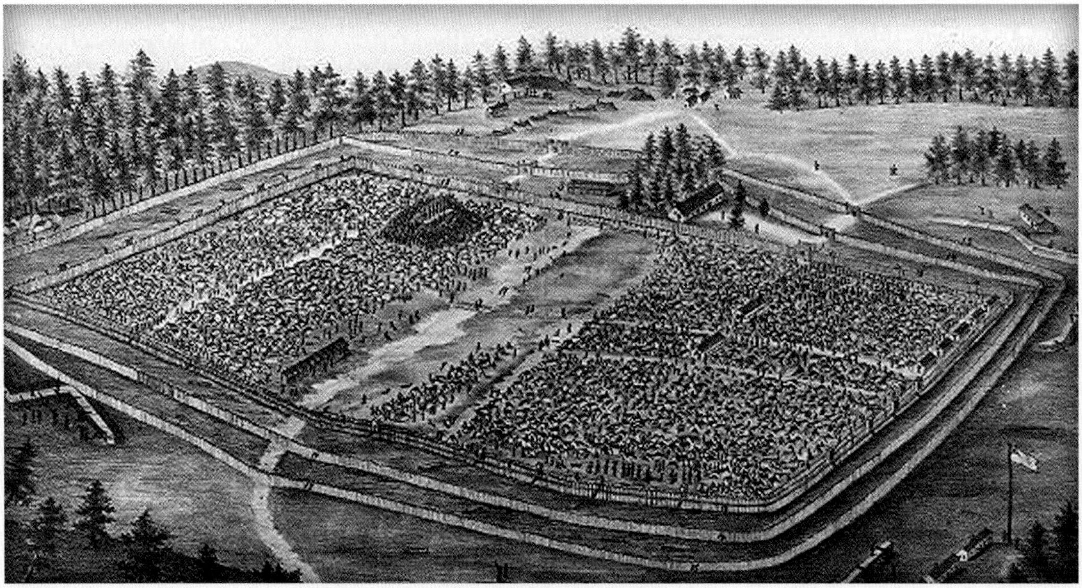

This drawing shows the overcrowding and lack of shelter at Andersonville Prison.

GA

# Andersonville Prison

There are few place names in American history that evoke the horror of Andersonville. While conditions were harsh in prison camps in both the north and south during the Civil War, this place epitomized man's inhumanity to man on an awful scale—on any given day scores of men would die here, with a total of almost 13,000 Union prisoners succumbing to starvation and disease.

The idea for this prison actually came about to alleviate the overcrowding in the prison camps around Richmond, Virginia. The original 16.5 acre camp—called Camp Sumter—opened in February of 1864 and was meant to house 10,000 prisoners. By June, an additional ten acres had to be added, but by August, 32,000 men were packed into a stockade that offered no shade from the blistering Georgia sun, a filthy, contaminated stream which was often the only source of water, and so few rations as to turn the strongest men into walking skeletons within months.

To make matters worse, a group of prisoners calling themselves the Raiders formed a gang to prey upon their fellow soldiers. They would beat and kill the other prisoners, especially the new ones, stealing their food, blankets, money, and anything else of value. Finally rising up against the Raiders, the prisoners rounded up the offenders, held a trial, and hung the six ringleaders.

Of course, death could also come at the hands of the Confederate soldiers. The "Dead Line" was a light fence placed about twenty feet from the stockade wall, and to cross that line resulted in immediately being shot by guards in watchtowers. For some prisoners who could no longer tolerate the suffering, stepping over the Dead Line meant a swift and merciful death.

Then there was the commandant of the camp, Captain Henry Wirz. While some documentation has him pleading for more food and supplies for the prisoners, others paint a picture of him as the devil incarnate. While the truth usually lies somewhere between the extremes, the fact remains that he was put on trial after the war for his alleged brutality. Wirz was found guilty, and was the only Confederate soldier to be executed for war crimes.

For every devil there is often an angel, and the angel of Andersonville Prison was Father Peter Whelan. Father Whelan was an Irish Catholic priest from Savannah, and from June to October of 1864, he volunteered to not only tend to the spiritual needs of the prisoners, he borrowed money to buy flour to make bread for those in the prison hospital. "Whelan's Bread" no doubt saved many lives, and after the war, his compassion was often spoken about by former prisoners. Unfortunately, he died in 1871 from a lung disease that he most likely contracted at Andersonville.

With so much death and suffering concentrated on this small piece of land, it should not come as any surprise that shadows of the past have been witnessed here. Even though Captain Wirz was hung in Washington, D.C., people have reported seeing his figure walking along Highway 49, headed toward the prison. Others have seen the transparent figure of Father Whelan and heard the voice of a priest administering the last rites. Both Union and Confederate soldiers have appeared, often amidst a strange fog. Then there are the sounds of gunshots, moaning, and screams.

Arguably the most unnerving experience is the horrible stench that suddenly arises out of nowhere, both on the grounds of the former prison camp and in the adjacent cemetery. It has been described as the foul smell of filth, disease, and death, like that of a field hospital.

Are all these experiences simply a static imprint, the result of residual energy lingering like a snapshot to occasionally be glimpsed by those who are sensitive, or are witnesses simply at the right place at the right time? Or are the unfortunate spirits of former prisoners still held captive as they seek a way to finally escape beyond the ultimate Dead Line? They say time heals all wounds, and we can only hope that with time, all the tortured souls of Andersonville will find peace.

## The Bottom Line

**The History:** The most infamous Civil War prison camp where 13,000 Union soldiers died.

**The Haunting:** The former commandant, a priest, and numerous soldiers have been seen. There are the sounds of gunshots, voices, screams, and moaning. The terrible stench of death can suddenly fill the air.

## Recommendations

**In addition to the former prison grounds, visitors can go to the Andersonville National Cemetery and the National Prisoner of War Museum. Markers are set up to show where the stockade wall once stood and the distance to the Dead Line. Many states erected monuments to their dead, who are buried in the cemetery. (The prisoners were initially buried in mass graves, and their bodies were moved when the cemetery was established.) The infamous Raiders are also buried here. This entire site may very well be an extremely active historic haunt, but please use the utmost respect when walking these grounds.**

## Visitor Information

**Andersonville National Historic Site**
496 Cemetery Road
Andersonville, GA 31711
(229) 924-0343
www.nps.gov/ande/index.htm

**Events:**

The park hosts various special events, and the two largest occur on Memorial Day weekend in May and POW/MIA Recognition week in September. There is also a luminary in the prison site, a candlelight tour in the cemetery, and living history weekends.

**Hours:**

The park grounds are open every day of the year from 8am – 5pm, allowing access to both the historic prison site and Andersonville National Cemetery.

The National Prisoner of War Museum, which also serves as the park's visitor center, opens at 8:30am and closes at 5pm. Open every day of the week year-round, except Thanksgiving Day, Christmas Day, and New Year's Day.

**Admission:** Free

**Directions:**

From their website—From the north, via I-75: Follow I-75 south to Exit 135 (Perry). Head southwest on GA-224 from the interstate to Montezuma, approximately 20 miles. Just outside Montezuma, turn right on GA-26 and follow to the intersection of GA-49. Turn left on GA-49 and head south approximately 6 miles to Andersonville. The park entrance will be on the left.

From the south, via I-75: Follow I-75 north to Exit 101 (Cordele). Head west on US-280 from Cordele to Americus, approximately 30 miles. In Americus, turn right onto GA-49 and head north approximately 10 miles to Andersonville. The park entrance will be on the right, after passing the park exit and employee entrance.

From Columbus area: Follow GA-520/US-280 toward Cusseta. Turn left on GA-26 and head east to Buena Vista, approximately 16 miles. Continue on GA-26 to Ellaville, approximately 15 miles. In Ellaville, turn right onto US-19 then left onto GA-228. Follow GA-228 east to Andersonville, approximately 12 miles. In Andersonville, turn left on GA-49 and head north approximately 1 mile. The park entrance will be on the right.

From Albany area: Follow US-19 north toward Americus, approximately 36 miles. In Americus, turn right onto US-280 and continue east through downtown Americus to Tripp Street. Turn left on Tripp Street/GA-49 and head north approximately 10 miles to Andersonville. The park entrance will be on the right, after passing the park exit and employee entrance.

III

# Hawaii

PEARL HARBOR: PACIFIC AVIATION MUSEUM, FORD ISLAND

KING KAMEHAMEHA'S KONA BEACH HOTEL

PELE

A Japanese photo of the actual attack on Pearl Harbor.

# Pearl Harbor: Pacific Aviation Museum, Ford Island

Some of the most recognizable words in American history were spoken by President Franklin D. Roosevelt when he said, "December 7th, 1941—a date which will live in infamy."

The sneak attack by the Japanese on Pearl Harbor began at 7:48am that fateful Sunday morning and consisted of 353 Japanese planes sinking or damaging eight battleships, several destroyers and cruisers, as well as destroying 188 aircraft, most of which never had a chance to leave the ground. However, the real toll came in the cost of human lives—2,402 killed and 1,282 wounded.

The Japanese goal was to eliminate the U.S. Pacific Fleet as a threat to Japan's plans of extending their empire. In reality, the infamous attack galvanized our nation into a war machine, the likes of which had never been seen. "Remember Pearl Harbor" became the rallying cry that drove men to enlist and women to work in factories to produce everything the soldiers needed for victory.

The military story of Pearl Harbor actually began in 1918 when Ford Island was purchased by the U.S. Army to be used as an airfield. The Navy also began using the base in 1923, but when the Army eventually shifted operations to the new Hickam Field, Ford Island became the sole domain of the Navy. By December of 1941, the hangars were filled with Navy planes and the fleet was lined up around the island—all poised like sitting ducks for the Japanese pilots.

It is still possible to relive that day of infamy thanks to a museum that opened on December 7, 2006. One of the buildings that survived the devastating attack—Hangar 37—was converted into the Pacific Aviation Museum containing WWII aircraft. Subsequently, Hangar 79, which still has Japanese bullet holes in its glass doors, opened as an aircraft restoration facility. Through films, photos, sounds, dioramas, many original artifacts, and a flight simulator, visitors can see what the area was like prior to the attack, understand what transpired on December 7, 1941, and learn about other key aspects of war in the Pacific.

While in the museum—and in fact, anywhere on the island—visitors might also see misty figures that vanish into thin air, or catch the phantom sounds of the actual battle that mysteriously have been replaying over the decades. Visitors and people based on the island have also claimed to have seen men in uniform, heard shouting and people running, had electronic devices turn themselves on and off, and experienced overwhelming feelings of anxiety sweeping over them.

That terrible day in American history ended thousands of lives, and forever changed the lives of millions more. If intense human emotion and suffering of a single person can leave an imprint on a place, then it would not be surprising if Pearl Harbor offered many glimpses into the world that has passed, as well as the world beyond. Every year, fewer and fewer WWII veterans remain to stand up and be counted, but here among the aircraft they flew, on the island on which they fought and died, something just might remain to remind the living of what happened here, and honor the brave men who once stood up to defend their country.

## The Bottom Line

**The History:** The site of one of the most famous and pivotal days in history, the sneak attack on Pearl Harbor on December 7, 1941. The battle claimed thousands of lives.

**The Haunting:** Misty figures and soldiers in uniform have been seen and the sounds of battle can still be heard.

## Recommendations

**The Pacific Aviation Museum is on an active Military Base, so expect tight security. While cameras are allowed, no bags of any kind are allowed on the shuttle bus to the museum. The Aviator's Tour is strongly recommended as you will see about twice the number of aircraft—and get a chance to shoot a rivet and earn a "Rosie the Riveter" souvenir! The flight simulator takes you off the deck of a carrier and into a dogfight. The exhibits include the actual Stearman N2S-3 in which former President George H.W. Bush soloed, and the Aeronca 65TC, a civilian aircraft which technically was the first American plane engaged in combat during World War II, when Japanese pilots on their way to Pearl Harbor fired at a flight instructor and his student. As for the paranormal aspects, things can be experienced anywhere on Ford Island, not only in the museum, so stay alert.**

## Visitor Information

**Pacific Aviation Museum**
319 Lexington Boulevard
Honolulu, HI
(808) 441-1000
www.pacificaviationmuseum.org/

**Hours:**

The museum and ticket office are open daily 9am – 5pm. The Museum is closed Thanksgiving, Christmas, and New Year's Day.

**Admission:**

Tickets can be purchased online. You can print your voucher and go directly to board the shuttle bus at the USS *Arizona* Memorial Visitor Center. Or tickets may be purchased at the USS *Arizona* Memorial Visitor Center. The museum has a restaurant and gift shop.

Adults $15, children (4-12) $8. Adult Hawaii resident and military $10. Child Hawaii resident and military $5.

Aviator's Tour: Guided behind-the-scenes tour, Hangar 37 and Hangar 79: Adults $35, children $28. Adult Hawaii resident and military $30. Child Hawaii resident and military $25.

**Directions:**

From Honolulu/Waikiki area: Head west on Ala Moana Boulevard/Nimitz Highway. Stay slightly left to take Interstate H1 W ramp. Merge onto Interstate H1 W. Take exit 15A, Highway 99 West Arizona Memorial, Stadium. Fourth traffic light, turn left Kalaloa Street. Arrive at Arizona Memorial Pl.

The past lives on at this sacred Hawaiian site. *Courtesy of the King Kamehameha Kona Beach Hotel.*

# King Kamehameha's Kona Beach Hotel

While the Kona Beach Hotel is not an historic building, the ground itself may very well be the most historic site in Hawaii. Over a thousand years ago, a temple was built where human sacrifices were made to the god of war. In 1812, King Kamehameha the Great rebuilt the temple, called it Ahu'ena Heiau, and dedicated it to the god of peace and prosperity. In 1975, a one-third scale model of the Ahu'ena Heiau was built, and today the site is on the register of National Historic Landmarks.

The temple was not the only structure on the site, as King Kamehameha also lived here, so there were many other buildings necessary for the royal residence, along with gardens and fish ponds. To recall this regal past, the hotel features many historic artifacts from the time of King Kamehameha, including a rare feathered cape and helmet, weapons, musical instruments, and objects from daily life. There are also royal portraits and a large mural depicting Kamehameha and his son Liholiho, who became king upon his father's death in 1819.

The new King Kamehameha II also made this place famous, as it was here that one day he ate and drank with women—something that was previously forbidden by the strict kapu law. Previously, the breaking of any kapu law usually meant death, so this was a major act of reform. As a further rejection of the ways of the past, King Kamehameha II then destroyed the Ahu'ena Heiau temple.

However, there are some things that were not destroyed here—like the spirits of the ancient Hawaiians who may actually be buried across the grounds and beneath the hotel. Guests and staff have heard sounds in the rooms and hallways they can't explain, like chanting and men shouting battle cries. People have even seen what they assumed were actors dressed like Hawaiian warriors, until they disappeared before their eyes.

This was once a sacred place of worship and bloody sacrifice, and has witnessed over a thousand years of human drama. If you believe in the ancient ways, or that this place was used for burials, then it still is a sacred place. Many Hawaiians believe that ghosts only torment the living when they have done something wrong, and can actually

## Recommendations

**While some seasons can be rainier than others, is there really ever a bad time to visit Hawaii? If you do want more than beautiful beaches, hula dancers, and luaus, there are historic sites and many natural wonders to explore on land and in the sea around the Big Island, so check with the hotel's guest services to see what's available and make your plans. There are lava flows, mountains, the Puako Petroglyph Archaeological Preserve, Mauna Kea Observatories, and lots of strong Kona coffee to keep you going on your adventures! Or you can just relax at the hotel and commune with the ancient spirits of Hawaii...**

## Visitor Information

**King Kamehameha's Kona Beach Hotel**
**75-5660 Palani Road**
**Kailua-Kona, HI 96740**
**(808) 329-2911**
**www.konabeachhotel.com**

**Directions:**
**The hotel is 17 miles from Kona International Airport at Keahole: Head south on Kupipi Street toward Keahole Airport Road. Turn left toward Keahole Airport Road and continue straight onto Keahole Airport Road. Turn right at HI-19. Turn right at Palani Road. The hotel will be on the right.**

be helpful to those who show respect to the land and their ancestors. So here's a word of advice when staying at the Kona Beach Hotel and visiting the temple—unless you want to come face-to-face with an ancient, angry Hawaiian warrior, stick with the respect approach!

### The Bottom Line

**The History:** The site of an ancient temple where human sacrifices were performed. King Kamehameha rebuilt the temple and had his royal residence here. A modern hotel was built on the site.

**The Haunting:** Ancient Hawaiian warriors have been seen and heard in the hotel and on the grounds.

## Pele

There are many strange things happening on the islands of Hawaii, not the least of which are numerous sightings of a mysterious woman who looks very real and may even speak to you, and then vanishes. This woman can be young and beautiful, old and ugly, dressed in a lovely white or red traditional Hawaiian dress, or dirty modern clothes, and can often be accompanied by a dog. She may be seen walking along a highway, standing by a volcano, or might even accept a ride in your car and disappear before you reach your destination.

For many generations, people from all walks of life, from lifelong residents to first time visitors, have seen and talked to this woman who can appear in so many forms. And who is this female spirit who comes and goes where and when she pleases, and seems to prefer the places where lava flows? Many believe she is Pele, the ancient Hawaiian goddess of fire and volcanoes.

If you believe in ghosts, but can't quite wrap your brain around the idea of a goddess, it might be possible to reconcile the sightings with religion. This could be a case where several different spirits of young and old women roam various parts of Hawaii, but the old imbedded beliefs in the island goddess has led to any sighting of a female to be attributed to the powerful, elusive, fire-loving Madame Pele.

Of course, who can say what forces of nature and the supernatural are at work on Hawaii? There is a power and majesty to these islands and if you take the time to leave the crowded tourist areas and spend some quiet moments in the shadow of a volcano or by a tranquil waterfall, you can't help but feel a strong energy. And if you happen to see an enchanting young woman along a lonely stretch of road or a weathered old woman who asks for a ride to the nearest lava flow, be kind and respectful—ghost or goddess, you don't want to take any chances!

### Recommendations

**Pele is said to reside on the Mount Kilauea volcano on the Big Island at Volcano National Park (www.nps.gov/havo/index.htm), but has been seen for hundreds of years all across the islands. Chances are if you don't ever leave the poolside lounge chair at your hotel, you won't have a very good opportunity to encounter something unusual. See as much of the natural side of Hawaii as you can, and if you see a mysterious figure don't look twice, just take her picture! And a word of warning, bad luck is said to follow anyone who takes rocks from Madame Pele's volcanoes, and if that sounds farfetched, just check the Internet for the thousands of stories about people returning rocks they took because they experienced bad luck!**

# Idaho

OLD IDAHO PENITENTIARY

OASIS BORDELLO MUSEUM

BJ'S BAYOU RESTAURANT

Photo by Peter Wollheim, *Courtesy of the Old Idaho Penitentiary.*

# Old Idaho Penitentiary

Idaho was a young territory in 1870. It was only ten years old then, but it already had the need of a prison. At first, just a single-cell house was built in Boise, but over the years, inmates quarried local stone to make several large additions. The place became the state penitentiary in 1890, and went on to hold as many as 600 inmates at a time. Bad conditions sparked riots in 1971 and 1973, finally prompting the closure of the old pen. In total, over 13,000 people would be incarcerated there over the years, with 215 being women. Deaths inside the walls numbered 110—some by natural causes, some by the hands of other inmates, and the worst of them at the gallows.

Now on the National Register of Historic Places, the former penitentiary is a museum that offers visitors the chance to see what life behind bars was really like, from the cells, to Death Row, to Solitary Confinement—which inmates called "Siberia"—to those dreaded gallows.

A fitting exhibit for a place that once housed violent criminals, there is the J. Curtis Earl Memorial Exhibit, displaying thousands of years of weaponry from his private collection. There are also special events and programs throughout the year. Or, you could just come to the Old Idaho Penitentiary to try to see a ghost.

One of the restless spirits is believed to be Raymond Snowden, who later came to be called the Idaho Jack the Ripper. Snowden was sentenced to the gallows for the brutal stabbing murder of a woman. In 1957, he was said to have hung by his neck for a full fifteen minutes before he died. But even death didn't set him free, as his ghost has been seen and felt in the building called the 5 House.

Then there was Douglas Van Vlack, who in 1937 was sentenced to be hung for the murder of his wife and two policemen. On the day of his execution, he broke free from his guards and managed to climb up to the rafters of the New Cell House. After pondering his fate for half an hour, he decided he didn't want to die at the end of a rope. Shouting, "I have a right to choose the way I die," Van Vlack then jumped three stories down to the concrete floor, dying five hours later from his injuries. (In a bizarre twist, prison officials actually considered hanging the unconscious man, but decided to wait to see if he died on his own!)

Is Van Vlack one of the many other apparitions seen in this prison, and could he be responsible for some of the many inexplicable noises? And who is it that has touched and grabbed visitors? There are also many reports of sudden overwhelming feelings of being watched, depression, anxiety, and dread.

One special word of caution—if you are feeling uncomfortable inside the prison and decide to catch your breath in the beautiful rose garden (a prison project begun in 1917 and still maintained by the historical society), think again. Six of the executions were carried out there and many of the sightings occur on that spot!

Of course, it's impossible to know all that went on behind the walls of the old pen, but enough is known about the ruthless criminals and their awful crimes to give you goose bumps just reading about them. If you are brave enough, you can take the next step and visit the Old Idaho Penitentiary, and just perhaps, experience this darker side for yourself.

### The Bottom Line

**The History:** Prison built in 1870 and expanded over the years. Housed over 13,000 inmates, with 110 deaths, included 10 executions. Closed in 1973 and now operated as a museum.

**The Haunting:** Many apparitions, noises, feelings of dread, and being grabbed.

### Recommendations

**Call or check the website for special events and exhibits, such as a recent exhibit highlighting escape attempts. Be sure to ask about the amazing story of serial killer Lyda Southard, the "Lady Bluebeard" who poisoned several husbands. The staff recommends dressing appropriately for the weather and wearing comfortable shoes. While this is a fascinating historic haunt, just keep in mind you aren't dealing with Casper the Friendly Ghost here!**

### Visitor Information

**Old Idaho Penitentiary**
**2445 Old Penitentiary Road**
**Boise, ID 83712-8254**
**(208) 334-2844**
**www.idahohistory.net/OLDPEN.HTML**

**Hours:**
**Open Daily, Year-Round Noon – 5pm. Closed State Holidays (open on Memorial Day and Labor Day) Last Admission at 4:15pm. Summer Hours: 10am – 5pm.**

**Admission:**
**$5 Adults, $4 Seniors, $3 Children (ages 6-12), Discount for groups of 10 or more, must be the ages of 6 and up.**

**Directions:**
**From their website—From the intersection of Broadway and Warm Springs Avenue, travel east on Warm Springs for about 1.5 miles then turn left onto Old Penitentiary Road.**



# Oasis Bordello Museum

## "No Frills: $15 for 8 minutes."

This is the first line of the price list posted in the Madame's room of the former Oasis Bordello. Now a museum, the old bordello rooms are on display exactly as they were the day it was raided in 1988—right down to the dishes in the sink, the bag of groceries on the kitchen counter, the magazines in the waiting room, and the boxes of red light bulbs in the pantry.

The building was constructed in 1895 as the Bi Metallic hotel and saloon in the town of Wallace, and the town was built on the profits of the richest silver mine in the world. Over a billion ounces of silver have been mined in the last 100 years, and operations continue to this day. Mining towns are not usually known for tea parlors and libraries, and Wallace was no exception, boasting dozens of bars and five brothels. Of those five, only the Oasis still exists, in spirit, at least.

Speaking of spirits, many visitors taking the guided tour have reported strange paranormal experiences—seeing, feeling, and hearing what may be the ghosts of former saloon and brothel "employees" and their customers. But you don't have to just take the word of the human visitors. A blind tourist brought her guide dog, but the highly trained and sensitive animal absolutely refused to go down into the basement. Other dogs have since reacted the same way, whining and crying pitifully, and refusing to go down those stairs.

However, there is no reason to fear the Oasis Bordello Museum, as for over a hundred years, everyone has had a good time here!

## The Bottom Line

**The History:** Wallace was built for miners of the world's richest silver mine. This building was constructed in 1895 as a hotel and saloon, and became a brothel until it was raided in 1988. It's now a museum, preserving everything exactly the way it was the day it closed.

**The Haunting:** Visitors have seen, heard, and felt many strange things. Dogs refuse to go into the basement.

## Recommendations

The entire town of Wallace is on the historic registry, so take the time to look around at the beautiful Victorian homes that silver built—and make sure you take the silver mine tour. The museum is a real time capsule, and the owners have gathered firsthand accounts that are woven together into their fascinating guided tour. There is a gift shop offering coffee mugs, tee shirts, calendars, and pictures of the bordello. The mayor declared Wallace the Center of the Universe, and placed a manhole cover to commemorate it. It's around the corner from the museum, ask for directions. The film *Dante's Peak* was filmed in Wallace.

## Visitor Information

**Oasis Bordello Museum**
**605 Cedar Street**
**Wallace, ID 83873-2232**
**(208) 753-0801**
**http://myweb.cebridge.net/jmmayfield/**

**Hours:**
**Guided tours on the half hour, Monday-Saturday 9:30am – 6:30pm, Sunday 10am – 5pm. Closed during the winter, reopens in May.**

**Admission:**
**$5 per person**

**Directions:**
**Wallace is about 75 miles from Spokane, WA. From I-90: Take exit 62 for ID-4/Burke toward I-90/Wallace. Turn right at Residence Street. Continue onto Bank Street. Turn right at Cedar Street. Take the 1st right to stay on Cedar Street and the museum will be on the right.**

# BJ's Bayou Restaurant

In 1892, Idaho's first Secretary of State, Martin Petry, opened a first class hotel in Roberts. At the time, Roberts was a big town, big enough to support three newspapers, and was a stop for both the stagecoach and train. Over the years, the hotel changed hands many times, and served many purposes, including an emergency hospital and a bordello. In June of 1976, the collapse of the Teton dam caused the hotel to be flooded, along with the rest of the town, and the damaged building sat empty for many years.

In the 1980s, BJ and Cherillee Berlin purchased the property in order to turn it into both a home and a restaurant featuring Louisiana cooking (BJ is from New Orleans). It was during the restoration that they believe all the spirits were stirred up.

Just how many spirits are there?

"There are at least 15 ghosts here," Cherillee asserts.

Among them is a Chinese man who died here in the late 1800s. There are two women and two pre-teen children who may have died in a fire in 1887. There are two younger children who can be heard running around. There's also a pre-WWI soldier on the balcony. Then there's Sam.

"Sam is the most obnoxious of them all," Cherillee says. "He's the one who opens and closes doors and slams doors and stomps his feet and walks up and down the halls and talks to my oldest daughter."

No one knows who Sam is or why he is there, but he is one spirit they wish would leave. As for the others, as long as they don't bother the Berlin family, the family won't bother them—and that goes for any bodies that may be buried on the property. Several people have said that bodies are buried in the courtyard, and strongly urge that they be dug up, but that's not happening while the Berlins own the place. There's no sense risking stirring things up even more!

So, if you happen to be in the vicinity of Roberts, Idaho, and have a taste for some crawfish, alligator, and gumbo, stop by the very haunted BJ's Bayou restaurant and leave an extra seat open at your table. Perhaps one of the 15 permanent residents will join you...

## Recommendations

**For a unique experience, they hold a special dinner theater type of event for Halloween. In addition to dinner, guests are treated to a series of skits that attempt to explain who some of these ghosts are and why they are there. Spirits of another kind are available in their Voodoo Lounge, offering a full bar and extensive wine list. And if ghosts don't scare you, check out their pet alligators.**

## Visitor Information

**BJ's Bayou Restaurant**
**655 North 2880 East**
**Roberts, ID 83444-5080**
**(208) 228-2331**

**Directions:**
**The restaurant is about 15 minutes north of Idaho Falls. Take I-15 North to exit 135 for ID-48 toward Roberts. Turn right at East 627 N/N Berrett Road/ID-48. Turn left at North 2880 E/N Bassett Road.**

## The Bottom Line

**The History:** A first class hotel built in 1892 by Idaho's first Secretary of State, Martin Petry. Also served as an emergency hospital and bordello. Flooded when the Teton dam collapsed in 1976. Renovated in the 1980s and reopened as a Louisiana-style restaurant.

**The Haunting:** At least 15 different ghosts have been seen and heard, including a Chinese man, a soldier, women and children, and the obnoxious Sam.

# Illinois

LINCOLN'S TOMB

FORT DE CHARTRES STATE PARK

CONGRESS PLAZA HOTEL

Lincoln's Tomb, Oak Ridge Cemetery, Springfield, Illinois, 2006. *Photo by Robert Lawton*

# Lincoln's Tomb

As Illinois is known as the Land of Lincoln, it is only fitting that any discussion of historic haunts in this state includes one of America's greatest Presidents. Lincoln's assassination in April of 1865 brought a tremendous outpouring of grief. Mourners lined the route of his funeral train as it brought his body back to Springfield for burial. While his body arrived on May 3, Lincoln's journey was far from over.

As construction of his permanent tomb took years, his body was initially placed in a receiving vault. In December it was moved to a temporary vault, and the coffin was opened to make sure Lincoln's body was still there. In 1871, he was moved into the tomb which was still under construction, and at that time his body was viewed again.

Then in 1874... well, you get the picture. To make a long story short, Lincoln's body was moved a total of seventeen times and viewed on six occasions, the last viewing taking place in 1901 when witnesses claimed his face was still clearly recognizable. In that same year his body was finally (we can only hope!) lowered into its permanent resting place in a steel cage covered in concrete ten feet under the red granite cenotaph. One might ask why take such precautions? Because someone attempted to steal Lincoln's body to hold it for ransom!

In 1876, Jack Hughes and James "Big Jim" Kennally (also spelled Kenealy in some texts) hatched a plan to get a fellow crook out of jail. The three men were counterfeiters, and Hughes and Kennally thought that if they took the beloved President's remains and hid them, they would be able to demand the release of the prisoner. Their plan just might have worked, had it not been for a tip that led to a member of the Secret Service going undercover and gaining their confidence. They allowed the thieves to enter the tomb and start to move the coffin, then law enforcement agents sprung into action. Unfortunately, they didn't spring fast enough, and Hughes and Kennally managed to escape, although they were apprehended soon after.

So much for Lincoln being able to rest in peace!

The imposing tomb incorporates a 117-foot-tall granite obelisk, and there are several bronze statues of Lincoln. In addition to the President, the polished marble and bronze crypt also holds his wife and three of their sons. Additionally, there are plaques containing sections of Lincoln's famous speeches. In all, it is a magnificent structure for a man who came from such humble beginnings, and Lincoln no doubt would have looked upon it and asked, "Is all this for me?"

Upon reflection, perhaps that is exactly what he is doing, because almost from the day of his burial (the one in the tomb, that is) visitors to Oak Ridge Cemetery have seen the figure of man fitting Lincoln's description walking by this massive granite monument to his life. Witnesses still report a tall figure moving about the area of the tomb. Over the years, many people have also heard the sounds of sobbing, whispers, voices, and footsteps. Are these sounds the imprints of the energy of grief that has been so focused on this spot?

If Lincoln does still walk the grounds of the cemetery, he is not alone, as a young boy and a woman in a red cape have also been seen here. It should also be pointed out that Lincoln's phantom funeral train has been glimpsed approaching the station in Springfield. In fact, that train has been seen over the years in many places along its route, as far back as in New York. Again, we can only surmise that the enormous amounts of emotional energy directed at this train somehow left behind psychic imprints.

No one can say for sure if the President's spirit has not yet found peace, but if you do visit his tomb and glimpse a very authentic-looking Lincoln reenactor, look more closely. He just may be more authentic than you imagined.

## The Bottom Line

**The History:** The tomb of Abraham Lincoln, built in the 1870s. Lincoln's body was moved and viewed many times and almost stolen before being buried under concrete.

**The Haunting:** Since the 1870s, Lincoln's ghost has been seen walking around his tomb. There are also the sounds of weeping, footsteps, and voices.

## Recommendations

**Don't just come to Springfield for Lincoln's tomb. Be sure to see his house (which is allegedly haunted by Mary Lincoln, but don't expect the staff to talk about it), and the Presidential Library and Museum. Try to visit the cemetery when there won't be as many tourists so you will have some quiet time to test the paranormal waters. If that isn't possible, people in crowds have still reported strange sensations and experiences upon entering the tomb. For a moving experience, attend one of the flag-lowering ceremonies during the summer.**

## Visitor Information

**Lincoln's Tomb State Historic Site**
**Oak Ridge Cemetery**
**1441 Monument Avenue**
**Springfield, IL 62702-2662**
**(217) 782-2717**
**www.state.il.us/hpa/hs/lincoln_tomb.htm**

**Events:**

**There are a number of special events held here. The "American Legion Lincoln's Birthday Pilgrimage" on February 12, the "Veterans of Foreign Wars Annual Pilgrimage" on the Sunday nearest Lincoln's birthday; the "Sons of Union Veterans Lincoln's Death Anniversary Services" on April 15, and "Boy Scout Sunday" on the last Sunday in April. Every Tuesday evening from June 1 through August 31, Civil War reenactors from the 114th Illinois Infantry conduct flag-lowering ceremonies at the site.**

**Hours:**

**May-Labor Day, Monday-Sunday 9 – 5pm, Post Labor Day-November, Tuesday-Saturday 9 – 5pm, December-February, Tuesday-Saturday 9 – 4pm, March-April, Tuesday-Saturday 9 – 5pm.**

**Directions:**

**From I-55 Bus. in Springfield, take Eastman Street heading west. Turn right at Monument Avenue to Oak Ridge Cemetery.**

The gatehouse and front wall.

# Fort de Chartres State Park

Illinois has the unique distinction of having a French powder magazine as the state's oldest building. This structure was part of the third Fort de Chartres built in Prairie Du Rocher from 1753-56. The first French fort was begun in 1718, but there was a problem with log palisades and wooden buildings here—flood waters from the Mississippi caused significant damage in only five years.

A second fort was planned farther back from the river, and construction was underway in 1725. Unfortunately, it wasn't far enough away from the river as it was still on the flood plain, and once again they used logs. By 1742 this fort was also in bad shape, and in 1747 the French garrison transferred to Kaskaskia.

In 1753, the French decided to build yet another Fort de Chartres, and as they say, the third time's the charm. Actually, the real charm was stone—limestone walls to be exact—and this third fort promised to have much greater longevity. However, in just ten years, French rule came to an end with the signing of the Treaty of Paris, giving control to Great Britain. It took a while for British troops to arrive, but in October of 1765 the 42nd Royal Highland Regiment occupied Fort de Chartres, renamed it Fort Cavendish and immediately made it known that the French in the area were not exactly welcome.

Many of the French settlers left for St. Louis and the British settled in for what looked to be a very long stay. However, after only a few years they realized they didn't really need to expend manpower at this remote fort, and in 1771, the British marched away again. As sturdy as the stone walls were, the mighty Mississippi proved stronger, and with no one to keep the fort maintained, walls began to fall the next year. To add insult to injury, local people started harvesting the stones for other buildings, and by the dawn of the twentieth century, all that remained was the powder magazine.

In 1913, the state came to the rescue and over the next few decades they restored sections of the fort. Today, the old fort is a museum that immerses you into the life of the French soldiers with exhibits and living history events. And if you can believe some eyewitness accounts, the fort might just also give you a glimpse into a dead history event.

There was a full moon on the 4th of July in 1889, and a local woman and her neighbor were sitting on her porch at midnight. From the ruins of the fort they clearly saw a large procession of soldiers in colonial uniforms, dozens of wagons, and a casket. Despite the large number of wagons and men, the procession moved in absolute silence toward an old cemetery a few miles away. The woman's dog must have seen the spectral parade, as well, as it barked so loudly it awakened another neighbor, who got out of bed and also saw the men, wagons, and casket. Then this bizarre funeral entourage disappeared and did not return.

It was later discovered that this was not the first time this procession was seen, and it may not be the last. There are different legends about whose funeral this is, and when it will appear again. Because of the 1889 sighting, some say it can only be seen at midnight on the 4th of July, during a full moon, that falls on a Friday. That seems to be quite a set of rules to impose upon the ghosts!

What is more likely is that this is just a residual haunting—albeit one of extraordinary magnitude—that can be glimpsed around the anniversary of some actual funeral, or perhaps at any time of year. You just might have to be the right person in the right place at the right time.

One final note—if you have a dog, you may want to bring him along. There was a full moon on the 4th of July in 1997, and while no funeral procession was seen, exactly at midnight all the coyotes in the area started to howl. Were they just baying at the moon, or like the barking dog in 1889, can their eyes see through the veil between worlds to a night long ago when one soul crossed from the living to the dead at Fort de Chartres?

## The Bottom Line

**The History:** The first fort here was built in 1718. The oldest building in Illinois is in the third fort built by the French here in 1753. Taken over by the British in 1763, abandoned in 1771. Purchased by the state in 1913, some sections were reconstructed.

**The Haunting:** A long, ghostly funeral procession of men and wagons, which must be one of the largest sightings in the country.

## Recommendations

The fort's biggest event is undoubtedly their annual Rendezvous in November which usually features over 1,000 eighteenth-century reenactors displaying military drills, music, and crafts. (Sorry, no pets allowed at this event.) Dust off your pre-1820 flintlocks, as this event also has a shooting contest. There is a Kid's Day, and Colonial Crafts and Trades Day as well. Why just look at the fort when you can actively participate in one of these events? If you want to try to glimpse the ghost funeral on the road between the fort and the cemetery, pick a quiet spot and just wait and watch rather than driving back and forth all night—sound advice for any ghost hunt!

## Visitor Information

**Fort de Chartres State Park**
1350 State Route 155
Prairie Du Rocher, IL 62277-2006
(618) 284-7230
www.ftdechartres.com

**Hours:**
Open Wednesday-Sunday, 9am – 5pm. Closed on major holidays.

**Admission:**
There is no set Admission, but there is a suggested donation box.

**Directions:**
From St. Louis and the north: Take I-255 S/IL-3 S/US-50 W. Take exit 6 on the left to merge onto IL-3 S toward Columbia. Turn right at Co Road 1/Kaskaskia Road. Turn right toward Kaskaskia Road. Turn left at Stringtown Road. Turn right toward Levee Road. Turn left at Levee Road.

*Courtesy of the Congress Plaza Hotel.*

# Congress Plaza Hotel

The World's Columbian Exposition, also known as the Chicago World's Fair, was held in 1893 and drew over 26 million visitors. All of those tourists needed places to stay, and one of the hotels built to accommodate them was the Auditorium Annex. The name derived from Louis Sullivan's Auditorium Building, which was across the street, and the two buildings were designed with similar facades.

The hotel initially comprised only the North Tower, but the real surprise wasn't above ground. Connecting the Annex with the Auditorium Hotel was an underground marble passageway called "Peacock Alley." The South Tower was built between 1902-07, and included the Gold Room, which would become the first ballroom to have air conditioning. Another ballroom was later added to the North Tower, and along with other public rooms the hotel became the place for events for the cream of Chicago society.

In 1908, the now 1,000-room hotel had clearly grown beyond the status of a simple annex, and took the name Congress Hotel, as it's across the street from Congress Plaza. Over the decades, many famous, and infamous, people would stay, work, and play here, including many presidents (Teddy Roosevelt's words spoken here coined the famous "Bull Moose" nickname for his newly created Progressive Party), gangster Al Capone had his headquarters here, and band leader Benny Goodman broadcast a radio show from the hotel. Business as usual came to an abrupt end during WWII when the government bought the hotel for the army to use as a headquarters. After the war, the property returned to private hands and once again got back to the business of welcoming guests and hosting important political and social events.

The Congress Hotel may also host enough ghosts to have earned it the reputation as being the most haunted place in Chicago. The most frequently experienced activity is the sound of a party coming from the ballroom late at night. Security has often been called, but when they unlock the doors and open them, the sounds abruptly end and all they find is a dark and empty room.

There are many other strange sounds throughout the hotel, and people have been startled when appliances and other electrical devices suddenly turn themselves on and off. Many ghosts have been seen in the hallways by guests and staff, perhaps none more distinctive than "Peg-Leg Johnny." This particular apparition is dressed in ragged clothing and limps along with his peg leg. After a rash of sightings, research that was conducted did reveal that long ago a vagrant with a peg leg had been murdered in the hotel!

There is one legend that doesn't appear to have any basis in fact. There is a hand-like section of plaster coming out of a wall that looks like it's holding onto the iron framework, and the story that arose was that someone was accidentally walled up during construction. This alleged "Hand of Mystery" may make for a spooky tale, but when looking for ghosts in the Congress Hotel, there's no need to make up any stories!

## The Bottom Line

**The History:** Built in 1893 to accommodate all the tourists for the Columbian Exposition. The hotel has hosted many presidents, gangster Al Capone, and numerous other famous people.

**The Haunting:** Phantom parties take place in the ballroom. Many spirits are seen, including Peg-Leg Johnny.

## Recommendations

Ghosts aside, this reasonably priced hotel is in the ideal location on Michigan Avenue to enjoy many of Chicago's attractions. When making reservations, ask for the floor where Peg-Leg Johnny is most often seen, or for one of the more paranormally active rooms. The hotel has convention facilities and restaurants, so if you're looking for a haunted location for your next event, why not add a little spice to that dull meeting?

## Visitor Information

**The Congress Plaza Hotel and Convention Center**
520 South Michigan Avenue
Chicago, IL 60605
(312) 427-3800
www.congressplazahotel.com

**Directions:**

**From their website**—From N/S on the Dan Ryan Expressway: I-90/94 Exit at Congress Parkway downtown. Follow Congress Parkway to Michigan Avenue. Turn right on Michigan Avenue. The Congress Plaza Hotel is on the corner.

**From the West on the Eisenhower Expressway:** I-290 Follow to Congress Parkway East to Michigan Avenue. Follow directions above.

**Driving South on Lake Shore Drive:** Route #41 Stay in right lane, exit at Randolph onto Michigan Avenue. Turn left on Michigan Avenue and keep straight seven blocks to corner of Congress Parkway and Michigan Avenue. The Congress Plaza Hotel is on the Southwest corner.

**Driving North on Lake Shore Drive:** Route #41 Stay in left lane, exit at Balbo onto State Street. Turn right on State Street and keep straight to the corner of Congress Parkway and State Street. Turn right onto Congress Parkway and drive just two blocks to Michigan Avenue. The Congress Plaza Hotel is on the Southwest corner.

**Driving East on the Stevenson:** I-55 Stay on the Stevenson to Lake Shore Drive. Exit at Balbo onto State Street. Turn right on State Street and follow directions above.

**Car parking is located directly West of the Hotel:** Park One Parking OFFICIAL HOTEL PARKING has two entrances: Valet is recommended, 525 South Wabash (one Way from North to South) and 63 East Congress.

# Indiana

HANNAH HOUSE

STORY INN

BRISTOL OPERA HOUSE

*Courtesy of Bob Newkirk of Indy Ghost Hunters.*

# Hannah House

Not every person who fought against slavery carried a musket; some simply opened their doors to runaway slaves. There were harsh penalties for anyone caught helping or harboring runaways, and the more a person had, the more he stood to lose.

Alexander Hannah had a lot to lose, as he had hundreds of acres of land in Indianapolis, farms and businesses, a beautiful home, and he played a prominent role in civic affairs. He built this house in 1858, and added another wing and several outbuildings in 1872 when the 51-year-old bachelor finally tied the knot.

One can only wonder, before his bride, Elizabeth, came to live in the house, did Alexander Hannah tell her the awful secret of what had happened there years before? If he didn't tell her, she probably quickly realized that something was very wrong in this place.

One night when a group of slaves was hiding in the cellar, an oil lamp was accidentally knocked over. The lamp burst into flames and the fire spread with deadly speed, killing many of the trapped slaves. Hannah knew he would be in deep trouble if the bodies were discovered, so he buried them all in the cellar where they died, so no one would ever know.

However, this type of awful tragedy tends to leave an indelible residue, and the truth will be told by the restless souls. Hannah died in 1895 and the property was sold in 1899. This new owner, and subsequently his descendants, experienced inexplicable smells of death, cold spots, the sounds of moaning coming from the cellar, and the figures of the slaves themselves. Mr. and Mrs. Hannah have also been seen, both in the house and on the property. Are they there to try to protect their secret?

Amidst the horror of this event, the acts of kindness and courage cannot be forgotten. From the slaves who risked their lives for freedom, to the man who risked all he owned to help them, we can only hope that their spirits will someday find the courage to move on.

## Recommendations

Unlike many historic haunts where you might get a chance to spend an hour on a guided tour, at the Hannah House you can spend the night conducting your own investigation. For all those armchair ghost hunters, here's your chance to put your money where your mouth is, and test your investigative skills and psychic abilities. However, if you aren't yet ready for an overnight adventure, you still can experience the place on their monthly guided tour. And if you really don't want to get too far from an armchair, you can attend one of the lively dinner theaters held here.

## Visitor Information

**Hannah House**
3801 Madison Avenue
Indianapolis, IN 46227-1309
(317) 787-8486
info@thehannahmansion.org.

**Events/Hours/Admission:**
To learn about all your options for visiting the Hannah House, it's best to call or go to their website for the latest schedule of events and prices.

**Directions:**
From their website: Hannah House can easily be reached from 465 by exiting on the US31 North exit, also known as East Street. The third light down is National Avenue – go right. The very next light is Madison Avenue. The house sits on the corner of this intersection.

## The Bottom Line

**The History:** A house built in 1858 by a prominent Indianapolis man who helped runaway slaves, many of whom were killed in a tragic fire and buried in the cellar.

**The Haunting:** The figures of the slaves and the Hannahs are seen. There are cold spots, the smell of death, and the sounds of moaning coming from the cellar.

# Story Inn

It's always a wonderful thing when an old building is preserved and becomes an inn, but it is nothing short of remarkable when an entire village is turned into an inn!

In 1851, President Fillmore granted land to Dr. George Story. Dr. Story opened a medical office there, and a new village grew to include two general stores, a church, a one-room schoolhouse, mills, a slaughterhouse, a blacksmith, and a post office. From 1880-1929 the settlement of Story was the largest in the area, but then the depression hit, and in the following decade, half the population left to look for work. In retrospect, that loss of people turned out to have some positive effect, as their abandoned farms became Brown County State Park and the Hoosier National Forest.

Other than the general store, about the only business left in the village was the production of bathtub gin, and even that dried up after Prohibition was repealed. As if the economic outlook for recovery wasn't gloomy enough, in the 1960s, the U.S. Army Corps of Engineers created a large reservoir, Lake Monroe, that cut off the main route to Bloomington on the Elkinsville Road. However, like the creation of all the parkland, the town's isolation would eventually have benefits. Quite simply, nothing ever changed there, so the village of Story became something of an enormous nineteenth-century time capsule.

In the 1980s, that time capsule became a unique bed and breakfast, and all of the buildings are now part of the Story Inn, which offers rooms, cottages, and a restaurant serving breakfast, lunch, and dinner. As their clever motto reads, the old village is "One Inconvenient Location Since 1851," but it is worth the drive, because where else could you rent an entire town?

When reviewing the history of this place, it's clear that for many years it teetered on the edge of becoming a ghost town. However, in an ironic twist of fate, even though all of the buildings have been saved, it is still something of a ghost town, primarily thanks to the Blue Lady. While the Blue Lady appears in the former general store (now the restaurant with rooms upstairs) as a figure draped in white, she is said to make her appearance whenever a blue light is turned on. She has one other bizarre characteristic—she likes to pinch women's rear ends!

The current owner, Richard Hofstetter, was skeptical of these ghost stories when he purchased the inn/village in 1999, but his wife, Angie, became a believer the day she got pinched. Richard was also surprised when he started going back over the decades of entries in the numerous guest books that had piled up in the attic. Guests with no prior knowledge of the Blue Lady consistently wrote about feeling a presence, seeing the figure of a woman, and yes, getting pinched! Most of this activity took place in the room that now bears the name of this "cheeky" ghost.

Who was this woman in life? No one knows for sure, but it is believed that she was one of Dr. Story's wives—and what a handful she must have been!

The Story Inn provides a truly unique experience in so many ways. It's an historic original 1851 village surrounded by a beautiful forest, with just enough of a spooky side to add the right amount of mystery to your journey. While there's no guarantee the Blue Lady will make an appearance or pinch you, it's best to stay alert and watch your back(side)!

## The Bottom Line

**The History:** An entire 1851 village that was turned into an inn.

**The Haunting:** The Blue Lady has been seen and felt—in the form of getting pinched.

## Recommendations

**If you want to get away from it all in a beautiful nineteenth-century setting with great food, this is the place. They are also very pet friendly (just ask their cats, dog, and horses) and pets are allowed in several of the cottages. Of course, for your best shot at a paranormal experience, request the Blue Lady Room, but be sure to book well in advance.**

## Visitor Information

**Story Inn**
6404 South State Road 135
Nashville, IN 47448
(800) 881-1183
storyinn.com

**Directions:**

**From Nashville: Drive three miles East on SR46/135. Turn right (South) at the SR46/135 split, onto 135 South, and proceed ten more miles.**

# Bristol Opera House

Many of America's earliest theaters have met the wrecking ball and been replaced with multiplexes. That's unfortunate from an historic perspective, and a haunted one as well, as theaters just seem to be one of those places that, if they last long enough, are bound to acquire a ghost or two. Perhaps spirits are drawn to all the drama and emotion that gets stirred up when the lights go down and the curtain goes up, or perhaps they were simply once "theater people" and still want to be part of that life, even in death.

One of the surviving theaters is the Bristol Opera House. Construction began in 1896, and in 1897 they hosted their first performance. The building would go on to have a number of uses, including a motion picture cinema starting in 1915, and for a time there was even a skating rink! Age and hard times eventually took their toll, and by 1940 the theater was in such bad shape it was just used for storage. By 1960, plans were in place for this old theater to have a date with that wrecking ball.

Fortunately, the Elkhart Civic Theatre stepped in and saved the Bristol Opera House from demolition. The building was renovated and performances began again in 1961. Since then, a lot of feet have crossed the stage, but not all of them have been from living actors.

The predominant ghost is that of a former handyman who lived in the theater. Initially, everyone referred to his mischievous spirit as Percy, until a psychic informed the staff that he prefers Percival. There is also a little girl they call Beth, who has been seen peeking through the curtain. There are at least three other distinct spirits of a woman and two men. Altogether, this group of paranormal occupants makes a variety of noises, moves objects, touches people, messes with anything electrical, and even manifests as solid figures from time to time.

Some have claimed that the sub-basement of the Bristol Opera House contains a portal between the world of the living and the dead. Maybe, maybe not. All that we can be certain of is that all the world is a stage—and you can never tell who or what is lurking behind the curtain…

## Recommendations

To experience the old Bristol Opera House you have to attend one of the performances, so don't be the last to arrive or first to leave if you want some relatively quiet time to test out your sixth sense in the auditorium. And remember, don't ask Percy to give you a sign, it's Percival!

## Visitor Information

**Bristol Opera House**
Elkhart Civic Theatre
210 East Vistula Street (SR 120)
Bristol, IN 46507-8613
(574) 848-5853

**Directions:**
From I-80/I-90: Take exit #101/Bristol/Goshen (toll) – go 0.8 mi. Turn Left on State Road 15 (IN-15) toward Bristol/Goshen – go 0.6 mi. Continue to follow IN-15 – go 0.9 mi. Bear Right on East Vistula Street (IN-120) – go 0.2 mi. Arrive at 210 East Vistula Street, Bristol, on the right.

## The Bottom Line

**The History:** A theater built in 1896 that also served as a cinema and skating rink. Scheduled to be demolished in 1960, it was saved, restored, and reopened for performances.

**The Haunting:** Percival and at least four other spirits make their presence known in a variety of ways.

# Iowa Haunts

VILLISCA AX MURDER HOUSE

OLD JAIL MUSEUM

MATHIAS HAM HOUSE

# Villisca Ax Murder House

IA

History isn't all about battlefields, documents, and old houses—sometimes it's about murder. There is something irresistibly intriguing and compelling about an unsolved crime, especially when it involves an ax.

While the town of Villisca claims the title of the "Pork Center of Southwestern Iowa," in June of 1912 more than pigs were slaughtered here. Josiah Moore, his wife, their four children, and two visiting children were all brutally murdered in their beds. Suspects abounded, but no one was ever convicted of the bloody crimes.

On the evening of June 9, the Moore children attended a church function, and invited two of the Stillinger girls to come over afterward and spend the night. It was a fatal decision. Early the next morning a neighbor noticed there wasn't any activity at the usually bustling household. That was because Mr. and Mrs. Moore and the six children, ranging in age from 5 to 12, had all been killed sometime in the night.

In addition to the extreme violence of the crimes—the murderer had continued to strike the victims after they were dead—there were some bizarre and distinctive things the perpetrator had done. The windows were covered over with skirts and aprons, all the mirrors were turned around, the victims faces were covered, one of the Stillinger girls had been suggestively positioned after her death, and a slab of bacon was found near her body.

Accusations flew and every possible scenario and suspect was considered. The townspeople were put in a panic, and previously open doors were locked and double bolted, and citizens carried guns. Were the murders a crime for hire as an act of revenge? Were they the twisted act of a serial killer who had struck in a similar manner in other locations? Was it the prominent businessman, the traveling preacher, a friend or relative, or a vagrant? We will probably never know, but one thing is for certain, the awful crimes have left their mark on this house.

In the 1930s a couple rented the house and were looking forward to their first child. However, the pregnant woman became hysterical after repeatedly hearing footsteps and sounds, not to mention seeing a man with an ax at the end of her bed. When the husband also heard footsteps coming up the stairs, they quickly packed up and left.

Other occupants have had similar trouble. One man slept in the barn as he refused to spend the night in the house. Late one night some guests fled in terror. Then there are the sounds of children's voices and of crying, the doors that open and close on their own, the overwhelming feeling that you are not alone—everything you would expect of a house where so many people met a swift and bloody end.

For students of crime, this case offers an amazing amount of material on which to test your detective skills. For fans of historic haunts, the Villisca Ax Murder House offers the opportunity to spend the night and test your paranormal detective skills. Can you solve a century-old crime? Can you contact the spirits of the unfortunate children and adults who died here, and learn from their phantom lips the name of their murderer? Take a trip to Villisca, Iowa to find out for yourself, if you dare…

## The Bottom Line

**The History:** The site of a brutal ax murder of eight people in 1912.

**The Haunting:** Footsteps, crying, children's voices, the apparition of a man with an ax.

## Recommendations

**Depending on your level of courage, you can take a daylight tour of the house or go all the way and spend the night. Don't forget a visit to the cemetery where the victims are buried. The ax used in the murders is in the collection of the state museum in Des Moines. The house does not have any heat or electricity, so plan accordingly.**

## Visitor Information

**Villisca Ax Murder House**
**323 East 4th Street**
**Villisca, IA 50864-1146**
**(712) 621-4291**
**www.villiscaiowa.com**

**Hours:**
**April 1 to November 1: Monday-Friday 10am – 4pm, Saturday-Sunday 1-4pm. Call to verify times, and for the schedule of overnight stays. During the winter, visits are by appointment only.**

**Admission:**
**Daylight tours of the museum and house are $10. Overnight stays are $300 for up to 5 people, additional people are $60 each.**

**Directions:**
**From their website—Villisca Ax Murder House/ Olson Linn Museum. I-29 exit 35, then east on US 34 for 45 miles, then south on US 71 for three miles. Turn left onto U Avenue, then left onto 4th Street. To tour the house you have to meet Darwin at the Olson-Linn Museum, a large, white building on the southeast corner of the town square, at the corner of 4th Street and 4th Avenue. The Villisca Ax Murder House is several blocks away, on the northwest corner of 2nd Street and 6th Avenue.**

The Egyptian Revival style jail built in 1858.

# Old Jail Museum

When talking about jails, the conversation usually centers on the criminals incarcerated there, not the architecture. However, thanks to its Egyptian Revival style, the old County Jail in Dubuque deserves special mention. Completed in 1858, it was designed by John Francis Rague, who is primarily known for the former State Capitol at Springfield, Illinois, and the former State Capitol at Iowa City, Iowa. And what was the price tag for this elegant-looking jail with its eighteen-inch-thick limestone walls? It cost $40,000 to build, which was quite a sum of money at the time.

The building contained living space for the Sheriff, offices, and three tiers of cells. A special cell block was in the basement, and was used for the more troublesome prisoners, as well as captured Confederate soldiers during the Civil War. The most notable prisoner may have been the infamous outlaw, Butch Cassidy, but his stay was very brief. He was suspected of robbing a bank in Illinois, but with no evidence and no witnesses willing to testify, he was released after just four hours.

A new jail was built around 1958, and today, the old jail is a National Historic Landmark and a museum operated by the Dubuque County Historical Society, and there are some very unique pieces of local history on display. There's the family cradle of Julien Dubuque—the early French Canadian settler in the area for whom the city is named, a passenger wagon from the 1860s from the Dubuque-based A. A. Cooper Wagon Works company, and the ACME Life Saving Device that saved twenty-seven people from the 1946 Hotel Canfield fire in which nineteen people died.

They also have a unique sound and light show on "The Hanging of Patrick O'Connor," which uses actual artifacts and the "ghost" of O'Connor himself. Of course, this particular ghost is part of the production, but that doesn't mean the real thing doesn't exist…

O'Connor had lost his leg in a steamboat accident, and obtained a wooden leg thanks to the charity of others. In an attempt to obtain even more charity, he set fire to his own cabin, but the flames spread to his neighbor's house as well. He then tried to shoot a man in Galena, Illinois, and almost met the noose from an angry mob that had learned about O'Connor's repeatedly violent and drunken behavior.

He narrowly escaped being lynched by another mob in Dubuque in May, 1834, when he shot his room mate in the chest for no apparent reason. The man had returned from the store with supplies and simply wanted O'Connor to open the cabin door. Though freely admitting to the murder, he believed that he could get away with it because of the lack of a formal legal system in the Iowa Territory. Nonetheless, a speedy trial was held, and even though O'Connor was allowed to pick his own jury, he was found guilty and sentenced to be hanged. The execution took place on the 20th day of June, about sixty feet from where the jail was built two decades later, and his body was buried on the spot (although the remains were later moved two times).

If there's one thing you learn studying cases of hauntings, it's that events that took place on the land can have an effect on whatever is built there many years later. Not that a jail containing a century's worth of violent criminals doesn't present many opportunities for ghosts, but the hanging death of an angry murderer certainly adds an extra paranormal layer.

Although the current staff asserts that nothing unusual occurs in the old jail, others claim to have been terrified by the specter of Patrick O'Connor. Apparently, he stills takes delight in bullying other people. If you visit the jail and hear the sound of a wooden leg or feel as though an angry presence is watching you, just remind him of the trouble that kind of behavior got him into before.

### The Bottom Line

**The History:** An Egyptian Revival-style jail built in 1858, which briefly held Butch Cassidy, built on the site of an execution. Now operated as a museum.

**The Haunting:** The intimidating ghost of a murderer has been seen and felt.

### Recommendations

The details of the murder and execution are fascinating, so make sure you take in the twenty-minute show on your visit. The haunted Mathias Ham House is also operated by this organization, so take advantage of the discount and visit both places. The old jail is one of only a few Egyptian Revival style buildings left in the country. The museum has a gift shop.

### Visitor Information

**Old Jail Museum**
E. 8th Street
Dubuque, IA 52001
(563) 585-2048
www.mississippirivermuseum.com/features_historicsites_jail.cfm

**Hours:**
Open Wednesday-Sunday from Memorial Day through Labor Day, 11am – 4pm. The Old Jail Museum is also available for field trips, group visits, and private functions at any time by appointment.

**Admission:**
Adults $5, Children $3.50, 6 and under Free. Receive a discount when purchasing Old Jail Museum tickets in conjunction with the National Mississippi River Museum and Aquarium or the Ham House historic site.

**Directions:**
From the North: Heading North on US-151/US-52 /US-61 in Dubuque, exit onto White Street toward Port of Dubuque. Turn left at East 7th Street. Turn right at Iowa Street. Turn left at East 8th Street. The Old Jail will be on the right.

From Illinois and the East: Merge onto Great River Road/US-151 S/US-61 S/WI-35 S. Continue to follow US-151 S/US-61 S. Entering Iowa. Take the 9th Street-11th Street exit toward US-52 N/IA-3 W. Turn right at E. 11th Street. Turn left at the 3rd cross street onto Iowa Street. Turn right at E. 8th Street. The Old Jail will be on the right.

## Mathias Ham House

Twenty years before John Francis Rague designed the old County Jail in Dubuque, he was the architect of a small stone house overlooking the Mississippi River. It was built for Mathias Ham, who had made money in lead mining, as well as several other business endeavors. As Ham's family and fortune grew, additions were constructed, creating a twenty-three-room mansion with fourteen-foot ceilings, all manner of European and American decorative arts, and a variety of architectural styles. Ham even had a tower from which he could keep an eye on his shipping interests on the river.

Ham's first wife died in 1856, and he remarried four years later. His second wife died in 1874, and he passed away in 1889. There were five Ham children, and two of the daughters continued to live in the mansion after his death. In the 1890s, one of the sisters died, leaving only Sarah.

It must have been especially terrifying then, when someone broke into the house one night when Sarah was all alone. She heard the intruder walk up to her door, but she was prepared to defend herself. Sarah fired two shots through the door. When help arrived, they followed a trail of blood from her door, out of the house, and down to the river, and there discovered the body of the thief who broke into the wrong mansion.

In 1964, the Ham House became a museum, and right away visitors and members of the staff detected a strong presence in the house. Powerful cold spots can sweep through you at any time, and lights seem to have a mind of their own. There are also the sounds of voices, footsteps, and of someone running down the stairs to the basement. Some windows open on their own. All in all, the paranormal activity at the Mathias Ham House has earned it the reputation as the most haunted place in Iowa.

Do the spirits of Ham and his wives and children still linger in their beautiful mansion, unwilling to leave the life of luxury they knew? Does the ghost of the thief return to the house looking for the person who shot and killed him? Do the building stones themselves act like storage units for all of the tumultuous energies of life, and of death? There's only one way to find out—enter the mansion and see for yourself who still lurks in its shadows.

## The Bottom Line

**The History:** A stone home first built in 1839, and expanded into a twenty-three-room mansion. In the 1890s, a thief was shot and killed.

**The Haunting:** Considered one of the most haunted places in Iowa, there are all the classic symptoms of a haunting—cold spots, footsteps, voices, and a very strong presence.

## Recommendations

The life of a prominent family during the Victorian era comes to life here, thanks to the costumed interpreters who give the guided tours. Check out the ten-minute film, *Lead Rush*, about the local lead mining industry, narrated by Kate Mulgrew, famous local actress and Star Trek captain. The property also contains the 1833 Settlers Log Cabin (the oldest building in Iowa) and a one-room schoolhouse.

## Visitor Information

**The Mathias Ham House**
**2241 Lincoln Avenue**
**Dubuque, IA 52001-1424**
**www.mississippirivermuseum.com/features_historicsites_ham.cfm**

**Hours:**

**Open Wednesday-Sunday from Memorial Day through Labor Day, 11am – 4pm (last tour begins at 4pm). The Mathias Ham House is also available for field trips, group visits, and private functions at any time by appointment.**

**Admission:**

**Adults: $5, Children: $3.50, Children 6 and under admitted free. Receive a discount when purchasing Ham House tickets in conjunction with a visit to the National Mississippi River Museum and Aquarium or the Old Jail Museum.**

**Directions:**

**From US-151 North: follow US-151 N/US-61 N. Take the Kerper Boulevard exit toward Greyhound Park/Eagle Point District. Turn left at Kerper Boulevard. Turn left at Hawthorne Street. Turn left at Lincoln Avenue. The Ham House will be on the right.**

**From Illinois and the east: Great River Road/US-151 S/US-61 S/WI-35 S. Continue to follow US-151 /US-61 S. Entering Iowa. Turn right onto the US-35 S/US-61 S/US-151 S ramp. Take the exit toward Eagle Point District/Kerper Boulevard/Greyhound Park. Merge onto East 16th Street/Riverview Park Drive. Continue to follow E. 16th Street. Turn right at Kerper Boulevard. Turn left at Hawthorne Street. Turn left at Lincoln Avenue. The Ham House will be on the right.**

# Kansas

FORT LEAVENWORTH FRONTIER ARMY MUSEUM

MINE CREEK BATTLEFIELD

HOLLENBERG PONY EXPRESS STATION

Artillery practice at Fort Leavenworth.

# Fort Leavenworth Frontier Army Museum

In 1827, Colonel Henry Leavenworth established a fort to provide protection for the Santa Fe Trail. At its inception, Cantonment Leavenworth as it was called, had 14 officers and 174 enlisted men. It is doubtful any of those men could have envisioned how the fort would grow and someday become the oldest, and one of the most important, army facilities west of the Mississippi.

The historical role of Fort Leavenworth and its soldiers is impressive—protecting settlers, fighting Indians, trying to keep the peace between the pro-slavery and free soil factions, bringing the Mormons back under federal control, as a recruitment camp during the Civil War, as a post for the Buffalo Soldiers, as a military prison, as a school with the likes of George C. Marshall, Dwight D. Eisenhower, Douglas MacArthur, Colin Powell, and George S. Patton, the site of one of the original National Cemeteries, as a VA center and Old Soldiers Home, to a modern facility encompassing thousands of acres and over a thousand buildings.

Surely, such a history may have left a little bit of paranormal energy here or there? In fact, just about all of the old fort buildings have a ghost story or two to tell. There's the phantom party that can be heard in the Chief of Staff Quarters, the priest, Father Fred, who died in a church fire who continues to appear in the house built on the site, Phil Sheridan's angry wife, the Lady in Black, and the apparitions of numerous soldiers and prisoners who still walk amongst the living just about anywhere at anytime.

Of particular note is The Rookery building at 14 Sumner Place. Construction began in 1827, making it the oldest house in Kansas. It is also quite possibly the most haunted house in Kansas. The building is still used as military housing, and over the years residents have complained about a man in a nightshirt waking them up at night. There's also a woman who appears to rush at people with arms extended as if about to attack. Then there's a talkative old woman and an angry little girl. With all these extra residents, it's a wonder that anyone gets any sleep here!

Then there is the tragic tale of Catherine Sutler, who arrived at the fort in 1880 with her husband and two children. While gathering firewood, the children were carried away by the river. Everyone gave them up for dead, except Catherine. Night and day she searched for her children, even when frigid winter weather set it. She died of pneumonia that winter, not knowing that in the spring her children would be found alive, having been saved and protected by the Fox Indians. Catherine was buried in the National Cemetery, and her distraught figure has been seen wandering around there, often carrying a lamp, still searching for her beloved children.

Many other things have been experienced in the cemetery. The figure of an Indian has been seen, and while some believe it to be Chief Joseph of the Nez Perce, who was held prisoner here in 1877, Chief Joseph died in 1904 in Washington. Of course, it makes for a better ghost when it is a famous chief!

Clearly, however, with a place that has had so many sightings of so many different ghosts, there's no need to embellish the stories. As with any site, there's no guarantee that the ghosts of Fort Leavenworth will make an appearance for you, but if you visit the museum and take the tour, you have a good chance of at least having a brush with some piece of the fort's long, haunted history.

### The Bottom Line

**The History:** The oldest army post west of the Mississippi, established in 1827. The fort and its soldiers played key roles throughout our country's history.

**The Haunting:** Numerous apparitions of soldiers, women, Indians, and children.

### Recommendations

**You will need a photo ID to enter the fort!**

Begin your visit at the Frontier Army Museum. From there, you can use a provided map to take a driving tour of seventeen points of interest, each of which has an audio description. Take a look for some of the graves of famous men and women in the cemetery. **And don't forget to bring that photo ID!**

### Visitor Information

**Fort Leavenworth – Frontier Army Museum**
Reynolds Avenue
Fort Leavenworth, KS 66027
(913) 684-3767
http://usacac.army.mil/cac2/csi/FrontierArmyMuseum.asp

**Hours:**
The museum is open to the public 9am – 4pm Monday through Friday, and 10am – 4pm on Saturdays. The museum is closed Sundays and all federal holidays.

The National Cemetery is open 7 days a week from dawn to dusk.

**Admission:** Free

**Directions:**
From highways 7, 73, and 92 in Leavenworth: Turn north onto Grant Avenue. Turn right at Reynolds Avenue. Take the 2nd left to stay on Reynolds Avenue. The museum will be on the left.

# Mine Creek Battlefield

In the fall of 1864, Confederate General Sterling Price hoped to bring Missouri into the Confederacy. His army fought several battles in the state, but after a defeat at the Battle of Westport (the site of present-day Kansas City), he was compelled to retreat into Kansas.

The retreat of Price's 7,000 men did not go smoothly due to the 500 wagons full of supplies. As all of those wagons were attempting to cross Mine Creek, which was swollen by heavy rains, Union forces attacked in what would be one of the largest cavalry battles of the Civil War. Although the Union forces only numbered about 2,600, they carried revolvers and seven-shot Spencer carbines, which certainly leveled the playing field against the Confederates and their single-shot muskets.

The Union onslaught brought great confusion to the Confederate forces. The situation was made worse by the fact that many of Price's men were actually wearing captured Union uniforms, so at times it was impossible to distinguish friend from foe. As a prime example of this, in an attempt to rally his forces, Confederate General Marmaduke thought he was riding up to a group of his men. They were, in fact, Union troops and Marmaduke was captured. By the time the brief, half-hour battle was over, a thousand Confederates were captured, between 400-500 men were killed, and the rest were running in full retreat. This Union victory, in contrast, cost only 100 killed or wounded.

The campaign not only ended many lives, it ended the Confederate hopes of taking Missouri. Another objective of this campaign had been to discourage voters in the north and prevent Lincoln from being re-elected. To the contrary, the decisive Union victories only helped Lincoln gain a second term.

Today, it is difficult to stand on this ground and imagine the bloody battle that took place here...or is it? Over the years, many people have heard the sounds of battle—gunfire, horses, sabers clashing, men shouting, moaning, and crying out. Others see shadowy figures on the battlefield, and get the distinct impression they are not alone. Perhaps, then, it would be more difficult to stand on this ground and imagine that nothing remains from the desperate battle in which so many men were killed and wounded.

### The Bottom Line

**The History:** The site of one of the largest cavalry battles of the Civil War. The Union victory ended the Confederate hopes of taking Missouri and stopping Lincoln's re-election.

**The Haunting:** Shadowy figures and the sounds of gunfire, horses, sabers clashing, men shouting, moaning, and crying out.

### Recommendations

**There are many living history and special programs throughout the year; call or visit the website for the latest schedule. The store offers a wide selection of Civil War and Kansas history books. Stop by the visitor center first to familiarize yourself with the battle, then walk the battlefield along one of the trails. Places like this afford excellent opportunities to bring your cameras, recorders, and meters to test for paranormal activity. But please, as always, do so discretely and respectfully, as you are on ground where men bravely fought and died.**

### Visitor Information

**Mine Creek Battlefield**
**20485 KS Highway 52**
**Pleasanton, KS 66075-4023**
**(913) 352-8890**
**www.kshs.org/places/minecreek/**

**Hours:**
**First Wednesday in April through last Saturday in October. 10am – 5pm, Wednesday – Saturday. Closed all state holidays.**

**Admission:**
**$3 adults, $1 students; KSHS, Inc., members, children five and under admitted free.**

**Directions:**
**Two miles south on U.S. 69, one-half mile west on K-52 in Pleasanton, Kansas.**

## Hollenberg Pony Express Station

"**WANTED:** Young, skinny, wiry fellows not over eighteen. Must be expert riders, willing to risk death daily. Orphans preferred."

Few things in American history were of such short duration, yet so long in memory as the fabled Pony Express. The 1860 advertisement above says it all—this was a dangerous job over treacherous terrain, facing bad weather, Indians, and everything else the untamed west could dish out.

The route ran 2,000 miles from St. Joseph, Missouri to Sacramento, California, and the Pony Express was only in operation for eighteen months, beginning in April 1860. It was claimed that just one bag of mail was ever lost, with 35,000 pieces of mail making it to their destinations. In total, the Pony Express would have 183 riders, ranging in age from 11 to over 40, and they cut down the delivery of mail to California from several months to ten days.

Because of the fast pace, fresh horses were needed every ten to fifteen miles, so stations were required all along the route. In 1857, Gerat Hollenberg built a six-room structure in what is now Hanover, Kansas, to cater to the wagon trains heading west. The combination grocery store, tavern, and post office became a perfect fit for the Pony Express Riders, and it actually became the biggest station along the route.

Unfortunately, what began as a great experiment, ended in financial disaster for investors when the telegraph lines were completed in October of 1861 and the Pony Express became obsolete. Of the 163 stations, Hollenberg's is the only original structure remaining at the site where it was built. This place offers a unique

Hollenberg Pony Express Station.

glimpse into a legendary era, when courageous young men risked storms and arrows to get the mail across the great expanse of the American west. And if you're lucky, you might also just glimpse one of those young men.

Hollenberg Pony Express Station became a national historic landmark managed by the Kansas State Historical Society, and over the years, visitors and staff have claimed to see the Pony Express riders, and hear the sound of galloping horses and the riders calling out as they approach the station. There are inexplicable cold spots, strange sounds, and the feeling that you are not alone.

Perhaps these stories are the result of overactive imaginations, or perhaps there is some truth to the tales of these phantom riders. In this case, it would only be fitting if the Pony Express men somehow lived on to allow visitors a chance to experience the romance and bravery of these western legends.

## The Bottom Line

**The History:** Built in 1857 as a store for settlers heading west, Hollenberg's is the only original Pony Express station remaining at the site where it was built.

**The Haunting:** Pony Express riders are seen and heard approaching the station. Inside the station are cold spots and strange sounds.

## Recommendations

If the weather is bad, use the handicap parking which is closer to the visitor's center (recommended by the facility). The center has two videos you can watch, and there's a gift shop and picnic area. If the center is closed, you can still walk the grounds. In June they have a Pony Express Re-Ride celebration, and in August there is an all-day festival featuring a reenactment of a Pony Express ride and a variety of pioneer living-history demonstrations. Even Santa comes to visit during the Christmas open house in December.

## Visitor Information

**Hollenberg Pony Express Station**
2889 23rd Road
Hanover, KS 66945-8901
(785) 337-2635
hollenberg@kshs.org
www.kshs.org/places/hollenberg/index.htm

**Hours:**
Open the first Wednesday in April through the last Saturday in October, call or check the website for exact dates: Wednesday to Saturday: 10am – 5pm. Closed all state holidays. Group tours by appointment.

**Admission:**
$3 adults, $1 students; KSHS, Inc., members, and children five and under admitted free.

**Directions:**
Four miles north of U.S. 36 on K-148, one mile east on K-243 in Hanover, Kansas.

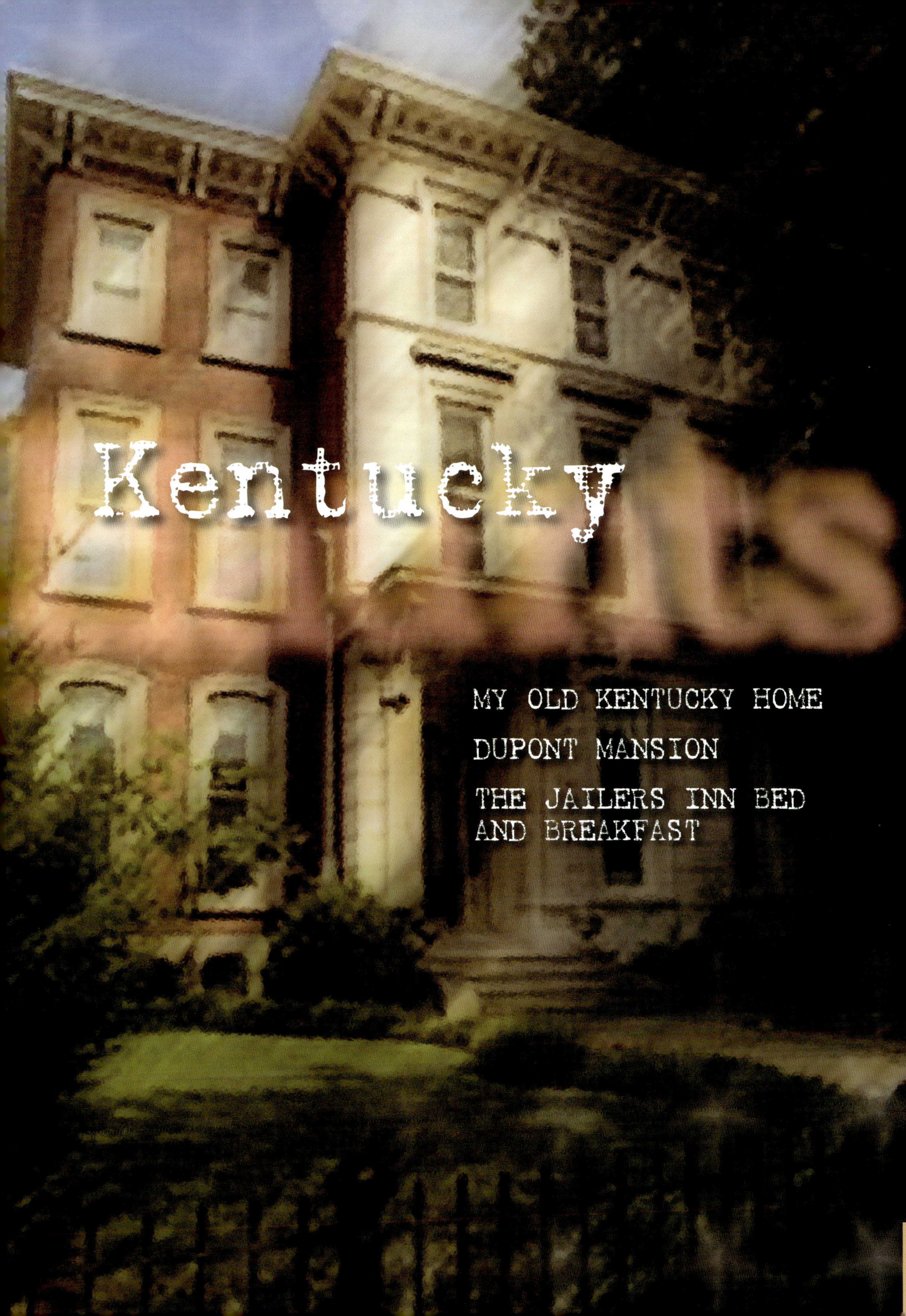

# Kentucky

MY OLD KENTUCKY HOME

DUPONT MANSION

THE JAILERS INN BED AND BREAKFAST

This iconic home represents the state on its quarter.

## My Old Kentucky Home

There are few old American songs that are as instantly recognizable as "My Old Kentucky Home" by Stephen Foster, but just what home was he writing about? It is believed that the house that inspired the song was Federal Hill, a Georgian-style mansion in Bardstown, built between 1795 and 1818 by Judge John Rowan.

Rowan was a prominent lawyer who also went on to serve in both the U.S. Congress and Senate. However, despite a life of law, he shot and killed a man in a duel in 1801. Remarkably, the fatal shooting came about when Rowan and Dr. James Chambers argued over who was the greater expert in classical languages! Rowan then made an insulting remark about Chambers' wife, for which he later publicly apologized, but Chambers insisted on satisfying his honor with pistols. Fortunately for Rowan, he turned out to be as good with a gun as he was with Latin, and the doctor was shot and killed—or should we say *offa quod iuguolo*. As times were quite different then, the murder didn't affect Rowan's ability to get elected to high office.

While tragedies hit all families, Rowan's seemed to be particularly hard hit. In 1833, a cholera epidemic claimed the lives of four family members and twenty-six slaves. One of the victims, one of Rowan's sons, had just been chosen to serve as Secretary of State for President Andrew Jackson, and had only stopped by to see his family on his way to Washington, D.C.

Another of Rowan's sons had stayed awake one night caring for one of his children who was sick. Taking a break, he sat on a window sill in his bedroom, with one leg out the window. In a truly bizarre accident, the man dozed off and died in a fatal fall out of the window. His wife, Rebecca, who witnessed the tragedy, would never again sleep in that bedroom.

Why was there so much bad luck at Federal Hill? Well if you are superstitious, you might conclude that it had to do with the use of the number 13 in the construction of the original house. In honor of the 13 colonies, Rowan had his home built with 13 rooms, with 13 windows in the front of the house. Then there were the 13 steps between floors, the walls that were 13 inches thick, and the ceilings were 13 feet high.

Of course, many family members led happy lives at Federal Hill, so if there was bad luck, perhaps it ran its course. However, not everything here has remained in the past. Over the years, Rebecca Rowan has been seen walking the halls. Has the widow's grief bound her to this house? There have been many other strange sights and sounds here, but arguably none so unnerving as what takes place at Judge Rowan's grave.

Rowan's final request before his death in 1843 was that no marker should be placed at his grave. He said that his parents had no markers, and he thought it would dishonor their memory if he had an elaborate monument. However, once he was dead, family members completely disregarded his wishes and ordered a large obelisk to mark the site of their prominent relative's final resting place. But resting in peace was not on the judge's agenda.

Shortly after the obelisk was erected, it was found lying on the ground. Workmen stood up the monument and put it back in its place, but a short time later it fell over again. Was the ground settling; was there a flaw in the design? No reason could be found, and when the obelisk toppled over yet again—this time directly onto the grave—many workmen refused to go near it, fearing that they, too, would incur the judge's wrath. It is not known just how many times the obelisk has fallen over the years, but it certainly has happened often enough to be beyond mere coincidence.

Thanks to a fundraising campaign led by Kentucky's school children, "My Old Kentucky Home" was purchased from a Rowan descendant in 1923 and it opened as a state park in 1936. Today, it is one of the most popular parks in Kentucky, and it gives visitors the chance to get a taste of what life was like for a wealthy southern family. And if you tour the house and visit the cemetery, you might also get a taste of what death is like for them, too.

## Recommendations

**Costumed guides do an excellent job of bringing the past to life here, and the antique furnishings are superb. Call or check the website for one of their special events. Keep an eye open for Rebecca in the house, and check out the cemetery for the judge's obelisk. And don't be surprised if, after your trip, you can't get the song "My Old Kentucky Home" out of your head!**

## Visitor Information

**My Old Kentucky Home**
**501 East Stephen Foster Avenue**
**Bardstown, KY 40004-0323**
**(502) 348-3502**
**http://parks.ky.gov/findparks/recparks/mo/history/**

**Hours:**
**Open Thursday to Sunday during the winter period of January 2 to February 28 and open daily from March 1 to December 30, 9am – 4:45pm.**

**Admission:**
**Free**

**Directions:**
**From Louisville: Take I-65 South to the KY-245 exit, Exit 112, toward Clermont/Bardstown. Merge onto KY-245 toward Clermont/Bardstown. Turn Right onto N. 3rd Street/US-150/US-31E. At the traffic circle, take the 3rd exit onto E. Stephen Foster Avenue. The park will be on the right.**

## The Bottom Line

**The History:** The home of a prominent lawyer and politician, first built in 1795. Legend maintains it was the inspiration for Stephen Foster's song, "My Old Kentucky Home."

**The Haunting:** A grieving widow still walks the halls, and an angry judge keeps knocking over his grave stone.

*Courtesy of the Dupont Mansion.*

# DuPont Mansion

When speaking of the financial royal families of America, the names of Rockefeller, Morgan, Astor, and Carnegie invariably arise, as does the name DuPont. The DuPont family fortune began with the production of gunpowder, which stands in stark contrast to the elegant mansions they erected. One such mansion was built in Louisville in 1879 to accommodate relatives who came from the family's main business in Delaware to work in the DuPont's ventures in Kentucky.

The three-story Italianate-Renaissance structure had the best of everything in its parlors, dining room, and ten bedrooms, including fourteen-foot-high ceilings, decorative molding, and hand-carved Italian marble fireplaces. Despite affording the opportunity to live right in the middle of the lap of luxury, at least one family member chose to spend most of his time in a suite at the Galt House Hotel.

Alfred V. DuPont was a bachelor, and to put it mildly he was a very energetic bachelor, and the women he preferred weren't the kind you brought home to meet the family. One of these women, Maggie, a Madame at a local bordello, became pregnant with Alfred's child in 1893. Of course, he did what any wealthy gentleman of his era would do when confronted with a pregnant mistress from a bordello—he told her to get lost. In response, Maggie employed what was most likely some of the family-made gunpowder and shot him in the chest, killing him. To protect the family, the DuPonts persuaded officials to rule the death a heart attack, but the truth eventually surfaced.

As for the fate of the mansion, it hit hard times when it was divided into apartments and it was not kept in the best shape for most of the twentieth century. In the 1990s it was doubtful the structure could be saved, but after enough work to make the building stable, it was sold to the Warrens who worked their magic. They brought the mansion back to all its Victorian glory, earning the Louisville Historical League's Historic Preservation

Award for their work. As it is now a bed and breakfast, you don't need to be a relative of the DuPonts to spend the night in their former lap of luxury.

While history has all but forgotten Maggie, Alfred has made sure his memory lives on. In 1998, a workman who had been hired to do some repairs was alone in the mansion one night. At the bottom of the staircase, a man suddenly appeared in front of him. This was one well-dressed ghost, as he wore a nineteenth-century tuxedo. There was also something else very distinctive about this apparition—he had a bloody bullet hole in his chest! The man in the tuxedo appeared surprised by the workman (and the feeling was mutual!) and quickly vanished.

Years later, an interior decorator was coming down that same staircase when the man in the tuxedo appeared in front of her. On two other occasions on those stairs, she felt a hot breath on her neck, and then felt a hand grabbing her rear end. It looks like even death has not curbed Alfred's appetite for women! You would think he would have learned his lesson, but perhaps because he hasn't, he is bound to this house.

It may be a puzzle to some as to why Alfred has chosen to return here, but in a way, though, it makes sense. By appearing in the DuPont mansion in a tuxedo, with a bullet hole, there can be no doubt as to the identity of this ghost. As to why he has chosen to stick around—as he doesn't exactly seem to feel guilty about his former behavior, he is probably simply trying to recapture those lost days of being a wealthy playboy. And let's be honest, what man wouldn't?

## The Bottom Line

**The History:** A mansion built by the DuPonts in 1879. Recently restored and turned into a B&B.

**The Haunting:** Alfred V. Dupont appears in his tuxedo, complete with bullet hole.

## Recommendations

If you want to spend the night in a luxurious mansion, just minutes from the best of what Louisville has to offer, this is the place. And ladies, if you ever wanted to meet a man from one of America's wealthiest families, here's your chance!

## Visitor Information

**DuPont Mansion**
1317 S. Fourth Street
Louisville, KY 40208-2313
(502) 638-0045
www.dupontmansion.com

**Directions:**

From their website—Arriving from Airport and I-65: From the airport go south on Terminal Drive. Turn left to stay on Terminal Drive and follow signs to I-65. Merge onto I-65 N toward downtown Louisville. Go approximately 5 miles and take exit 135 (St. Catherine Street West). Follow St. Catherine Street for four blocks and turn left onto Third Street. Drive .3 miles and turn right onto W. Ormsby Avenue. Drive one block and turn left onto S. Fourth Street. DuPont Mansion is on the left at 1317 S. Fourth Street.

Arriving from the North on I-65 South: Take I-65 S through downtown Louisville. Approximately 2.5 miles south of the Kennedy Bridge crossing the Ohio River, take the St. Catherine Street West exit 135. Turn slightly right onto St. Catherine Street at the end of the ramp and drive three blocks. Turn left onto Third Street. Go .3 miles and turn right onto W. Ormsby Avenue. Drive one block and turn left onto South Fourth Street. DuPont Mansion is on the left at 1317 S. Fourth Street.

Arriving from the East on I-64 or I-71:Take I-64 W or I-71 S to Louisville. I-71 merges into I-64 near downtown. Take I-64 W to I-65 S and exit at St. Catherine Street West (exit 135), south of downtown. Turn slightly right onto St. Catherine Street at follow the Directions: above.

Arriving from the West on I-64 East: Take I-64 E into downtown Louisville and exit onto I-65 S. Drive approximately 2.5 miles south of the Ohio River and take the St. Catherine Street West exit 135. Follow Directions: above.

*Courtesy of the Jailer's Inn.*

# The Jailers Inn Bed and Breakfast

Spending the night in jail isn't typically something you would want to do on vacation, or any other time for that matter, but at the Jailer's Inn in Bardstown, incarceration is elevated to a new level.

The Old Nelson County Jail was built in 1819 with limestone walls that are thirty inches thick. An addition was put on the back of the building in 1874, and the original section was converted into a residence for the sheriff. Remarkably, this jail was still in use until 1987, making it the oldest operating jail in the state, and it was listed on the National Registry of Historic Places.

Over the years, at least two outlaws of note passed through the doors of the old jail, one voluntarily, the other as a prisoner. Jesse James spent a considerable amount of time in Bardstown, but then no one there would arrest him. The sheriff had ridden with James when they were with Quantrill's Raiders during the Civil War, and the sheriff's wife was James' cousin, so the wanted man was a welcomed guest.

Then there was John Dillinger, the notorious bank robber of the early 1930s. He was a most unwilling overnight guest at the old jail. Due to the high-profile nature of this dangerous criminal, he was brought in under an assumed name and quickly removed the next morning, so as not to attract any undue attention as they transported him.

Today, this historic jail is a bed and breakfast where guests are free to come and go as they please, and no paroles are necessary. Unfortunately, the same can't be said for the ghosts, as they don't seem able to leave the old jail...

This place has been called one of the most haunted houses in America, and one of the spirits perpetrating this haunting may be a convicted murderer. Martin Hill shot his wife in 1885, and for that he was sentenced to hang. The site of execution was to be the courtyard behind the jail, but fate intervened before the hangman could do his work. Hill became very sick and died an extremely painful death in his jail cell, but according to witnesses he has not yet left the building. A newspaper article written in 1909 tells of the many people who continued to hear the phantom moaning and Hill's voice crying out in agony.

More recently, staff and guests have witnessed lights and other electrical things go on and off by themselves. In the Colonial Room, a man woke up late at night and wanted to use the bathroom, but before he could reach for the lamp on his side of the bed, the lamp on the far side came on by itself! Apparently, someone was trying to be helpful, but the frightened man didn't see it that way.

A woman was looking in the mirror and saw a man standing behind her. She spun around, but there was no one there. Yet, when she turned back to the mirror, there was the man again! Other people, particularly women, have reported being tapped on the shoulder or having their hair touched. There are voices, whispers, screams, footsteps, a baby crying, and all sorts of inexplicable sounds.

Perhaps the best encounter will remain a mystery: A couple checked in one day, and the husband made a point that he was a complete skeptic and there were no such things as ghosts. The next morning their room was empty, and the keys and a note were on the bed. The note simply read, "My husband got scared and we had to leave."

## The Bottom Line

**The History:** A jail originally built in 1819 with an 1874 addition. Jesse James stayed here as a guest, John Dillinger as a prisoner.

**The Haunting:** A convicted murderer who died in his cell can still be heard crying out. Lights and appliances turn on and off. People have been touched and a man has been seen.

## Recommendations

**Many places in Bardstown are thought to be haunted and there is a "Spirit Walk" through town, which includes the old jail. Of course, if you are serious about ghosts, why stand on the sidewalk listening to stories when you can spend the night and have your own experiences? All of the rooms are elegantly furnished with antiques, except the Jail Cell Room which has two of the original jail beds (and a water bed if you decide not to be that original). If you have a ghost hunting group, you can have the place all to yourselves by renting all the rooms. If not, just remember that some people are actually there to sleep at night!**

## Visitor Information

**Jailer's Inn Bed and Breakfast**
**111 West Stephen Foster Avenue (Highway 150/62)**
**Bardstown, KY 40004-1415**
**(503) 348-5551**
**www.jailersinn.com**

**Directions:**

**From Louisville: Take I-65 South to the KY-245 exit, Exit 112, toward Clermont/Bardstown. Merge onto KY-245 toward Clermont/Bardstown. Turn Right onto N. 3rd Street/US-150/US-31E. Enter next roundabout and take 1st exit onto W. Stephen Foster Avenue/US-31E/US-62. 111 W. Stephen Foster Avenue is on the Left.**

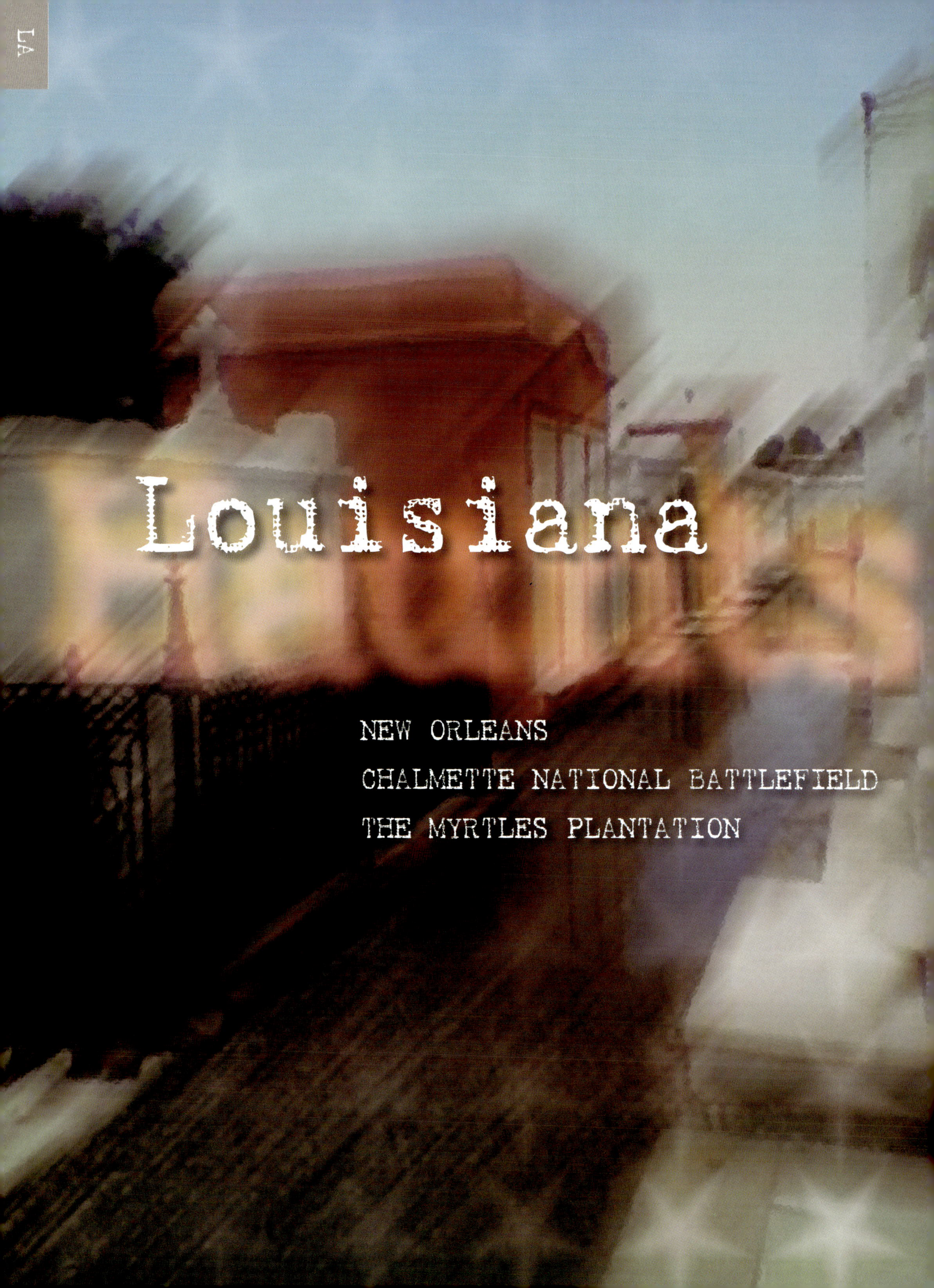

# Louisiana

NEW ORLEANS

CHALMETTE NATIONAL BATTLEFIELD

THE MYRTLES PLANTATION

St. Louis Cemetery #1.

## New Orleans

Take many different cultures and languages, a couple of wars, several epidemics, lots of criminals, prostitutes, and corrupt politicians, sweltering heat and humidity, slaves, voodoo, pirates, and a few natural disasters, mix thoroughly and let sit for a couple of hundred years and what do you get? The very haunted city of New Orleans. And to come here to see only one or two haunted places is like going to a sumptuous buffet wearing blinders. You need to see the big paranormal picture here, and the picture is very, very big.

The city was founded by the French in 1718, and builders soon realized the area between Lake Pontchartrain and the Mississippi was prone to flooding, so levees also had to be built. There were high hopes for establishing a thriving port city, but they were missing one crucial component—women! To solve this dilemma, prostitutes in France were given a choice, go to jail or be shipped to New Orleans. This didn't create much of a scandal at this point in the town's development, given the fact that many of the men were released convicts, so no one could claim to be better—or worse—than the next person. Things began to change, however, and in 1728, in order to attract a less "professional" female population, a group of nuns supervised the arrival of more respectable women to marry some of the more respectable men.

The town began to grow and families and businesses were established. Then in 1768, France gave Louisiana to Spain. Spanish rule didn't sit too well with the citizens of New Orleans, and they ran the governor out of town. Spanish soldiers (led by an Irishman!) put a bloody end to the little rebellion, and Spain continued to rule until Louisiana was given back to the French in 1800. This governmental ping pong continued, when Napoleon sold the vast Louisiana Territory to the United States in 1804.

Any hopes for long term stability were short-lived as the War of 1812 brought the threat of a British attack (see Chalmette National Battlefield story). After the war, New Orleans really began to prosper, but everything didn't run smoothly. There was great tension and conflicts between the established Catholic residents and the influx of American Protestants. There were the numerous devastating epidemics of cholera and yellow fever. Then came something far worse than the diseases, conflicts, and floods—Yankees!

After Union gunboats blasted their way up the river in 1862, New Orleans surrendered and was occupied by federal troops for the remainder of the Civil War. To describe how the residents felt about their military governor, General Benjamin Butler, one only needs to point out that chamber pots were made with pictures of Butler on the bottom.

The post-war years saw a series of ups and downs, scandals, and financial hardships, but throughout all the struggles, New Orleans continued to maintain its unique identity. Even after the devastation of Hurricane Katrina in 2005, the people persevered and you can still count on great food, jazz music, wild revelers at Mardis Gras, and arguably more haunted locations than anywhere else in America.

There are many ghost tours you can take which include places not open to the public. For a more personal paranormal experience, the following are just a few suggestions as to where to eat, sleep, and visit with some of the ghosts of New Orleans.

## Visitor Information

**Arnaud's Restaurant**
813 Bienville Street
New Orleans, LA 70112-3121
(504) 523-5433
www.arnauds.com

**Muriel's Restaurant**
801 Chartres Street
New Orleans, LA 70116-3206
(504) 568-1885
www.muriels.com

**Le Pavillon Hotel**
833 Poydras Street
New Orleans, LA 70112-1015
(504) 581-3111
www.lepavillon.com

**St. Louis Cemetery #1**
Bounded by Basin, St. Louis, Conti, and Treme Streets.

## Arnaud's Restaurant

Arnaud's Restaurant: A New Orleans institution for generations, this restaurant was opened in 1918 by a French wine salesman, Arnaud Cazenave. Arnaud sought perfection in the food, the service, and the dining experience. It is believed he is still making his presence known, as objects in the restaurant move on their own as if someone is making sure everything is just right. Arnaud's daughter, Germaine, managed the restaurant after her father's death, and she, too, may still haunt the place. The restaurant operates the Germaine Cazenave Wells Mardi Gras Museum, and contains some of her elaborate dresses. A white, misty figure has been seen in this museum, and many think it is Germaine.

## Muriel's Restaurant

Pierre Antoine Lepardi Jourdan built his dream home in 1789. Unfortunately, Jourdan was a gambler and he actually lost the house in a poker game in 1814. However, he couldn't bear to leave, so he committed suicide in a second floor room, where the Séance Lounge is today. While there are many ghost stories here involving slaves, a woman, a little girl, and someone who throws glasses, the predominant spirit is that of Jourdan, himself, who can still be seen wandering through the building.

## Le Pavillon Hotel

This elegant, centrally located hotel opened in 1907 on land that was once a canal in a desolate and dangerous area. Today, it is a step back into refined luxury, with crystal chandeliers, antiques, and a hand carved marble bathtub that belonged to Napoleon (in the European Palace Suite). But don't let this graceful façade fool you, as Le Pavillon is considered the most haunted hotel in New Orleans. Staff and guests have seen dozens of apparitions, including a couple and a gentleman in 1920s-style clothing, and a young girl. Many guests have awakened to find figures standing by their beds. One unfortunate man actually woke up to find an old woman sitting on his bed. She had her hand on his face and said, "I'll never let you go." He promptly checked out!

## St. Louis Cemetery #1

If you like spooky graveyards, this just might be the most haunted cemetery in the country. Despite its small size, it's estimated that since 1789 over 100,000 people have been buried here. There are soldiers from the Battle of New Orleans, yellow fever victims, politicians, musicians, and famous people from all walks of life. The trouble is, a lot of them are still walking even though they're dead! The most famous is no doubt Marie Laveau, known in the nineteenth century as the Voodoo Queen. She has been seen in her turban, still chanting spells. There is also the spirit of Marie's snake, and various dogs and cats. Then there's Henry, a man in a white shirt who looks completely solid, yet vanishes into thin air. It's said that someone sold Henry's tomb while he was away, so when he died he was buried in potter's field, but he still walks among the vaults looking for better accommodations! There are many, many other sightings, as well, so be prepared!

An early 1900s view of the cemetery.

# Chalmette National Battlefield

It is an interesting bit of irony that one of America's greatest military victories came two weeks after the war was over, but that doesn't detract from what happened at the Battle of New Orleans, also known as the Battle of Chalmette Plantation.

It was 1815, and the Treaty of Ghent had been signed to end the War of 1812. However, it had not yet been ratified, and British and American forces around New Orleans had not yet received word of the treaty. What these two armies did know on the morning of January 8 was that British Major General Sir Edward Pakenham and his 8,000 men, including Native Americans and black soldiers from the West Indies, were about to collide again with an equally diverse enemy—under the command of Andrew Jackson was a collection of no more than 4,000 militia, volunteers, Choctaw Indians, free blacks, and pirates!

Famous pirate Jean Lafitte had offered the services of his Baratarians—smugglers who operated in the swamps and bayous of an area called Barataria—to the United States. He and his men would help fight the British, but of course, he wanted something in return—official pardons for their many pirating indiscretions. Jackson needed skilled fighters, and although at first skeptical, a deal was struck and Lafitte kept to his word and brought his pirates to Jackson's army.

The British wanted control of the lands gained in the Louisiana Purchase, and one step in their plan was to take New Orleans. At the very least, seizing that important port city would be a huge bargaining chip in any peace negotiations. Pakenham's forces had been slowed in their advance on New Orleans by repeated engagements with Jackson's men. This precious time gave the Americans the chance to strengthen their defenses with earthworks and artillery at a site about six miles southeast of New Orleans.

A dense fog enshrouded the landscape on the morning of January 8 as the highly trained and more numerous British troops moved on the American positions. The British advanced under the perfect cover, but the fog suddenly lifted and made them easy targets. In a remarkable blunder, the British had forgotten to bring ladders to scale the earthworks, making them even more vulnerable. Pakenham was mortally wounded by grapeshot, and other officers and troops were dropping in great numbers under the American's relentless hail of lead from their muskets and cannons.

Although Pakenham had ordered General Lambert to keep up the fight, Lambert believed the cost in human lives was too great and ordered a retreat. Indeed, the British suffered a casualty rate of twenty-five percent, with over 2,000 men being killed, wounded, and captured. Remarkably, Jackson's men were relatively unscathed, with only thirteen killed, fifty-eight wounded, and thirty captured. It was a stunning defeat of crack British troops by a ragtag American army.

So, two weeks after the signing of the treaty, the Americans had won the day, saved New Orleans, and secured all the territory in the Louisiana Purchase, opening the door to westward expansion. The battle also made Jackson a national hero, which would help send him to the White House in 1829 as our seventh President. It was the last major battle ever fought between the British and the Americans, and it helped galvanize the national spirit and put forth the idea that America was no longer the inferior of its European counterparts.

Speaking of the national spirit, another type may linger on the battlefields of Chalmette, and in the National Cemetery. On the battlefield, the sound of cannon fire has been heard, as well as loud voices shouting commands to troops. In the cemetery, there are also voices, and a British soldier has been seen walking among the graves. Some visitors to the park have even felt a hand touch them, when no one else is near.

The Battle of Chalmette marked several endings and a number of beginnings in American history, but perhaps for some, the story goes on and on as if it was again the foggy morning of January 8, 1815...

### The Bottom Line

**The History:** One of America's greatest military victories, although the battle was won two weeks after a treaty had been signed. With the aid of Indians, free blacks, and pirates, a superior British force was defeated. New Orleans was saved and lands of the Louisiana Purchase were secured.

**The Haunting:** The sound of cannon fire and orders being given to the troops. A British soldier is seen wandering through the cemetery.

### Recommendations

**You should visit at least twice, once when it is quiet and you can contemplate the events and what may linger. The second time, go in January for the anniversary of the Battle of New Orleans which is commemorated with reenactors, cannon firings, and more. The visitors center has films and exhibits on the War of 1812. Kids can earn a badge with the Junior Ranger program. The bookstore also has period music, reproductions of items from the period, and children's books. Special programs are offered throughout the year.**

### Visitor Information

**Chalmette National Battlefield**
**8606 West St. Bernard Highway**
**Chalmette, LA 70043-4204**
**(504) 589-2636 ext. 1**
**www.nps.gov/jela/Chalmettebattlefield.htm**

**Hours:**
**Chalmette Battlefield and Jean Lafitte National Park are open daily: 9am – 4:30pm; closed December 25 and Mardi Gras.**

**Admission:**
**Admission is free but donations are accepted at the visitor centers.**

**Directions:**
**The Chalmette Battlefield and National Cemetery are just a few miles east of downtown New Orleans on LA-46.**

## The Myrtles Plantation

David Bradford was a successful attorney with a beautiful home in Pennsylvania. Life was good with his practice and his family, until he got on the wrong side of the Whiskey Rebellion. It is believed that George Washington ordered a bounty placed on Bradford's head in 1794, and he was forced to leave his family and beat a hasty retreat. He eventually made his way to Louisiana where he bought 600 acres of land and built a house, calling his estate Laurel Grove.

In 1801, Bradford received a pardon from President John Adams and he was finally able to be reunited with his wife and children. Laurel Grove remained in the family after Bradford's death, in the care of his son-in-law, Clark Woodruff, who expanded the plantation. However, after the death of Woodruff's wife and two of his children, he lost interest in Laurel Grove and in 1834 sold the property and all its slaves to Ruffin Grey Stirling, a wealthy landowner who already had several plantations.

Obviously, the eight-room home would not do for a man of his stature, so Stirling greatly expanded the structure and brought fine furnishings over from Europe. He also renamed his mansion Myrtles, after the beautifully blooming crape myrtle trees. Unfortunately, it seemed as though only tragedies awaited the Stirling family at the Myrtles Plantation. Just a few years after his estate was completed, Ruffin died of consumption. Five of his children would also die before reaching adulthood. His son-in-law was murdered on the front porch by someone who rode up on horseback and shot him. During the Civil War, the Stirling family fortune was lost in the waves of destruction.

The Myrtles Plantation.

Ruffin's wife, Mary Cobb, somehow managed to keep the Myrtles Plantation, and passed it onto her daughter and son-in-law, Sarah and William Winter. But tragedy still stalked the residents of this house. William went bankrupt and the property was sold, but Sarah managed to buy it back two years later. Then in 1871, William was shot dead on the porch. Sarah died in 1878 at the age of 44, and her mother passed away in 1880.

The house remained in the Stirling family until 1886 when, probably due to debts, it was sold several times, finally ending up in the possession of Harrison Williams in 1889. Williams did well with the plantation and it looked as though the Myrtles would finally smile kindly on its occupants. Unfortunately, that was not to be as the Williams' eldest son accidentally fell into the river and drowned. The property stayed with various Williams' family members until the 1950s, and has since had several different owners, each of which, no doubt, added their own layers of history to the place. Guests now have the opportunity to appreciate that history, as the Myrtles Plantation was transformed into a bed and breakfast, and a restaurant.

Given the long and colorful history of the plantation then, is it any wonder that the Myrtles has gained the reputation as being one of "America's Most Haunted Homes?" One reason for that is the figure of an African-American woman wearing a green turban that has been witnessed on many occasions over the years, and may have actually been photographed. Guests also report that someone tucked in their covers at night, as though someone was watching over them. Various legends arose to explain this activity, and all the versions involve the same person—a slave girl named Chloe who was involved in a terrible tragedy.

The stories claim that Clark Woodruff took a slave girl named Chloe as his mistress, and took her away from the harsh conditions of working in the fields and put her to work in the house. Chloe liked to eavesdrop on the family, and after being caught several times, Woodruff taught her a lesson by cutting off part of her ear. To hide her partial ear, Chloe took to wearing a green turban.

Chloe became very worried that she would be sent back to the fields, so she devised a plan to make herself appear to be indispensable to the family. She baked a birthday cake for two of the children, and added the liquid of boiled oleander leaves. This was only supposed to make the children sick, and then Chloe would cure them with other herbs. Unfortunately, the plans went terribly awry, and Woodruff's wife and two of his children died from the poison. The terrified Chloe confessed to the other slaves in hopes that they would hide her, but instead they killed her by hanging her from a tree. From that day, Chloe's turbaned spirit has haunted the Myrtles.

It's a great story, the only problem is that there is no record of a slave named Chloe, and Mrs. Woodruff and her children are listed as dying from yellow fever. Could the details of this story have been distorted over time, and the real name of the slave girl and circumstances of the poisoning confused? It certainly wouldn't be the first time that facts were muddied by the retelling and passage of time. However, whether her name was Chloe or something else, it does not alter the fact that a turbaned slave girl still walks the halls and grounds of the Myrtle Plantation.

The spirits of Mrs. Woodruff and her two children are also said to have remained, and are believed to be attached to a mirror, or more accurately, trapped inside the mirror. Handprints from these unhappy souls have appeared, even after the glass was replaced and re-silvered.

Let us not forget the one documented victim of murder, William Winter. There are legends that claim his spirit can be seen crawling or walking up the staircase. This same staircase may also have a young blond girl who can be seen skipping up and down, singing or humming. There are countless other reports of sights and sounds that can't be explained, and it has been estimated that there are as many as a dozen separate entities at the Myrtle Plantation. Of course, to be really convinced, all you need to see is one!

## The Bottom Line

**The History:** A plantation begun in 1796 by a man fleeing punishment for his role in the Whiskey Rebellion. Owned by several families, many of whom suffered various personal and financial tragedies. The house was looted during the Civil War, and there was a murder on the porch in 1871. The place is now a bed and breakfast and restaurant.

**The Haunting:** Witnesses have seen, and possibly photographed, a slave girl in a green turban. A man and a girl have been seen on the staircase. Faces and handprints appear in mirrors. There are many other inexplicable sights and sounds that have led to the Myrtles Plantation earning the title of one of America's Most Haunted Homes.

## Recommendations

You can experience the Myrtles Plantation through one of their tours or by dining in the restaurant. For the full experience, however, you must spend the night in one of their beautiful rooms. When you aren't trying to contact one of the twelve spirits, relax on the 120-foot veranda in an oversized rocking chair, or simply sit back and admire the Baccarat crystal chandeliers, Carrera marble mantles, and fine furnishings.

## Visitor Information

**The Myrtles Plantation**
7747 U.S. Highway 61
P.O. Box 1100
St. Francisville, LA 70775
(225) 635-6277
(800) 809-0565
www.myrtlesplantation.com/

**Hours and Admission:**

Historic Tours: Daily from 9am – 5pm, every hour and half hour. $8 for adults, $4 for children 12 and under.

Mystery Tours: Friday and Saturday at 6pm, 7pm, and 8pm. $10 per person, and reservations are recommended.

Carriage House Restaurant Hours:
Lunch: Monday thru Saturday from 11am – 2pm;
Dinner: Monday thru Saturday from 5pm – 9pm;
Sunday Brunch: 11am – 2; Closed Tuesdays

**Directions:**

From Baton Rouge: Take I-110 North for 5.8 miles to US-61 North. In 22 miles, turn left at Jackson Road/LA 10, then an immediate left at US-61 South.

# Maine

FORT KNOX STATE HISTORIC SITE

1794 WATCHTIDE BY THE SEA

CAPTAIN FAIRFIELD INN

A circa 1870 painting of Fort Knox.

# Fort Knox State Historic Site

The British and Americans fought over the territory of Maine during the Revolutionary War and the War of 1812. Disputes about the border with Canada continued until the Webster-Ashburton Treaty of 1842, but the American government was still worried about British incursions, so they authorized the building of a fort.

Overlooking the Penobscot River, construction of Fort Knox—named after General Henry Knox—was begun in 1844, and it was the first fort in Maine to be built of granite, not wood. The batteries of cannons were designed to defend against hostile ships, and the shot furnaces insured a hot reception for any vessel foolish enough to tempt fate. These furnaces would heat the projectiles, which would then set fire to any wooden ship. Of course, once the age of ironclads began, the furnaces became obsolete.

During the Civil War, volunteers from Maine garrisoned the fort until they completed their training and were sent to active theaters of the war. Fort Knox did not see any action during this time. In fact, it never did.

So what was the federal government going to do with a massive granite fort that cost over $1 million to build and never saw battle? In 1923, they sold the fort and 125 acres to the state for only $2,121! In 1970, Fort Knox was named a National Historic Landmark, and today it is a popular State Historic Site that offers a wide variety of programs and activities. And some of those activities are paranormal.

For example, in the 1980s, a tour guide had a man in her group dressed in a very authentic-looking Civil War uniform. She simply assumed he was a reenactor at some event the fort would be holding. However, after the tour she discovered there were no reenactments being held that day, and no one in the fort was wearing such a uniform. Later, she was shown a photo of Sergeant Leopold Hegyi, and she was certain he was the soldier she had seen. It turns out that Hegyi had been at Fort Knox, but after thirteen years of service, he died in his house by the fort and was buried in a local cemetery. Over the years, this soldier has been seen many times, so it appears as though Sergeant Hegyi is still on patrol.

Figures and voices have been recorded, especially in Two Step Alley which is particularly active. One night, an employee saw a dark figure at the end of the hallway and thought it was a straggler from the evening's event. He called out to the man—who was definitely solid enough to block out the light behind him, but received no response. The man continued to walk away from him, so he reached down for his flashlight, but when he turned it on, the figure had vanished.

There are literally "hundreds of stories" from visitors and staff of strange sounds and figures, of physically being touched, and of experiencing that intensely creepy feeling of a strong presence. Could all of this activity be attributed to Sergeant Hegyi, or are there many spirits here, as several psychics have asserted? Chances are you will not be alone on your tour, so be prepared for both psychic and physical encounters.

Fort Knox was built out of fear of a British attack, but now the fear is within…

## The Bottom Line

**The History:** A large granite fort constructed in 1844 for $1 million.

**The Haunting:** A soldier is still on duty and people are physically touched.

## Recommendations

There are many great events held here each year, including the Pirate Festival, Scottish Tattoo (that means music, not ink), Cannon Firings, and battle reenactments. There's also the breathtaking 420-foot-high Observation Tower of the Penobscot Narrows Bridge, which opened to the public in 2007, and is the only one like it in Western hemisphere.

To indulge in the spooky side, every year the fort also hosts the Paranormal/Psychic Faire for ghost hunters and lovers of the bizarre. During Halloween season there is the popular "Fright at the Fort" where all sorts of creepy things jump out of the shadows. For the real deal, the Alcove, just off the Officer's Quarters and Two Step Alley have the most reports of paranormal activity. This is really such a cool place in such a beautiful location—definitely worth the trip!

## Visitor Information

**Fort Knox State Historic Site**
711 Fort Knox Road
Prospect, ME 04981-3125
(207) 469-7719
www.fortknox.maineguide.com

**Hours:**
Fort Knox: May-October, 9am to Sunset; Penobscot Narrows Observatory: May-Oct, 9am – 5pm, July-Aug till 6pm.

**Admission:**
Fort Knox: $3 Adults, $1 Children 5 11, Children under 5 are free.

Penobscot Narrows Observatory: $5 Adults, $3 Children 5 to 11, Free Children 4 and under. Observatory fees include Admission to Fort Knox.

**Directions:**
From their website—From Belfast: Proceed north on US Route 1, through Searsport and Stockton Springs, immediately before crossing the Penobscot Narrows Bridge, take a left onto Route 174. Fort Knox will be approximately 1/4 mile up on your right.

From Bar Harbor: Follow US Route 1 south across the Penobscot Narrows bridge, immediately adjacent to the town of Bucksport. Once over the bridge take a right onto Route 174. Fort Knox will be approximately 1/4 mile up on your right.

From Bangor: On Route 1A South, follow Route 1A South through the towns of Hampden, Winterport, Frankfort and Prospect. In Prospect Center, take a left onto Route 174. Follow Route 174 approximately 4 miles. Fort Knox will be on your left. On Route 15 South, follow Route. 15 South through the city of Brewer and the towns of Orrington and Bucksport. In Bucksport, take a right onto US Route 1 South and proceed over the Penobscot Narrows bridge. Immediately upon exiting the bridge take a right onto Route 74. Fort Knox will be approximately 1/4 mile up on your right.

# 1794 Watchtide By the Sea

This beautiful colonial cape was originally built in Prospect, Massachusetts, but it was not relocated. So how did this house end up in Searsport, Maine, if it never moved? Because back in 1794, when this place was built, this land was part of Massachusetts, as Maine did not become a state until 1820.

The builders were a group of six craftsmen, and they are known because they also built just about every other eighteenth-century house that is still standing in town. Obviously they did good work, as this home has withstood over two centuries of the rugged Maine coast's wind and weather.

The first famous person to be connected with this house was General Henry Knox, Revolutionary War hero and the first Secretary of War, whose ownership of the property began in 1794. Interestingly, he also acquired Sears Island, which at the time was called Brigadier Island. However, it was not named for General Knox, but for British Brigadier General Samuel Waldo, his wife Lucy's grandfather. Lucy's loyalist parents did not approve of Henry's rebel sentiments, and they literally turned their back on their daughter. They moved back to England and never saw her again.

As Searsport became known as "the home of the famous sea captains," it isn't surprising that other owners of the property included sea captains and master mariners. In the early twentieth century, Massachusetts residents George and Rose Pettee bought the property for a summer home. George was a teacher at Andover Academy, and his daughter, Frances, attended Wellesley College. In 1917, Frances and three college roommates turned the home into the College T House, a tea house that eventually became the famous College Club Inn.

For twenty years the College Club Inn was the most popular place to stop when traveling along the Maine coast. It was a favorite of Eleanor Roosevelt who loved the view, the food, and the peaceful atmosphere. Unfortunately, the inn was unable remain open during WWII when travel restrictions were in place, and it once again became a private home.

In 1994, the property was purchased by Nancy-Linn Nellis and her husband Jack Elliott. They converted the place into a bed and breakfast and christened it the "Watchtide...by the Sea!" And it wasn't long before they were watching something other than the sea—they were seeing ghosts.

Nancy had no idea the house was haunted when they bought it, but quickly became convinced one morning when a friend, Jane, was visiting.

"I walked out of my dressing room one morning and spied her [Jane] in the dining room looking at the Winslow Homer painting we had just hung," Nancy explained. "I said hello to her and we exchanged some pleasantries—all the while she kept looking at the painting while I stood in the dressing room door. About half an hour later Jane arrived in the kitchen and my husband asked when she had come down. She replied, 'Just now.' To which I replied, 'Yes, but she was down here about half an hour ago.'"

Jane insisted she had not been downstairs yet that morning and wanted to know what Nancy was talking about. Nancy explained about seeing and speaking to the woman in the dining room, thinking it was Jane. Jane was stunned and frightened, and clearly not trying to pull a prank. If it wasn't Jane, and no other women were in the house, that left only one option—the Watchtide had at least one permanent resident of the ghostly variety.

Actually, there are at least two such residents, as a guest described seeing a middle-aged couple in her room. The man had blond or white hair, and they were both dressed in clothing from the late eighteenth or early nineteenth century. They weren't threatening, just inquisitive, as they just stood quietly and stared at her. They were no doubt wondering what this strange woman was doing in their house!

This couple apparently enjoys music, and radios will suddenly turn on by themselves. This can happen any time of day or night, regardless of whether or not anyone (anyone living, that is) is in the room. The most remarkable incidences of this phenomenon are when several radios in the house will suddenly come on at the same time!

Then there's the really bizarre activity—the sudden appearances of small puddles of water, often under chairs. The water is clear, and the puddles are small, but no earthly reasons could ever be found for their mysterious appearances. A previous owner told Nancy that in addition to the puddles, she used to find toilet paper strewn around the house, as well. If there were no dogs or other people in the house at the time, it can only be concluded that something there enjoys playing pranks.

When Nancy and Jack retired in 2006, they sold the property to Patricia and Frank Kulla, who undertook a complete renovation of the house and grounds. Did all of these changes settle the spirits of the Watchtide, or did they stir up more activity? You'll just have to drive up the beautiful Maine coast to spend the night and find out for yourself.

### The Bottom Line

**The History:** A home built in 1794 once owned by General Henry Knox. It was a popular inn in the early twentieth century where Eleanor Roosevelt stayed.

**The Haunting:** A couple in 200-year-old clothing appears, plays pranks, and likes to turn on the radios to listen to music.

### Recommendations

**Watchtide is listed on the National Register of Historic Places and is ideally located overlooking Penobscot Bay, within an hour's drive of Rockland, Bangor, Deer Isle, Bar Harbor, and Acadia National Park. There's nothing like starting the day with one of their impressive breakfasts on the sun porch and strolling through the gardens. Ask for the Eleanor Roosevelt Room if you want to sleep where a former first lady slept.**

### Visitor Information

**1794 Watchtide By the Sea**
**190 West Main Street**
**Searsport, ME 04974-3514**
**(207) 548-6575**
**(800) 698-6575**
**www.watchtide.com**

**Directions:**

***From their website*—Driving from the south: Take I-295 north and I-95 north to Exit 113, Route 3 in Augusta. Follow Route 3 east to Belfast, then Routes 1 and 3 east approximately 4.5 miles to the inn.**

***From Bangor:* Take Route 1A south to Route 1 west. Driving from Bar Harbor or St. Stephens, N.B., Canada, take Route 1 west. The inn is one mile west of the Searsport village center, on the ocean side.**



## Captain Fairfield Inn

James Fairfield was born in Arundel in 1784. His father was a sea captain, and he chose to follow the same life. It was a good living for a time, as Fairfield sailed to Charleston, New Orleans, and European ports. Then came the War of 1812 when he was captured by the British on November 1, 1814.

Fairfield was sent to the dreaded Dartmoor Prison in England, where he managed to survive both the deprivations and the massacre in which the British fired upon the unarmed American prisoners. After his release, he returned to his wife, Lois, and their home in Kennebunkport.

The beautiful Federal-style house had been a gift from Lois' father, and was constructed between 1813-1815. The couple shared the house with James' sister Polly and her husband, Joseph Lord, who had been a fellow prisoner in Dartmoor. It was the ideal situation, as the men were away at sea for such long periods of time, the women were able to keep each other company.

Unfortunately, this happy situation was not to last long. Joseph Lord was lost at sea in 1817, James died of pneumonia in 1820 at the age of only 36, and Lois died the following year. Polly remarried and stayed in the house, which allowed for a rather amazing event to occur.

Soon after he was married, James had his portrait painted in one of his ports of call. As he was eager for his new bride to have the picture and he would be away for a long time, he sent the painting on another ship. When James finally returned home he was very disappointed to find that his portrait had not been received, as the ship was lost at sea.

Fast forward to 1822, when James' former employer, Tobias Lord, was asked to come aboard a Swedish ship in Portland's harbor. Imagine his shock when he found that the Swedish crew had found a sealed tin canister floating out at sea and opened it to discover the portrait of James Fairfield that had been lost so many years before! And how did the Swedish crew know to contact Tobias Lord? Because in the painting, James is holding an envelope on which his employer's name and address had been written: Messieurs Tobias Lord and Co., Kennebunk, Maine!

The incredible journey of James' portrait finally came to an end when it was delivered to his sister Polly at the house they had shared. It now hangs in the Brick Store Museum on Main Street in Kennebunk, and if you look closely, you can see the surface is rough and creased from the salt water.

It all seems to be a remarkable series of events that finally led to James' portrait coming home, but was it all just coincidence, or was some other force at work? Had James, after his death, somehow directed the Swedish crew to find and return the painting? Stranger things have certainly happened—indeed, they have happened at the Captain Fairfield Inn.

In 1991, the stately historic structure was being converted into a bed and breakfast. During the renovations, Captain James Fairfield, himself, made an appearance. He was seen floating in the basement, and from that time he has been seen throughout his home. He is never threatening—and anyone who has ever read the collection of his tender letters to his wife would realize he was a kind soul. In fact, his presence always evokes a warm and comforting feeling. Even when his figure does not make an actual physical appearance, he can quite often be felt.

The Captain Fairfield Inn was once a beautiful home filled with warm, loving people. Now it is a beautiful inn welcoming couples looking for a romantic getaway. In retrospect, not much has really changed here—but then again, isn't that what a historic haunt is all about?

## The Bottom Line

**The History:** The home of a sea captain built around 1813, with an amazing story of the captain's portrait.

**The Haunting:** The captain is still seen and felt throughout the house.

## Recommendations

**A replica of the good captain's portrait hangs above the fireplace in his beloved home, and of course, you do have a chance of seeing him in the flesh—correction—in spirit. The original portrait and Fairfield's letters to his wife are in the Brick Store Museum, so make a point of stopping by. The inn has lovely gardens and a scenic view of the Green River. Their four-course breakfasts are wonderful. This place is everything that's good about a historic, haunted inn.**

## Visitor Information

**Captain Fairfield Inn**
**8 Pleasant Street**
**Kennebunkport, ME 04046**
**(800) 322-1928**
**www.captainfairfield.com/**

**Directions:**

***From their website*—Take the Maine Turnpike (I-95) to Exit 25 (formerly exit 3) for Kennebunk-Kennebunkport. Once you've left the tollbooth, turn left onto Route 35. You will be on Route 35 for 5 1/2 miles in total. While on Route 35, you will encounter a small rotary; go half way around to stay on 35. You will also go through the center of Kennebunk, where you will need to turn left and then immediately bear right, again staying on Route 35—watch for signs. At the junction of routes 35 and 9 (there will be a traffic light at the intersection and a Sunoco station on your left), turn left. Go over a small bridge, and you'll enter Dock Square. Take your first right (at the monument) onto Ocean Avenue. Take your fifth left off of Ocean Avenue, and onto Green Street. The inn is on the second block, on the right.**

# Maryland

USS CONSTELLATION

ANTIETAM NATIONAL BATTLEFIELD

THE PRY HOUSE FIELD HOSPITAL MUSEUM

*Courtesy of Historic Ships in Baltimore.*

# USS Constellation

For all its varied landscapes, the story of America could be written by tracing the history of its seagoing vessels. From the fledging navy and merchant fleets, to becoming the greatest maritime power in the world, this country's military and commercial endeavors on the world's oceans have defined us as a nation.

A wonderful example from the age of American sailing ships sits today in Baltimore's Inner Harbor. The sloop-of-war, the USS *Constellation*, was the last all-sail vessel built for the U.S. Navy, and was commissioned in 1855. The ship was to carry more than the name of its illustrious predecessor, a frigate built in 1797, as eight pieces of timber from the old ship went onto the construction of the new vessel.

The *Constellation* began her century of service with three years in the Mediterranean. In 1859, she became the flagship of the African Squadron. Their mission was to capture slave ships, free the slaves, and bring them to safety in Liberia. The Civil War saw the *Constellation* acting against Confederate ships in Europe and the West Indies. Beginning in 1871, the ship began a long career as a training vessel for naval cadets, earning the nickname of the *"Cradle for Admirals."*

Occasionally, her role as a cradle was suspended while she took on special assignments. In 1878, the *Constellation* brought artwork and exhibits to France for the Paris Exposition. In 1880, her guns were removed so she could carry thousands of barrels of potatoes and flour to famine victims in Ireland. In 1892, she carried artwork from Europe to New York for the Columbian Exposition. At this point, her days of sailing were all but over, and she became a stationary training vessel.

The *Constellation* would undergo many repairs and modifications over the years, but not all of them were for the sake of modernization. In 1914, by order from Acting Secretary of the Navy Franklin D. Roosevelt, the ship was altered to appear as the original *Constellation* would have looked in 1814. It was then put on display to commemorate the 100th anniversary of the writing of the "Star Spangled Banner," and later for the 150th anniversary of the signing of the Declaration of Independence. She was decommissioned in 1933, but returned to active status during World War II. Finally decommissioned for the last time in 1955, she underwent many years of restoration and preservation by a private, non-profit organization.

After the *Constellation's* most recent restoration, completed in 1999, about fifty percent of the original ship still exists. Of course, the question remains, what else still exists on the old sloop-of-war? On this account there appears to be a lot of confusion and misinformation, attributing deaths on the 1797 frigate with restless spirits on this *Constellation.* Perhaps the explanations are erroneous, but the sightings remain:

In the 1800s, the ship's purser, Moses Safford, recorded an odd incident. He wrote that a sailor in the brig wouldn't stop singing. When asked why, the sailor replied that the cook's helper wanted to dance to his songs. A reasonable explanation, except for the fact that the cook's helper had fallen overboard two weeks earlier and his body was never found! Safford was reluctant to even report this incident, had it not been for another odd occurrence that night: Someone had precariously stacked several buckets, which despite rough and stormy seas that night, never fell over, as if someone was holding them up.

Several sailors in old-style uniforms have been seen walking or running across the deck.

A man in a captain's uniform and a young boy are also seen.

A twentieth-century night watchman apparently returns to keep an eye on the ship.

The smell of gunpowder accompanies a shadowy figure.

Visitors have spoken to someone in an old uniform, assuming he was a costumed guide, only to find out such a person did not exist.

Whether you visit the USS *Constellation* to see guides dressed as former sailors, or hope to see former sailors mistaken for guides, you are in for a fascinating trip back in time. From chasing down slave ships, to confronting Confederates, to training future admirals, this ship offers the unique experience of literally walking through history.

## The Bottom Line

**The History:** The last all-sail ship built for the Navy and commissioned in 1855. The ship saw 100 years of service capturing slavers, blockading Confederates, transporting artwork and food, and as a training ship for naval cadets.

**The Haunting:** Various sailors are seen, as is a captain, a young boy, and a night watchman. People have spoken with a knowledgeable man dressed like a sailor, only to find out no such man exists.

## Recommendations

**Plan your visit so you can hear the cannon, which is fired every day at noon. While the top deck was replaced, much of the lower decks are original. Note the Captain's quarters, and compare them to where the sailors slept. (It was good to be the Captain.) Free audio tours are available for both children and adults. There are special events, and overnight programs are available.**



## Visitor Information

**The USS *Constellation* Museum**
**301 East Pratt Street**
**Baltimore, MD 21202-3134**
**(410) 539-1797**
**www.historicships.org**

**Hours:**

**January-February 10am – 4:30pm, March-May and September-October 10am – 5:30pm, June-August, Monday-Thursday 10am – 5:30pm, Friday-Sunday 10am – 7pm, November-December 10am – 4:30pm.**

**Admission:**

**There are four ships in the harbor available for tours, and there are discounts for tickets for multiple ships. For the USS Constellation only, tickets are $10 for adults (15-59), seniors $8 (60+), children (6-14) are $5, children 5 and under, and military personnel w/ID are free.**

**Directions:**

**From their website—From the North: Via I-95 South: Take I-95 South through the Ft. McHenry Tunnel (toll) to exit 53 (I-395 North, Downtown). After exiting follow signs to the Inner Harbor. Take a left on Light Street—the Inner Harbor will be on your right. The USS Constellation Museum is located on Pier 1 between the Light Street and the Pratt Street Pavilions of Harborplace.**

**Via I-83: Follow I-83 South to the merger of I-83 and I-695 West. Continue on I-695 West/I-83 South about one mile to Exit 23A (I-83 South, Downtown). Proceed on I-83 South until the expressway ends at Exit 1 (Fayette Street), at which point it becomes President Street. At the next light, Lombard Street, turn right. Follow Lombard Street six blocks to Light Street. Make a left turn onto Light Street and travel one block to Pratt Street. Turn left onto Pratt Street. The Inner Harbor will be on your right. The USS Constellation Museum is located on Pier 1 between the Light Street and the Pratt Street Pavilions of Harborplace.**

**From the South: Via I-95: Take I-95 North to Exit 53 (I-395 North, Downtown). After exiting follow signs to the Inner Harbor. Take a left on Light Street—the Inner Harbor will be on your right. The USS Constellation Museum is located on Pier 1 between the Light Street and the Pratt Street Pavilions of Harborplace.**

**From the West: Via 1-70: Proceed on I-70 East to Exit 91A (I-695S, Glen Burnie). Take I-695 to Exit 11A (I-95 North, Baltimore). Proceed on I-95 North to Exit 53 (I-395 North, Downtown). After exiting follow signs to the Inner Harbor. Take a left on Light Street—the Inner Harbor will be on your right. The USS Constellation Museum is located on Pier 1 between the Light Street and the Pratt Street Pavilions of Harborplace.**

***Parking is available in garages and open lots around the Inner Harbor.***

Casualties near the Dunker Church after the Battle of Antietam.

# Antietam National Battlefield

Abraham Lincoln needed a victory in 1862. He had drafted the Emancipation Proclamation, but knew if he announced it after a string of Union defeats, it would simply look like a ploy to rally fading support in the north.

Union General George McClellan was as slow and cautious as Confederate General Robert E. Lee was bold and decisive. Lee's Maryland Campaign was designed to bring the war to the north and possibly sway the residents to the Confederacy, as well as the sentiments of the European powers. For all of Lee's careful planning, however, a simple mistake could have cost him dearly, had McClellan acted swiftly.

There were 90,000 men in the Union's Army of the Potomac, which should have been more than enough to defeat the 55,000 men in the Army of Northern Virginia. The opportunity was never greater than when two Union soldiers happened upon a copy of Lee's battle plans (Special Order 191) wrapped around three cigars. The plans detailed Lee's decision to split his army between Harpers Ferry, West Virginia, and Hagerstown, Maryland. Had McClellan acted immediately, he might have defeated one of the smaller forces, then turned his attention to the other and destroyed the Army of Northern Virginia. Instead, he waited eighteen hours to make a decision, and by then the opportunity was lost.

On the morning of September 17, by the town of Sharpsburg along the Antietam Creek, the two armies collided. Fierce fighting took place near the Dunker Church, the Bloody Lane, Miller's cornfield, and a stone bridge over the creek. Just when it looked as though the Union troops might deal a crushing blow, a Confederate division from Harpers Ferry arrived with crucial reinforcements.

Men were falling at an alarming rate throughout the day, and by battle's end, there were an astonishing 23,000 casualties, making it the single bloodiest day in a very bloody war. There were some skirmishes the following day, but they were mostly to cover Lee's retreat. McClellan once again had the opportunity to pursue the battered and much smaller enemy, but he chose not to and Lee slipped back into Virginia. The war would drag on, but the battle was over, the campaign was over, and Lincoln had enough of a victory to announce the Proclamation on January 1, 1863.

An enormous price was paid at Antietam by both sides, and to stand on the battlefields today can be a chilling experience just imagining what transpired there. It can also be chilling when you hear the sounds of gunfire, smell the smoke of battle, hear men crying out and shouting, all when no one is visible. Strange blue lights have been seen by the bridge where so many brave men lost their lives. Both Union and Confederate soldiers have been seen across the fields, only to vanish in the blink of an eye. Some people claimed to have heard the Gaelic chant of the Irish Brigade near the Bloody Lane where they lost sixty percent of their men. During the battle, the bodies in Bloody Lane stacked up like firewood, and this may be the location where the most eerie sights and sensations are experienced by visitors.

In short, Antietam Battlefield still vibrates with the energies of battle, of life and death, of the desperate struggles and terrible suffering endured by so many thousands of men. Go to Antietam and learn about the courageous men who fought and died here. Tour the battlefield and try to comprehend the awesome scope of events. And if in a quiet moment you see a weary soldier still fighting on, take a moment to pray that he finds the peace he deserves after all these years.

## The Bottom Line

**The History:** The bloodiest single day of the Civil War.

**The Haunting:** The figures of soldiers and the sounds of battle are everywhere.

## Recommendations

If you are unfamiliar with the battle, do some reading beforehand as you will get more out of your visit. Absorb all you can at the visitor center and don't be afraid to ask questions as the staff is very knowledgeable. There is a viewing area which overlooks the battlefield and helps put it all into perspective. The self-guided driving tour is excellent, but make sure you stop and walk around at each location to better appreciate everything. Strange things can happen anytime, anywhere, so be prepared.

## Visitor Information

**Antietam National Battlefield**
Visitor Center
5831 Dunker Church Road
Sharpsburg, MD 21782
(301) 432-5124
www.nps.gov/anti/index.htm

**Events:**
There are various interpretive programs and events, and several yearly special programs: Memorial Day Commemoration, Saturday of Memorial Day Weekend; Independence Day Commemoration (First Saturday in July); Anniversary of the Battle of Antietam (Sharpsburg), September 17; The Memorial Illumination (First Saturday in December).

**Hours:**
Open All Year. Opens at 8:30am, and depending on the season, closes between 5pm – 7pm. Closed Thanksgiving, Christmas, and New Years Day.

**Admission:**
Three Day Pass: $4 Per Person, $6 Per Family.

**Directions:**
Traveling East on Interstate 70: Exit 29A onto Route 65 south. Ten miles south on the left is the Visitor Center.

Traveling West on Interstate 70 from the Baltimore/Washington area: Exit 29 onto Route 65 South towards Sharpsburg. Travel about 10 miles south to the Park Visitor Center entrance which will be on your left side.

Optional Route: Exit 49 onto Alternate Route 40 West towards Middletown. Continue through Middletown, over South Mountain to Boonsboro. Turn left onto Route 34 to Sharpsburg. When you enter town, turn right (north) onto Route 65 and the Park Visitor Center will be on your right a mile north of Sharpsburg.

Traveling North-South on Interstate 81: Exit 1, Route 68, six miles east to Route 65. Turn right at light on Route 65. Five miles south on the left is the Visitor Center.

*Courtesy of the National Park Service.*

# The Pry House Field Hospital Museum

Realizing a great battle was about to begin, the family of Philip Pry fled to Keedysville. Pry stayed behind, and what a transformation he would see on his property!

The quiet farm became a center of activity as Union General George McCellan made the Pry House his headquarters for the bloody battle of Antietam. After the battle, thousands of wounded soldiers needed to be cared for, and many private homes were turned into field hospitals. Pry's barn accommodated about 500 wounded enlisted men, while wounded officers stayed in the house. Two generals—Hooker and Richardson—were given special treatment according to their rank, but unfortunately Richardson, who had taken canister shot to the stomach at Bloody Lane, died of his wounds in a second-floor bedroom on November 3, 1862.

Amidst all this carnage and suffering, some good was done. For several weeks, the Pry house was the headquarters of Dr. Jonathan Letterman, the medical director of the Army of the Potomac. It was here that he organized the structure of the medical corps and methods for battlefield evacuations. Dr. Letterman became known as the "Father of Battlefield Medicine," and modern armies today still use his system.

While the Pry family did return safely to their home, they were eventually forced to leave it once again because of the fortunes of war. However, it was not due to another impending battle, but rather to the fact that the huge Union Army had eaten every scrap of food in the area, so it became impossible for Pry to feed his own family. They were truly eaten out of house and home!

The Pry House Field Hospital Museum now occupies the building, with displays of the Battle of Antietam from a medical perspective. There's also another unique perspective here—one of glimpses of the past. In the 1970s, there was a fire in the Pry House, and firemen reported seeing a woman standing in a second-floor bedroom window. This was obviously a problem, but not in the manner you might think. You see, the second floor had already collapsed, so there was no earthly way for a flesh-and-blood woman to be standing by that window.

After the place became a museum, one witness saw a woman in Civil War-era clothing on the second floor. It quickly became evident that she was also not from this world when she walked into a wall!

Do we know the identity of this woman? Some have speculated that she was the wife of General Richardson.

She had come to the Pry House to care for her wounded husband, and was there when he died—in the same bedroom where a woman was seen during the fire. Does her grief keep her tied to this house, or does she stay because her husband's spirit also lingers here?

There were also reports from a museum employee who watched in amazement as all of the doors in the house slammed shut, from front to back. After he opened all the doors again, they then proceeded to slam shut, this time from back to front! Even if it had been a windy day, once the front or back door had closed it would have blocked any wind from closing the interior doors of the house. Obviously, someone there doesn't like open doors.

If trauma and tragedy are ingredients for ghosts, then surely a field hospital from America's bloodiest battle would have seen more than its share of both. If the Pry House and its grounds do have restless spirits, perhaps they will find comfort in the fact that it is now a museum that honors those who tried their best to alleviate the suffering of the wounded.

## The Bottom Line

**The History:** A farmer's house that became General McClellan's headquarters during the battle of Antietam, then a field hospital after the battle. It was here that Dr. Letterman structured the medical corps and methods for battlefield evacuations, earning him the title of the "Father of Battlefield Medicine."

**The Haunting:** A woman in a Civil War-era dress is seen on the second floor. Doors slam and other inexplicable things occur.

## Recommendations

Of course the Pry House should be included in your visit to the Antietam Battlefield. Try to imagine what this place was like when 500 wounded men were being treated here. Several years ago, the remains of some soldiers from the Irish Brigade were found at Bloody Lane, so look for the artifacts from these soldiers which are now on display in the museum. Living History events are held throughout the year.

## Visitor Information

**The Pry House Field Hospital Museum**
18906 Shepherdstown Pike (MD Route 34)
Keedysville, MD 21756
(301) 416-2395
www.civilwarmed.org/VisitUs/PryHouse.aspx

**Hours:**
Open daily June-October; and weekends only during May and November. Hours of operation are 11am – 5pm.

**Admission:**
Admission is free, however a $2 donation per person is suggested.

**Directions:**
From Antietam National Battlefield: Head south on Bloody Lane, to Richardson Avenue. Continue south on Richardson and then turn left at MD-34/Shepherdstown Pike. The museum will be on the left in 1.5 miles.

# Massachusetts

- BOSTON COMMON AND CENTRAL BURYING GROUND
- OLD YARMOUTH INN
- STURGIS LIBRARY
- STONE'S PUBLIC HOUSE

Boston Common in 1848.



# Boston Common and Central Burying Ground

Boston Common is America's oldest public park, dating back to 1634, when the land was designated as a common area where people could bring their cattle to graze. So then, why should a former cow pasture be haunted?

Boston Common was also a place where criminals and heretics were hung from trees, and later gallows were erected to do their grisly work until 1817. The bodies of the executed men and women were buried in the park, and in fact, many bodies of the poor were also buried there. It has been said that it would be impossible to take a walk through any of the park's forty-eight acres without walking over graves!

While you may not know who you are stepping on in the grassy fields and pathways, there are marked stones in the Central Burying Ground, which is also in the park. The land for this cemetery was purchased in 1754 because the King's Chapel and Granary burial grounds were filling to capacity. One of the claims to fame of the Central Burying Ground are the graves of both American and British soldiers killed in 1775 at the Battle of Bunker Hill (which was actually mostly fought on Breed's Hill, but that's another story). Artist Gilbert Stuart is also buried here.

Another claim to fame in the old burial ground is the many spirits that have been witnessed over the generations. One of the most frequently seen figures is that of a little girl, who at first appears real and solid, but then slowly fades into thin air. And there's no need to search for these ghosts in the dead of night, as they are not shy about appearing in broad daylight.

Such is also the case for the spirits seen throughout the rest of Boston Common. Again, there have been encounters with all manner of ghosts, but two are of particular note. A pair of older ladies dressed quite nicely in clothing from the 1830s have been seen strolling through the park or sitting on a bench, only to vanish before astonished onlooker's eyes. Some believe these women may have been sisters who once lived near the park, and still continue to take their daily constitutionals.

Boston Common and the Central Burying Ground are steeped in history, and bodies, and visitors may see for themselves that the two go hand in hand here, and sometimes slip back into the world of the living.

MA

## The Bottom Line

**The History:** The oldest park in America, the land was first used as a public cow pasture in 1634. Executions were conducted here by hanging, first from trees, then from gallows, until 1817, and the bodies were buried within the park. The Central Burying Ground contains the graves of both American and British soldiers killed at the Battle of Bunker Hill.

**The Haunting:** Many spirits are seen throughout the park, both day and night. A little girl is most often seen in the Central Burying Ground, and two women in 1830s clothing walk through the park.

## Recommendations

On a warm sunny day at the Boston Common, it may be difficult to imagine that this was once a place of execution, and that bodies are buried everywhere. In addition to the Central Burying Ground, the park contains many things to see, such as the Brewer Fountain, Parkman Bandstand, Frog Pond Skating Rink, and the Soldiers and Sailors Monument dedicated to Civil War soldiers. And speaking of the Civil War, don't miss the magnificent monument honoring Robert Gould Shaw, the colonel of the all-black, 54th Massachusetts Volunteer Infantry, made famous in the movie, *Glory*. Boston Common is where the Freedom Trail begins, which is a wonderful 2.5-mile walk covering sixteen sites along a path to Bunker Hill.

## Visitor Information

**Boston Common**
**Bound by Tremont, Beacon, Charles, and Boylston Streets**
**www.cityofboston.gov/FreedomTrail/bostoncommon.asp**

**The Central Burying Ground is on the Boylston Street side of Boston Common.**

**Hours:**

**Boston Common is always open. The Central Burying Ground is generally open from 9am – 5pm.**

**Parking is located in the Boston Common Garage located on Charles Street between the Public Garden and the Boston Common. See directions below.**

**Admission:**

**Free Admission to the park; there is a fee for skating: $4, free for children 13 and under.**

**Directions:**

**From their website—From the West: Follow the Mass Pike to Boston and look for signs for downtown. Get off at Prudential Center/Copley Square exit. Bear right for Copley Square. This is Stuart Street (East Route 9.) Follow Stuart Street to Charles Street (1/2 mile.) Take a left onto Charles Street. Park at the Boston Common Garage, straight ahead.**

**From the North: Take Route 93 South. Follow signs for Storrow Drive. Get on Storrow Drive and take the Back Bay/Downtown exit. Once off the ramp, you will take a left at lights and then a quick right onto Arlington Street. Keep the Public Garden on left and take first left onto Boylston Street, and first left onto Charles Street. Park at the Boston Common Garage, straight ahead.**

**From the South: Take 93 North to the East Berkeley Street Exit, follow road to your second left. (Be sure and not take first left as that would be a U-turn.) This is East Berkeley Street. Follow this street and take a right onto Washington Street. Take a left at the second set of lights onto Marginal Street. Take your next right (in front of convenience store) onto Tremont Street. Take next left onto Charles Street South. Follow Charles through one set of lights. Park at the Boston Common Garage, straight ahead.**

**Public Transportation: Located near two T stops. On the Green Line: "Park Street" and on the Red Line: "Charles Street." Both stops are about a five-minute walk to us.**

*Photo by author.*

# Old Yarmouth Inn

Old is a relative term. In some parts of the country, a building from 1896 could be the oldest building in town. Then there's Cape Cod, where age takes on a different dimension. Imagine an inn that was built over 300 years ago that not only is still standing, but it still continues to welcome visitors!

The Old Yarmouth Inn was established in 1696 and is the oldest inn on Cape Cod. It was strategically built at the halfway point on the road between Plymouth and Provincetown. As that trip would have taken a day and a half, the Old Yarmouth Inn was the perfect location to stop for food, lodging, and of course, something to drink. This inn must have many tales to tell, but unfortunately the old records burned in a fire. However, there may be a few ghosts ready and willing to tell their tales to staff and guests.

The ghost stories reach back for generations. There is the story of a doctor who had his office in the building, along with both his family and his mistress. Talk about one-stop shopping! At night, after his family had fallen asleep, he would sneak down the back stairs to her room. It is believed that some of the sounds and footsteps are from the doctor still making his rounds. Another possibility is that the mistress died in a fire, and she, too, haunts the place.

On Thanksgiving night in 1999, a guest awoke to find a man standing next to his bed. This was no shadowy form, as he was able to describe the man as being a "jowly individual with big full cheeks and a calm manner. He was dressed in late 19th century clothing with a flounced white blouse with large cuffs and full sleeves." Although startled, the guest did not feel any fear, but the jowly gentleman looked quite surprised that someone was in "his" room!

Another visitor in 2002 awoke to the feeling of someone sitting on his bed. He tried to ignore it, but this spirit was determined to get his attention and next put its hands on the man's feet. When that still failed to make the man sit up and take notice, the mischievous entity grabbed the bedposts and started shaking them. That was the last straw and the man jumped out of bed and spent the rest of the night outside on the deck! The next morning the owner's mother, who was in the room across the hall, was able to confirm that something was making quite a racket in that room all night.

There are also cold spots, objects that fly through the air, voices that whisper your name, and lights and appliances that go on by themselves. There are most likely more spirits here than those of the doctor and mistress, perhaps many more given its long history. Over the centuries, how many old or sick travelers checked into the inn, but never checked out? There is a secret room in the attic; could it have harbored runaway slaves, and perhaps now has some spirits attached to it?

If the original records still existed, perhaps we would find some answers to the strange activity here. Or, why not dine at the Old Yarmouth Inn, and when a figure appears next to you, ask him to tell his story, because here, dead men just might tell tales…



### The Bottom Line

**The History:** Built in 1696, it is the oldest inn on Cape Cod.

**The Haunting:** The figure of a man in nineteenth-century clothing, beds shake, footsteps, lights and appliances turn on, and objects fly through the air.

### Recommendations

**While rooms are no longer available for spending the night, there are several lovely dining rooms and a tavern. Reservations are recommended during the busy seasons. The staff can point out the oldest sections of the building, and you can just imagine chilled travelers warming themselves by the old fireplace. There are many haunted sites in town, so you can really make a day of it.**

### Visitor Information

**Old Yarmouth Inn Restaurant and Tavern**
**223 Route 6A**
**Yarmouthport, MA 02675-1717**
**(508) 362-9962**
**www.oldyarmouthinn.com**

**Hours:**
**Lunch Tuesday-Saturday 11:30am – 2:30pm. Dinner nightly from 4:30pm. Sunday brunch 10am – 1:30pm.**

**Directions:**
**From the Mid-Cape Highway/Route 6 East: Take exit 7 for Willow Street toward Yarmouthport/W Yarmouth. Turn right at Willow Street. Turn right at Massachusetts 6A E to #223.**

## Sturgis Library

When one thinks of historic sites, libraries generally don't come to mind, but remember that not all library buildings were originally built to house books. Many public institutions were once private homes, and Cape Cod boasts one of the country's most unique. The Sturgis Library in Barnstable holds the distinction of being America's oldest public library building, with part of the structure dating all the way back to 1644!

Even though people came to America for religious freedom, factions inevitably developed among congregations in their new land, and groups split from their churches and went off to form new churches. Such was the case in 1644, when Reverend John Lothrop—who was quite liberal for his time—and his parishioners left Scituate and moved to Barnstable. Reverend Lothrop built his house, and until his church could be built, the front room was used for services. This also gives the Sturgis Library another distinction, as Lothrop's congregation makes the building the oldest in America, that is still standing, where religious services were held regularly.

The house was expanded over the years and was the home to many interesting people. Arguably the most important resident, after Lothrop, of course, was William Sturgis. Going to sea at the tender age of 15, he learned his trade quickly and came back just four years later as the captain of a ship! Sturgis went on to become a successful businessman as a partner in a company engaged in the lucrative China trade, and he bequeathed his home to be used as a village library. In yet another mark of distinction, in 1867, the Sturgis Library opened as the first public library on Cape Cod.

With such a long and distinguished history, could anything else possibly add to the historic significance of the Sturgis Library? Well, yes, if Reverend Lothrop were still here.

There have been reports of seeing and hearing someone walking between the shelves of books. Others have felt a presence, as if someone was watching them, even though they were alone. Could the liberal clergyman be pleased that his humble home has become a center for learning, and does his curiosity bring him back to see how America has changed? Or is it some other former resident who has finally found the time to catch up on his reading?

## The Bottom Line

**The History:** One of the oldest homes on Cape Cod, built by Reverend Lothrop in 1644. It is the oldest library building in America, the oldest standing building to hold regular religious services, and the first public library on Cape Cod.

**The Haunting:** Is Reverend Lothrop the figure that is seen and heard walking through the library?

## Recommendations

You must see Lothrop's Bible from 1604, which traveled the Atlantic with him to America in 1634. While conducting services aboard ship, he spilled hot wax on the Bible which burned holes in several pages. Imagine what it was like at the moment the wax spilled, crossing the rolling ocean to a wild new country! The Bible is on display in the Lothrop Room, which is where services were held in 1644. The library has an excellent collection of genealogy and Cape Cod history, so spend some time with a good book in a room over 365 years old.

## Visitor Information

**Sturgis Library**
3090 Main Street
Barnstable, MA 02630
(508) 362-6636
info@sturgislibrary.org
www.sturgislibrary.org/

**Events:**
There are history and ghost tours conducted by CAIPRS (Cape and Islands Paranormal Research Society) that begin in the library parking lot. To reserve your space or for more information, call (508) 771-2725, or go to: www.caiprs.com/

**Hours:**
Monday, Wednesday, Thursday and Friday 10am – 5pm, Tuesday 1pm – 8pm, Saturday 10am – 4pm, closed Sundays and holidays.

**Directions:**
From their website—From Route 6 (the Mid-Cape Highway): Take Exit 6 to Barnstable. Turn Left at the end of the exit, onto Route 132 (heading North). At the end of Route 132, take a Right onto Route 6A ("The Old King's Highway"). The Library is approximately 2.5 miles further East on the Left side of Route 6A (3090 Main Street), just past Saint Mary's Church (on the Right). Parking is available to the right or left as you come into the driveway. A larger lot is available behind the Library, at the end of the driveway. Overflow parking is also usually available at Saint Mary's Church, just across the street.

Traveling West on Route 6A towards Barnstable: The Library is on the Right side of Route 6A, about 300 yards past the Barnstable County Court House (on the Left in the Village center).

*Photo by David Francis IPR/MA.*

# Stone's Public House

John Stone was a farmer who owned land in what was then known as Unionville. Perhaps he would have done well for himself with farming, but his prospects certainly improved when he learned that the railroad would be coming to town—right through his land. Seizing the opportunity, Stone built a hotel by the tracks in 1834, called the Railroad House.

Stone ran the hotel for three years, then leased it to several different managers. After Stone died in 1858, the hotel was sold. Over the next century it went through a series of owners, and by 1976, was in serious need of repair. Enter Leonard "Cappy" Fournier who purchased and restored the old hotel, now known as Stone's Public House in Ashland.

Fournier was the first person on record to declare that the place was haunted, claiming that doors opened and closed on their own, and lights turned on and off. While he was the first, he certainly hasn't been the last. Below is a compilation of some of the spooky activity.

A little girl has been seen looking out the kitchen and the second floor windows. There is an old blood-stained girl's dress in the attic. Is the little girl the former owner of this dress, and if so, what happened to her? There is a record of a 10-year-old girl who was killed by a train in 1862. As the accident occurred by the hotel, perhaps the girl was carried into the hotel, hence both her dress and her spirit may have been left in the hotel?

There is a legend from the time of John Stone of a gambler who was suspected of cheating and was killed in the hotel. The story purports that this has lead to the unfortunate gambler's spirit left to search for his stolen money. Employees of the hotel who were complicit in the murder are also still wandering the halls, trapped by their guilt.

John Stone is also believed to be still in residence, keeping careful watch over his former property.

Doors open and close, glasses have been thrown from shelves, and people have been tapped on the shoulder and have felt hands on their neck.

## The Bottom Line

**The History:** Originally a hotel built by John Stone in 1834. Restored in 1976 and now operated as a bar and restaurant.

**The Haunting:** John Stone may still be watching over his property. A little girl is seen looking out of windows. A murdered gambler and those complicit in the crime may still haunt the building. Doors open and close, glasses are thrown, and lights go on and off.

## Recommendations

**Enjoy lunch, dinner, or Sunday brunch by a roaring fire or out on the patio. There is live entertainment, artist's work on display, and special events throughout the year. Or, sit at the bar and sip some liquid spirits, and see what other spirits join you.**

## Visitor Information

**Stone's Public House**
**179 Main Street**
**Ashland, MA 01721**
**(508) 881-1778**
**http://stonespublichouse.com**

**Hours:**
**Closed Mondays. Tuesday through Saturday: 11:30am – 1am, serving food until 11pm; Sunday: 11am – 1am, Brunch until 3pm, serving food until 10pm.**

**Directions:**
**From Boston on I-90 Westbound: Take exit 12 to merge onto MA-9/Worcester Road toward Framingham. Turn right at Country Club Lane. Turn left at Gates Street. Slight left at Parker Road. Take the 1st right toward Salem End Road. Turn left at Salem End Road. Take the first right onto Badger Road. Continue on Myrtle Street. Myrtle Street turns slightly left and becomes Main Street, and Stone's Public House is at 179 Main Street.**

**From I-90 Eastbound: Take exit 12 and follow Directions: above.**

# Michigan

THE HENRY FORD ESTATE

THE LANDMARK INN

NATIONAL HOUSE INN

*Photo by Dave Parker.*

# The Henry Ford Estate

Any discussion of American history in terms of technology and industry must include Henry Ford. Thanks to his adoption of assembly line manufacturing, he was able to produce the affordable Model T automobile which revolutionized the life of the average American. In 1914, he made another unprecedented move—he began paying his workers $5 per day, which was double the standard wage. This kept valuable workers from leaving—a practice today's companies might want to consider—and it also allowed these workers to actually afford to buy the cars they were making.

Throughout his life, Ford would hold 161 patents, grow his company into an automotive giant, and become one of the most famous men in the country. With his fortune he could have built a palace in Detroit's most fashionable neighborhood. Instead, he and his wife, Clara, chose privacy over high society, and built a secluded mansion on 1,300 acres in Dearborn.

The initial plans were to spend no more than $250,000 on the estate, but you know what happens to building budgets. By 1916, the Fords were living in their new 31,000-square-foot mansion, called Fair Lane, with its own hydro-electric Powerhouse, a man-made lake, hunting lodge, indoor pool, bowling alley, skating house, and even a "Santa's Workshop" for Ford's grandchildren. The total cost? Just a bit over budget, to the tune of about two million dollars!

For the next thirty years, life was good there for the extended Ford family. Henry passed away peacefully in his bedroom at the age of 83 in 1947, and Clara died a few years later. Two years after her death, the family sold the estate to the Ford Motor Company to use for the company's archives. The company then donated the house and 210 acres to Michigan University to establish the Dearborn Campus.

Since the 1970s, with the help of over 250 volunteers annually, Fair Lane is open to the public, so everyone can see what millions of dollars in automobile industry profits could buy in the early twentieth century. The public might also get a chance to see something else—or someone else to be more precise—the Ford family's trusted butler. No, he isn't a 100-year-old man still on duty. He is, in fact, quite dead, but he still appears to take his job very seriously and has been seen and heard rushing through the halls. Many people who have seen the phantom butler in uniform have identified him from photographs, so there's no doubt he is still on the job. And they say good help is hard to find!

In addition to the eternally tireless butler, witnesses have heard doors and windows opening and closing on their own, felt cold spots, experienced the sensation of being watched, and feeling a strong presence. Most often these sensations occur in Henry's bedroom, the room in which he died, and some speculate that he and Clara are still in the home they loved for so many years.

Figures have also been seen in and around the cars in Ford's personal collection. Speaking of cars, while visiting Dearborn, don't miss the Henry Ford Museum which is just down the street. In their amazing collection they have the Ford limousine in which President Kennedy was shot, and some claim to have seen JFK himself by the car. The museum also has the chair in which Lincoln was shot, and similar claims have been made about seeing this assassinated president, as well.

It is impossible to imagine the history of the twentieth century without the American dream of a car in every garage, made possible in great part by Henry Ford. The grand estate of Fair Lane is as much a testament of our love of the automobile as it is of one man's love of his work and home. And if the Fords and their butler—and perhaps many others—still reside here, so much the better, as it fulfills the American historic haunts dream of a ghost in every house.

## The Bottom Line

**The History:** Estate built in the 1910s by Henry Ford from his fortune gained in the automotive industry.

**The Haunting:** The Ford's butler is still seen and heard rushing about, doors and windows open and close, cold spots, and a strong presence in the room where Ford died.

## Recommendations

**The residence is simply magnificent and there is so much to see, but don't neglect the beautiful grounds and the Powerhouse. Look for the cornerstone of the Powerhouse, which was laid by Thomas Edison in 1914. Enjoy a meal in the restaurant in the room where the indoor pool once was, and shop in the gift shop which is on the porch. Be sure to make time to also visit the Ford Museum and Greenfield Village.**

## Visitor Information

**The Henry Ford Estate**
4901 Evergreen Road
Dearborn, MI 48128-2406
(313) 436-9196
www.henryfordestate.org

**Hours:**

January-March, Tuesday-Sunday: Tours are offered at 1:30pm only.

April-December: Tuesday-Sunday: Tours begin at 10:30am, 11:30am, 12:30pm, 1:30pm, and 2:30pm. Closed Thanksgiving, Christmas, and New Year's days.

**Admission:**

Guided tours: Adults $12, Senior (62 and older) $11, Student (with I.D) – $11, Children (6-12) – $8. There are special group rates and packages available, which include a meal. Catered events and weddings are also available.

The gardens are open Tuesday-Saturday, Mid May through Labor Day from 9:30am – 5pm. $2 admission includes a walking map.

**Directions:**

From MI-39N/S: Take exit 6 toward US-12/Michigan Avenue. Stay straight onto Southfield Road. Merge onto Michigan Avenue/US-12 W. Turn slight right onto Evergreen Road, then U-turn on Evergreen, and the estate will be on the right.

*Photo by Daniele Carol. Courtesy of the Landmark Inn.*

# The Landmark Inn

The village of New Worcester was founded in 1849, several years after iron ore was discovered nearby, but a year later was renamed Marquette. Rail lines began carrying the ore into Marquette to be shipped out via Lake Superior. In the following decades, while the iron ore was heading out of town, steamships started bringing tourists in, and a popular summer destination was born.

To accommodate this influx of vacationers, plans were made to build the Northland Hotel in 1910. However, things progressed rather slowly, to put it mildly, and it wasn't until 1917 that the foundation was begun, and not until 1930 that the hotel opened for business!

Once it was finally accepting guests, the hotel accumulated quite a list of notable people. Amelia Earhart stayed in room 502, and today you can request her room which is now named in her honor. Or, you could ask for the Abbott and Costello Room, or one of the many other rooms where famous musicians such as Louis Armstrong, Duke Ellington, the group Peter, Paul, and Mary, and the Rolling Stones stayed. For movie buffs, there are the rooms where Jimmy Stewart, Lee Remick, and George C. Scott stayed while filming *Anatomy of a Murder.*

Unfortunately, the glamorous days of the rich and famous came to an end as the old hotel was not maintained properly, and the Northland closed in 1982. In 1995, the building underwent extensive renovations by a team specialized in historic restorations, and when complete, the now re-named Landmark Inn once again opened its doors for travelers…and possibly a few ghosts.

Local legends talk about a spinster librarian who fell in love with a sailor in the 1930s. They planned to marry after he took one more voyage on Lake Superior. Unfortunately, a terrible storm hit the ship and all hands were lost. The poor librarian died of a broken heart, and she can still be seen waiting for her lost love in the window of a sixth-floor room, now known as the Lilac Room. From the very first night the newly renovated hotel opened, the Lilac Room has been the scene of all manner of bizarre activity, and the front desk often receives calls from the room when it is empty.

Another legend involves the murder of a woman. During financial negotiations as the original structure was being built, an escort was hired to obtain some important information by using her feminine charms. The man who had divulged the information to her suffered financially as a result, and in revenge, killed her and buried her body in the unfinished basement. It is claimed that people hear this woman crying out for help.

Another active location is the North Star Lounge, where people's clothing has been pulled and glasses fly off of shelves. Then there are the hallways where people feel they are being watched, locks that refuse to open, then open effortlessly, and just about every other kind of paranormal activity you can imagine. It is impossible to say who still remains in this historic hotel that has seen so many visitors come, but not all of them go. It's certainly worth a stay to see if you can shed some light on the mysterious occupants, and perhaps even convince the librarian that she is long overdue for checking out.

### The Bottom Line

**The History:** A hotel which began construction in 1917, but didn't open until 1930. Many famous people stayed here. Renovated in 1995.

**The Haunting:** The ghost of a heartbroken librarian and a murdered woman.

### Recommendations

**The National Trust for Historic Preservation named Marquette, Michigan, as one of the twelve best heritage travel destinations in the country, and there are a wide variety of events throughout the summer and winter. The hotel has a restaurant, pub, and lounge, offering everything from drinks to high tea to gourmet meals. You can request one of the historic rooms, like Amelia Earhart's, or one of the known haunted rooms, like the Lilac Room.**

### Visitor Information

**The Landmark Inn**
**230 N. Front Street**
**Marquette, MI 49855-4221**
**(888) 752-6362**
**(906) 228-2580**
**www.thelandmarkinn.com**

**Directions:**
**From routes 28 and 41 in Marquette, exit on S. Front Street and head north for 8 blocks.**

*Courtesy of the National House Inn.*

## National House Inn

The stagecoach line from Detroit to Chicago was established in 1833, and it was a long, tiring trip that took several days. The town of Marshall was ideally located at the halfway point of the journey, so in 1835 Colonel Andrew Mann built an inn to accommodate the weary travelers. While stagecoaches were eventually replaced by trains after the railroad began service in 1844, it was still good for the inn's business as there was a train station right in town. Things were good for many years, but by 1878, the place was forced to close. As the railroad now had dining and sleeper cars, there wasn't any reason for passengers to get off in Marshall.

The sturdy brick building was converted to a factory that made windmills and wagons. Then in 1902, a veterinarian, Dr. Dean, turned the place into an upscale apartment house. Dean's Flats did well for most of the twentieth century, but gradually deteriorated due to neglect. In 1976, a major restoration was undertaken, the rooms were decorated with antiques, and the oldest hotel in the state was back in business. Today, the National House Inn operates as a lovely Bed and Breakfast, in a town that has a National Historic Landmark District with 850 structures.



As if that wasn't enough history, the old inn had a secret room that was believed to have been used for the Underground Railroad. During Prohibition, this room was used to store and sell illegal liquor.

A stagecoach and railroad hotel that harbored runaway slaves and bootleggers seems to be an ideal location for ghosts, yet there are no documented old stories about haunted activity. However, immediately after the renovations were complete and the house was filled with antiques, a phantom resident did begin to appear—the Lady in Red. She does not appear to be bound to any particular location in the inn, as she has been seen both upstairs and downstairs, in the halls and common areas.

The Lady in Red is by no means a threatening presence; she simply seems to be going about her business, whatever the business of a ghost may be! Of course, the big questions are who was this woman in life, and why is she here? Was she connected with the early days of the inn, was she a resident of the apartments, or did she enter the house attached to one of the many antiques? Why does she appear wearing red; is this some clue to her former existence?

The mysterious Lady in Red may have been wandering through this house for over 170 years, or her spirit may have been awakened by the renovations, which often provoke dormant ghosts. Whatever her story, she is here at the National House Inn, and she just might be waiting for the right guest to whom to tell her story.

## The Bottom Line

**The History:** The oldest hotel in Michigan, originally built in 1835 as a stagecoach inn.

**The Haunting:** The Lady in Red began to appear soon after the place was renovated.

## Recommendations

Marshall has the largest Historic Landmark District in Michigan, so if you gravitate toward nineteenth-century Americana you will love this place. There are a great variety of events throughout the year (www.marshallmi.org) so you can time your visit according to your special interests. The inn overlooks the beautiful Fountain Circle, and as it is only two blocks to the historic downtown shops and restaurants, you can leave your car and not have to drive for your entire stay. The inn also has a large gift shop, garden, and working fireplaces. Rooms are spacious and beautifully decorated with antiques, so you can forget the twenty-first century for a while.

## Visitor Information

**National House Inn**
102 South Parkview
Marshall, MI 49068-1495
(269) 781-7374
www.nationalhouseinn.com

**Directions:**

From their website—From I-94, exit 110 (old 27): Go south to the Fountain. The National House Inn is on the right side of the road about 1/4 of the way around the Fountain Circle. (The National House Inn is on the southwest corner of the Fountain Circle.)

From I-69, exit 36 (Michigan Avenue): Go east. Go though the first light and continue traveling east to the Fountain. Just before reaching the Fountain you will see The National House Inn is on the right side of the road. (The National House Inn is on the southwest corner of the Fountain Circle.)

# Minnesota Haunts

FORT SNELLING

THAYER'S HISTORIC BED N' BREAKFAST

FOREPAUGH'S RESTAURANT

MN

Fort Snelling in 1889.

# Fort Snelling

Built on a bluff overlooking the confluence of the Mississippi and Minnesota Rivers, Fort Snelling has played a rather significant role in history, considering its humble beginnings as a frontier outpost. Completed in 1825, the fort was named for its commanding officer, Colonel Josiah Snelling, who was considered to be a competent officer—when he was sober and not suffering the effects of chronic dysentery which finally killed him in 1827.

The main purposes of the fort were to keep the British and other non-Americans off the rivers, keep whites from trespassing on Indian lands, enforce the law, protect travelers, and try to keep the peace between the Ojibwe and Dakota tribes. In addition, soldiers built mills, planted crops, and generally tried to promote the best a frontier settlement had to offer. Unfortunately, it was also the scene of the worst aspects of early American history.

In the 1830s, John Emerson worked at Fort Snelling, and he owned a slave named Dred Scott. As slavery was illegal in Minnesota, this situation lead to the famous U.S. Supreme Court case, in which Scott argued for his freedom. The ensuing Dred Scott Decision by the court essentially stated that African Americans brought to this country as slaves could never be citizens and were not protected by the rights granted by the U. S. Constitution.

Another shameful chapter in the fort's history came in 1862. Local Dakota Indians were tired of broken promises from the government and led an uprising, killing hundreds of white settlers. Over 300 captured warriors were sentenced to hang, but President Lincoln reduced that number to 39 of the worst offenders. In December, the largest mass execution in the history of the country took place in Mankato when 38 were hung in a single day. In addition, at Fort Snelling's Pike Island, 1,600 Indian elders, women, and children were interned, and hundreds of them died during the brutal winter months. After all the Indians were eventually forcibly removed from the state, the fort continued to be a headquarters in the campaigns against the western tribes.

By 1851, Fort Snelling was no longer on the frontier which had expanded westward, so it was sold to a developer. However, with the start of the Civil War, it was back to military use to train soldiers. Even during WWII, the old fort trained over 300,000 troops. With the building of highways after the war, Fort Snelling's existence was threatened, but public efforts preserved the site, and in 1960, it was the first place in the state to be designated a National Historic Landmark.

Today, thanks to the Minnesota Historical Society, costumed guides bring visitors back to the frontier days and present what life was like for soldiers, settlers, and Indians from 1820-1840. And if you are sensitive or just plain lucky, you might also witness some of the people of the past—or at least shades of them—as staff and visitors have reported transparent, white figures wandering around the fort grounds, especially near the walls and tower. Voices have also been heard, some in a whisper, others like a loud moaning. Additionally, there are many cases of visitors experiencing a heavy feeling and a strong presence, which can occur anywhere on the old fort grounds.

Fort Snelling does indeed represent both the good and bad of America's expanding frontier in the nineteenth century, but the best way to honor all of those who lived, suffered, fought, and died here is to visit and learn about their lives and how events at the fort influenced the nation. It is no wonder with such a long history of strife that something from the past remains here, but hopefully in time, the spirits will all move on to new frontiers.

## The Bottom Line

**The History:** A frontier fort completed in 1825. The famous slave Dred Scott lived here, and 1,600 Indians were held prisoner, with many of them dying.

**The Haunting:** Transparent white figures are seen, voices are heard, and uncomfortable feelings are experienced.

## Recommendations

With the enormous Mall of America and the airport nearby, you may have difficulty imagining a time when this area was on the edge of a wild frontier. However, stepping into the fort is like stepping back in time. They offer an impressive list of special events, history walks, and lectures spanning the breadth of American history, wars, and crafts. The popular "Little House in the Big Fort Day Camps" was named Best Camp for Kids by Nickelodeon. In 1820, the fort's doctor started keeping weather records. Still kept to this day, it is one of the oldest and most complete histories of weather observations in the nation. There are many ways to enjoy and appreciate the fort, so call or visit their website for all the latest information. And keep your camera and recorder handy just in case something from the past decides to manifest!

## Visitor Information

**Fort Snelling**
345 Kellogg Boulevard West
St. Paul MN 55102-1903
(612) 726-1171
www.mnhs.org

**Hours:**
Memorial Day weekend through Labor Day: Tuesday through Saturday 10am – 5pm; Sunday noon to 5pm. September and October: Saturday 10am – 5pm.

**Admission:**
$10 adults, $8 seniors and college students, $5 children ages 6-17; free for children age 5 and under, and MHS members.

**Directions:**
At the junction of Minnesota Highways 5 and 55, one mile east of the Twin Cities International Airport.

*Courtesy of Thayer's Historic Bed & Breakfast.*

MN

# Thayer's Historic Bed n' Breakfast

The Thayer was first built in 1895 as an inn for people traveling on the railroad, and was named after the original owners, Gus and Caroline Thayer. When current owner Sharon Gammel first saw the old hotel in 1993, it had fallen on hard times, but she knew she had to have it. After two long years of hard work restoring and decorating, the Thayer was once again ready to greet travelers. Today, it is a bed and breakfast on the National Register of Historic Places and many people still come and go—it's just that not all of them are alive…

"I would estimate that at any given time there are ten to twelve spirits here," Sharon pointed out, also noting that some are long-time residents, while others make brief appearances, never to return.

There's Lily, who arrived at the Thayer when a friend gave Sharon a portrait of the woman. Lily has been particularly accommodating to guests who take part in Sharon's ghost hunting classes, as she has been known to regularly "tap or nudge participants."

Another ghost also arrived attached to an old photo of a couple on their wedding day. Late one night, six couples—who had previously scoffed at the idea of the place being haunted—returned to the inn after dinner and none of their keys would work, until someone apologized to the ghosts and asked if they would please open the door! One couple was still completely skeptical, said their "good-nights" and went to their room. They never came down for breakfast, and when one of the staff checked, found the room empty. It wasn't until the next day that Sharon found out what had happened.

When the couple got into bed their room grew icy cold. Suddenly, all the lights went on at once (they all have separate switches), and the figure of a man slowly materialized at the foot of their bed, forming from the waist up. When the man looked completely solid, he raised his top hat and bowed. Then he vanished, all the lights went out, and the room was warm again. The once skeptical couple fled as fast as they could!

Sharon is a cat lover, and her favorite cat was an enormous, brown, 38-pound Maine Coon, named Cocoa Bear, who passed away, leaving her only two cats. One day a four-year-old boy asked if it was okay to go upstairs and pat the cats. He returned a few minutes later and asked Sharon, "Ma'am, how many cats do you have?" She had already told the boy there were two, but told him again, and then the boy went back upstairs. Again, and again he returned to ask how many cats she had, growing increasingly frustrated each time for some unknown reason. Finally, he blurted out the source of his annoyance.

"You have three cats. One of them is a really big kitty named Cocoa Bear, and he wants you to know he's okay. He's big and soft and I don't know how you could miss such a big kitty like that!"

Other guests have encountered Cocoa Bear, as well as some cats who have passed on, but are obviously still using some of those nine lives.

This former railroad hotel has clearly not lost the energy of people, and pets, coming and going; it's just that now they all stay way past check-out time. Could the Thayers ever have imagined that into the twenty-first century their establishment would still be going strong? Why don't you spend the night and ask them yourself—maybe they are still here, too!

### The Bottom Line

**The History:** A former hotel for railroad travelers built in 1895.

**The Haunting:** At any given time there may be the spirits of 10-12 people, and several cats.

### Recommendations

**You really can immerse yourself in the spiritual world here, as in addition to the hauntings, Sharon Gammel offers psychic readings and ghost hunting classes (assisted by Lily, of course). Then there are Sharon's delicious breakfasts, which may just be good enough to raise the dead! They also host a variety of period murder mystery dinner theaters, which by the way, seem to also stir up the paranormal activity, especially the 1895 version. This is definitely a place where you not only can get great hospitality, but can indulge your paranormal curiosity. (And don't forget to pat Cocoa Bear!)**

### Visitor Information

**Thayer's Historic Bed n' Breakfast**
**60 West Elm Street**
**Annandale, MN 55302-1153**
**(800) 944-6595**
**www.thayers.net**

**Directions:**

**From Minneapolis: Take I-394 West. At exit 3, take ramp right and follow signs for US-169 North Take ramp right for SR-55 West/ Olson Memorial Highway toward Buffalo. Pass McDonalds on the right. Arrive at 60 Elm Street W, Annandale. (The last intersection is Harrison Street W/W. Harrison Street W. If you reach Maple Avenue N, you've gone too far.)**



## Forepaugh's Restaurant

Haunted locations are often dirty, dark, and dilapidated, so it is a great pleasure to satisfy your paranormal curiosity while dining on exquisite cuisine in an elegant mansion. While Forepaugh's Restaurant in St. Paul is not your ordinary haunt, the story behind the haunting is all too familiar.

Joseph Forepaugh made a fortune with his dry goods business, so he bought five lots along Irvine Park and built a magnificent mansion. It was 1870, he was only 36, he was rich, and had a wife and two daughters. Life should have been a bed of roses, but he was prone to depression that he couldn't seem to shake.

To combat that depression, Forepaugh decided to go to Europe for several years, and in 1886, the mansion was sold to General John Henry Hammond, a retired Civil War veteran. Forepaugh returned with his family to St. Paul in 1889, and promptly built another mansion on Summit Avenue. However, the dark cloud over Forepaugh could not be dispelled, and on July 8, 1892, he walked into Irvine Park with a gun and shot himself in the head. The family claimed he was worried about his business, but it turned out that the bed of roses appears to have had a servant girl in it.

There are two versions of the story concerning this servant, Molly. One account has Molly hearing about Forepaugh's death and then committing suicide by hanging herself in the Summit Avenue house. Another version has Molly hanging herself years earlier in the first mansion, after Mrs. Forepaugh caught the lovers in the act and forced Joseph to promise to break off the affair. Molly's death was what then weighed so heavily upon him, led him to sell the house and leave the country, and eventually ended in his suicide, as well.

Whatever the chain of events, the result was the suicide death of two people who loved one another and could not be together in life, so now they are together in death. Members of the restaurant staff and guests who have come for dinner or a special event have seen a handsome man in 1890s clothing walking around the place as if he owned it—which just might be the truth! Molly has also been seen on many occasions, and it is comforting to know she does not appear to be an unhappy spirit.

There are also strange noises that can often be heard upstairs. On one occasion, convinced that there was an intruder, a police K-9 unit was brought in. At first, the usually fearless dog refused to go up to the third floor (where Molly may have hung herself), but he eventually did and no one could be found. There are also cold spots, lights that turn on and off, and objects and furniture that move by themselves.

It is a sad story about a tragic love that led to two untimely deaths, but if Molly and Joseph are happily reunited in death, who are we to judge fate? While dining at Forepaugh's Restaurant, take a moment to raise a glass of wine to the lovers and wish them well, and they may just appear and do the same for you!

## The Bottom Line

**The History:** A beautifully restored mansion built in 1870. The owner later committed suicide, as did the servant girl with whom he was having an affair. Now a first-class restaurant.

**The Haunting:** Forepaugh and Molly have been seen and heard throughout the building.

## Recommendations

The restaurant has been named one of the best in St. Paul, and this truly is a beautifully restored mansion. Many members of the staff have had ghostly encounters, so ask if they wouldn't mind sharing their stories.

## Visitor Information

**Forepaugh's Restaurant**
276 South Exchange Street
St. Paul, MN 55102-2417
(651) 224-5606
www.forepaughs.com

**Hours:**

Brunch: Sunday 10am – 2pm; Dinner: Monday-Thursday 5pm – 9pm, Friday-Saturday 5pm – 10pm, Sunday 5pm – 9pm.

**Directions:**

From I-35E N: Take exit 106A for Grand Avenue. Slight right onto Grand Avenue, then turn left on Exchange Street S.

From I-35E S: Take exit 105 toward St. Clair Avenue. Merge onto W. Pleasant Avenue. Turn left at St. Clair Avenue. Slight left at 7th Street W/Fort Road. Slight right at W. Forbes Avenue. Continue onto Exchange Street S.

From I-94E: Take exit 241B for 5th Street. Turn right at N. Smith Avenue. Take 3rd left onto N. Walnut Street. Take 2nd right onto Exchange Street. S.

From I-94W: Take exit 243 for US-61/Mounds Boulevard toward Kellogg Boulevard. Keep right at the fork, follow signs for Mounds Boulevard N/US-61 and merge onto Mounds Blvd/US-61 N. Turn left at 3rd Street E. Continue onto E. Kellogg Boulevard. Turn left at Jackson Street. Take the 2nd right onto Shepard Road. Turn right at Old Chestnut Street. Turn left at Exchange Street S.

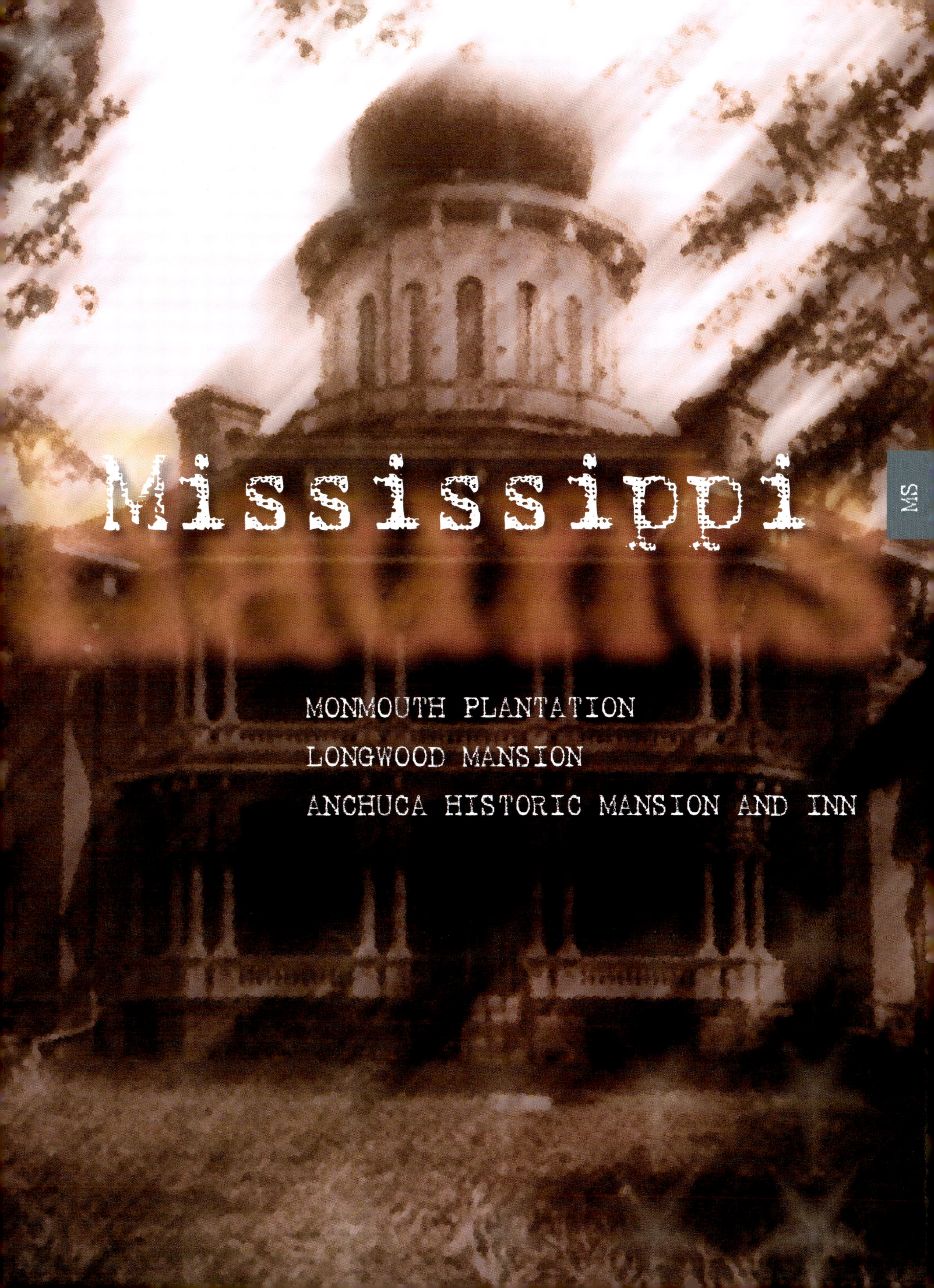



# Mississippi

MONMOUTH PLANTATION

LONGWOOD MANSION

ANCHUCA HISTORIC MANSION AND INN

Photo by National Park Service, 1972.

MS

# Monmouth Plantation

Natchez, Mississippi is one of the most remarkable historic haunts in the country. You can tour, sleep, and eat in dozens of amazing haunted antebellum mansions. The following places are only two examples, and don't expect to see and experience all the city has to offer in just one trip.

In 1818, Natchez's postmaster, John Hankinson, built a brick house on thirty acres of land. Unfortunately, he and his wife didn't have long to enjoy their beautiful home as they both died in a yellow fever epidemic. The house was sold at auction in 1825, then resold in 1826 to John Quitman, who would go on to distinguish himself in the Mexican War and hold many political offices, including that of Governor of Mississippi. General Quitman expanded and renovated the house at Monmouth Plantation in 1853, converting it to a white stucco, Greek Revival mansion.

Though born in New York, Quitman was pro-slavery and believed the south had the right to secede, and he voiced his opinions as a Congressman in Washington, D.C. Soon after he and other southern politicians spoke out, many of them came down with a mysterious illness and died. Quitman was also sickened, but survived. However, two years later in 1858, he died a slow death in his home from what some believed were lingering complications from that sickness. At the time, it was suspected that abolitionists had poisoned the politicians, but it is now believed to have been National Hotel Disease, a type of food poisoning brought on by poor sanitation.

Mrs. Quitman died the following year, so it was left to their three married daughters to hold down the plantation during the Civil War. Ironically, Natchez was spared the destruction of other southern cities because it was occupied by Union troops in 1862 after the fall of New Orleans. Many of the plantation's slaves escaped, and some even joined the Union army. The mansion was occupied by Union soldiers in 1863, at which point many of the general's belongings were stolen. Quitman's daughters were forced to sell much of what was left after the war.

But even through war and financial troubles, the mansion managed to stay in the hands of family members until 1924. For the next five decades the property would change hands a number of times, and time and neglect eventually took a terrible toll. By 1977, the place was in desperate need of major renovations. Fortunately, Lani and Ron Riches bought Monmouth Plantation, and through their extraordinary efforts were able to rescue this antebellum jewel and convert it into a luxury inn that has been named "One of the 10 Most Romantic Places" in the country.

Would General Quitman have approved of his house being saved from the wrecking ball and restored to its former elegance? One would hope he would have been pleased, but when renovations first began, some unseen presence began angrily stomping up and down the stairs and down the hallways. Workman not only complained of the heavy footsteps, they felt an unnerving, strong presence, as if the old general himself was inspecting their work to make sure they did it right.

Once the renovations were complete and the inn was opened for business, the stomping gradually faded, but that didn't mean General Quitman was resting in peace. One night a guest awoke to find the general, in uniform, standing by the bed, staring at him as if to determine if the man was worthy of spending the night in his house. Apparently, the man passed inspection as the general walked to the other side of the bed and vanished. Other guests have also reported that the general had visited them in the night, as well.

Can we blame General Quitman for still keeping an eye on his beloved home? When a man pours his heart and soul into a place, is it any wonder his spirit sticks around for the ride?

## The Bottom Line

**The History:** A house built in 1818, later owned by a general who became governor of Mississippi. Now an inn, named one of the most elegant and romantic in the country.

**The Haunting:** The general still inspects his home and the guests.

## Recommendations

**There are less expensive places to stay in Natchez, but if you want one of the most elegant and romantic historic haunts in the country, set on a stunning 26 acres of gardens, this is it. You can stay in the main house, or one of the many other buildings on the property. Whatever your choice, you will not be disappointed by the service, food, or the total "antebellum immersion" experience of the luxury accommodations. The staff can arrange anything from a carriage ride to a hot air balloon excursion lifting off from the front lawn. Look for the piece of furniture that the family had to sell after the Civil War to pay their taxes. It was found in Europe in 2006 and returned to the house! And make sure you and your room are ready for a midnight inspection from the general!**

## Visitor Information

**Monmouth Plantation**
36 Melrose Avenue
Natchez, MS 39120-4005
(800) 828-4531 or (601) 442-5852
www.monmouthplantation.com/



**Hours:**

A house tour is given daily at 10am, and a garden tour is conducted daily from 4pm – 6pm. Closed for tours only on New Year's Eve and New Year's Day.

**Directions:**

From their website—From Baton Rouge, LA: Highway 61 North to Natchez. After entering city limits, continue straight. At fifth traffic light, take a left on Melrose-Montebello Parkway. Go through the flashing light, then at next traffic light, take a left on John Quitman Boulevard. Monmouth is on the left.

From New Orleans, LA: Travel I-10 West to the I-55 exit. Travel north to Brookhaven. (Highway 84) Take Highway 84 West to Natchez. Take a left on Highway 61 South. Enter city limits. Go through four traffic lights. Continue one block more and turn left on Junkin Street. At the second traffic light, turn right on John Quitman Boulevard. Monmouth is on the left.

From Jackson, MS: Travel on I-55 South to Brookhaven. (Highway 84) Take Highway 84 West to Natchez. Take a left on Highway 61 South. Enter city limits. Go through four traffic lights. Continue one block more and turn left on Junkin Street. At the second traffic light, turn right on John Quitman Boulevard. Monmouth is on the left.

From Highway 84 (Louisiana): Cross Mississippi River Bridge from Vidalia, Louisiana. Take left at first light. (Canal Street) Go to the fifth traffic light and take a right on State Street. Monmouth is on the right in the tenth block.

Longwood Mansion in 1936.

MS

# Longwood Mansion

Longwood in Natchez is the tale of two houses, of two vastly different eras, and of eight sides. It is the largest octagonal house in America, and construction began in 1860 when life was good for plantation owners in the south. However, the gilded world they had built on the backs of slaves was about to come crashing down.

Dr. Haller Nutt was born in 1816 on Laurel Hill Plantation in Jefferson County, Mississippi. He would own several different plantations during his life, and developed a strain of cotton that proved to be very successful. His plantations also grew sugar cane, and thanks to these crops grown by the labor of his 800 slaves, he amassed a personal fortune estimated at over $3 million.

Nutt hired Philadelphia architect Samuel Sloan to design the unique eight-sided, 30,000 square foot Oriental Revival-style mansion with a sixteen-sided cupola and onion-shaped dome. It was to be six stories tall, each floor was to have eight rooms around the central rotunda, and it was to be filled with the finest European antiques and furnishings. Construction progressed until the spring of 1861 when the Civil War began. Sloan and his workers fled Mississippi and returned to Pennsylvania to fight for the Union. Slaves completed the basement level in 1862 so the family could move in, and though Nutt was loyal to the Union, he remained in Natchez in his unfinished mansion with his family until the bitter end.

Many of the expensive items he had ordered from Europe were seized in Federal blockades. His crops were burned, his land seized, and both armies confiscated anything and everything they needed. In 1864, distraught at the loss of his fortune and weakened by all the devastation of war, Nutt succumbed to pneumonia at the age of only 48, leaving his widow, Julia, and their eleven children.

"Nutt's Folly," as the mansion came to be called, remained in his family's hands for a time after his death, but with the five top floors unfinished, they could only occupy the finished ground floor. With Haller and his fortune gone, the mansion was never completed and today remains in the state it was when work was halted. In 1970, the house was donated to the Pilgrimage Garden Club which operates tours in many of Natchez's antebellum mansions.

Unfinished business is often the reason behind a haunting, and it may be the unfinished state of his dream home that has kept Dr. Nutt bound to the property. He has been seen on many occasions strolling through the gardens, especially during tours. Is he keeping an eye on visitors to make sure they don't damage his beloved home, or is he simply waiting for someone to finally finish it? Mrs. Nutt has also made appearances to staff and tour groups, but she prefers to be indoors, particularly on the staircase.

While it is unfortunate that Nutt was never able to finish this unusual and magnificent house because he lost his fortune and his life due to the war, to his 800 slaves and their descendants the war didn't arrive a minute too soon. While the finished floor of Longwood stands as a reminder of the opulence of the pre-war era, the barren, unfinished floors stand as a testament to the price the south paid for secession. And the ghosts of Mr. and Mrs. Nutt still stand by to keep an eye on their unfinished business.

### The Bottom Line

**The History:** The largest octagonal house in America, unfinished due to the start of the Civil War.

**The Haunting:** The original owners still keep an eye on their home and appear to staff and tour groups.

### Recommendations

**During Spring and Fall Pilgrimage in Natchez (March-April, and October), dozens of antebellum mansions, many of them private residences, are open to the public, which presents a marvelous opportunity so see some of the finest southern homes on a single trip. Don't be fooled by the fact that only one of the six floors is finished—the tour is fascinating and visitors often say that Longwood was the best part of their trip.**

### Visitor Information

**Longwood Mansion**
140 Lower Woodville Road
Natchez, MS 39120-4412
(601) 442-5193

**Tours of the house are run by:**
Natchez Pilgrimage Tours
(Located in the Visitor's Center)
640 S. Canal Street
Natchez, MS 39120
(601) 446-6631
(800) 647-6742

**Hours:**
Tours every 30 minutes 9am – 4:30pm. New Year's Eve 4 – 4:30pm and New Year's Day 10am – 5pm.

**Admission:**
Individual Ticket Prices: Adults $10, Children (6-13) $8
Discount Packages: Visit any three mansions (except for The Briars, Dunleith, and The Towers) 3-House Ticket: Adults $24, Children $18.

**Directions:**
From 61/84/425/John R Junkin Drive in Natchez, turn onto Lower Woodville Road.

# Anchuca Historic Mansion and Inn

Vicksburg is another of those special historic haunts where it seems that everywhere you turn there's a ghost story. This is most likely due in great part to the battles that have been waged here and the thousands of lives that were lost.

It is ironic that a town that has seen so much conflict was named after a pacifist minister, Newitt Vick, who had been a conscientious objector during the Revolutionary War. From the Indian Wars to the 47-day Siege of Vicksburg in 1863, people have suffered and died here with an intensity that has obviously left a paranormal mark.

Anchuca was built in 1830 by a local politician, J. W. Mauldin, and the original design was a simpler Primitive Colonial Style. The next owner was a coal and ice merchant, Victor Wilson, who added the Greek Revival front to the structure, making it the first building in Vicksburg to have those stately columns. At the time, one of his daughters described the view from the property as like "a sea of water" and from the front of the house one could look up the river "as far as the eye could

*Courtesy of Anchuca Mansion and Inn.*

MS

see." Wilson enjoyed that view, as he was able to watch his barges go down the river. (The course of the river changed in 1876, then the Corps of Engineers created the Yazoo Canal, so the original river view is gone.)

During the long, brutal siege in 1863, many of Vicksburg's buildings were damaged or destroyed, but Anchuca survived relatively unscathed—if you consider seventeen cannonball hits and every window shattered to be "unscathed." Because this house managed to somehow escape total destruction, others who had lost their homes sought shelter here. After the battle, the place became a hospital for wounded soldiers, as did every other structure in the area that could provide some shelter. As a reminder of those grim days, heavy rains in Vicksburg will still turn out bones from amputated limbs and from some of the 7,000 horses that also died.

There is also another Civil War connection with this house—in 1868, it was purchased by Joseph Emory Davis, the older brother of Jefferson Davis, the President of the Confederacy. Jefferson Davis spoke from Anchuca's balcony in 1869, in what would be one of his last public speeches. Joseph died in the home the following year at the age of 87, and his life's story is a true reflection of the country's early history, from his humble beginnings to becoming one of the wealthiest planters in the south.

In the 1950s, the house was first opened for tours and the slave quarters became an antique shop. Since 2008, Anchuca has been a beautiful bed and breakfast that offers guests southern hospitality at its best, in a neighborhood that has the highest concentration of antebellum buildings. Though all of the original furnishings were destroyed during the Civil War, there are many lovely period antiques that create an atmosphere of the nineteenth-century elegance the early owners of Anchuca once enjoyed, and may still be enjoying...

Guests have seen and sensed a woman in nineteenth-century clothing by the master bedroom. Jane, as she has come to be called, may have been the wife of Victor Wilson. Perhaps all the tragedies she endured during the war, as well as losing her husband in 1865, have left her to search for happier times here.

Another ghost appears to haunt the Davis Suite. The massive bed in this room was built in New Orleans in 1858, and has no doubt seen its share of births and deaths. A few years ago an engineer was staying in the room for several weeks, and after a few days the housekeeper asked one of the owners, Tom Pharr, if she should still change the sheets on the bed, as the guest didn't sleep on the bed, he slept on the couch. Tom explained that the engineer was just a very neat and orderly person, and he probably was just making his own bed, but the housekeeper insisted the bed was untouched.

Tom asked the engineer if there was a problem with the bed, perhaps it was too hard or too soft for his liking? After some hesitation, the engineer admitted there was a problem, but not with the mattress. He said that on the first night after he fell asleep, he was awakened by what sounded like someone slapping the pillow next to his. He turned on the light and there was an indentation in the pillow, as if someone had hit it. When this happened again, and again, the skeptical engineer decided that someone didn't want him in that bed, so he spent the rest of his stay on the couch!

An ironing room had been set up in the former slave quarters on the second floor, and one warm day Tom heard his housekeeper scream. The terrified woman came running out and told him that as she was busy ironing, an icy cold wind "done blew through me to the bone." She was so shaken by the incident they had to move the ironing to another room, and that room is now the Aunt Sarah Courtyard Suite.

Other guests have reported footsteps on the porch and feelings of a strong presence, and one woman who is particularly sensitive felt "surrounded by good feelings" from the many spirits of Anchuca. There is much to surround yourself with here, whether it is the history, the ambience, the food, or the spirits. Vicksburg has so many tales to tell, and so many of them can be heard at Anchuca.

Note: Great Story, Wrong Building There is a misconception about a ghost story at Anchuca that is often repeated on websites and in books.

**The story goes:** Richard Archer had five daughters, and one of them was as stubborn and headstrong as he was, and even looked like him, which earned her the nickname, Archie. She fell in love with a man beneath her social station and her father forbid the marriage and sent the man away. Archie barely spoke to her father from that day, and refused to ever again sit down at the dinner table with him. Instead, she took all her meals standing up by the fireplace in the parlor. Reports from eyewitnesses dating back at least fifty years tell of a woman in a brown, nineteenth-century dress standing by that fireplace. Is it Archie, who is still so stubborn that she won't leave until she is reunited with the man she loved?

While the story is true, the events did not take place at this Anchuca. There was a plantation house called Anchuka (with a "k"), and that was where the Archers lived. That house was dismantled and its pieces were used to build Grey Oaks (privately owned) in Vicksburg, and that's where the lady in brown is seen by the fireplace. The confusion arose when a former resident of the plantation house Anchuka, was living in this East First Street house (which was previously known as the Wilson or Davis House) in 1952 and for sentimental reasons decided to name it Anchuca (a Choctaw word meaning "happy home"), with the difference in spelling to distinguish the two places...which obviously hasn't worked all that well!

## Recommendations

**Anchuca can be experienced through a tour, a meal, or an overnight stay, but it's best to do all three! Co-owner Tom Pharr is a wealth of information about the history of Vicksburg which will really help you to appreciate this historic house, the Spring Field neighborhood, and the city of Vicksburg. Fellow owner Chris Brinkley is the restaurant's chef, and people come from far and wide just to dine here—and don't forget to pick up a copy of their cookbook. Look for the original ceiling medallions in the Entry Hall and the Ladies Parlor which were made of marble dust, horse hair, and molasses, and the eighteenth-century Sevres porcelain and gilded bronze chandelier in the Gentleman's Parlor. While sightings and experiences can occur anywhere, ask for the Davis or Aunt Sarah Suite for a better chance of encountering one of the ghosts of Anchuca.**

## Visitor Information

**Anchuca Mansion**
**1010 First East Street**
**Vicksburg, MS 39183**
**(888) 686-0111**
**www.anchucamansion.com**

**Hours:**

**Cafe Anchuca: Lunch: Thursday-Sunday 11am – 2pm, Supper: Thursday-Saturday 6pm to 8pm, Library Bar: Thursday-Saturday 5pm to 8pm. Tours are offered daily from 9:30am to 3pm, $6 per person.**

**Directions:**

**From their website—Traveling east on I-20: Take exit 1A (Washington Street). Go north 2.6 mile to South Street. Turn right and proceed three blocks to Cherry Street. Turn left, go pass the Old Court House Museum and turn right on First East Street. Anchuca is immediately on the right.**

**Traveling west on I-20: Take exit 4B (West Clay Street). Go west 2.5 miles to Cherry Street. Turn right and proceed five blocks to First East Street. Turn right, Anchuca is immediately on the right.**



## The Bottom Line

**The History:** A magnificent antebellum home first built in 1830, struck by seventeen cannonballs during the Civil War. Jefferson Davis gave one of his last speeches from the balcony.

**The Haunting:** A woman is seen by the master bedroom, indentations appear on a bed, and there are footsteps and icy breezes.

# National Military Park

While in Vicksburg, you must see the National Military Park and visit with its many ghostly Civil War soldiers. The park also has the largest and finest collection of battlefield art and monuments, including thirty-six Tiffany bronzes, all valued at between $3-4 billion.

# McRaven House

Don't miss the tour of the McRaven House, which has been called the most haunted place in Mississippi.

## Visitor Information

**National Military Park, Visitor's Center**
Clay Street
Vicksburg, MS 39183
(601) 636-0583
www.nps.gov/vick/index.htm

**Hours:**

Open All Year except Thanksgiving Day, Christmas Day, and New Year's Day.
8am – 5pm.

**Admission:**

Per Vehicle – $8 (valid 7 days), Per Individual – $4 (Pedestrian, biker, motorcycle, jogger, etc.), Bus Passenger/Church Van – $4per person

**Directions:**

From their website—From the east: Take Interstate 20 west to Vicksburg, Mississippi. Use exit ramp 4B. Follow Clay Street (US-80) west 0.25 miles to park entrance.

From the north: Take Interstate 55 south to Jackson, Mississippi. (To save time, use Interstate 220 bypass on west side of Jackson.) Take Interstate 20 west to Vicksburg (approximately 40 miles). Use exit ramp 4B. Follow Clay Street (US-80) west 0.25 miles to park entrance.

From the south: Take Interstate 55 or US Highway 49 to Jackson, Mississippi. Take Interstate 20 west to Vicksburg, Mississippi, (approximately 40 miles). Use exit ramp 4B. Follow Clay Street (US-80) west 0.25 miles to park entrance.

From the west: Take Interstate 20 east to Vicksburg, Mississippi. Use exit ramp 4B. Follow Clay Street (US-80) west 0.25 miles to park entrance.

## Visitor Information

**McRaven House**
1445 Harrison Street
Vicksburg, MS 39180-3637
(601) 636-1663
www.mcraventourhome.com

**Hours:**

9am – 5pm Monday-Saturday, 10am – 5pm Sunday

**Directions:**

From their website—From the Military Park or Tourist Information Center: Drive west on Clay Street and turn left at traffic light #6; turn left at the 2nd stop sign. The house is at the very end of Harrison Street. Parking is on right.

From the State Welcome Center by the river: Drive north on Washington Street and turn right at traffic light #26, then at traffic light #19 turn left. The next intersection is traffic light #18, turn right and proceed to the stop sign and drive straight on to the end of the street. House at the very end of the street, and parking is on the right.

There are also several historical ghost tours of Vicksburg.

# Missouri

LEMP MANSION

JEFFERSON BARRACKS

THE PARLOR B&B

The Lemp Mansion c. 1892. *Courtesy of the Lemp Mansion.*

# Lemp Mansion

MO

The history of St. Louis, Missouri, could be characterized by two things. It became the "Gateway to the West" for settlers, and it had breweries—a lot of breweries. By 1870 there were over fifty breweries employing thousands of St. Louis residents and making vast fortunes for their owners. Mansions sprung up across the city to house generations of these brewing dynasties as beer and money flowed freely.

The earliest record of local beer production is from 1809, and the brews first made were all dark English-style beers. In 1840, it would be a German immigrant, John Adam Lemp, who would brew the country's first lager beer and set St. Louis on the path to this highly lucrative industry.

Kings of industry need suitable castles, so in the 1860s John's son, William, purchased a house on DeMenil Place and transformed it into a magnificent thirty-three-room Victorian mansion. The Lemp Mansion also boasted a very unique feature—a passageway to underground caves, whose cool constant temperatures were ideal for brewing. But all work and no play makes a cave a very dull place, so the Lemps had a portion of these caves converted into a theater and heated swimming pool!

Just as royal families look to marry with other royalty, William's daughter, Hilda, married Gustav Pabst, of Milwaukee brewing fame. Other family members worked hard at expanding the business, and life should have been good for the Lemps. Unfortunately, William's son, Frederick, may have worked too hard. Frederick was a talented young man poised to take over the family business, but died of heart failure and complications from other illnesses in 1901. From that point, tragedy relentlessly dealt the family fatal blows.

William Lemp never recovered from his son's death. On February 13, 1904, he ate breakfast as usual, and then went back to his bedroom and shot himself in the head. In 1906, Mrs. Lemp died of cancer. In 1920, William's daughter, Elsa, also committed suicide by shooting herself. When news of his sister's suicide reached William, Jr., he had an odd reaction, simply stating, "That's the Lemp family for you." His words were rather prophetic as it turned out, as the house claimed another victim when William, Jr. shot himself in the heart in December of 1922.

As remarkable as it seems, there was still one more suicide to be committed in the Lemp Mansion. William's brother, Charles, apparently grew into an eccentric recluse who was deathly afraid of germs so he always wore gloves. He should have been more afraid of revolvers, as in May of 1949 he shot himself to death in bed.

Only brother Edwin appears to have escaped a tragic fate, as he lived until the ripe old age of 90, finally passing away in 1970. With all of the Lemps now gone, the mansion became a boarding house, but it was difficult to keep tenants as they complained of ghostly activity. By 1975, the neglected building was in serious need of renovation. It was at this point that the property was purchased by the Pointer family who returned the mansion to its former glory and turned it into an inn and restaurant.

It was during these renovations that it became clear that the place was most definitely haunted. In fact, some workers were so frightened they actually left and refused to return. Over the years, the inn and restaurant staff has experienced countless odd occurrences, and guests have also had their share of ghostly encounters. The following are just a few examples:

Staff and guests have seen solid figures they assumed were real people, until they vanished into thin air.

Objects move and are thrown by unseen forces.

There are many voices, footsteps, music, and other sounds where no one is visible.

Locked doors suddenly swing open, while unlocked doors refuse to open.

There are sudden cold spots, people feel as though they are being watched, and strange anomalies appear on photographs.

Activity can occur at any time of the day in any room in the mansion, and while it is never threatening, it can certainly be unnerving when the person you are about to speak to dissolves into nothingness, or something starts pounding on your bedroom wall in the middle of the night.

The Lemp Mansion represents the triumphs and tragedies of an American family. From a humble immigrant grocer turned millionaire brewer, to troubled souls who ended their own lives, it's a sad tale that reinforces the old adage that money can't buy happiness. To many Americans, unlimited amounts of money and beer would be heaven on earth, but to the Lemps, it may just have been a path to their own private hell that endures to this day.

## The Bottom Line

**The History:** German immigrant John Adam Lemp brewed America's first lager beer in St. Louis in 1840, and then proceeded to build a brewing empire. His son, William, bought the mansion and transformed it to a Victorian gem. Unfortunately, the family was devastated by four suicides. The Lemp Mansion has been an inn and restaurant since the 1970s.

**The Haunting:** In 1980, the Lemp Mansion was named one of "America's Ten Most Haunted Places," and today there's every reason to keep it on that list. Staff and guests see figures of men and women who vanish, hear all manner of sounds and voices, and witness objects moving on their own. The suicides have clearly created many paranormal disturbances.

## Recommendations

**For the ultimate experience, you should spend the night. If you are brave enough, you can even choose one of the suicide bedrooms. If you aren't quite that brave but still have some courage, you can join a ghost hunt and search for the Lemp's spirits. For those who are curious, but are bordering on being big chickens, you can at least stop by for lunch or dinner.**

## Visitor Information

**Lemp Mansion**
**3322 DeMenil Place**
**St. Louis, MO 63118**
**(314) 664-8024**
**www.lempmansion.com/**

**Events:**
**Tours of the mansion are available. Haunted tours are conducted every Monday night. Special events include Murder Mystery dinners and a Halloween party. Catered events and weddings are also welcome. Ghost hunts are conducted on a regular basis by Supernatural Investigations. For the latest schedule and fees of the Lemp Mansion Experience, go to: http://supernaturalinvestigations.com/lempmansion1.html**

**Hours:**
**Call or visit the website for reservations for the inn. The restaurant is open on the following schedule: Lunch: Monday-Friday, 11am – 2:30pm; Dinner: January through August, Thursday-Saturday 5:30pm – 10pm; September through December: Tuesday-Saturday 5:30pm – 11pm; Sundays: Family Style Chicken Dinner 11:30am – 6pm.**

**Directions:**
**From the north: From I-55 S take exit 206C for Arsenal Street. Turn left at Lemp Avenue. Turn right at DeMenil Place.**

**From the south: From I-55N take exit 206B toward 3200 S/Broadway. Turn left at Utah Street. Turn left at DeMenil Place.**

# Jefferson Barracks

In 1826, a new military post was needed to replace Fort Bellefontaine, which had been established in 1805 as the first U.S. military post in the recently acquired Louisiana Territory. Several army officers scouted locations along the Mississippi River and a suitable site was agreed upon ten miles south of St. Louis. On July 10, 1826, 6 officers and 245 enlisted men arrived at what would become one of the most important military posts during America's inexorable push westward.

The post was initially named Cantonment Miller, in honor of the governor, but was changed the following year to honor Thomas Jefferson, who had died in 1826. Over the years, a veritable Who's Who of army notables were stationed here, including Stephan Kearny, Zachary Taylor, Jefferson Davis, Robert E. Lee, Ulysses S. Grant, William T. Sherman, and Phil Sheridan. The post became the first "Infantry School of Practice," as well as the site of the first permanent U.S. Army unit of cavalry.

Jefferson Barracks' soldiers would first be tested in the Black Hawk War in 1832, but they would also serve rolls in Mexican War, Civil War, Spanish-American War, Philippine War, World War I, and World War II. During the Civil War, the post had a hospital for both Union and Confederate soldiers, and by war's end, over 18,000 men had been treated there, and those who did not survive are buried in the Jefferson Barracks National Cemetery. In 1912, the first successful parachute jump took place here. During World War II, the post became the site of the first Army Air Corps training base. After 120 years of service, the post was decommissioned in 1946.

Some of the old post housing gave way to a townhouse development, and today Jefferson Barracks is the site of two county parks, an Air National Guard base and a veteran's hospital. Some of the original buildings are also used as museums and a visitor center, and some of the original soldiers have not yet left their posts...

Not surprisingly, many ghosts stories were connected with one of the hospital buildings. Many years ago during a Halloween party, several security guards at the gate admired the authentic-looking Civil War uniform one of the guests was wearing. Later, when one of the guards mentioned this man to one of the organizers of the party, he discovered that none of the guests wore such a costume. However, at least one guest did encounter this mysterious Union officer, who spoke a few words with difficulty, then vanished!

As far back as the Civil War, there have been reports of misty figures of men walking around the post, phantom footsteps, lights going on and off, and all manner of inexplicable activity.

The Powder magazine in 1957 before restoration. *Courtesy of The Library of Congress.*

Another story involves the powder magazine, built in 1857, which is now a museum. During WWII, several guards on duty encountered another guard who seemed determined to keep everyone away from the magazine. The only problem was that this particular guard had a bloody bullet hole in his head, and had been killed long ago in a raid. Rather than admiring the ghostly soldier for his continued diligence, most of the witnesses dropped their guns and ran!

When one considers the tragedies and intense emotions that were experienced here, how many people lived and died on the old post grounds, and how many thousands of bodies fill the cemetery, it only seems natural that boundaries between the living and the dead occasionally get a bit blurry. There is a saying that old soldiers never die, they just fade away, but all of the unusual activity at Jefferson Barracks proves that they never fade completely away...

## The Bottom Line

**The History:** A military post established in 1826 which saw involvement in every war through WWII. The site of a Civil War hospital and a National Cemetery.

**The Haunting:** Civil War soldiers, a guard with a head wound, misty figures, many inexplicable sights and sounds.

Need a ride? *Courtesy of the Parlor Bed & Breakfast.*

# The Parlor B&B

Jeanette Schrum was raised to not believe in ghosts. When her grandmother was young, she went outside one night and was terrified when she suddenly "felt arms and legs all over" her. The next morning she discovered that she had, in fact, encountered the long johns drying on the clothesline. As a result, she would always tell her granddaughters, "If you are going to be afraid of something, just make sure it isn't a pair of underwear!"

So when Jeanette bought this house in Ironton eleven years ago and heard that the place was haunted, she didn't believe a word—until things started to happen, which was almost immediately. Nothing was ever threatening, but there were "many shadows moving around the house." Objects would go missing, any type of battery went dead very quickly, and even though she set all the clocks on Sunday, by mid-week they all had different times.

## Recommendations

**Start with the visitor center and museums. While most of the ghost stories are connected with the original buildings, allow plenty of time to explore the grounds as activity can occur anywhere at any time. The park hosts special events, guided tours, and educational programs, so call or check the website for the latest schedule.**

## Visitor Information

**Jefferson Barracks**
**251 Cy Road (end of S. Broadway)**
**Lemay, MO 63125-4262**
**(314) 544-5714**
**www.co.st-louis.mo.us/parks/j-b.html**

**Hours:**
8am to one half hour past sunset, except when reservations are issued. Museum buildings are open from noon to 4pm Wednesday through Sunday.

**Admission:**
Free. Admission fees may apply for special events.

**Directions:**
From Illinois I-255/50, after crossing the river take the second exit, the Telegraph Road exit and go north to Kingston, turn right to South Broadway, to Cy Road.

From St. Louis Take I-55 S to exit 204 for Broadway. Turn left at South Broadway/MO-231 S. Turn left at South Broadway. Continue onto Grant Road. Turn right at Cy Road.

"Whatever is here is very mischievous, but certainly means no harm," Jeanette emphasizes about the spirits she didn't believe existed.

What is behind all of this activity? The house was built between 1901-1907 by an architect, Charles Tual, for his wife. There are no records of tragedies occurring in the house, although it was briefly used as a funeral parlor in 1961. While only four or five bodies were laid out here, one of them happened to be Jeanette's great-grandfather! Stories of the ghosts actually go back at least as far as the 1920s, so could something have possibly occurred on this land before the house was built?

The Battle of Pilot Knob during the Civil War took place here, as is evidenced by the cannonball holes in the courthouse a block away, and the grapeshot Jeanette found in her rose garden. There were over a thousand Confederate and 184 Union casualties during the battle, so could they account for the "many shadows" in the house?

A 13-year-old girl who lived in the house said that every night a man stood over her bed. Rather than be afraid of this man, she felt as though he was there to protect her. Could he have been a soldier who died there, a family man who misses his own daughter? Jeanette encounters a similar feeling from a female spirit in the dining room. Whenever this woman is around, Jeanette gets a "warm and wonderful feeling." She thought, perhaps, that this might be her beloved grandmother. If so, wouldn't that be an ironic twist—the woman who adamantly refused to believe in ghosts, has become one!

Another common occurrence is the doorbell ringing when no one is there. Even after the old doorbell was removed and a brand new one was installed, it would continue to ring at all hours. Even after a third system was installed it kept ringing. Not even removing the button stopped this doorbell!

Jeanette's husband often sees a woman dressed in old-fashioned clothing with her hair up in a bun. People passing by have seen a child peering out a window. Then there are all those persistent shadows.

There really isn't anything to be afraid of at the Parlor B&B. Whether or not there are soldiers, children, and women's spirits here, they are existing in peace and harmony. Jeanette is comfortable with all of her guests, and she is quite glad that she never sold the place as everyone had urged her to do. People don't always choose buildings, sometimes buildings choose them, and Jeanette is just the right person to welcome all souls to the Parlor Bed and Breakfast.



## Recommendations

**For a romantic experience you can take a champagne carriage ride from the front doorstep, or a not-so-romantic ride in their 1974 Cadillac hearse. Fort Davidson State Historic Site is nearby, where you can see where the main action took place during the Civil War battle. Bring your cameras and recorders, as you never know what you might capture in the house. See if you feel the friendly female presence in the dining room, and watch for all those shadows!**

## Visitor Information

**The Parlor Bed and Breakfast**
**203 South Knob Street**
**Ironton, MO 63650-1503**
**(573) 546-2670**
**(866) 550-6142**
**www.theparlorB&B.com**

**Directions:**
**From I-55S in St. Louis: Take exit 174B to merge onto US-67 S toward Bonne Terre/Farmington. Take the State Highway W ramp to Doe Run/ Farmington/MO-221. Turn right at West Columbia Street/MO-221 S. Continue to follow MO-221 S. Turn left to stay on MO-221 S. Turn left at MO-21 S. Turn right at E. Russell Street. Take the 1st right onto S. Knob Street. The Parlor B&B will be on the right.**

## The Bottom Line

**The History:** A home built between 1901-1907, on land where a Civil War battle was fought.

**The Haunting:** Many shadows, a friendly woman, a child, and all sorts of electrical anomalies.

# Montana



OLD MONTANA PRISON MUSEUM

GARNET GHOST TOWN

CHICO HOT SPRINGS RESORT

The Old Montana Prison.

# Old Montana Prison Museum

MT

There's an old saying about inmates running the asylum, and in the mid-twentieth century, one inmate ran the Montana Prison in Deer Lodge—or at least he thought he did. Paul "Turkey Pete" Eitner was a likable man who earned his nickname tending to the flock of turkeys raised in the prison. As he grew older, Turkey Pete's mental faculties began to fail, and the guards and fellow inmates humored him in his various "business" activities. For example, he "sold" the turkeys to another prisoner, and then decided he wanted to "buy" the prison and run it himself. Special "checks" were printed so Pete could "pay" the guards and take care of all the expenses.

Pete's other businesses supposedly included a coffee crop in Brazil, as well as selling pink alligators, ships to the navy, and—you're going to love this—selling grasshopper legs to Fidel Castro!? When Turkey Pete passed away in 1967 at the age 89, his funeral became the first that was ever paid for by the prison. Also, Cell #1, where Pete spent the last forty-nine years of his life, was officially retired from use as a cell and converted into a barbershop.

Of course, not all of the inmates were so lovable. In the nineteenth century, Montana was a rough and dangerous place, especially after the discovery of gold in 1862 drew hordes of prospectors, as well as ruthless outlaws to prey upon them. Vigilante justice was the prevailing law of the land, but more civilized men soon realized that a proper prison was needed.

The Montana Territorial Prison began operations in July of 1871, and it was the prisoners themselves, who would make over a million bricks for the various structures they would build. One of the more notorious criminals that was to be incarcerated here was at least one member of Butch Cassidy's "Wild Bunch," as well as countless thieves and murderers—some of whom met their fate on the prison gallows.

In addition to some bloody escape attempts, overcrowding and poor conditions led to violent riots, including one in 1959 that required the National Guard to be called in to restore order. However, it wasn't until 1979 that the outdated prison was closed, but that doesn't mean all the inmates left...

The buildings were turned into museums by the Powell County Museum and Arts Foundation, and include a classic car museum, Desert John's Saloon, a doll and toy museum, and the Old Montana Prison Museum where visitors can see what it was like to do hard time. Self-guided and guided tours take you to Turkey Pete's cell, where many claim Pete still resides. Then there is the menacing presence in "the Hole," where prisoners were held in solitary confinement. Staff and visitors have heard heavy footsteps, heard both male and female voices (women were also incarcerated here), experienced unnerving chills and felt a strong presence, and have taken many inexplicable photographs. In short, the over 20,000 violent men and women who lived and died here have left quite an impression on the old prison!

## The Bottom Line

**The History:** A prison built by the inmates in 1871, closed in 1979 and converted into a museum complex. The scene of executions, riots, and bloody escape attempts.

**The Haunting:** Footsteps, voices, a menacing presence, and Turkey Pete has not yet left his cell.

## Recommendations

There are many original artifacts on display such as shackles and weapons the prisoners fashioned out of anything they could get their hands on. Look for the concrete shoes weighing twenty pounds that prisoners who were a threat for trying to escape were forced to wear. Look for the mustache forms—permission forms that inmates had to fill out in order to grow a mustache! There is one section of the brick wall where prisoners scratched dates and their names. And of course, don't forget to say hi to Turkey Pete in Cell#1.

## Visitor Information

**Old Prison Museum**
1106 Main Street
Deer Lodge, MT 59722
(406) 846-3111
www.pcmaf.org/prison.htm

**Hours:**

Open early March through mid-December. In the spring and fall the hours are 10am – 4pm, Wednesday-Sunday. During the summer the hours are 9am – 6pm. It's best to call for the latest seasonal schedule.

**Admission:**

Spring and fall admission is $8 adults. Children 10-15 $4, under 10 free, and includes both the Old Prison and Car Museum. During the summer the admission is $1 more but includes all 5 museums. Seniors, military, and AAA receive a $1 discount.

Guided tours are available during the summer months only. Self-guided tours are available year round.

**Directions:**

From Butte: Take I-90 West to exit 187 for I-90 toward Deer Lodge. Merge onto I-90 BUS W, and the museum will be on the right.

An 1890s view of Garnet.

# Garnet Ghost Town

MT

Any place that has the word "ghost" in the name should probably be considered haunted, although the term can simply apply to any abandoned town. However, Garnet isn't just any abandoned town, as it has a wealth of spirits still roaming its streets and buildings.

Garnet began as a mining town in the late 1800s, and by 1898 the town had a population of over 1,000 men, women, and children. While there was still plenty of gambling, drinking (in their thirteen saloons), and prostitution, there were also miners with families, the kids went to school, and many people found employment in the four hotels, four stores, two barbershops, butcher shop, doctor's office, and laundry. Unfortunately, after mining 60,000 ounces of gold, 50,000 ounces of silver, and 60,000 ounces of copper (and some garnets, of course), the rich veins were played out.

By 1905, the boom had gone bust, and only about 150 people remained in Garnet. Then the town was hit by a devastating fire in 1912 and many of the commercial buildings that had been destroyed were not rebuilt. During WWI, the last remaining residents left town to seek other jobs, and a ghost town was born.

One last spark of hope occurred in 1934, when the price of gold doubled from $16 to $32 an ounce. The abandoned buildings and mines once again sprang to life, but the call for manpower during WWII ended that brief resurgence. The town was stripped of anything that could be carried away, and Garnet looked like a place that was doomed to crumble into dust and be forgotten.

However, realizing that treasure comes in more forms than gems and precious metals, efforts began in 1970 to try to preserve this piece of American history. With the help of the Bureau of Land Management and the Garnet Preservation Association, the buildings in this ghost town are being stabilized and preserved. Today, Garnet is not a commercialized representation of an old Montana mining town, it *is* an old Montana mining town—or at least a skeleton of the town—just as it was when gold and good times were plentiful.

Garnet presents fans of historic haunts with a very unique opportunity to experience an isolated ghost town in every sense of the word, as spirits have been seen and heard throughout the thirty remaining original buildings. For example, many people have heard music and laughter in Kelly's Saloon, but the sounds abruptly stop when they reach the door. Even in the middle of winter when no one else is around, the lone caretaker has reported sounds of the old days in the saloon.

The J.K. Wells Hotel is another center of paranormal activity. Many people claim that the second floor is particularly intense, thanks in part to one male spirit who isn't very friendly. There are many footsteps echoing throughout the hotel, as well as the sounds of doors slamming, even in sections that no longer have doors!

If you are serious about your pursuit of paranormal activity and are tired of crowded tourist towns with mobs of would-be ghost hunters, Garnet is the place for you. Think of it this way—at any given time, there are far more ghosts than people here!

## The Bottom Line

**The History:** A mining town from the late 1800s that was abandoned and became a true ghost town.

**The Haunting:** The name says it all; this is a ghost town!

# Chico Hot Springs Resort

Long before tourists discovered the hot springs, Native Americans were enjoying their many benefits. When miners first came to the area, they saw the springs as a rare opportunity to wash their clothes, and themselves. In 1876, one clever farmer channeled the hot water into his greenhouse. However, for people to get the most out of the springs, a hotel was needed, but after many years of ideas and plans, it wasn't until 1900 that Percie and Bill Knowles finally built a hotel.

Soon many notables such as Teddy Roosevelt and artist Charlie Russell were arriving at the Emigrant train station to await transportation to this luxurious new hot springs hotel. Much to Percie's dismay, her husband, Bill, added a bar that brought in even more tourists. Bill died in 1910, from drinking too much, and Percie was finally able to create the health resort she had been wanting. Hiring Dr. George Townsend in 1912, the hotel became a famous hospital renowned for its healing waters.

After Dr. Townsend retired in 1925, business declined. Percie grew ill in the late 1930s, and spent most of the last four years of her life in a hospital. After her son died in 1943, a series of owners tried all different types of resorts, offering everything from gambling to a dude ranch. It wasn't until 1974 that owners Mike and Eve Art decided to restore the place back to its original style and purpose—a place where people could enjoy the beautiful scenery, the good food, and of course, soak in the warm, healing waters.

## Recommendations

For the ultimate ghost town experience, you can rent one of two old miner's cabins, both of which are haunted. As creepy as this place may be during the day, imagine spending the night! If you are very adventurous, you can ski, snowshoe, or snowmobile to Garnet during the winter. The town comes to life one day every summer on Garnet Interpretive Day, with costumed "residents," musicians, craftsmen, food, gold panning, and many other activities.

## Visitor Information

**Garnet Preservation Association**
3255 Fort Missoula Road
Missoula, MT 59804
(406) 329-3883
www.garnetghosttown.net

**Hours:**

Garnet is open year-round. Wheeled vehicles are allowed on the road from May 1 through January 1. Please note that visitors may want to park in the designated parking lots and ski or snowmobile to the town instead of driving on snow-bound roads in late fall. In winter, the tour to Garnet is a popular snowmobile and cross-country ski trip.

Visitor Center Open Summer: daily from 10am – 5pm. Winter: weekends from 11am – 3pm. Rangers lead guided tours from late-May through September, seven days a week from 10am – 4pm.

**Admission:**

$3 a person over 12 years of age. Entrance fees to help protect, preserve, and interpret Garnet Ghost Town.

**Directions:**

From their website—From Montana Route 200: Turn south at the Garnet Range Road located between mile markers 22 and 23, about 30 miles east of Missoula. Follow the Range Road approximately 12 miles to Garnet where the parking area is located.

From Interstate 90: Take either Drummond or Bearmouth exit. Then follow the North side frontage road to Bear Gulch Road which is located 10 miles west of Drummond or 5 miles east of Bearmouth. Approximately 7.5 miles up Bear Gulch Road is the Cave Gulch Road Junction. From here, Garnet and the parking lot are 3 miles up Bear Gulch or 4 miles up Cave Gulch.

One might initially think that all the ensuing paranormal activity was the result of something being stirred up during the renovations, but reports of ghostly activity have been around at least since the early 1960s. The most active spirit by far is that of Percie Knowles, who has been seen as a white, misty figure floating several inches above the floor, as well as manifesting as a clear, solid-looking old woman with her hair up in a bun, wearing a long dress.

It's usually the night watchmen who encounter this stern-looking female apparition, who silently glides through hallways and locked doors. One guard followed Percie to the third floor, where all the rooms were vacant that night, or so he thought. He smelled a sweet floral perfume by room 349 and unlocked the door and opened it. No one was inside, yet the rocking chair was moving back and forth. The very shaken guard later discovered that 349 was Percie's room, where she spent her very last days at the resort in that rocking chair!

As creepy as Percie can appear, she literally pales in comparison to the tall man who floats through the rooms in the staff's quarters. Dressed in old-fashioned clothing and preferring to hover near the ceiling, he has terrified many employees—even driving one poor man to throw himself out of bed and crawl from his room in the middle of the night to avoid the apparition that was approaching him.

The kitchen is also the scene of a lot of activity, with plates, pots, and pans banging together in the middle of the night. Staff has often found plates and silverware scattered about the kitchen, long after everyone else had gone. There are also many accounts of cold spots, and inexplicable sights and sounds.

Perhaps Percie, who suffered from senility in the end, does not yet know she is dead and believes she is still running the health resort that she poured her heart and soul into for so many years. And does Bill still haunt the place with regret, finally looking to replace his liquor with the healing waters? And what of the hospital's patients, and all the guests and staff over the years? Do they, too, return to his place to search for the peace they have yet to find in death? There is so much to explore, with both the natural and supernatural, at this resort—just remember if your nerves do become rattled by a floating apparition, you can soothe them in the hot springs' pools.



## Recommendations

**Most of the activity takes place in the Main Lodge in the dead of winter during the dead of night, but activity can occur anywhere at anytime. Staying in room 349 might offer the best chance to meet Percie. But don't let all the ghosts keep you from enjoying all this resort and valley have to offer, from fine dining, to hiking, horseback riding, and dog sledding. After a long day at Yellowstone Park, a warm soak in the hot springs pools is just the ticket. Much of the movies *A River Runs Through It* and *The Horse Whisperer* were filmed nearby in the town of Emigrant. Actor Peter Fonda and writer Christopher Paolini live in the area.**

## Visitor Information

**Chico Hot Springs Resort and Day Spa**
**1 Old Chico Road**
**Pray, MT 59065**
**406-333-4933 in Montana**
**(800) 468-9232 outside Montana**
**www.chicohotsprings.com**

**Directions:**

**From their website—From the Gallatin Field Airport in Bozeman, Montana (Approximate total travel distance – 62 miles): After leaving the airport, turn left onto the Frontage road toward Bozeman, accessing I-90 East at the 19th Street exit, approximately 6 miles. Take I-90 East for 31 miles to the second Livingston, Montana exit, 333 (Yellowstone National Park exit). Turn left at the light at the end of the off ramp. You are now on highway 89 traveling South. Travel 23 miles on highway 89 to the flashing yellow light located at Emigrant, Montana; turn left and travel 1.2 miles to the stop sign and turn left. Travel .5 miles and turn right onto the Chico road. Chico Hot Springs is located 1.6 miles at the end of the paved road.**

**From Billings, Montana (Approximate total travel distance: 140 miles): Take I-90 West for approximately 115 miles to Livingston, Montana exit 333 (Yellowstone National Park exit), then follow Directions: above.**

**From the North Entrance of Yellowstone National Park, Gardiner, Montana (Approximate total travel distance: 34 miles) Travel highway 89 North approximately 31 miles to the yellow flashing light at Emigrant, Montana. Turn right, then follow Directions: above.**

## The Bottom Line

**The History:** A resort built in 1900 that became a hospital famous for its hot springs.

**The Haunting:** The original owner, Percie, floats around the main lodge, as does the figure of a man.

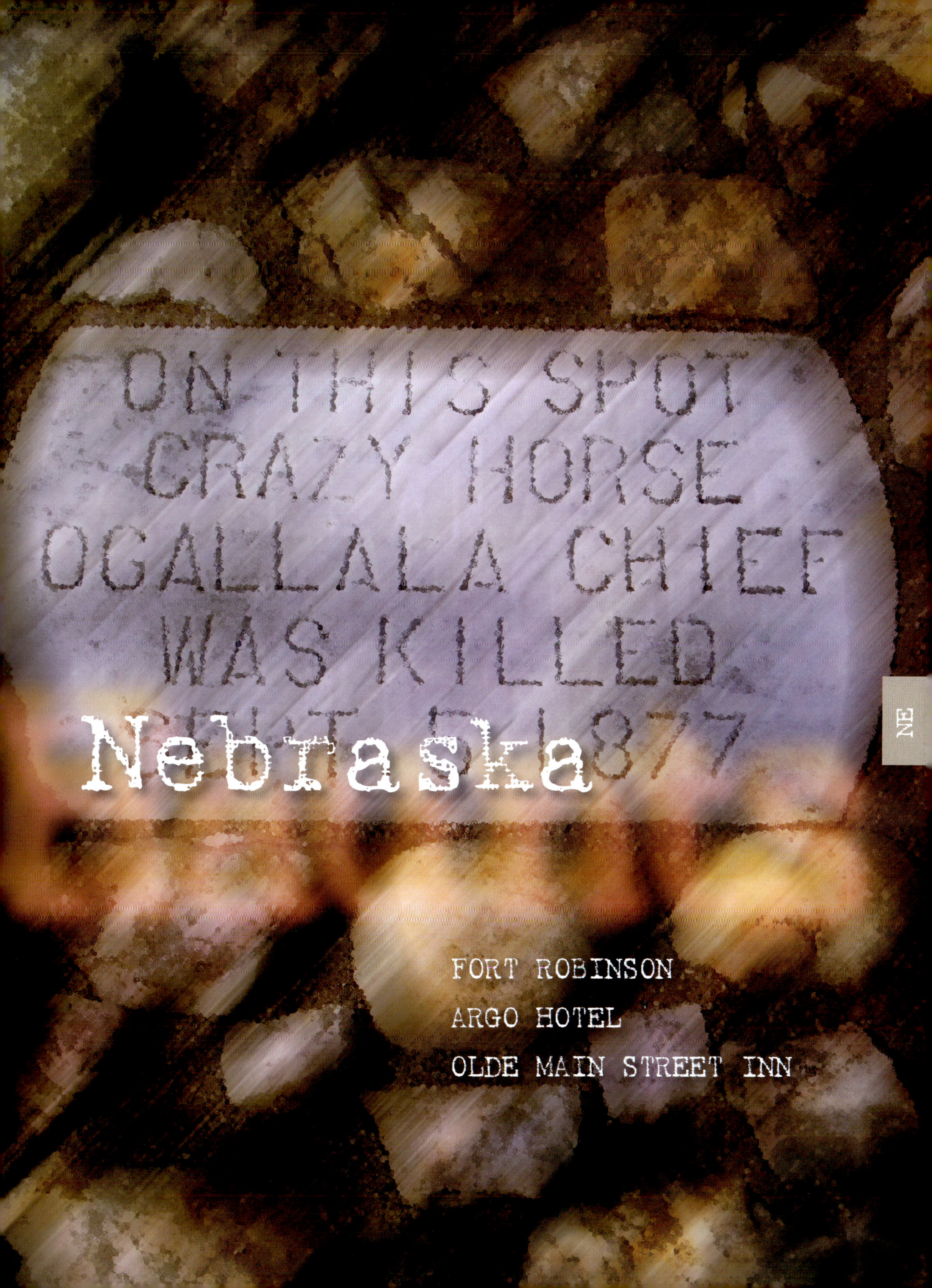




# Nebraska

FORT ROBINSON

ARGO HOTEL

OLDE MAIN STREET INN

Monument that marks the spot where Crazy Horse was killed.

# Fort Robinson

NE

The 22,000 acres of Fort Robinson State Park are now a place for families to enjoy horseback riding, swimming, and all sorts of leisure activities. However, in 1873 this land was not such a happy place as it became the location for the Red Cloud Agency, where 13,000 Lakota Indians were sent to live. Understandably, the Lakota were angered by their treatment, and an army camp was quickly established on the site in March of 1874 to try to avert hostilities.

First called Camp Robinson, it was named for Lt. Levi H. Robinson, who had been killed by Indians while he was gathering firewood just a month earlier. The camp would play a pivotal role in the Sioux Wars and it was here that the famous Crazy Horse surrendered in May of 1877. In September, Crazy Horse was fatally wounded by a guard, and a monument now marks the site of his death.

In the ensuing years, Fort Robinson was expanded and played important military roles well into the twentieth century. The U.S. 9th Cavalry regiment—known as the Buffalo Soldiers—was posted here in 1885. In World War I, the fort became a center for breeding and training horses and mules. In World War II, K-9 dogs were trained here, and German prisoners were held in the fort from 1943-1946.

From Indians, to soldiers, to horses, dogs, and German POWs, the next stage in the fort's history was beef, when the army turned over the facility to the Department of Agriculture for cattle research from 1948-1971. However, during that time part of the land also became the state park and the Fort Robinson Museum was established in the 1905 post headquarters building and opened to the public.

Several of the fort's buildings are still standing, and visitors can see the officer's quarters and guardhouse, as well as the old cemetery. Visitors have also seen many authentic-looking army soldiers and Indians, and the reason they look so authentic is because they are—they are the shades and spirits of the past who appear very real and very solid, until they disappear, that is.

Such appearances of the ghosts of the people who lived and died here can occur at any time of the day. Visitors often think they are seeing reenactors, until they find that no one else can see that Indian warrior or army private, or they fade from sight. Given the long history of struggle and turmoil here, it isn't surprising that so many spirits still walk the grounds and buildings here, possibly right next to you…

## The Bottom Line

**The History:** Site of the Red Cloud Agency, Crazy Horse's death, and an Army fort that operated from 1874 through WWII.

**The Haunting:** Very realistic ghosts of soldiers and Indians are seen throughout the park and buildings.

*Courtesy of the Argo Hotel.*

# Argo Hotel

The town of Crofton was planned in 1892, and its name was chosen by pulling a name out of a hat. Crofton had been written on a piece of paper in honor of one of the resident's home town, The Crofton Courts in England.

This small Nebraska town would have other English connections, as with the Englishman, J.T.M. Pierce, who started a railroad that brought in workers, and the English financier who backed the project. Unfortunately, Mr. Pierce was a fraud and he took off leaving behind all his debts and the unfinished railroad. With work no longer available, many people left Crofton and dismantled and carted away their buildings with them. The town's future looked bleak.

When the railroad finally was built in 1906, the town prospered. By 1910 there was a variety of over forty businesses in town, but there wasn't a decent hotel. Nick Michaelis decided to make the town an offer—if they supplied the water and sewer lines, he would build a hotel, and even put in electric lights! It was an offer Crofton couldn't refuse.

Michaelis named his new hotel The Argo, after the ship that had brought his ancestors to America. The hotel

## Recommendations

The best way to familiarize yourself with the park and its history is to take the informative horse-drawn wagon tour. For an overnight experience in the park, there is a campground, or you can actually stay in the 1909 enlisted men's quarters or the officer's quarters that date between 1874 to 1909. Look for the plaque and stones marking the site of Crazy Horse's death. There is so much to see and do here, including beautiful scenery, the military museum, a playhouse, rodeos, kayaking, biking, an indoor swimming pool, herds of buffalo and longhorns, and mammoth bones and other fossils at the Trailside Museum of Natural History. If you are bored here, it's your own fault! Remember, if you see an authentic-looking soldier or Indian, keep your eye on him!

## Visitor Information

**Fort Robinson State Park**
3200 U.S. Highway 20
Crawford, NE 69339-3112
(308) 665-2900
www.ngpc.state.ne.us/parks/guides/parksearch/showpark.asp?Area_No=77

**Hours:**

Park activities run from Memorial Day to Labor Day. Museum: Memorial Day-Labor Day: 8am – 5pm Monday-Saturday, 9am – 5pm Sunday. Open Memorial Day, 4th of July and Labor Day. September-May: 10am – 5pm Monday-Friday, Closed weekends. Closed all state holidays in the off season.

**Admission:**

All Nebraska state parks are $4 per day per vehicle, or $20 for the year. Museum: $2 for adults. Children with adults free. Admission fees are waived for NSHS members. Call or check the website for lodging and camping rates.

Fort Robinson Restaurant serves breakfast, lunch, and dinner daily during the summer season. Snacks are available at the Sutler's Store in the Activities Center.

**Directions:**

The park is located 3 miles west of Crawford on Highway 20.

did very well as visitors and traveling salesmen were brought by wagon from the train station every morning and evening. The hotel changed hands and in 1923 the new owners, the Hoigs, renamed it The New Meridian Hotel after Highway 81—also called The New Meridian Highway—which ran through town.

In 1932, the Hoig's granddaughter, Lorraine Gettman, came to live with them for a couple of years. She moved to Hollywood in 1937 and became a classic girl-from-small-town-America success story. After winning a beauty contest, Lorraine signed a contract with MGM, and then Warner Brothers and Columbia (where she changed her name to Leslie Brooks), and appeared in about two dozen films.

In 1935, the hotel was sold to a German couple who turned the hotel into a clinic, calling it the New Meridian Sanatorium. The sanatorium operated for twenty-seven years, and at its height had forty-two employees. In 1962, the building became the home/office of a local doctor, Charles Swift, who lived there until 1992. The house was vacant until 1994 when the current owner, Sandra McDonald, and her brother purchased the property with the intent to restore the old hotel back to its former grandeur.

However, the renovations ended up being more extensive than originally planned—then again, aren't they always!—but their hard work paid off. On December 31, 1994, the Argo Hotel rang in the New Year in a grand style. Five years later, the hotel was accepted onto the National Historic Registry, and continues to welcome diners and overnight guests who want to experience the hospitality of 100 years ago.

Guests might also experience one of their resident ghosts. There is a baby who has been heard crying, and rumor has it that many years ago during some renovations, the skeleton of a tiny child was found in a burlap bag in a wall. Witnesses have also seen and heard a woman who appears to be crying out for her child, so it is likely these two ghosts are related. Did a mother and child die of natural causes here when it was a clinic or doctor's office? If so, why was the child's body hidden in the wall? Is there some darker secret surrounding these two spirits?

Objects have been seen moving on their own, icy cold spots can suddenly engulf you, and glasses have shattered. Others have felt as if they were being touched. Even though all the electrical lines were replaced, the lights continue to mysteriously flicker. Are these signs that many other spirits roam the halls of this old hotel and sanatorium? Perhaps you will be able to unlock the paranormal secrets of The Argo Hotel...



## Recommendations

**This beautiful historic, haunted hotel fittingly has 13 guest rooms. If you are adventurous, the hotel has a special package that includes a hot air balloon ride. While nothing here is threatening, if you are too timid for an overnight stay you can enjoy a fine dinner (there's even a romantic private dining room for two) or drinks and dancing in the Speakeasy Lounge. Look for the name Argo imprinted in the original bricks on the upper east side of the hotel.**

## Visitor Information

**The Argo Hotel**
**211 West Kansas Street**
**Crofton, NE 68730-4138**
**(402) 388-2400**
**www.theargohotel.com**

**Hours:**
**Dining room, lounge, and bar hours vary by season, so please call or check the website for the latest days and times.**

**Directions:**
**From their website—Located 4 miles west of U.S. Highway 81. Nebraska Highways 12 and 121 meet on the west edge of town. Crofton is located 14 miles Southwest of Yankton, South Dakota, and is reachable from the north, south, east or west by these highways.**

## The Bottom Line

**The History:** A hotel built in 1912, which also served as a sanatorium and doctor's office for many years. Restored and reopened as a hotel and restaurant in 1994.

**The Haunting:** A mother searches for her child, and a crying baby can be heard.

# Olde Main Street Inn

The first building on this site was destroyed in a fire. In 1890, the Hotel Chadron was built here by Peter and Margaret O'Hanlon. That same year they had a very important guest—General Nelson Miles, who stayed at the inn while he investigated the massacre at Wounded Knee.

In 1901, the inn was owned by the YMCA, but in 1931 it reverted back to a hotel. In 1951, new owners changed the name to the Hub Hotel. In 1969, Eva Gore bought the old place and gave it to her daughter, Jeanne Goetzinger, who renovated the building and renamed it, yet again, the Olde Main Street Inn.

It wasn't long before Jeanne realized the place was haunted, and by a rather mischievous man who liked to move objects, open and close doors, and play games with the staff and guests. His footsteps are often heard, and he does seem to be particularly partial to anyone who's Irish! The man is not alone, either, as a woman in a red satin dress has appeared, most often in the first-floor hallway near the rest rooms.

For years the identities of these two spirits was a mystery. Then one day the son of a former owner came to visit, and told Jeanne that his uncle, Jack, had been a real prankster. Jack had a sister, Anna, and her description fit that of the woman in the red dress. From that day, Jeanne and the staff have referred to their "guests" as Jack and Anna, and it doesn't appear as if either of them has plans to check out.

Today, the Olde Main Street Inn welcomes both ghosts and ghost hunters, as well as offers the opportunity to experience an historic hotel. Perhaps Jack and Anna are alone here, or perhaps they have company, maybe from the building that burned down on this site, or from the many people who stayed here in its more than a century of operation. Of course, there are no guarantees that anything paranormal will happen during your stay, but if you have an open mind—and you happen to be Irish—you never know what might happen at the Olde Main Street Inn.

## Recommendations

**General Miles Suite is room 204. The dining room also serves dinner, and you can have spirits of another kind in their Longbranch Saloon. Jeanne is open to paranormal investigations, so give her a call. Chadron is only about 25 miles from the haunted Fort Robinson in Crawford, so include it in your plans.**

## Visitor Information

**Olde Main Street Inn**
**115 Main Street**
**Chadron, NE 69337-2353**
**(308) 432-3380**
**www.chadron.com/oldemain/**

**Directions:**
**From Highway 20 in Chadron, turn north onto Main Street. Go 0.2 miles, the inn is on the left.**

## The Bottom Line

**The History:** A hotel built in 1890 where the general investigating the massacre at Wounded Knee stayed.

**The Haunting:** Jack likes to play pranks and Anna is seen in a red dress.

# Nevada

GRIMES POINT HIDDEN CAVE ARCHAEOLOGICAL SITE

CAL NEVA RESORT

GOLD HILL HOTEL

# Grimes Point Hidden Cave Archaeological Site

U.S. Route 50 runs from Ocean City, Maryland to Sacramento, California, but obviously there are some less populated stretches of road between the coasts. In fact, one section in Nevada was named by *Life* magazine as "The Loneliest Road in America." Fallon is the westernmost town on that lonely length of road, but it is worth a drive to experience something very unique.

Fallon is the site of a Naval Air Station, alfalfa and cantaloupe farms, and the Churchill County Museum. While the museum has interesting items from early settlers, its main attractions are the thousands of prehistoric artifacts from the Native Americans who were in this area at least 8,000 years ago. For more evidence of this ancient habitation, visitors can tour an outside museum of sorts, just seven miles east of town.

Grimes Point Archaeological Site contains many fascinating ancient Indian petroglyphs—figures and shapes carved into rocks. A vast lake, Lake Lahontan, once covered thousands of square miles in this area, and nomadic Indians came here and left evidence of their tools and what they ate, and also took the time to carve these symbols, so the site must have had some special significance to them. In the 1920s, a cave entrance was discovered nearby. Archaeologists uncovered over 2,500 artifacts inside (many of which are now in the county museum). These artifacts prove that the Indians used this cave for storage and shelter for many thousands of years.

What were these people like? What did these symbols and figures signify? Why were these sites chosen?

A star-shaped petroglyph.

Perhaps this became sacred ground because of some natural earth energy here. Visitors have reported that sitting quietly among the petroglyphs can evoke visions or experiences of higher consciousness. Glowing figures have also been seen in and around the cave. Is there a concentration of both spiritual energy and spirits at this ancient Indian site?

There is unquestionably a type of magic to places like this, even if it's nothing more than to inspire the imagination to travel back through the millennia to picture what this land and the people were like. Then again, who knows what forces flow through this land, and what layers of energies were added by sacred ceremonies reaching back at least 8,000 years. It is indeed worth a trip down this loneliest of roads, as it may lead to a spiritual journey you never could have anticipated.

### The Bottom Line

**The History:** Ancient Indian sites dating back at least 8,000 years.

**The Haunting:** Glowing figures, visions, a sense of altered consciousness.

### Recommendations

**Start your visit at the Churchill County Museum where you can see the ancient artifacts and get a better understanding of how the Indians lived. Guided tours of the cave are available on the second and fourth Saturday of each month, and begin at the museum. The petroglyphs can be viewed on a quarter-mile self-guided trail, but there are many hundreds of petroglyphs to be found nearby with a little more exploring—just bring plenty of water and bug spray. Take the time to sit quietly for a while and see if you sense or experience anything unusual.**

### Visitor Information

**Grimes Point/Hidden Cave Archaeological Site**
US 50, Fallon, NV
(775) 885-6000
www.nv.blm.gov/carson/Recreation/Rec_grimes_pt.htm

**Hours:**
Guided public tours: The second and fourth Saturday of each month. Meet at the Churchill County Museum, 1050 S. Maine Street, Fallon, Nevada. Sign up begins at 9:30am, the tour leaves at 10am. The museum hours are 10am – 4pm daily except Thursdays, noon to 4pm Sundays. For more information, telephone (702) 423-3677 during these Hours.

**Admission:** Free

**Directions:**
From Fallon, go east on US 50 approximately 7 miles until you see the archaeological site sign.



# Cal Neva Resort

Where is Nevada's oldest casino? Most people would assume it is in Las Vegas, but years before gambling came to the famous strip, there was Cal Neva on Lake Tahoe. The original lodge was built in 1926 and was modeled after a cabin in the Will Rodgers' play, *Lightnin*. Due to the stunning 180-degree views of the lake, the place came to be known as the "Lady of the Lake."

The rich and famous flocked to Cal Neva to escape the public eye, but on occasion their behavior here only drew more attention. For example, in 1930 during the Depression when many people didn't know where their next dollar was coming from, silent film star Clara Bow lost $13,900 in Cal Neva's casino! Unwanted attention was also brought to the resort during Prohibition when the place was raided several times for illegal liquor.

However, Cal Neva could be a place to draw attention and to be "discovered." Judy Garland performed here in 1935 when she was 13, and it is said her appearance led to her MGM movie contract. The rest, as they say, is Hollywood history.

In May of 1937, the resort was destroyed in a suspicious fire. Cal Neva could have become a distant memory, but it was rebuilt so quickly no one had time to forget—100 men reconstructed the resort from the ground up in just 40 days!

Movie stars continued to frequent the place, along with gamblers and gangsters, and in 1960, it would even have a celebrity owner—none other than the Chairman of the Board himself, Frank Sinatra. Sinatra's grand opening was attended by Marilyn Monroe, Joe and John F. Kennedy, and several high profile mobsters. Even the FBI got in on the act by setting up surveillance and keeping an eye on everyone. One can only imagine what they saw that night!

Marilyn Monroe loved Cal Neva and the little private cottage overlooking the lake where she usually stayed. There are rumors that the week before she was found dead in Los Angeles, she tried to kill herself in that cottage—or was it another murder attempt? Are the mysterious circumstances surrounding that week the reason why so many have seen and felt her presence at Cal Neva? Is she trying to convey some sort of message about her death? Claims of Marilyn Monroe's ghost have come from many different hotels and locations and its doubtful she is responsible for every blond apparition, but a woman fitting her unique description has been seen by Cal Neva's pool, and even after death she should be easy to distinguish from other women!

Frank Sinatra has also made several post-mortem appearances at the resort he once owned—often by that same pool. He came and went as he pleased in life, so why not choose to do the same in death? Is he also the man that is seen and felt on the showroom stage that Sinatra built?

Other paranormal hotspots include the tunnels that were built so that the rich and famous could have some privacy as they moved around the resort. In addition to voices and strange sensations in the tunnel, there is a light that goes on and off by itself. The light is supposed to be a 24-hour light, so it doesn't even have a switch. Electricians have repeatedly examined the bulb, socket, and wiring and can't find any reason for the erratic behavior. One of the tour guides believes it is Marilyn Monroe who keeps playing with the light, as it seems to go off when her name is mentioned.

The most intense location is Room 101, and is said to be so paranormally active that many employees refuse to enter, and it's the last room that will be rented out. Supposedly, an employee learned he had a terminal illness and rather than face a slow, painful death, chose to commit suicide by hanging himself in that room. It may turn out that it was an unfortunate choice, for if you believe the many stories of strange occurrences here, the poor man is suffering still.

Today, Cal Neva continues to be a popular destination for its elegant accommodations, spa, casino, and breathtaking views of Lake Tahoe and the mountains. While indulging yourself in all this resort has to offer, pause a moment to reflect on the colorful history of this former playground of movie stars and mobsters. And during your stay, you may yet have a chance to meet some Hollywood stars—it's just that there are no guarantees they will be alive!

## Recommendations

**This land was sacred to the local Indians and the resort may have been built on a burial ground. Several suicides and least one murder have been connected with Cal Neva owners, guests, and employees. All this may add up to many layers of paranormal activity here, in addition to Marilyn and Frank. Ask for Room 101 or Marilyn's cottage for the most active places. The resort offers specials throughout the year, such as skiing packages, so call or check the website. If you want to impress people with your swimming prowess, you can tell then you swam from Nevada to California, which is easily accomplished as the pool straddles the state line!**

## Visitor Information

**Cal Neva Resort, Spa and Casino**
**2 Stateline Road**
**Crystal Bay, NV 89402-7702**
**(800) 233-5551**
**Reservations: (800) 225-6382**
**www.calnevaresort.com**

**Directions:**

**From Reno: Take I-80 E to exit 15 to merge onto US-395 S toward Carson City. Take the exit toward Mt. Rose Highway/NV-431 W. Keep right at the fork, follow signs for NV-431/Mt. Rose/No Lake Tahoe and merge onto Mt. Rose Highway/NV-431 W. Turn right at Mt. Rose Highway/NV-28 W/Tahoe Boulevard. Continue to follow Mt. Rose Highway/NV-28 W. Entering California. Turn right at Stateline Road.**

**From Sacramento, CA: Take I-80 E to exit 188B for CA-89/CA-267 toward Sierraville/Lake Tahoe. Turn right at CA-267 E. Turn left at CA-28 E/N Lake Boulevard. Continue to follow CA-28 E. Turn left at Stateline Road.**



## The Bottom Line

**The History:** Nevada's oldest casino, first built in 1926 and once owned by Frank Sinatra.

**The Haunting:** The ghosts of Frank Sinatra and Marilyn Monroe.

Boom times for Gold Hill.

## Gold Hill Hotel

Gold Hill Hotel is oldest hotel in Nevada, and it was built here because of the discovery of the famous Comstock Lode and the ensuing mining boom. Construction on the hotel most likely began around 1859 and it was first called the Riese House. In January of 1862, severe flooding caused part of the structure to collapse, but it was rebuilt. Another building was soon added when Horace Vessy leased the property in 1862, and the renamed Vessy Hotel did a booming business for twenty years.

Unfortunately, mining booms do often go bust. The combined populations of Gold Hill and nearby Virginia City had approached 40,000 during the good times, but by 1930 only a few hundred people remained. Still, the hotel hung on. In 1887, the place was under new management, becoming the Capitol Hotel. Just a few years later, Vessy's building was gone, but the original structure was still welcoming guests. During the twentieth century, the old hotel began to show signs of its age, but a complete renovation begun in 1958—a century after it was first built—gave hope that the hotel might be around in another 100 years.

In 1986, another extensive renovation took place, along with a new addition. There is now a saloon offering lunch, dinner, and spirits—but they are not to be confused with the other spirits at Gold Hill...

The most often experienced ghost is that of Rosie, who may at one time have practiced the world's oldest profession. She acquired her name due to the strong smell of roses that accompanies her presence, most often in Room #4. Rosie likes to turn the lights on and off and move objects and guest's belongings.

The ghost in Room #5 is decidedly male, as the smell of tobacco and alcohol are his trademarks. "William" is believed to be one of the miners killed in a fire, but more on that in a moment. There are also the spirits of many children that can be heard running and laughing in the upstairs hallway of the original building.

Now, back to that fatal fire. Just behind the hotel was the Yellow Jacket mine. In 1869, a terrible fire in the mine killed at least thirty-five men, and many of their bodies were never recovered. The hotel has a cabin by the mine entrance, and it is reputed to be extremely haunted, with a wide variety of paranormal activity. Do the lost souls of those miners come here to try to tell the living about their awful fate?

The unfortunate truth about the many discoveries of silver and gold across the country is that it makes a lucky few very wealthy, and an unlucky many very dead. Silver and gold fever and all of its ensuing vices clearly leaves impressions in the paranormal realm—which you can experience firsthand at the Gold Hill Hotel.

### The Bottom Line

**The History:** The oldest hotel in Nevada. A fatal fire occurred in the mine right behind the hotel.

**The Haunting**: A woman, children, and miners killed in a fire all haunt the original building and miner's cabin.

### Recommendations

**Stay in the Miner's Cabin for your best shot at a creepy experience. Rosie is in Room #4, and William likes Room #5. There is a lot to learn in this area about mining booms and busts, and how they affected so many lives. A better appreciation of the history will help you to better appreciate why Virginia City is one of the most haunted places in the country.**

### Visitor Information

**Gold Hill Hotel**
**1540 Main Street**
**Virginia City, NV 89440**
**(775) 847-0111**
**www.goldhillhotel.net/**

**Directions:**
**In Virginia City, go south of town on North Main Street/NV-342 S for about one mile.**

New Hampshire
AMERICA'S STONEHENGE
MARGARITA'S MEXICAN RESTAURANT
THE 1875 INN AT TILTON
NH

# America's Stonehenge

Did an ancient civilization build these structures?

In the United States, structures that were built a couple of centuries ago are considered to be very old. When listing places many thousands of years ago, we naturally think of Rome, Greece, or Egypt. Certainly, you would turn heads in a discussion of ancient sites if you brought up New Hampshire, but there is a site in Salem that is far more ancient than the Coliseum or the Parthenon.

America's Stonehenge is a megalithic site covering thirty acres, containing walled pathways, chambers, and standing stones. Carbon dating has shown that charcoal found in one of the stone walls was from 2000 BC. Of course, there's no telling how long the walls were standing before the charcoal was produced; these results indicate that the site is at least 4,000 years old.

Who built this ancient site, and what was its purpose? As to who moved and placed these massive stones—some weighing many tons—there is speculation ranging from some unknown Native American tribe, to Celts, to Phoenicians. As of yet, there is no definitive proof who built America's Stonehenge, but there are clues as to why it was constructed.

The view from within one of the stone chambers.

Around the main concentration of buildings there are large, pointed stones standing upright. From a modern viewing platform (where an ancient viewing platform or building most likely once stood), one can view various astronomical events marked by these stones, such as the sunrises and sunsets at the equinoxes and solstices. The significance of some stones has yet to be determined, but who can say what holidays or positions of the stars were important to the builders?

One star that has been important to cultures around the world is Polaris, known as the North Star, which has guided travelers for thousands of years. But due to the fact that the Earth wobbles on its axis, Polaris was not always the North Star. To be specific, from 3942 BC to 1793 BC, the star closest to the North Pole was Thuban (also known as Alpha Draconis). This is important because a few of the standing stones point to positions of Thuban, thereby adding weight to the argument that the site was constructed at least four millennia ago.

NH

Unfortunately, our ability to uncover the mysteries of this ancient site has been compromised by the ignorance of modern man. In the 1800s, quarrymen carted away tons of the stones to use in local construction projects. It's estimated that between twenty to fifty percent of the stones were lost in the process. Also, subsequent owners altered the site, such as William Goodwin who purchased the property in 1937 and reconstructed some walls according to what he believed to be historically accurate.

Were sacrifices performed on this stone table?

Fortunately, enough remained intact that we can still stand in awe of the builders of this unique and mysterious complex of structures. For example, there is the so-called Oracle Chamber which has a stone-lined speaking tube that extends under a massive slab of carved stone known as the Sacrificial Table. A person could be concealed in the Oracle Chamber, and when speaking through the tube his voice would seemingly magically appear to be coming from the table.

While we can only wonder what transpired within these chambers thousands of years ago, we do know what they were used for in the years prior to the Civil War, when Jonathan Pattee lived on the site. Pattee was an abolitionist, and these remote, ancient chambers where the perfect hiding spot for runaway slaves on their way to freedom in Canada.

In 1958, the site was opened to the public under the name Mystery Hill Caves, and was changed to its current name in 1982 to reflect its similarity to the British megalithic site in terms of its astronomical alignments. Research continues to be conducted to try to determine who and when the site was constructed, but the mysteries of this hilltop location remain.

Something else mysterious may also remain here, according to numerous eyewitness accounts. People have experienced strange sensations and cold spots, and electronic equipment behaves erratically. Figures have also been seen moving about the stones—most notably the clear figure of a man entering the Oracle Chamber, only to vanish into thin air.

Are these figures ghosts of the recent past, or ancient impressions of the enigmatic builders? Many people have reported feeling unusual energies in certain locations—is this caused by natural Earth anomalies, or by spirits of sacrificial victims who met their fate on the stone slab more than 4,000 years ago?

There are few sites in this country that can claim to be this old, and perhaps no others that have such extensive stone structures and astronomical standing stones. A trip to America's Stonehenge is a journey back to a time when the pyramids of Egypt were young and many of the world's great civilizations didn't exist. Yet here, on a hill in New Hampshire, some people had the skill and knowledge to carve and move massive slabs and set up a ring of calendar stones. There is something quite mysterious here, and that mystery may extend into a hidden world of spirits and energies that are beyond our comprehension.

## The Bottom Line

**The History:** One the oldest complexes of structures in the United States with carbon dating indicating the site is at least 4,000 years old. Also contains astronomically aligned standing stones.

**The Haunting:** Cold spots, strange sensations, figures moving throughout the site, particularly by the Oracle Chamber.

## Recommendations

**Allow plenty of time to explore this site. Bring a camera, a compass, and a note pad to record your own observations and thoughts. For an extra added experience, try to visit during one of the equinoxes or solstices and watch the sun rise or set over the stones, as people did thousands of years ago. For even more excitement, public ghost hunts are held every October.**

## Visitor Information

**America's Stonehenge**
**105 Haverhill Road**
**Salem, NH 03079**
**(603) 893-8300**
**www.stonehengeusa.com**

One of the astronomically aligned standing stones.

**Hours:**
**Open daily year round, 9am – 5pm. Last admission at 4pm. Closed on Christmas and Thanksgiving Day. See website for special events.**

**Admission:**
**Adults $9.50; Seniors (65+) $8.50; Ages 6-12 $6.50; Children 5 and Under Free.**

**Directions:**
**From I-93: Take I-93 to exit 3. Follow route 111 east for approximately 5 miles. Watch for their sign just past the North Salem Village Shops. Turn right at the traffic lights (the Gulf gas station should be on your left side at the intersection). Follow this road for 1 mile. Entrance is on the right.**

**From I-95/ 101: 101 West to Exit 7 (Route 125 South) to Route 111W (Do *not* take 111A). Follow Route 111W for approximately 9 miles. Turn left at blinking light (Sunoco Gas/Dunkin Donuts is on left). At top of road turn left onto Haverhill Road. Entrance is located approximately 1/2 mile on right. If you miss this turn, you can turn left at the next set of lights (Gulf gas will be on right) and follow approximately 1 mile.**

**From 495: Take Exit 50 (Route 97) and follow Route 97 North. Turn right at Hampstead Road (97 Shoppes Plaza is located on right). Follow approximately 4 miles. Hampstead Road changes to Shannon Road and then to Haverhill Road. America's Stonehenge is located on the left.**

The police station in the early 1900s. *Courtesy of the Concord Police Department.*

# Margarita's Mexican Restaurant

When was the last time you heard of anyone enjoying the food they had in jail? There is a place in Concord where people line up to sit in a jail cell and eat and drink all they want, and can't wait to come back again.

Margarita's Mexican Restaurant is obviously no ordinary restaurant, as it occupies the former police station. As of 1883, the Concord Police Department had never consisted of more than nine men, but as the force expanded, it needed a new facility. In 1890, a two-story brick building was constructed and was used by Concord's finest until 1976. In 1981, the building was turned into Margarita's, but in a stroke of restaurant genius, they kept the sixteen jail cells, which now serve as small, private dining rooms.

While this feature would already place Margarita's on the list of the country's most unique dining experiences, the restaurant has yet another interesting feature—George, the ghost. Over the years, staff and patrons have witnessed objects moving, felt cold spots, seen faucets turn on and off, and even claim to have watched food being thrown and drinks consumed by some invisible entity. While some of these incidents may be blamed on the tequila, enough sober witnesses have reported inexplicable occurrences over the past three decades.

While the name George has been given to this alleged entity, no one knows for sure his true identity. There is the unsubstantiated belief that George was a former inmate who hung himself in one of the cells and now amuses himself by causing harmless mischief. And George may not be alone, as some people have felt that there is actually more than one restless spirit in the old jail.

Has eighty-six years of being a police station and jail left an indelible impression on this building? Clearly, something strange seems to be going on here. But even if George doesn't pull out your chair for you or sample your drink, how could you resist the opportunity of being the first on your block to have great Mexican food in a haunted jail cell?

The old jail cells provide a unique dining experience.

## Recommendations

The food is good no matter where you sit, but for the most unique experience call ahead to reserve one of the jail cells. Keep an eye out for objects moving on your table, and if you get a sudden chill, just ask George to move to a different cell.

## Visitor Information

**Margaritas Mexican Restaurant**
1 Bicentennial Square
Concord, NH 03301
(603) 224-2821
www.margs.com

**Hours:**
Sunday-Thursday 4pm – 10pm, Friday and Saturday 4pm – 11pm.

**Directions:**
From I-93 South: Take exit 14 for Loudon Road/NH-9. Turn right at Loudon Road/NH-9 and then continue to follow NH-9. Turn left at North Main Sreett/NH-9/US-202/US-3. Turn right on School Street. Turn left on North State Street. Turn left on Warren Street. Turn right at Bicentennial Square/Odd Fellows Avenue.

From I-93 North: Take exit 13 for US-3. Take the slight left at Manchester Street/US-3/Water Street. Continue to follow US-3. Turn left at NH-9/Pleasant Street/US-202. Turn right at North State Street. Turn right on Warren Street. Turn right at Bicentennial Square/Odd Fellows Avenue.

## The Bottom Line

**The History:** This 1890 building was a police station containing sixteen jail cells. The police moved out in 1976, and the restaurant began operation in 1981.

**The Haunting:** Objects moving and cold spots, perhaps the actions of George, a former prisoner?

# The 1875 Inn at Tilton



In 2001, when owner Joanna Oliver was trying to gather historic information that might help with renovations of the structure, she did not exactly get the response she expected from a local historian. Instead of supplying Joanna with old documents and photos, he handed her a book of matches and said, "Here, this is what you should do with that place."

Fortunately, Joanna didn't take his advice and burn it down. Instead, she replaced the foundation, solidified the structure, and beautifully restored the inn's twelve guest bedrooms and restaurant, so that people could once again enjoy this lovely place.

The 1875 Tilton Inn.

Not much is known about the history of the building and its owners, other than it was originally built as an inn in 1875, and at one point the police station was housed in the basement. The other known history is somewhat more tragic—the building was hit by two fires, and one of them in the nineteenth century claimed the life of a 12-year-old girl named Laura, and it is her ghost that is most often seen.

This is a photograph of a girl named Laura, who may have died in a fire at the inn. Does Laura's ghost still haunt the place?

For example, a guest in the Samuel Sanborn room saw a young girl sitting on her bed. Another guest in the Mary Baker Eddy room saw a girl leaving his room and then she promptly disappeared. Still another guest saw this girl in his room and in the hallway. One woman stepped out of her shower, and came face to face with Laura! While such encounters are obviously unnerving, Laura isn't trying to scare anyone. She is probably just a confused little girl looking for someone to communicate with.

Over the past several years, many paranormal investigators have found evidence of other spirits, as well, perhaps as many as a few dozen. Whether these are traveling spirits who come and go, or who are permanent residents along with Laura remains to be seen—both literally and figuratively!

The Tilton area is ideally located to explore both the lakes region and the White Mountains, along with many other New Hampshire natural wonders. A stay at the 1875 Tilton Inn also offers a chance to explore some supernatural wonders!

## Recommendations

**Once a month the inn hosts a Paranormal Night, which includes dinner, a tour, and very entertaining stories of the ghostly occurrences told by owner, Joanna Oliver. When making reservations, ask for the rooms where Laura was most recently seen.**

## Visitor Information

**The 1875 Inn at Tilton**
**255 Main Street**
**Tilton, NH 03276-5113**
**(603) 286-7774**
**www.1875inn.com**

**Events:**
**Paranormal Night is $25 per person. The Olive Branch Tavern serves dinner Friday to Sunday, Sunday Brunch, and also has a special Pub Menu. Some small pets are allowed in the rooms.**

**Directions:**
**From their website—Take Interstate 93 to Exit #20. At the end of the Ramp, go right; towards Tilton Center. Approximately 1 and 1/2 miles ahead on the right will be the 1875 Inn and Olive Branch Tavern, next to the Tilton Town Hall.**

## The Bottom Line

**The History:** An inn built in 1875 where a fatal fire occurred.

**The Haunting:** A girl killed in a fire is seen throughout the inn. There may be dozens of other spirits, as well.

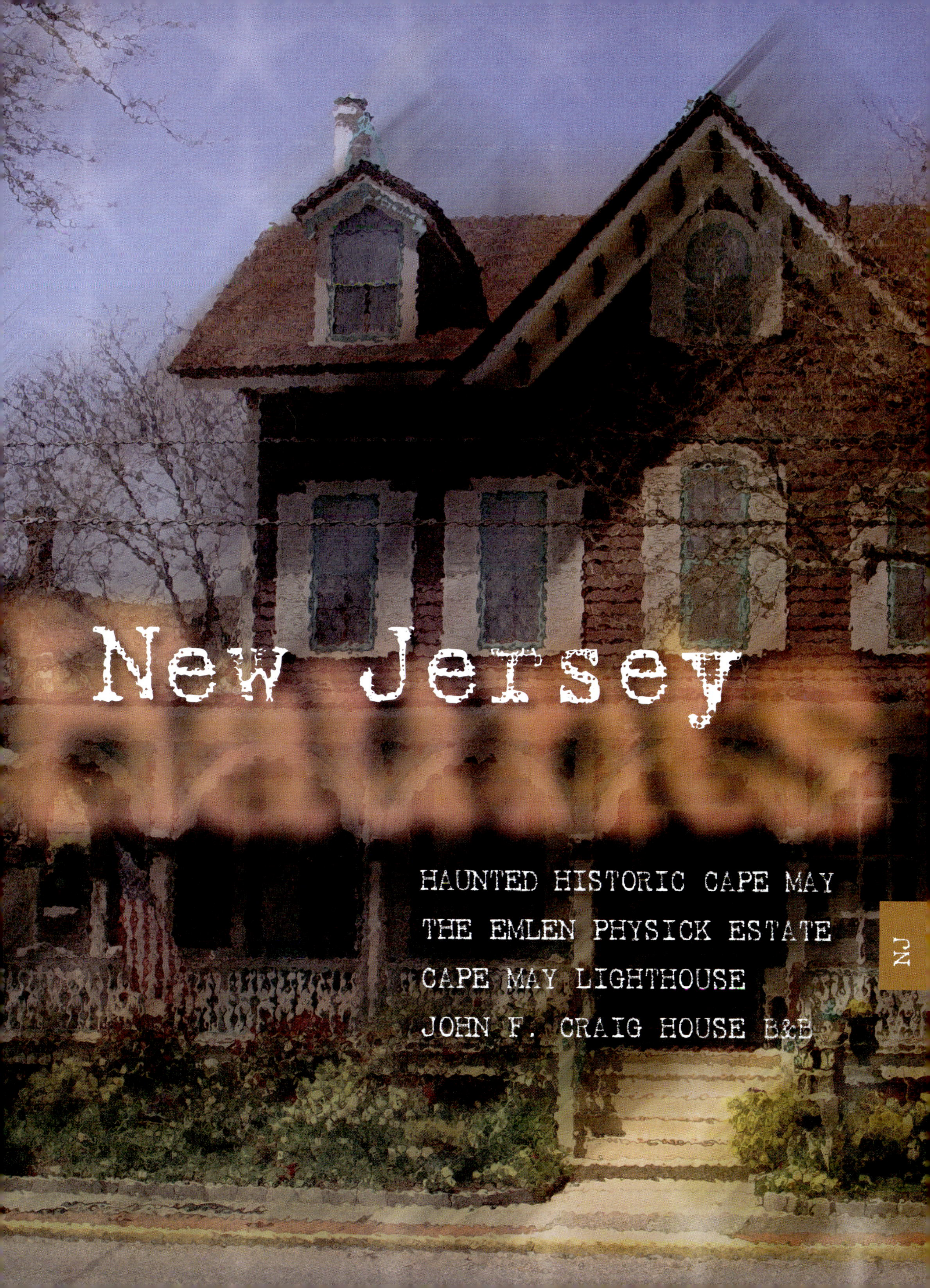
New Jersey
HAUNTED HISTORIC CAPE MAY
THE EMLEN PHYSICK ESTATE
CAPE MAY LIGHTHOUSE
JOHN F. CRAIG HOUSE B&B
NJ

# Haunted Historic Cape May

It's not that there aren't other interesting historic haunts in New Jersey, it's just that when you have an entire beautiful seaside resort town that probably has more ghosts per square foot than anywhere else in the state, why bother going anywhere else?

Cape May became the country's first seaside resort in 1761, and soon tourists from the hot, disease-riddled cities were seeking its clean air and ocean waters. Roads and eventually railroads brought in even more tourists, and large resort hotels sprang up. The town suffered economically during the Civil War when they lost all their southern visitors, and it did take many years for business to spring back, but when it did it was bigger and better than ever.

Money poured into town, giving rise to elegant homes and gambling houses, and tourists enjoyed all manner of dances, concerts, and entertainment. Unfortunately, this gilded era came to a disastrous end in 1878, when a terrible fire swept through town destroying many of the original buildings and large resorts. The growth of other seaside resorts in the late nineteenth century added another challenge to the town. Finally, a storm in 1962 threatened an end to old Cape May and its lovely Victorian buildings. However, like a Phoenix from the ashes, and floodwaters, the town was galvanized to action to save and preserve what was left.

Lucky for us they did, because Cape May today is a Victorian architectural showpiece, and it also happens to be extremely haunted by residents, tourists, shipwreck victims, and perhaps even a pirate or two. You would be hard pressed to go into any restaurant, shop, or inn that doesn't have at least one ghost story. The following are just a sampling of some of beautiful Cape May's historic haunts.

NJ

# The Emlen Physick Estate

During the early 1970s, this place was known as Cape May's original haunted house. That was because the once-grand estate now looked downright spooky, as it had fallen into a terrible state of disrepair. Fortunately, the house has been fully restored to the architectural showpiece it once was, but don't be too hasty to remove the title of haunted house—the spirits of former occupants and their faithful, four-legged friends may not yet have left the building.

Dr. Emlen Physick (1855-1916) was a man who was born into a famous family. His great-great grandfather was Philip Syng, Jr., a silversmith who made the inkwell used by the signers of the Declaration of Independence. His grandfather, Dr. Philip Syng Physick, has the distinction of being known as the Father of American Surgery. Emlen also followed the medical path, but not to carry on any proud family tradition. He would not receive his inheritance unless he obtained a medical degree, so he dutifully obeyed.

Emlen and one of his beloved dogs. *Courtesy of the Emlen Physick Estate (MAC).*

However, the new Dr. Physick never agreed to actually practice, so without even treating a single patient he promptly "retired" from medicine. With his share of the family fortune, the young doctor hired the famous architect Frank Furness and built this magnificent estate on twenty-two acres. Completed in 1879, the eighteen-room house is a beautiful example of Victorian "Stick-Style," and exhibits many of Furness' quirky trademarks, including upside-down chimneys and oversized features. The estate also contained a carriage house, greenhouse, Hill House (used as Physick's workshop), and other small buildings. Physick never married, and lived in the house with his mother, Mrs. Ralston, and her spinster sister, Emilie Parmentier. He was very fond of dogs, of which there were many on the estate grounds over the years.

Today, standing on those grounds amongst the flowers and blossoming trees, looking at this magnificent home, it is very difficult to imagine that this once-dilapidated structure had a date with a wrecking ball. In response, the Mid-Atlantic Center for the Arts and Humanities (MAC) was formed in 1970 to save the Physick Estate and restore it for future generations to enjoy. To be accurate, though, it seems that a generation from the past is also still enjoying "their" home.

The history of the haunting goes back at least to the 1950s, when an owner moved out because she was afraid of all the ghostly activity. Soon after the house was opened as a museum, the staff began encountering all sorts of inexplicable sights, sounds, and sensations. They suspected that some of Emlen's relatives were still in residence, but it wasn't until they invited psychic medium and author Craig McManus (www.craigmcmanus.com) in to investigate that they got a clearer picture of the family members who just don't seem to want to leave.

To summarize, it appears as though Dr. Physick is still here, as is his Aunt Emily, who is a lot more energetic and active than her nephew. Dr. Physick's mother, Frances Ralston, may not be here in spirit, but she has left residual energy in her former bedroom, which some sensitive people might interpret as a presence. Mrs. Ralston had an invalid younger sister Isabelle, or Bella, who died in the house in 1883, and her spirit also inhabits the mansion. And what man's home is complete without his best friends? It seems that Dr. Physick's beloved dogs are also still running around the house and grounds.

The Carriage House also has its share of spooky sounds and sights, which may be attributed to a former groomsman or servant, or both. In short, there is no shortage of apparitions, disembodied footsteps, phantom music, cold spots, and all other manner of paranormal activity here. In New Jersey's most haunted town, the Emlen Physick Estate is the crown jewel of historic haunts!

## The Bottom Line

**The History:** A beautiful Victorian mansion built in 1879 in the Stick Style by architect Frank Furness. Today it is the only house museum in Cape May.

**The Haunting:** Most of the Physick family and their dogs are still here.

## Recommendations

Don't just drive by and look at this house; take the tour! There are just so many fascinating things you can learn and so much to admire in terms of architecture, artwork, clothing, and everyday objects from the Victorian period—well, everyday objects of extremely wealthy people, that is. Look for the old Ouija Board and spirit devices that were used as a type of parlor game. The mansion is exquisitely decorated for Christmas, and the grounds are beautiful in the spring when everything is blooming. The Carriage House has changing exhibits, and after a long day of touring you can treat yourself to an elegant tea or lunch in the Carriage House Tearoom. For your best shot at a ghostly encounter, sign up for one of the Midnight Tours with Craig McManus.

## Visitor Information

**Emlen Physick Estate**
1048 Washington Street
Cape May, NJ 08204-1737
(609) 884-5404
(800) 275-4278
www.capemaymac.org

**Hours:**
Times vary by day of the week and season, so please call or check the website for the latest tour schedule.

**Admission:**
Tickets for the Emlen Physick Estate are available at the Carriage House Visitors Center, and are $10 for adults; $5 for children (ages 3-12). Combination Tours: Guided trolley tour of Cape May's Historic District, followed by a guided tour of the Emlen Physick Estate are $18 for adults; $9 for children ages 3 to 12. The Midnight Tours are $25 per person, and should be booked well in advance as they fill up very quickly.

**Directions:**
From the Garden State Parkway South: Travel to the end of the Parkway then merge onto US-9 S to 109 S. Turn left at Sidney Avenue. Turn right at Washington Street. The Physick Estate is on the left.

Photo by author.

# Cape May Lighthouse

Lighthouses have an enchanting, almost magical quality. While warning ships at sea to stay clear, these tall, silent sentinels have the power to attract people on land. They also seem to have the uncanny ability to attract ghosts...

The first lighthouse at Cape May was built in 1823, and was only 68 feet tall. It stood about 100 yards out from the present lighthouse and the encroaching sea brought it tumbling down. The site is now completely under water, but occasionally one of its bricks washes ashore. The second lighthouse was 78 feet high and was built in 1847, but as it was not designed and constructed properly it was demolished.

Finally in 1857, the Army Corps of Engineers began work on a proper lighthouse, and when completed and lit on Halloween night of 1859, the tapering brick tower would stand 157-feet-tall and contain 199 steps up to the light. The cost was substantial for the time—$40,000 for the lighthouse and keeper's buildings and $30,000 for the massive Fresnel lens for the beacon. The keepers had to carry heavy containers of whale oil to the top to light that beacon, but in 1938 the original oil lamp was replaced by an electrical light, and the need for lighthouse keepers ended. Today, that light still flashes every 10 seconds and can be seen as far as 24 miles out to sea.

When the U.S. Lighthouse Service was discontinued in 1939, management was turned over to the U.S. Coast Guard. During WWII, Nazi U-boats wreaked havoc with shipping off of Cape May, and the light was turned off so the enemy couldn't use it as an aid to navigating these waters looking for prey. After the war, the beacon was lit again, but budget cuts forced the Coast Guard to look for other groups to manage the old lighthouse. Fortunately, in 1986, the Mid-Atlantic Center for the Arts was able to lease the lighthouse from the state, and after an initial restoration, was able to open the lighthouse to the public the following year. Restoration and maintenance projects are now ongoing, ensuring both public access, and the preservation of a sparkling historical gem.

The Cape May Lighthouse now attracts almost 100,000 visitors a year, and this power of attraction apparently also extends to the ghostly realm, as well. Visitors and staff often hear footsteps ascending the stairs when no one is around. Children's laughter and voices echo up the tower. One woman who found the climb to the top very challenging, later told a staff member she couldn't have done it if it hadn't been for the little girl's voice that kept encouraging her, telling her she could make it. She commented that it was a great idea, but where were the speakers they used to pipe in the girl's voice? The woman simply refused to believe that there was no speaker system in the lighthouse, and that no children were on the site at the time!

Others have seen a woman in a nineteenth-century dress, sometimes holding a lantern, and believe that she may have been a keeper's wife who is there to watch over these children. Some have sensed a more recent male spirit—unfortunately perhaps too recent, as a man managed to slip through the security railings and jumped to his death from the top of the lighthouse in 1995.

What is it about lighthouses that attract so many ghosts? In the final analysis, perhaps it is the same thing that draws tourists. They are beautiful beacons of strength and solitude, and can anyone, living or dead, ask for more?

## The Bottom Line

**The History:** The third lighthouse on this site, built in 1859.

**The Haunting:** Little children, a woman with a lantern, and a suicide victim.

## Recommendations

You simply can't go to Cape May without visiting the lighthouse, it must be against some sort of law! The lighthouse takes on a variety of shadows and effects depending on the angle of the sun and weather, so for some great photos try different times of the day. Unless you are in fabulous shape, you will get winded climbing to the top, and have rubber legs descending; just take your time and stop frequently to admire the views. It is well worth reaching the top—and not only for your self-esteem—as a very knowledgeable guide can tell you fascinating details about the history of the lighthouse. Ask about the map that shows how many ships were sunk by U-boats in the area, you will be amazed. After you fully explore the lighthouse by day, you must return at night with the Ghosts of the Lighthouse Tour. And if you are sensitive, check out the grounds and beach here, as a variety of spirits have been encountered.

## Visitor Information

**Cape May Point State Park**
215 Lighthouse Avenue
Cape May Point, NJ 08212
(609) 884-5404
(800) 275-4278
www.capemaymac.org

**Hours:**

The park is open daily 8am – 4pm. Depending upon the season, the lighthouse may open at 9am, 10am, 11am, or noon, so please call or check the website for the schedule.

**Admission:**

$7 for adults and $3 for children 12 and under.

**Directions:**

The park is located off the southern end of the Garden State Parkway. Cross over Cape May Bridge onto Lafayette Street, Cape May. At the intersection, bear right onto County Route 606 (Sunset Boulevard), then left onto Lighthouse Avenue.

From Route 9, take County Route 626, Seashore Road and cross the bridge. Follow directions as above.

Photo by author.

# John F. Craig House B&B

It must be more than a coincidence that houses which have been moved and joined together tend to be haunted. When this occurs in a place like Cape May that seems to have ghosts everywhere, you can probably expect a very active house. Such is the case with the John F. Craig House Bed and Breakfast in Cape May, where many spirits come and go, and some are simply still residing in their former home.

The house that faces the street was built in 1866 in the Carpenter Gothic style, and was used as the model home for the development planned for the area. An older house from the 1830s was moved from Lafayette Street and attached to the back of the house, providing servants quarters. The original owner was George Richardson, the president of a local railroad, but he lost the house in the 1870s at a sheriff's sale, and later drowned at sea during a storm. A banker from Philadelphia was the next owner, and he was known for turning the place into something of a party house.

John Fullerton Craig was an Irishman who made a fortune in sugar, and he bought the house in 1891 as a summer cottage. Apparently, there was quite a scandal when John, who was a widower, married Emma the housekeeper, and she ended up inheriting the family fortune when John died in 1926. Emma was a stern woman, and she also had her elderly mother staying in the house, who lived to be almost 100. One can only imagine the turmoil and tension all this caused with the Craig children.

The house was sold out of the family in the 1950s, and eventually was opened as an inn. Current owners, Barbara and Chip Masemore, bought the house in 2002, and have been operating it as a stunningly beautiful bed and breakfast ever since. When asked if Barbara knew about the ghosts of the Craig house, she replied that she could definitely feel "a lot of different energies here." Guests describe similar feelings, and are also not always able to define these sensations as particular spirits. As one might expect, these feelings are quite different between the "old" and "new" houses that were joined together so long ago, but still manage to retain their separate energies.

Some of the identifiable ghosts are those of some boisterous fishermen in the back of the house by the staircase. They seem to be having a great time celebrating a good day of fishing, and perhaps, partying?

The stern Emma Craig is also believed to be keeping an eye on everything, and her spirit may be the most pronounced. John Craig himself may still be on the front porch smoking his pipe, wondering what happened to his view of the ocean, now obscured by all the buildings.

Many psychics and mediums have entered the Craig House and felt these various personalities and energies, but they are always accompanied by good feelings, never anything threatening or menacing. This is definitely one of those lovely homes where you couldn't blame anyone, living or dead, for not wanting to leave. For a taste of what Cape May used to be, you can't top the hospitality, décor, or spirits of the John F. Craig House.

## The Bottom Line

**The History:** A beautiful Carpenter Gothic style home built in 1866 that had an 1830s house attached to it.

**The Haunting:** Former owners, some rowdy fishermen, and countless other spirits who come and go.

NJ

## Recommendations

If you really want to delve into the world of the spirits here, they occasionally hold séances, so call for the next available one. Aside from being a simply gorgeous place with great food, it is ideally located so you can park your car and not need it again until you leave. Activity is spread throughout the house, so there's no need to request any particular room. Look for the photos of the Craig family along the main stairs, and look outside to see where the two houses where joined.

## Visitor Information

**John F. Craig House Bed and Breakfast**
609 Columbia Avenue
Cape May, NJ 08204-2305
(609) 884-0100
(877) 544-0314
www.johnfcraig.com

**Directions:**

From their website—From the West and North: Take your choice of routes to the Garden State Parkway. Go South on the Parkway and follow it to Exit 0, where it intersects with Route 109. Go straight and follow it over the big bridge at the Cape May, New Jersey Harbor. When you enter town you will be on Lafayette Street. Follow it to the First Traffic Light at Madison Avenue. Turn left on Madison and go to the blue Water Tower at the intersection of Columbia. Turn right on Columbia and follow it about six blocks and just beyond the war memorial is the Craig House. Our Cape May bed and breakfast is the (pretty) burgundy and teal house on your right, one building from the corner of Columbia Avenue and Ocean Street.

From the Cape May – Lewes Ferry: Upon exiting the Ferry you will be on Route 9. Follow it north to the intersection of Route 109. Turn right on Route 109 and follow the signs into Cape May, New Jersey. Then follow same directions as above.

From the Delaware Memorial Bridge: As you leave the bridge stay in the center lane and look for the Route 40 east exit. It will be a short distance and the last exit, to the right, before the NJ Turnpike. Follow Route 40 (it will turn frequently, but is well-marked) past Elmer to Route 55, south. Take Route 55 south to the end, about 39 miles, where it merges into Route 47. Follow Route 47 to where it merges with 347, then take Route 347 to the traffic light at Route 657. Turn left onto Route 657 and follow it to Cape May Courthouse, about 5 miles. You will cross over Route 9 in Cape May Courthouse, then at the next traffic light, turn right onto the Garden State Parkway, south. Follow the Parkway south to the end then use the directions above from the North and West.

When you arrive, pull along the yellow-lined loading zone directly in front to unload your things. Free Parking is available on the meter-free Columbia Avenue and adjoining streets.

# New Mexico

FORT UNION

DOUBLE EAGLE RESTAURANT

ST. JAMES HOTEL

*Photo by Nationalparks, Wikipedia, Creative Commons Attribution-Share Alike 2.5 Generic.*

# Fort Union

In a world crisscrossed with superhighways between cities blanketed in asphalt and concrete, it is truly an amazing moment when you can stand in the actual ruts made by the wheels of the wagons that traveled along the old Santa Fe Trail. Fort Union was established in 1851 by the intersection of the Mountain and Cimarron Branches of the Santa Fe Trail, and a visit here is like a step back in time.

Now a National Monument in the National Park Service, this site preserves sections of the three forts built here to protect travelers and to act as a major supply depot for military operations throughout the frontier. The fort was operational from 1851-1891, and in addition to fighting Indians and outlaws, the army had to fight battles in court. The fort had, in fact, been built on private land that had been part of the Mora Grant, but through a series of legal maneuverings and delays, the government never paid anything to the rightful owners of the land.

At its peak, Fort Union was like a small city sending out patrols and handling massive amounts of vital supplies. However, as the railroad stretched into the west, the need for Fort Union as a supply depot came to an end and the depot operations ceased in 1883. With its overall usefulness also waning, the old fort which had played so many roles in life or death dramas for forty years, closed in 1891. The fort became a National Monument in 1956, and now comprises 721 acres of land and buildings.

For all the turmoil and violence associated with Fort Union, it's interesting to note that one of the oldest ghost stories involves dancing. Even after the recreation building was demolished, soldiers reported seeing and hearing large parties going on. Perhaps the many wandering souls here were trying to recapture some of the happy moments before their deaths?

There is another old story about a dance at Fort Union, and while it is pure fiction, it is worth retelling by a campfire. The attractive sister-in-law of one of the officers stationed here was a terrible flirt. A young lieutenant fell in love with her, and before leaving on a dangerous mission, asked if she would marry him. She said yes, and assured him that if something happened to him, she would never marry anyone else.

The patrol did return, but the lieutenant was missing. The fickle woman showed no concern and soon announced she was marrying someone else. After the ceremony, as the new bride was dancing, the doors flung open and in walked the bloody, scalped corpse of the lieutenant. Taking hold of the terrified woman, he spun her in a dance—the Death Waltz—and she dropped lifeless to the floor. The awful specter then disappeared, and the lieutenant's scalped body was found a few days later.

While there is no evidence to support the fanciful tale of the Death Waltz, many visitors do see things that cannot be explained. For example, people report seeing a tall, bearded man in a Civil War uniform walking on the old parade ground and by the hospital. He looks very real and solid, and people simply assume he is a reenactor. However, when they follow the man, he can't be found. It's as if he simply disappears, which of course, is probably exactly what he's doing. Witnesses claim that he looks just like General Ulysses S. Grant, but as he died in New York and is buried there, that doesn't make any sense as to why he would haunt Fort Union. But who can say what makes sense in the ghostly world!

What does make sense is that if you love history and ghost stories, you should visit Fort Union. Stand in the ruts of the wagon wheels, walk the parade grounds and old buildings, and imagine what life was like when this was a remote outpost in very hostile territory. It may not be so hard to picture the soldiers, Indians, and wagon trains, and with any luck, the veil between worlds will temporarily pull back so you can experience them all firsthand!

## The Bottom Line

**The History:** Established in 1851 to protect travelers on the Santa Fe Trail. At one time this was the largest military base and supply depot in the southwest.

**The Haunting:** A bearded man in a Civil War uniform, sights and sounds of a dancing party.

## Recommendations

**Living history events take place during the summer, and in August there is "An Evening in Fort Union" when visitors are allowed to walk through the fort's ruins at night. There is a lot to explore here, so if you are sensitive, take the time to "feel your way around" all of the buildings and grounds. There are great photographic possibilities here with the ruins set against the blue sky, so be sure to bring your best camera.**

## Visitor Information

**Fort Union**
**NM 161**
**P.O. Box 127**
**Watrous, NM 87753**
**(505) 425-8025**
**www.nps.gov/foun/index.htm**

**Hours:**

**Open daily except Thanksgiving Day, Christmas Day, and New Year's Day. Winter Hours: Labor Day to Memorial Day 8am – 4pm. Summer Hours: Memorial Day to Labor Day 8am – 6pm.**

**There is a visitor center with exhibits about the fort and a film about the Santa Fe Trail. A 1.6 mile, self-guided interpretive trail enables visitors to tour the ruins with electronic narrations at each stop. Visitors may opt to do a shorter .5 mile self-guided tour.**

**Admission:**

**Entrance Fees: Individuals 16 years of age and older $3 for 7 days. Entrance fee is also valid for 7 day use at Pecos National Historical Park. A yearly pass is available for just $10.**

**Directions:**

**From their website—From Albuquerque (156 miles), Santa Fe (94 miles) or Las Vegas, NM (28 miles) take I-25 north, exit 366 at Watrous, 8 miles on NM 161.**

**From Denver (313 miles), Colorado Springs (243 miles) or Raton (95 miles) take I-25 south, exit 366 at Watrous, 8 miles on NM 161.**

The Old Mesilla Plaza. *Courtesy of The Library of Congress.*

# Double Eagle Restaurant

The plaza in Mesilla was the site of the confirmation of the Gadsden Purchase in 1853, which bought land from Mexico. This land became part of New Mexico and Arizona, and was used for a southern route for a transcontinental railroad. One of the finest houses on this plaza was also where the Secessionist Convention met and declared Mesilla the capital of the Confederate Arizona Territory in 1861. Then in 1881, Billy the Kid was jailed and tried here by Pat Garrett. For all its history, however, it is a private family tragedy that has had the most lasting impression on this house.

In the late 1840s, the wealthy Maese family moved from Santa Fe, where their business interests were being affected by the Mexican-American War, to this house on the plaza in Mesilla. The Senora Carlota Maese had great plans for her family, including the marriage of her eldest son, Armando, to a suitable member of an aristocratic family in Mexico City. Armando had other plans, as most young men do, and he fell in love with Inez, a beautiful young girl with a fatal flaw—she was a servant.

When Carlota discovered the two lovers in Armando's bedroom, she flew into a blind rage, grabbed a pair of long scissors and brutally attacked Inez. Armando tried to shield the woman he loved, and in doing so was mistakenly stabbed by his mother. Inez died right there in Armando's arms, then he collapsed and died three days later, never having regained consciousness. It's said that Carlota, severely traumatized by the results of her violent outburst, never spoke again.

This historic home remained a private residence until acquired by Robert O. Anderson in 1972. His efforts helped preserve this National Registered Historical site, and then the present owner, C. W. "Buddy" Ritter, a fifth-generation Mesilla decedent, completed a restoration in 1984. The décor and fine antiques, such as the seven-foot Baccarat crystal chandeliers, hearken back to the days when it was one of the finest homes in the area. All of the ensuing paranormal activity experienced by the staff and guests hearkens back to when a crazed mother killed her son and his lover.

While things can happen anywhere, possibly due to energies attached to some of the antiques, most of the strange happenings take place in the Carlota Salon, which had been Armando's bedroom and the scene of the tragic murders. The restaurant has motion detectors armed at night, yet when the staff returns in the morning they often find tables and chairs rearranged or knocked over, and glasses broken. There is no way anyone can physically enter that room without setting off those detectors, but perhaps the culprit is not hampered by a physical body.

People have also seen the ethereal figures of a man and woman in this room, and two overstuffed chairs show the impressions of two people being seated, when no one is there. There are voices and whispers heard when no one else is around. For no apparent reason, the air can suddenly be filled with the scent of lavender perfume. There is never anything threatening or malicious, just signs that a couple of young lovers are having some innocent fun.

Of course, there was nothing innocent about the awful crime committed here, but love does triumph over evil, and Armando and Inez are the (non)living proof of that!

### The Bottom Line

**The History:** A house built in the 1840s. The Gadsden Purchase was signed in the plaza, the house was occupied by Confederates in 1861, and Billy the Kid was held prisoner here in 1881. A woman murdered her son and his lover here.

**The Haunting:** Two young lovers create mischief throughout the restaurant.

### Recommendations

**You will be amazed when you enter this adobe building and find it to be decorated like a palace with museum-quality art. Of course, request to be seated in the Carlota Salon for your best chance to encounter Armando and Inez, and ask the staff about their many experiences. You have the option of a fine dinner with wine, or if you are really hungry, attempt one of their spicy twenty-ounce green chili cheeseburgers—but you may wish you were dead if you finish it!**

### Visitor Information

**Double Eagle Restaurant and Peppers Cafe**
On The Plaza in Historic Old Mesilla
**2355 Calle De Guadalupe**
**Mesilla, NM 88046**
(575) 523-6700
www.double-eagle-mesilla.com

**Hours:**
**Open Seven Days A Week. 11am – 10pm Monday-Saturday. Noon – 9pm Sundays. Seatings at 11am and 1:30pm Sunday Champagne Brunch.**

**Directions:**
**Take the Mesilla Exit #140 off Interstate 10 in Las Cruces, New Mexico, and turn west under the interstate onto Avenuenida de Mesilla (Highway 28). Go about a mile and follow the brown signs for the Plaza and turn right off Avenuenida De Mesilla onto Calle de Santiago. Go two blocks to the Plaza. The Double Eagle Restaurant is on the east side of the Plaza.**

# St. James Hotel

When talking about the Wild West, you are more apt to describe food as "grub" or "chow" rather than cuisine, and you certainly wouldn't picture a French chef among the rowdy cowboys. However, life is stranger than fiction, and Henri Lambert, personal chef to President Abraham Lincoln, headed west to find gold after Lincoln was assassinated. Things didn't work out so well with the gold, but he did open Lambert's Inn in Cimarron in 1872.

The hotel was not, however, where one sipped fine vintage champagne while eating crepes. Lambert's restaurant, rooms, and saloon were the scenes of at least twenty-six murders, and the tin ceiling of the old saloon still bears the marks of twenty-two bullet holes (over 400 bullet holes were found when the roof was replaced in 1901). Violence at Lambert's became so routine that it was said that every morning people in Cimarron would automatically ask, "Who was killed at Lambert's last night?"

Travelers along the Santa Fe Trail, gold miners, famous cowboys, gunslingers, and outlaws stayed and drank and gambled here; men such as Jesse James, Black Jack Ketchum, Clay Allison (who reputedly killed nineteen men), the Earps (on their way to Tombstone), Doc Holliday, Kit Carson, Billy the Kid, Pat Garrett, Bat Masterson, and Buffalo Bill Cody, who would become godfather to Lambert's son and teach him to shoot. Cody also met Annie Oakley at the hotel. Other famous guests included General Phil Sheridan, western artist Frederick Remington, Governor Lew Wallace, and western writer Zane Grey.

The existence of the inn, later renamed the St. James Hotel, was threatened when the railroad ended

The St. James Hotel in 1936. *Courtesy of The Library of Congress.*

the need for the old trails, and gold mining in the area began to dry up. The hotel fell on hard times and passed through a series of owners. Finally in 1985, the hotel was restored to its original elegance, the saloon was turned into a restaurant, and it was once again open to receive travelers along the new asphalt trails. To preserve the feeling of stepping back into the old west, none of the rooms in the main hotel have telephones, televisions, or radios (the rooms in the annex do, if you can't stand being that authentic). However, one thing they do all have is ghosts.

There's Room #17, said to be inhabited by the white, misty ghost of Mrs. Mary Lambert who was partial to rose-scented cologne and died in the hotel in 1926. Guests have often smelled roses upon entering that room, and sometimes it is so strong as to be overwhelming. At the St. James Hotel, however, if all you have to contend with is some strong-smelling cologne, you should consider yourself lucky.

There's the ghost of a very short old man known as the "Little Imp" who goes about the hotel taking things and knocking objects off of shelves and walls, and generally unnerving everyone wherever he strikes. But even he pales in comparison to what lurks in Room #18. Don't bother asking for that room, though, as it is kept padlocked.

It seems as though during the hotel's violent past, a man won the property in a poker game, but he didn't get to enjoy his winnings. As he returned to Room #18 that night, someone shot him in the back, and he bled to death in his room. He is apparently still very angry about his murder, and it is said that terrible things have happened to people trying to spend the night in his room, so the door was locked and no guests are allowed to stay there.

Other paranormal activity includes the figures of cowboys, cold spots, screams, lights going on and off, and batteries draining. This is all most likely the result of all the bullet holes—not the ones in the ceiling from the shots that missed, but from the ones that found their marks in the unfortunate murder victims of Lambert's Inn.

## Recommendations

**For the most historic and haunted rooms, give up the TV and radio for a few days and ask for a room in the old part of the hotel. If you like the scent of roses, ask for Mrs. Lambert's room. At the time of the writing of this book, the hotel was coming under new management, so you can ask about staying in Room #18 in case they changed the hotel's policy.**

## Visitor Information

**St. James Hotel**
617 S. Collinson Avenue
Cimarron, NM 87714
(575) 376-2664
www.exstjames.com

**Hours:**
Restaurant: Open Daily 7am – 9pm, 7 days a week; Bar and Lounge: 11am – 11pm.

**Directions:**
The hotel is just south of the town on South Collinson/Route 21. Cimarron can be reached from the east and west by Route 64, and from I-25/85 to exit 419 to Route 58 W.

## The Bottom Line

**The History:** A saloon and hotel first opened in 1872 by Lincoln's personal chef. The guest list is a "Who's Who" of the old west. At least twenty-six murders occurred here.

**The Haunting:** A very angry murder victim, the wife of the original owner, and a very short, mischievous old man have been witnessed here.

# New York

SARATOGA SPRINGS

FORT MONTGOMERY

THE OLD '76 HOUSE

The "temples" of Saratoga Springs.

# Saratoga Springs

A typical town may have a small park on the main street with a bandstand that has seen better days, a statue of some half-forgotten founder, or an old cannon with a cement-filled barrel that has become more of a climbing toy for kids than a war memorial.

However, Saratoga Springs is not a typical town, and Congress Park is by no means your average park. Located downtown on Broadway, entering the park is reminiscent of walking onto the grounds of an elegant European estate. Like temples to some deity, there are the columned structures housing the Congress and Columbian Springs, whose precious waters brought tourists and great wealth to the area.

In 1767, a wounded British soldier was brought by Native Americans to a spring (now known as High Rock Spring) that supposedly had medicinal properties. Settlers moved to the area around 1776, and tourists were not far behind. Saratoga Springs was established as a town in 1819, and the ensuing flow of tourists coming for the healing waters gave rise to many hotels, resorts, gambling houses, and the famous Saratoga Race Course for thoroughbreds, which opened in 1863 and is now the oldest continuously-operating sporting event of any kind in the United States.

The future looked dim for the resort town in the mid-twentieth century as many of the old hotels were demolished and the gambling houses closed. In the 1960s, however, the completion of Interstate 87 and the building of the Saratoga Performing Arts Center helped give rise to new waves of tourists. Some come for the concerts, some for the horses, some still come for the springs, but now others come for a new reason—the ghosts.

Canfield Casino.

## Canfield Casino

In addition to the springs, Congress Park contains the impressive former Canfield Casino, built in 1870 to lighten the bulging bankrolls of high rolling tourists. For example, in an age when the average worker was lucky to make $500 a year, men here would wager hundreds of thousands of dollars on a single bet! The building now houses the Saratoga Springs History Museum, and it is by the museum's roulette table where the figure of one of the old casino's former gamblers is still seen today. Could this man have lost his fortune on this table, and is still trying to recover it?

There is another figure from a time gone by that walks the halls of the Canfield Casino—a blond woman in a Victorian-era dress. As the casino never permitted women, what could her spirit be doing here? Perhaps when her belongings were brought into the museum and put on display, she came along with a favorite item from her past. In addition to these two figures, there have also been numerous reports of voices, cigar smoke, and other inexplicable occurrences throughout the building. Passersby have also noted lights going on and off and shades going up and down when the building is closed and empty.

## Recommendation

Whatever amount of time you have allotted for the Canfield Casino, double it so you can take a stroll through the park to see the gardens, ponds, and springs. The Inn at Saratoga provides an excellent central location from which to explore the town on foot. Request a room on the third floor if you want the best chance of having an unusual encounter. Only the gardens at Yaddo are open to the public, but they are stunning when in bloom. The Saratoga battlefield and museum are fifteen miles to the southeast in the town of Stillwater. One word of caution, this town is packed during racing season from the end of July through August, so either plan way in advance or go another time.

## Visitor Information

**The Saratoga Springs History Museum**
P.O. Box 216
1 East Congress Street
Saratoga Springs, NY 12866-6019

**The Canfield Casino in Congress Park**
Saratoga Springs, NY 12866
(518) 584-6920, (518) 581-1477 fax
www.saratogahistory.org

**Hours:**

The museum is open daily Memorial Day through Labor Day, 10am – 4pm. Closed Monday and Tuesday the remainder of the year.

**Admission:**

$5 Adults, $4 Seniors and Students, Children Under 12 Admitted Free.

**Directions:**

From the South: New York State Thruway to Exit 24 onto I-87 North to Exit 13N (Route 9). Drive north on Route 9 approximately 4 miles. Route 9 is Broadway in Saratoga Springs. Congress Park is on your right, by the intersection of Broadway and Congress Street.

From the North: I-87 South to Exit 15. Make right turn off ramp and travel 3 miles to intersection making a left turn onto Broadway (at The Prime Hotel) then travel one mile south. Congress Park is on your left, by the intersection of Broadway and Congress Street.

# Inn at Saratoga

While many hotels have come and gone in Saratoga Springs, the Inn at Saratoga claims the honor of being the oldest continuously-operated hotel in town. Opening its doors in 1843 as a boarding house to accommodate the growing influx of tourists arriving for the spring waters, the inn has undergone many changes with an eclectic variety of owners.

In 1846, Dr. Richard Allen provided his guests/ patients who stayed at the inn with supervised diets as part of his treatments that utilized the mineral waters. In 1866, another owner added the large, three-story addition to the rear. At one point in its history, a walkway connected the main building to yet another addition, bringing the total number of rooms to over 200.

Today, the inn has thirty-eight rooms and four luxury cottages, and strives to provide a refined Victorian experience for tourists interested in the wide variety of arts and entertainment available in the area. With such a long and colorful history, does the inn also have something to offer guests who are looking for an experience a little out of the ordinary, say for example, a ghost or two? In fact it does, and many employees will attest to experiencing inexplicable sights and sounds.

It appears as if the third floor is the most active, and over the years some of the housekeepers have reported seeing figures, hearing voices, and having doors opening and closing. Employees often hear voices on the basement level, as well. There are also many sightings in the lobby. The desk clerk will glimpse someone passing through or approaching the desk, only to look up and find no one there.

## Visitor Information

**Inn at Saratoga**
231 Broadway
Saratoga Springs, NY 12866
(518) 583-1890
www.theinnatsaratoga.com

**Directions:**

As listed on their website—From the South: New York State Thruway to Exit 24 onto I-87 North to Exit 13N (Route 9). Drive north on Route 9 approximately 4 miles. Route 9 is Broadway in Saratoga Springs. The Inn at Saratoga is on the left, at the corner of Broadway and Circular Streets.

From the North: I-87 South to Exit 15. Make right turn off ramp and travel 3 miles to intersection making a left turn onto Broadway (at The Prime Hotel) then travel one mile south. The Inn at Saratoga is on the right, at the corner of Broadway and Circular Streets.

From the West: New York State Thruway to Exit 27 – Amsterdam. After the Toll Booth take your first right turn. Follow Route 67 East signs through the City of Amsterdam. Head East approximately 20 miles into Ballston Spa, at the light you take a left turn onto Route 50 North. Route 50 North will bring you right into Saratoga Springs. Route 50 will intersect with Broadway (Route 9). At the light, make a left turn and the Inn at Saratoga is on the left.

From the East: Take Route 90 (Mass Turnpike to the NYS Thruway), then exit the Thruway onto Exit 787 North. Take 787 North to exit for Route 7 West. Take Route 7 West until you get to 87 North Exit (Adirondack Northway). Follow the Northway to the Saratoga Springs Exit 13 North. You may then follow the directions from the South.

Yaddo Gardens.

## Yaddo Gardens, Adelphi Hotel, & Saratoga Battlefield

Then there are the beautiful Yaddo Gardens, where one family's tragedies led to the establishment of an art school, and also resulted in quite a few ghosts in the house and throughout the grounds. There's the Adelphi Hotel, where a women in a blue Victorian dress is seen, and the famous Saratoga battlefield where phantom soldiers still stand guard.

With over two centuries of soldiers, people seeking cures, gamblers, and countless tourists, Saratoga Springs has seen its share of human drama. It has been suggested that underground springs attract spirits. If so, that explains why this area is overflowing with ghosts!

### The Bottom Line:

**The History:** A resort town built for the medicinal natural springs, first discovered by a wounded British soldier in 1767. The site of many gambling houses and the famous thoroughbred racetrack. The Battle of Saratoga took place fifteen miles from here.

**The Haunting:** Numerous reports of gamblers, women, in Victorian dresses, soldiers, and countless inexplicable sights, sounds, and smells.

### Visitor Information

**Yaddo Gardens**
Route 9P (Union Avenue)
Saratoga Springs, NY 12866
(510) 584 0746
http://yaddo.org/garden/home.asp

**Hours:**

Yaddo Gardens are open every day from 8am to dusk.

**Admission:**

The gardens are free of charge to the public. There is a $5 fee for guided tours.

**Directions:**

As listed on their website—From the City of Saratoga Springs: Proceed east from the center of the city on Union Avenue (NY Route 9P). Just after you pass the NYRA Thoroughbred race track you will come to a stoplight. Turn right at the light and follow the signs to the gardens bearing left as you go.

From all other areas: Travel Interstate 87 to Exit 14 in Saratoga Springs. Turn right on NY Route 9P North. At the first stoplight, turn left into Yaddo and follow the signs to the gardens bearing left as you go.

A "cannon-eye's view" from Fort Montgomery.

# Fort Montgomery

The year 1777 looked to be a dark time for the cause of American liberty. New York City had fallen into the hands of the British at the end of 1776. In February of 1777, British General Howe hoped to be warm and comfortable in Philadelphia by the time the next winter set in. As painful as the loss of these two cities would be, however, the real coup de grâce was to be seizing control of the Hudson River. The British saw the river as the key to cutting the lines of communication and supplies between the northern and southern halves of the rebellious colonies. They believed that if this campaign was successful, the war would come to a swift end.

The plan called for the bold and overconfident General John Burgoyne to move south from Canada. Colonel Barry St. Leger was to move from the west through the Mohawk Valley, and General Sir Henry Clinton and his forces would come north from New York City. These armies would sweep away all the rebels in their paths and they would have a glorious victory celebration when they all met in Albany, New York.

It was a great plan on paper, but then, the American patriots developed a knack for spoiling British parties.

One of the first pieces of the British victory puzzle to be lost was when General Howe decided that he and his 10,000 men would concentrate on taking Philadelphia instead of marching to New York. St. Leger became entangled in a long and unsuccessful siege of Fort Stanwix and had to turn back. General Clinton was slow to begin his campaign, and then ran into some stubborn resistance at a couple of forts on the west side of the Hudson River in October of 1777—Forts Clinton and Montgomery.

In early October when General Clinton sailed up the river with about 3,100 troops, he tried to make it look as though he was landing his soldiers on the east side of the river. However, the following morning under the cover of fog, the British forces—consisting of Hessian mercenaries, local Loyalists, and British regulars—came ashore at Stony Point and made their way toward the two forts.

The British began assaulting the forts from the west on land, and from ships in the river below late in afternoon of the 6th of October. They greatly outnumbered the American forces, and of those 600-700 defenders, only half of them were army regulars, the rest being local militia. Despite the uneven numbers, the fortifications and artillery initially helped hold back the British, but by evening it was obvious that it would only be a matter of time before the forts fell.

To prevent "further effusion of blood," British Lieutenant Colonel Mungo Campbell approached Fort Montgomery with a flag of truce and offered the Americans terms—if they surrendered immediately, they would all receive good treatment. The American officer, Colonel William Livingston, is said to have boldly replied to Campbell that if the British surrendered immediately, they would also be treated well.

Apparently, Campbell was not amused by the American sense of humor, and the attack was renewed. Unfortunately for Campbell, he was to discover just how determined the Americans were to fight on, as he was killed leading his men against one of the redoubts of Fort Montgomery. Fighting was fierce, and acts of bravery were recorded on both sides, although perhaps none can compare with that of American Lieutenant Timothy Mix.

As the British began to overrun Fort Montgomery, he prepared to fire his cannon. At that moment, a shot blew off his right hand. Without hesitating, he grabbed a match with his left hand and fired the cannon right into a group of about forty British troops, with deadly effect. (Remarkably, Timothy Mix survived, and lived until 1824.)

As night fell, the British gained entry into both forts and overwhelmed the defenders with their superior numbers in brutal hand-to-hand combat. At Fort Montgomery, the majority of this fighting occurred in the areas of the Round Hill and North Redoubts. An interesting and poignant fact to consider here is that this section of the fort was being attacked by New York Loyalists, so it was actually New Yorkers fighting New Yorkers.

Under the cover of darkness, some of the Americans were able to escape, but of the regulars and militia at the two forts, an estimated 350 were killed, wounded or captured—a staggering fifty percent casualty rate. And despite the promises of fair treatment, the prisoners were sent to the infamous Sugar House in New York City, and to floating prisons known as "hell ships" where many died of starvation and disease.

The British suffered about 190 casualties, but the Battle of Fort Clinton and Fort Montgomery was a satisfying victory for them. They occupied the forts until word came to retreat back to New York City, then they set fire to all the structures, exploded the powder magazines, and reduced both forts to rubble. They also severed the chain across the river.

However, ultimately the British campaign in New York would be a failure, as reinforcements never reached Burgoyne, who was compelled to surrender at Saratoga on October 17. It was a critical victory that helped convince France to join the patriot cause in 1778, and the rest, as they say, is history.

While there were several firsthand accounts describing the events of the battle and some excellent histories have been written, there is still one very intriguing mystery—what happened to all of the bodies from Fort Montgomery? According to the eyewitness account of an army chaplain named Dr. Dwight, who visited the sites of the forts a few months after the battle, the bodies were partially burned, others dumped in a pond where the water was at a "depth so small, as to leave them distinctly visible. Others had an arm, a leg, and a part of the body above the surface. The clothes which they wore when they were killed, were still on them; and proved that they were militia; being the ordinary dress of farmers. Their faces were bloated and monstrous; and their postures were uncouth, distorted, and in the highest degree afflictive."

There is no record of any proper burial taking place, which may account for the paranormal activity here. For example, one night people were arriving at the visitor's center at Fort Montgomery to attend a lecture. One man came in and complimented the staff on the authentic looking reenactor "dressed in an old hunting frock" standing close by on the grounds of the fort. He looked real and solid and just as if he had stepped out of the 1700s. However, there were no reenactors at the event that night, and when they searched the grounds he couldn't be found.

Another fascinating aspect of the history of this site is the fact that long before the first stone of the fort was put in place, Native Americans lived on this land, as was evidenced by the many artifacts that were unearthed here. Some believe the Indian's spirits still reside here.

The most active location is the visitor center where they hear footsteps and voices, and figures have often been witnessed. It's never anything threatening, but it certainly gives one the sense that history is literally still alive at Fort Montgomery, in more ways than one!

## The Bottom Line

**The History:** Fort Montgomery is an important Revolutionary War site that is more intact than most other contemporary battlefields.

**The Haunting:** Revolutionary War-era soldiers have been seen on the grounds. The presence of Native Americans has been felt. Many strange occurrences have been experienced in the visitor center.

## Recommendation

Fort Montgomery spreads over fourteen acres containing sections of the original fortifications, the foundations of soldier barracks and other buildings, and Indian rock shelters. To fully appreciate the scope of the battle and the brave acts of the soldiers who fought here, you must walk the grounds. The visitor center has many authentic battlefield artifacts on display. The theater shows an excellent fourteen-minute orientation film, and there's a large three-dimensional map that really helps in understanding the layout of the forts. Look for the enameled cuff buttons with the word "Liberty." Paranormal activity is the highest in the visitor center, and near the foundations of the barracks.

## Visitor Information

**Fort Montgomery State Historic Site**
Route 9W
Fort Montgomery, NY 10922
(845) 446-2134
http://nysparks.state.ny.us/sites/info.asp?siteId=36

**Hours and Admission:**

Visitor's Center Hours: are 9am – 5pm, Wednesday through Sunday. Rates for Visitor's Center and grounds: $3 per adult, $2 per senior/student, children 12 and under free. Parking is free.

Fort Montgomery grounds are open 7 days a week, sunrise to sunset. Attractions include audio-visual programs, demonstrations, group tours, hiking, interpretive signs, scenic views, and self-guided tours.

**Directions:**

From the East-Route 202, 6, or 9D to the Bear Mountain Bridge: In the traffic circle take your first right to 9W North. The entrance to Fort Montgomery will be on your right just after you cross the bridge.

From New York City: Take the Palisades Parkway north to the Bear Mountain Circle or take the New York State Thruway to Exit 16 in Harriman, then Route 6 toward Bear Mountain. At the circle the third right will be 9W North. The entrance to Fort Montgomery will be on your right just after you cross the bridge.

The Old 76 House.

# The Old '76 House

By the time Casparus Mabie began building his house on Main Street in 1753, Tappan was already an old town. The grant for a township had been issued in 1686, by 1691 there was a courthouse, and a church was built in 1694. Tappan was an important center in early colonial days, and Mabie's house would play an important role in the coming Revolution.

Patriots would meet at the house to discuss the latest news and share information, and it came to be known as the "listening post." George Washington and many of his generals dined at the house—events that were catered by Samuel Fraunces, of the famed Fraunces Tavern in Manhattan. Arguably, though, its most famous role would be as a jail, when British Major John André was held there for his trial and execution.

In September of 1780, Major André received the plans for West Point from the notorious American traitor, General Benedict Arnold. When the treasonous plot was uncovered, Arnold escaped to the safety of the British lines, but André was taken prisoner. He was brought to Tappan and held in Mabie's house.

On September 29, Major André was put on trial at the church across the street. The recommendation that the board of inquiry delivered to George Washington stated that this British officer caught in civilian clothes "ought to be considered as a spy from the enemy" and "ought to suffer death" as a consequence. Washington signed the death warrant and André's fate was sealed.

On October 2, André was taken from the Mabie house and led to the place of his execution. Ever the gentleman and brave soldier, he put the noose around his own neck, and tied a handkerchief over his eyes. As he had predicted, there was only a "momentary pang" as death was almost immediate, and his body was buried on the spot where he died.

The famous house became a tavern in 1800, and for most of the next 200 years the "1776 House" continued to serve the public, becoming one of the country's oldest such establishments. Today, the fully restored and expanded Old '76 House is a colonial gem, which is best appreciated while dining by one of its fireplaces, or perhaps gathering with family and friends for Sunday brunch. However, if it's more than just food and history you're looking for, you probably won't be disappointed—this two hundred and fifty-year-old house just might also have some of the country's oldest ghosts...

For example, several people have seen a man in a British officer's uniform who fits the description of Major André. Years ago there was a dishwasher named Baltimore who lived alone upstairs. He would often hear footsteps and voices throughout the house late at night and kept a rope ladder by his window so he could make a quick escape in case the ghosts ever came into his room!

Over the years, other employees have also heard footsteps and voices. On at least one occasion, the police were called because it sounded like someone was upstairs after the restaurant had closed, but no one was found. The early morning hours also seem to be popular with at least one ghost who has often been heard coming down the staircase from the second floor.

If you want a prime paranormal seat, request Table #2. Tablecloths on that table have been seen to move on their own. There was a loud sound of silverware crashing to the floor by Table #2, but when the staff came to see what happened, not a thing was out of place. The most common occurrence at Table #2 involves the glass flue. All of the tables are set in colonial style, and each has a candleholder with a glass flue. There has never been any problem with these candleholders, except at Table #2. The glass flue is often found laying on the table or the floor. No one can figure out why the flue repeatedly comes off of its base, or why it hasn't broken when it falls to the floor. No one has actually seen or heard it happen, but just about everyone on the staff has replaced the wandering flue. (Just in case you think that this particular candleholder is defective, they have switched it with other candleholders. On a different table, the flue remains in place, but whatever holder is on Table #2 invariably has the same problem!)

Don't hesitate to indulge in an excellent meal within the walls that once held Major André prisoner. In fact, it may be his famous restless spirit causing some of the haunted activity, as he still waits for George Washington to grant a pardon and spare him the noose. (Or, it may be the aroma of the delicious pumpkin soup on a cold winter's day that attracts him—because it tastes so good it's enough to bring anyone out their grave!)

There are few structures that survive today with the rich history of the Old '76 House, and fewer still that are open to the public. Enjoy the food, appreciate the history, and if you are seated at Table #2 and strange things happen, don't say you weren't warned!

## Recommendation

**Take the time to look at the beautiful Manse house set back from the road just to the north of the Old '76 House, and the church and old cemetery across the street (where other spirits have been seen wandering). To see the actual site of Major André's execution, turn left out of the front of the restaurant's parking lot and make your next left. Then turn left on Andre Hill. A monument marks the spot of the hanging. Ask for Table #2 for the best paranormal seat in the house.**

## Visitor Information

Old '76 House
**110 Main Street**
**Tappan, NY 10983-2427**
**(845) 359-5476**
**www.76house.com**

**Hours:**
**Open every day. Sunday: brunch 11am – 3pm, dinner 4pm – 9pm. Monday-Thursday: lunch 11:30am – 3pm, dinner 5pm – 9pm. Friday: lunch 11:30am – 3pm, dinner 5pm – 9:30pm. Saturday: lunch 11:30am – 3pm, dinner 5pm – 10pm.**

**Directions:**
**From the 287/New York State Thruway: Take exit 12 to Route 303 south. After passing over the Palisades Parkway, turn right onto King's Highway at the next light. The road winds its way to a stop sign. Make a left and the restaurant will be just past the next light on your right.**

**From the Palisades Parkway: Take exit 5S to go south on Route 303, then follow the Directions: above to Kings Highway.**

## The Bottom Line

**The History:** How can you resist the opportunity to visit one of America's most historic sites and have a great meal at the same time, and then take an after-dinner stroll to the site of the hanging of a notorious British spy? You really do feel like you are stepping back into colonial times with the architecture and décor, and you can easily picture George Washington being right at home wining and dining here.

**The Haunting:** People have seen a British officer, heard many inexplicable sounds, and witnessed objects moving. Ask for Table #2 if you want the best haunted seat in the house.

# North Carolina

MORDECAI HISTORIC PARK

USS NORTH CAROLINA

THE CAROLINA INN

# Mordecai Historic Park

Raleigh is one of the few capitals that was actually a planned city. In 1785, Joel Lane built a home here for his son, Henry, and then in 1788 he convinced officials that his property was the best location for the new state capital. Lane sold 1,000 acres just to the south of this house, and the city of Raleigh was officially established in 1792.

The Mordecai House. *Photo by Robert A. Strong.*

## Mordecai House

The house is known as the Mordecai (pronounced MordeKEY) House because of Moses Mordecai, who married not one, but two of Henry Lane's daughters—but fortunately not at the same time. Moses was a lawyer from a very prominent Jewish family, but after marrying Margaret Lane, adhered to her Episcopal faith. Moses and Margaret had three children, Henry, Jacob, and Ellen. Upon Margaret's death, he married her sister, Ann, and they had one child, Margaret. In 1824, Moses contracted with the State Architect, William Nichols, to remodel and expand the house into a Greek Revival mansion. Much of the growing city of Raleigh during the nineteenth and twentieth centuries was built on Mordecai land, and the mansion stayed in the family through his daughter Margaret's descendants until 1967, when it was purchased by the state.

The acquisition brought about the establishment of the Mordecai Square Historic Park, and the home contains many original furnishings and papers. Today the Mordecai House is the city's oldest building still on its original foundation, and it is a beautiful example of early North Carolina history. It is also one of the state's finest haunted houses!

A misty, grayish lady in a nineteenth century dress has been seen throughout the house. She is said to be Mary Willis Mordecai Turk, and she can also be seen and heard playing the piano. Another family member was seen by an employee who was alone in the house cleaning—or at least she thought she was alone. As she cleaned the woodwork in the dining room, she saw a woman walking toward her up the hallway from the library. The woman wore a long black skirt and white blouse, and looked perfectly real and solid.

The woman did not resemble any of the guides, yet still, she somehow looked familiar. The employee was a little put off when the woman ignored her and walked right by her as if she wasn't there, then turned into the parlor. Minutes passed, and the mysterious woman made no sounds in the parlor. Curious as to what she was doing in that room, and why she was even in the house in the first place, the employee entered the parlor, but found no one. Racking her brain, she finally realized where she had seen this woman—in the portrait of Margaret Lane!

Some have claimed to see Civil War soldiers around the grounds, and other figures from the long history of this place, so the property itself may be haunted. At least one other building in the park has also earned the titled of haunted house.

The Andrew Johnson House. *Photo by Robert A. Strong.*

## Andrew Johnson House

Andrew Johnson, the seventeenth president, was born in a small house in Raleigh in 1808. Built in the late 1700s, it was part of Casso's Inn where his mother worked, and it certainly speaks to his humble beginnings. In 1906, the building was purchased by the Colonial Dames of America, and it was moved several times before finally finding a permanent home in Mordecai Historic Park. It is considered to be the oldest house in Raleigh.

On one occasion a boy from a visiting school group became very agitated at the sight of "a man with a scar" at the house, although no one else could see him. A prolonged sighting occurred one night when an employee was leaving one of the other buildings in the park. It was long after closing and she was the only one there, but she had a strange feeling as she was passing the Johnson House. She saw a light on inside, and when she came up to the window she saw a lit candle hovering on the air.

Someone was obviously holding that candle, but they simply were not visible! After watching for some time, the candle began to move and went out of sight. Frightened, the woman started to quickly walk away, but she turned back to see that the phantom candlelight was now upstairs. It burned brightly for another minute or two, then was extinguished.

Was the man with the scar a former employee of the inn, or a member of the Johnson family? And who still resides inside this little house, lighting their way through the darkness with a candle? It is impossible to put a name to all the spirits who reside within Mordecai Historic Park. But be assured, there have certainly been enough interesting residents and human drama over the centuries here to create quite a cast of paranormal characters!

## The Bottom Line

**The History:** The Mordecai House was first built in 1785, and Mordecai land was used for the city of Raleigh. President Andrew Johnson was born in the small house that was moved to this park.

**The Haunting:** Two women are seen in the Mordecai House, a man with a scar and phantom candlelight are seen in the Johnson House, and Civil War soldiers appear throughout the park.

## Recommendations

**The Historic Raleigh Trolley Tours begin in Mordecai Historic Park, so plan your trip to include this informative tour, as well. You are allowed to get off the trolley and back on at any stop, so you can go at your own pace. Call or check the park's website for special events that cover a wide variety of topics.**

## Visitor Information

**Mordecai House and Andrew Johnson House**
**Mordecai Historic Park**
One Mimosa Street
Raleigh, NC 27604-1203
(919) 857-4364
www.nps.gov/history/Nr/travel/raleigh/mor.htm

**Hours:**

Park Tour Hours: Tuesday-Saturday: 10am – 3pm on the hour. (1pm – 3pm when a school group is on site), Sunday: 1pm – 3pm on the hour; One-hour tours begin every hour, last tour begins at 3pm. Tour times are subject to change please call for the latest information.

The Historic Raleigh Trolley Tours are narrated 1-hour tours around downtown Raleigh every Saturday from March-December.

**Admission:**

Admission for Park Tours: $5 for adults, $3 for seniors, $3 for youth (7-17), children (6 and under) are free.

**Directions:**

From Route 401 in Raleigh, exit onto Wake Forest Road and go south to Mimosa Street.

The U.S.S. *North Carolina* in 1946.

# USS North Carolina

In 1942, when the USS *North Carolina* arrived at Pearl Harbor, it was still a scene of devastation. One young sailor stationed there described his feelings when he first saw the new battleship, saying it was like a "ray of hope" in what were very dark days for America.

The *North Carolina's* keel was laid down in 1937 in the New York Naval Shipyard, and she was launched in June of 1940. This was the first of a new breed of battleships, and so garnered a lot of press and attention, earning her the nickname "*Showboat*." But this boat was not all show, as it would see action throughout the Pacific. In August of 1942 in the Solomon Islands, the *North Carolina* helped sink a Japanese carrier. In September, she was struck by a torpedo and six men were killed. Whether protecting other ships or pounding the coastline of an island with her big guns, *North Carolina's* battle record included every major offensive operation including Tarawa, Kwajelein, Truk, Iwo Jima, and Okinawa, earning her fifteen battle stars.

Immediately after the war, the ship was used for training for a short time, and then was decommissioned in 1947. Like so many of the planes and ships that fought in WWII, the *North Carolina* was destined to be cut up for scrap, but North Carolina school children mounted an effort to "bring the ship home." They raised $330,000 to buy her from the Navy, and in 1961 tugboats began maneuvering her up the river to Wilmington. Unfortunately, in a narrow stretch of the river the ship struck the Fergus Ark restaurant on Princess Street, inflicting so much damage it never reopened. But the restaurant was to be the last casualty the mighty *North Carolina* would inflict, as it became a museum and memorial to all North Carolinians killed in World War II.

Soon after the ship was restored and opened to the public, the staff began noticing strange things happening. Long after everyone else had gone, lone employees would hear voices and noises, such as the sounds of hatches opening and closing. Lights and televisions would go on and off by themselves. The air could suddenly turn icy cold and objects would move on their own.

Witnesses have also reported a young blond man, perhaps a sailor who lost his life on the ship? Another man has been seen looking out of the portholes. Then there are the overwhelming feelings of sadness, fear, or anxiety, experienced by staff and visitors.

In short, you never know who or what you will encounter on this ship, but suffice to say the traumatic effects of war still resonate within the battleship *North Carolina*, and the spirits of lost sailors may very well still be on duty.

This ship has so many stories to tell, and because it has been preserved you have the opportunity to learn about and appreciate what America's greatest generation sacrificed and accomplished.

## The Bottom Line

**The History:** The first battleship of its kind, launched in 1940. The ship saw action in every major offensive operation in the Pacific in WWII.

**The Haunting:** At least ten sailors died aboard ship, and at least two are still there.

## Recommendations

**This is a big ship! Allow at least two hours for your visit and wear comfortable and sensible shoes. It is a self-guided tour, so you can go at your own pace and if it isn't too crowded, you can have time alone to test your sixth sense. There are a wide range of special events for families and history buffs, including special behind-the-scenes tours, and if you have a big group—or just a big budget—you can rent the whole ship.**

## Visitor Information

**Battleship *North Carolina***
**1 Battleship Road**
**Wilmington, NC 28401-2577**
**(910) 251-5797**
**www.battleshipnc.com**

**Hours:**
**Open every day of the year, including all holidays. Summer Hours: (Memorial Day through Labor Day) 8am – 8pm, except Independence Day when the ship closes at 6pm to prepare for fireworks. Winter Hours: (After Labor Day weekend through Thursday prior to Memorial Day weekend) 8am – 5pm, except Christmas Day when the ship opens at noon.**

**Admission:**
**Adults (12 and over): $12. Seniors (65+): $10. Military (active duty or retired with ID): $10. Children (6-11): $6. Children (5 and under): Free.**

**Directions:**
**From their website—**From the South on 1-95 North: **After you cross the border from South Carolina into North Carolina, go approximately 14 miles. Take Exit 14 onto US 74 East towards Wilmington. After approximately 26 miles, US 76 merges with US 74. Continue to travel approximately 52 miles to Wilmington. When approaching Wilmington follow the signs to the Battleship Memorial and 421 North. (US76 East out of Florence SC may seem quicker but it is 2 lanes and US 74 East is 4 lanes and it is actually a quicker route to Wilmington and the Battleship Memorial.)**

From the North on I-95: **As you approach Benson NC, exit east on I-40 to Wilmington. Then follow the directions below, "From the West on I-40."**

From the West on I-40 **(Raleigh-125 miles): As you approach Wilmington (6 miles out), take exit 416 A (I-140/US 17 South) towards Myrtle Beach. At 7 miles you will cross the Dan Cameron Bridge with the temporary end of the highway in sight. Take the Battleship Memorial/ Wilmington exit, at the end of the off ramp, bear right onto US 421 South. Continue approximately 3 miles, passing thru the stop light and follow the Battleship Memorial sign. Proceed approximately 1 mile crossing over the S. Thomas Rhodes Bridge. Turn left at the sign "Battleship Memorial."**

# The Carolina Inn

Normally, you wouldn't want to stay in university housing, but The Carolina Inn on the University of Chapel Hill campus is unique—a AAA 4-Diamond hotel on the National Register of Historic Landmarks, whose profits all go to fund to the university's library.

The inn was built in 1924 by John Sprunt Hill, an alumnus and trustee, who wanted "to provide for the special wants and comforts of the University alumni... and University visitors." He certainly succeeded, as this elegant, Colonial Revival hotel which was designed to resemble Mt. Vernon, caters to the most finicky alumni. Hill donated the inn to the university in 1935, with the understanding that all profits would be put toward "the maintenance and support of the University library, and especially for the support of the collection of books and papers known as the North Carolina Collection." While some inns have libraries, few support them!

It is only fitting, then, that such an academic institution has an academic ghost. A physician with the International Health Division of the Rockefeller Foundation, Dr. William Jaccs, retired in 1948 and decided to live at the Carolina Inn. He remained there for the next seventeen years until his death in 1965. To be correct, however, he may remain there still.

Dr. Jaccs apparently had a wonderful sense of humor, and still does, as he likes to play pranks on guests who stay in his second-floor room, often locking them out. For example, one day the guest's key cards could not be made to work, so a maintenance man had to climb a ladder, go through the window, then take the door off of its hinges. Jaccs has also been held responsible for moving things, messing with the plumbing, and a variety of inexplicable sounds and smells.

However, the good doctor is most likely not the only ghost in the house. Witnesses have reported hearing a piano playing where there was no piano, and footsteps and voices where there weren't any people.

The case of the Carolina Inn does not appear to be one of unhappy spirits locked to the site of some tragedy. On the contrary, the "high-spirited" practical jokes and other activity speak to those who choose to be at the inn after death because they enjoyed their life here. Perhaps Dr. Jaccs knew that laughter was the best medicine, and he is still dispensing that medicine to this day.

## Recommendations

**Keep in mind the university's sporting events and other busy times before trying to make reservations. There is also a fine restaurant, bar, and afternoon tea. Ask for the doctor's room if you want a prime paranormal spot, but don't be surprised if he messes with you!**

## Visitor Information

**The Carolina Inn**
211 Pittsboro Street, Chapel Hill, NC 27516-2739
On the Campus of the University of North Carolina at Chapel Hill
(800) 962-8519 (919) 933-2001
www.carolinainn.com

**Directions:**

From their website—From I-40 WEST (Coming from the East – Road U Airport, Raleigh, Wilmington): Follow I-40 West to exit 273A, which takes you to Route 147 North (Durham Freeway). Merge onto NC-54 W via exit 273A toward Chapel Hill. Stay straight to go onto Raleigh Road/NC-54 BR W. Continue to follow Raleigh Road/NC-54 BR W. Turn slight right onto S. Columbia Street. Turn left onto W. Cameron Avenue. Turn left on Pittsboro Street.

From I-85 NORTH (Coming from the South Charlotte, Atlanta). Take I-85 North to I-40. Take I-40 E. toward Raleigh. Take the NC-86 exit, exit 266, toward Chapel Hill. Keep right at the fork to go on NC-86. Turn right onto W. Cameron Avenue. Turn left onto Pittsboro Street.

From I-85 SOUTH (Coming from the North – Virginia and Points North) Take I-95 S to I-85 S. Take 1-85 S to US-15. Keep left to take US-15 S/ US-15-501 S via exit 174B toward Chapel Hill. Take the exit toward UNC Chapel Hill. Turn onto Raleigh Road./NC-54 BR W. Continue to follow Raleigh Road/NC-54 BR W. Turn slight right onto S. Columbia Street/NC-86 N. Turn left onto W. Cameron Avenue. Turn left onto Pittsboro Street.

## The Bottom Line

**The History:** An inn built for the alumni and donated to the university in 1935.

**The Haunting:** A practical joking ghost who likes to lock guests out of his room.

# North Dakota

FORT ABRAHAM LINCOLN

FORT ABERCROMBIE

SAGE HILL B&B

# Fort Abraham Lincoln

Miti-ba-wa-esh, meaning On-a-Slant, was a Mandan Indian village built around 1575 on ground sloping down to the Missouri River. It was the Mandan women's job to build about 86 earth lodges in which 1,000-1,500 people lived. The Mandans were skilled in making pottery and working with animal skins, so their villages became centers of trade—until the population was devastated by smallpox in 1781.

Custer's House. North Dakota State Parks.

In 1872, when the railroad had been extended to the Missouri River, it was decided to build a military post by the Mandan village site. Fort McKeen was established to protect the western expansion movement, and shortly after, it was renamed Fort Abraham Lincoln. The fort quickly grew and in 1873 the 7th Cavalry under the command of the flamboyant Lt. Col. George Armstrong Custer arrived. By the following year, Fort Abraham Lincoln was the largest in the Dakota Territory, as well as being the most important.

In November of 1877, the Nez Perce, led by Chief Joseph, spent four days here during their long relocation journey. It was from this fort that the Black Hills Expedition left in its search for gold in 1874. A less successful mission also started here—the Centennial Campaign, begun on May 17, 1876. The campaign was undertaken by Custer and the 7th Cavalry in an attempt to get Indians back on their reservations. One of the locations they traveled to was a river called Little Bighorn, and the ensuing battle became popularly known as Custer's Last Stand. Custer and over 260 of his men were killed in that battle against Sioux and Cheyenne warriors.

The importance of the fort gradually declined in the 1880s. In 1883, the cavalry was transferred to another fort, and in 1891 Congress ordered that the fort be shut down for good. Ever resourceful, area residents dismantled Fort Abraham Lincoln the following year to reuse all the wood and nails for their homes and barns.

This once crucial military post and thriving Indian village may have been forgotten, had it not been for reconstruction projects first begun by the Civilian Conservation Corps in 1934. Thanks to all of these efforts, the site now has a replica of the Mandan village, a visitors center, military blockhouses, barracks, commissary, stables, and a reproduction of Custer's house. It also has quite a few ghosts.

At the Mandan On-A-Slant Village, visitors have heard sounds and voices speaking in a strange language. Perhaps some of this can be attributed to active imaginations, but there's one thing that can't so easily be explained. A descendant of the Mandans gave some visitors an excellent tour of his ancestors' village. The only problem is, they later discovered that this man had been dead for many years!

Then there's Custer's house, where many people have seen a woman looking out a window, but when they go inside the house is empty. Could this be Custer's wife, Libby, still waiting for her husband to return from the Little Bighorn? Legend has it that Libby had a premonition of her husband's fate, and actually fainted at what might have been the moment of his death.

Members of the staff feel uneasy in this house, as if they are being watched or are never alone. They will lock up the house in the evening with everything in order, then return in the morning to find objects and furniture moved, and an impression on one of the beds as if someone had sat there. Visitors who have no prior knowledge of the place report seeing figures and feeling a strong presence. Many have been convinced this house is haunted.

It is not uncommon for new structures to inherit old ghosts—especially if the building is an exact reproduction of the home with which the spirit was connected. Does Libby Custer haunt this familiar place, or is it another lady, or several other people? The grounds of the old fort and Indian village may have many stories to tell, if you are willing to listen.

## The Bottom Line

**The History:** The most important military post in the Dakota Territory, established in 1872. This was Custer's last home before his last stand.

**The Haunting:** A woman is seen and felt in the Custer's house. All manner of inexplicable things occur in the Indian village.

## Recommendations

Tour guides are all dressed in period costumes and it isn't hard to imagine that you're stepping back into 1875—especially if you happen to see Libby Custer! There are many special events throughout the year including Frontier Army Days in June, with military reenactments and activities for the entire family. Custer Christmas days are in December, and the very popular "Haunted Fort" days are held every October, when you get to hear all of the fort's best ghost stories. There's a gift shop and coffee shop. Plays are performed during the summer, including ones originally performed here in the 1870s. For the full experience, you can spend the night in one of the campsites or sleeping cabins. The park includes over 1,000 acres to explore by hiking or on horseback.

## Visitor Information

**Fort Abraham Lincoln State Park**
4480 Fort Lincoln Road
Mandan, ND 58554-7947
(701) 667-6380
www.parkrec.nd.gov/parks/flsp.htm

**Hours:**

The Fort Abraham Lincoln State Park is open daily year round. The interpretive sites, buildings, and tours run late April or early May-October, 9am – 5pm.

Tours of the Custer House and On-a-Slant run daily every half-hour starting a 9am with the last tour leaving at 5pm.

**Admission:**

An Interpretive Pass provides admission to all tours and special programs at On-a-Slant Mandan Indian Village, Fort Abraham Lincoln cavalry post, and the Visitor Center: $6 for Adults, $4 for Students. Costs for special events may vary. Entrance fee into the State Park is $5 per car.

**Directions:**

From Bismarck: Take I-94 BUS W/E. Main Avenue. Continue to follow I-94 BUS W. Turn left at E. Main Street. Turn left at 6th Avenue SE. Continue onto N. Dakota 1806 S/Fort McKeen Road. Continue to follow N. Dakota 1806 S. Continue onto Pleasant Valley Road S. Continue onto 20th Street/Township Road 12. Continue straight onto 46th Street. Turn left toward N. Dakota 1806 N/Fort Lincoln Road. The fort will be on the right.

# Fort Abercrombie

The Red River wagon trails were used by gold miners and settlers headed to western Canada, Montana, Washington, and Oregon. In 1857, Congress approved twenty-five square miles near where these trails converged to be used for a military outpost to protect travelers. The final decision on the location would be up to Lieutenant Colonel John J. Abercrombie, who arrived in 1858 and established the fort that would bear his name, but would also come to be called "The Gateway to the Dakotas."

Unfortunately, the initial site was prone to flooding, so it was moved to higher ground in 1859. The army regulars stationed there were ordered elsewhere when the Civil War began, and were replaced by Minnesota Volunteer Infantry in March, 1862. It wasn't much of a fort at the time, and the Minnesota men found only the barracks, commissary, and Officer's quarters, and they would soon wish the army had taken the time to build strong fortifications.

It wasn't the Confederates that attacked the garrison that year, it was the Dakota Indians. The government's empty promises of food and supplies left the Dakota people with empty stomachs. Tensions were running high, and hostilities were ignited when some Dakotas went to Andrew Myrick, a trader for the Lower Sioux Agency in Minnesota, and asked for some food on credit. Myrick—who was married to an Indian—nonetheless stated in response, "So far as I am concerned, if they are hungry let them eat grass or their own dung." Myrick's body was later found with his mouth stuffed with grass.

As the conflict spread in August of 1862, Fort Abercrombie came under siege for six weeks. The soldiers desperately tried to fortify the post, even using barrels of food and firewood to construct some makeshift defenses. The fiercest fighting took place by the stable and the commissary on two separate occasions in September. The siege was finally lifted on the 23rd when 500 reinforcements arrived.

Throughout the region, the army took thousands of Dakota men, women, and children prisoner, and condemned 307 men to death. President Abraham Lincoln reviewed the cases, and revised that number down to just 39, but when the sentence was carried out in Mankato, Minnesota on December 26, 1862, it was still the largest mass execution in American history.

The fort was abandoned in 1877, as it had outlived its usefulness, and the buildings were sold and removed. However a WPA project in 1939-1940 brought the original guardhouse back, and several blockhouses and the stockade were reconstructed. An interpretive center was recently added, and the Fort Abercrombie State Historic site now stands as a reminder to an unfortunate time in our history when settlers, soldiers, and Indians were locked in a terrible struggle.

There are other reminders here, too, in the form of the figures of both soldiers and Indians. Seen throughout the grounds over the span of many years, some of these figures appear very real and solid, while others are simply wispy or dark shapes. Nothing here is threatening, though, and these may just be the imprints or residual energies from those terrible times. But perhaps they are truly wandering spirits, looking for justice, or at least a little compassion, from someone… perhaps a visitor like you?

## Recommendations

**Fort Abercrombie was the first permanent U.S. military fort established in what was to become North Dakota. Call or check the website for the latest schedule of special events. Audio tours are available to more fully appreciate the site.**

## Visitor Information

**Fort Abercrombie**
**County Highway-22**
**Abercrombie, ND 58001**
**(701) 328-2666**
**www.history.nd.gov/historicsites/abercrombie/index.html**

**Hours:**
**The fort grounds are open year-round. The museum is open Mid-May to Mid-September, 9am – 5pm, Thursday-Monday.**

**Admission:**
**The fort site is free. Museum and Exhibits: $5 for adults, $2.50 for children 6-15, $1 for students in supervised school groups, $2 per person for groups of 20 or more.**

**Directions:**
**From Fargo: I-94 BUS E/Main Avenue/US-10 E. Entering Minnesota. Turn right at 8th Street S/US-75 S. Continue to follow US-75 S. Turn right at Co. Highway 1. Turn right at Co. Highway 22. Entering North Dakota. The fort will be on the right.**

## The Bottom Line

**The History:** The first permanent U.S. military fort established in what was to become North Dakota. Under siege for six weeks during the Dakota Wars of 1862.

**The Haunting:** Figures of Indians and soldiers are seen.

*Courtesy of Sage Hill Bed & Breakfast.*

# Sage Hill B&B

When the White School was built in Anamoose in 1928, it was one of the most modern buildings in the state. Named for local resident Colonel Samuel White, who led a battalion in the Spanish American War, the school had something most places only dream about today—a wind generator for power. Also unique for the time was the hot lunch program, and hot showers for the students who most likely didn't yet have indoor plumbing at home.

The three-story school building had 10,000 square feet consisting of two large classrooms, a library, gym, kitchen, stage, and various offices. There were also two barns to house the six horse-drawn school buses! The White School was so progressive, that meetings were held here to instruct rural teachers on the latest methods. At its peak, the school had about 100 students, but a declining population forced the school to close its doors in 1968.

In 1996, the old school was in need of serious repair, and with little money and even less experience, the new owners undertook the challenge of restoring the building and opening it as a bed and breakfast. In addition to the three guest rooms, the traveling superintendent's office became a small, intimate dining area, the former teacherage was converted to the dining room, and the gymnasium is now a reception hall.

Today, the Sage Hill Bed and Breakfast offers award-winning accommodations and dining, and there are still valuable lessons to learn in this old school—how to relax and enjoy yourself! There are also some paranormal lessons to be learned, as the owners discovered during the renovations.

The first thing they noticed was that furniture and objects would seemingly move on their own, and not just a short distance. Something placed in one room could later be found at the other end of the building on a different floor! There were also "darting figures" that could just be glimpsed out of the corner of their eyes, that would vanish when they turned to look. In the basement room where a coal-fired boiler once stood, a mysterious light often glowed. Then there was the cigar smoke; the smell would suddenly appear and be very strong, then just as quickly disappear. What was the message that this spirit or spirits was trying to convey?

The story of a tragedy at the school eventually came to light. One day the superintendent and a student were making the rounds of the school in a routine inspection. No one knows how it happened, but by the boiler in the basement the superintendent caught fire. The flames spread, and both the man and the boy were killed. It just so happened that this particular superintendent often enjoyed smoking cigars.

While experiences here can occur at any time, activity really picks up whenever the owners are working on renovations. Perhaps the former superintendent wants to make sure things are done right, i.e., his way?

As with any location, there are no guarantees as to when the ghosts will make their presence known. However, it is certainly worth the trip to the Sage Hill Bed and Breakfast to find out if the paranormal school is in session.

## The Bottom Line

**The History:** A former school built in 1928 converted to a bed and breakfast.

**The Haunting:** A superintendent who died in a fire still makes his presence known.

## Recommendations

**The restaurant has won awards for its cuisine, and a special award for its honey oatmeal bread. Lunch and dinner are available to the general public on a 24-hour advance reservation basis, and entrees are required to be pre-ordered. Parties of up to seventy-five people can be accommodated. Located in the Lakes and Gardens region, the area is known as a "bird watchers paradise," and there are many outdoor activities to enjoy. Even though there is a no-smoking policy, pay attention if you catch a whiff of cigar smoke!**

## Visitor Information

**Sage Hill Bed and Breakfast**
**2091 33rd Street Northeast**
**Anamoose, ND 58710-9428**
**(701) 465-0225**
**www.sagehillnd.com**

**Directions:**

**From their website—Sage Hill is located off Highway 52. It is approximately a one hour drive east from Minot. Traveling east or west down U. S. Highway 52, before entering or leaving the city of Martin, look for the light blue and white Department of Transportation tourist locator signs. The signs are on both sides of the highway and are located approximately 500 feet from the turn off intersection. The intersection is identified with a 911 street sign marked 21st Street NE. Turn north onto a graveled road and drive 4 miles. Sage Hill is a large slate blue cedar shake building.**

**If you want to save a few miles, the back way to Sage Hill is to exit Highway 52 at Anamoose. Drive north through town, over the railroad tracks, and just beyond the tracks is a cemetery on the right. Take a right just after the cemetery onto a gravel road and go 5 miles East.**

# Ohio

MANSFIELD REFORMATORY

FAIRPORT HARBOR LIGHTHOUSE

RIDER'S INN

Mansfield Reformatory.

# Mansfield Reformatory

In the late 1800s, the state of Ohio needed a facility for youthful offenders. The first stone was placed in 1886 in what was to grow into one of the largest castle-like structures in the country, encompassing 250,000 square feet. The impressive combination of Gothic, Romanesque, and Queen Anne architecture was supposed to inspire inmates to reform, but unfortunately, the fancy stonework did little to temper the brutality of many of the 154,000 prisoners that would enter these gates. The inmates represented the worst of humanity, and the over 200 men who died within these walls may still be imprisoned there as a result of their violent deaths.

If ever there was a Hollywood setting for a haunting, it is at the Mansfield Reformatory. In fact, Hollywood has used the prison for several movies, including *The Shawshank Redemption* and scenes from *Air Force One*. The prison was officially closed in 1990 and is now a museum that hosts tourists and ghost hunters from around the world—and there is more than enough here to see and experience.

However, the deaths that occurred at the reformatory were not all those of the prisoners. Guards were killed in escape attempts, and even the warden and his wife passed away here, possibly accounting for two of the many wandering spirits. Warden Arthur Glattke had a heart attack in his office in 1959, but his wife's death was far more suspicious. In November of 1950, Helen Glattke was allegedly reaching into her jewelry box where a loaded gun was also kept. Somehow, the gun managed to discharge and shot her in the chest. She died three days later of pneumonia, and her death was ruled to be accidental, but rumors spread that it had really been suicide or murder.

We may never know the truth, but perhaps Helen is still trying to tell us what really happened. In the Warden's Quarters people have heard a man and woman arguing—could this be a replay of the final moments leading up to Helen's "accidental" death? There is also the scent of roses, particularly in Helen's former room, which signals she is present. A man's footsteps have also been heard, perhaps the Warden himself pacing his quarters, pondering the mysterious circumstances of his wife's tragic end, or perhaps suffering from guilt?

Many of the other deaths at Mansfield Reformatory were no mystery at all—those of the inmates who committed suicide. Most of the suicides were by hanging, but one desperate man set himself on fire with chemicals he had stolen from the prison's workshop.

Then there were the murders—the stabbings and beatings of both prisoners and guards. For example, two inmates were put into a small cell in solitary confinement one night, but only one was alive in the morning. The other man's body was found stuffed under the bed. In 1932, one of the guards was beaten to death with an iron rod in solitary confinement during an escape attempt. One prisoner was hung in the West Wing Shower, which is one of the most paranormally active places. Other paranormal hotspots include solitary confinement, the infirmary, and the chapel. But ghosts can be seen, felt (with anything from the sense of being watched to being pushed or punched), and recorded anywhere at anytime.

In addition to the sheer number of paranormal encounters and the enormous size of the place, what makes Mansfield Reformatory unique among historic haunts is the access ghost hunters are granted here. Depending upon your level of interest, and nerves, you can take a daylight tour of the facilities, a nighttime ghost walk, or you can spend the entire night in prison and investigate every terrifying nook and cranny to your heart's content. Just remember, many of the spirits here were criminals who lived and died by violence, so be prepared for some nasty, negative entities. If you have the guts to see what the inmates here were really like, give up your freedom for a night for a taste of paranormal purgatory behind bars.

## The Bottom Line

**The History:** One of the country's largest castle-like structures, construction on this prison began in 1886. It closed in 1990, having housed over 154,000 inmates.

**The Haunting:** The ghosts of former prisoners, guards, the warden, and his wife. Staff and visitors have seen apparitions, recorded sounds, and have been pushed and punched.

## Recommendations

If you are aware of the potential consequences, by all means book one of the overnight ghost hunts, but do so well in advance as they sell out very quickly. There is so much to see here, don't expect to cover all 250,000 square feet in a two-hour tour. Note the massive 600-cell cellblock, which is the largest free-standing steel cellblock in the world. Movie buffs can see the actual sets used for *The Shawshank Redemption*. There is a gift shop, numerous special events, and you can even have your wedding and reception here—although that may send some mixed signals by getting married in a prison...

## Visitor Information

**The Ohio State Reformatory Museum**
100 Reformatory Road
Mansfield, OH 44905-1208
(419) 522-2644
www.mrps.org

**Hours:**

There are three different tours offered on Sundays beginning at 1pm and departing every 15 minutes on a rotating schedule. Weekday tours are conducted Tuesday-Friday at 2pm. Closed Monday and Saturday. Check the website or call for the latest available ghost walk and overnight ghost hunt schedule.

**Admission:**

Sunday tours are $8 for Adults and $6 for children ages 7-17. Additional tours taken on the same day are $5. Tickets are purchased on a first come first serve basis. Gates open and tickets are sold one half hour prior to 1pm. Each tour is approximately one hour long. Weekday tours are the same price and are also sold on a first come, first serve basis. Gates open and tickets are sold one half hour prior to the tour, which is approximately 1 ½ to 2 hours long. Ghost Walk Tours start promptly at 8pm and last approximately two hours. Tickets are $15 for adults and $8 for children (ages 12-17). Reservations can be made by mailing the Ghost Walk License with your payment. The overnight ghost hunts are $65 per person, which includes access to the building from 8pm until 5am and a late dinner of pizza and soda. Water, soda, coffee, and hot chocolate available throughout the evening. Overnight paranormal investigation for ages 21 and over and are limited to 100 people. Security for each hunt will be provided by a uniformed police officer.

The building contains hazards including, but not limited to: steep steps, uneven surfaces, and lead-based paint. It is not recommended for pregnant women. You must download and fill out the ghost hunt license agreement. Private Ghost Hunts are available on Friday and Saturday for $2,250 for 30 people or less. For more than 30 people the cost is $75 per person. Maximum of 100 people. Please see the website for rules and conditions.

**Directions:**

From Cleveland: Take I-71 South to Route 30 West, then take Route 30 to Route 545. Turn left at the stop sign at the end of the ramp.

Fairport Harbor Lighthouse. *Photo by Tony Bertone.*

# Fairport Harbor Lighthouse

The first lighthouse to sit on the hill overlooking the point where the Grand River enters Lake Erie was built in 1825. The thirty-foot brick tower and two-story house were constructed at a cost of $2,900, and the first keeper was Samuel Butler. Butler was an abolitionist, and the lighthouse was truly a beacon along the Underground Railroad where many runaway slaves stopped on their perilous journey to Canada and freedom.

In terms of commerce, the harbor thrived and saw thousands of ships every year. Unfortunately, the lighthouse did not fare so well and within ten years there were problems with the foundation. By the 1860s it was clear the structures needed to be replaced.

In 1869, $30,000 was appropriated to build a new sixty-foot tower out of sandstone, and construction was completed in 1871. A third-order Fresnel lens burned brightly in the tower for over fifty years, but times and technology changed. In 1925, a new modern facility was built nearby, and the old Fairport Harbor Lighthouse and its keepers became obsolete. Several times, plans were made to demolish the lighthouse, but concerned citizens fought to preserve it.

The Fairport Harbor Historical Society preserved the structures and opened them to the public as a museum in 1945—making this the oldest museum in the country to be housed in a lighthouse. The museum features artifacts from the lighthouse's history, the Coast Guard, and the Erie Indians who lived on this spot in the 1600s. It also has an unusual "attachment," the former pilothouse from the Great Lakes carrier *Frontenac*. It's somewhat ironic that this ship is now connected with the lighthouse, as the *Frontenac* had some rather unfortunate contact with another lighthouse. In 1958, the ship smashed into the Buffalo Breakwater Lighthouse, pushing it back twenty feet and tilting it at twenty-degree angle!

While the stories of the past are now preserved here, are there any spookier stories at the Fairport Harbor Lighthouse? In fact there are, in what must be considered one of the most unique and bizarre historic haunts on record. Over the years, many volunteers who were in the lighthouse after dark often felt an "eerie presence" and one curator, Pamela Brent, could have sworn she kept seeing a "wispy gray spirit of a cat."

"It would skitter across the floor near the kitchen, like it was playing. I would catch glimpses of it from time to time," said Brent. "Then one evening I felt its presence when it jumped on the bed. I felt its weight pressing on me. At first it kind of freaked me out. But ghosts don't bother me. They are part of the world."

But what part of the world did this particular cat come from, and why was it still here?

Skeptics discounted these ghostly tales of a presence and a phantom cat as simply imaginations running wild—until an amazing discovery was made in 2001. Air conditioning vents were being installed so a plumber had to squeeze through the dark, basement crawl space. As he was stretched out on his back, he leaned his head back on the floor of the crawl space, or so he thought at first. Something felt very strange under his head, so he leaned forward as best he could in the cramped space and aimed his light at the object. Imagine his shock and horror when he saw that his head had been resting on a cat—the mummified remains of a gray cat!

Could this dried-out feline be the earthly remains of the gray spirit cat? Research may have revealed an answer.

In 1871, the Head Keeper of the lighthouse was Captain Joseph Babcock, who had led an adventurous life. Babcock's mother was an Indian, and he had barely escaped death as a child during an Indian attack. Babcock also had an "illustrious career" during the Civil War. Two of his children were born at the lighthouse, but tragedy struck when one of his sons, Robbie, died of smallpox in the living quarters. Shortly after, his wife became very ill and was bedridden until her death. During her illness, she had many cats to keep her company, and one in particular was her favorite.

Babcock had found a small stray gray cat in the basement, and although he personally didn't care for cats, there was something about this one he liked. He gave the cat to his wife and it became her constant companion, spending all of its time on her bed. When his wife died, the gray cat disappeared and couldn't be found anywhere—until over a century later, that is!

Does this faithful cat still look for its former owner, or does it merely try to brighten the day of whoever is living there at the time by playing and jumping on the bed? Or, now that its mummified remains have finally been found, can the cat now rest in peace?

*Information supplied by the Fairport Harbor Historical Society: Pres. Dan Maxson, Helen Kasari, and John Ollila.*

## Recommendations

**This is a beautiful location on Lake Erie and different lighting conditions offer great photographic opportunities. Take the time to climb the sixty-nine steps to the top of the lighthouse. The staff is very knowledgeable and passionate about the history here, and can really add to your understanding and enjoyment of the place. Whether you are a lighthouse fan, are interested in the history of the Great Lakes, or simply love a good ghost story, this is an ideal location. If you plan on spending the night in the area, stay at the nearby haunted Rider's Inn.**

## Visitor Information

**Fairport Harbor Lighthouse and Marine Museum**
**129 Second Street**
**Fairport Harbor, OH 44077-5816**
**(440) 354-4825**
**www.fairportlighthouse.com**

**Hours:**
**Summer Hours: Wednesday, Saturday, Sunday, and legal holidays 1pm – 6pm. From the Saturday before Memorial Day through the 3rd weekend in September.**

**Admission:**
**Adults $3, Seniors $2, Ages 6-12 $1, Children Under 6 Years Old or Members Free. School Tours, (Children and Chaperones) $1. Small Tour Groups Minimum Charge $20.**

**Directions:**
**Take State Route 2 to the Fairport Harbor/ Richmond Street exit. Take Richmond Street North. Continue as name changes to High Street. The Fairport Harbor Lighthouse and Museum is located at the corner of High and 2nd Street.**

## The Bottom Line

**The History:** A lighthouse was first built on this site in 1825, and replaced in 1871. A new facility in 1925 made it obsolete, but it was preserved and turned into a museum in 1945.

**The Haunting:** A ghostly gray cat was often seen, and its mummified remains were found.

*Courtesy of Rider's Inn.*

# Rider's Inn

When land in northern Ohio was granted to Connecticut veterans who had fought in the Revolutionary War, toolmaker Joseph Rider made the move west. In 1810, he built a home and shop for his business, but later moved the structure four miles to a road in Painesville that was more heavily traveled by people heading farther west.

As customers would journey long distances to buy Rider's tools, he would accommodate them by letting them spend the night. Mrs. Rider was not thrilled about all these strangers in her home so she urged her husband to add an inn, which would also accommodate the many stagecoach passengers going from Buffalo to Cleveland. At the height of the stagecoach service, as many as 100 people a day would stop at Rider's Tavern for four hours. According to owner Elaine Crane, these people would spend one hour eating, two hours sleeping, and one hour drinking the products of Rider's still. Of course, some may have spent a little more time at that still, just to ease the pain of the bumpy stagecoach ride.

Unfortunately, Mrs. Rider #1 did not live to see her idea come to fruition with the addition of the inn. She died leaving Rider alone with their four children. But Rider was not a man to be without female companionship, and he soon remarried and had twelve more children. When Mrs. Rider #2 was completely worn out and died, Rider had quite a dilemma. He was having financial difficulties, he had sixteen children to feed, and the wealthiest available woman in town, Suzanne, was also known as the ugliest woman in town.

Nonetheless, Rider apparently overcame his aversion to her looks, in deference to her lucrative timber rights, and Suzanne became Mrs. Rider #3… But not for long. Just six weeks later, the blushing bride was found dead in the fireplace room, under what was described in the local newspaper as "strange and mysterious circumstances." However, no investigation was undertaken—especially now that Rider was one of the wealthiest men in town—and Suzanne was promptly buried.

The dirt above Suzanne's grave barely had time to settle before Rider married wife #4 just six weeks later. Six months after the ceremony, the latest Mrs. Rider presented her husband with twins. As Elaine summed up the situation, "You do the math." Either Rider was extraordinarily lucky and his twins survived being born three months early, or he was a cold, calculating murderer who solved all his problems with one homicidal act.

The Rider family—which finally totaled nineteen children—allowed the inn to be used as a stop on the Underground Railroad. Many people in the area helped runaway slaves, but it was not all for reasons of compassion. Ohio tobacco growers were in direct competition with Virginia tobacco growers, and the more slaves that left the plantations, the better it was for local business.

The inn was also used as a speakeasy during Prohibition, and there were a variety of owners in the twentieth century. In the 1980s, time had taken its toll on the old building, and it looked as though it would ultimately be demolished. Enter Judge Elaine Crane, who along with her mother, invested their time and money to restore the inn and return it to a place where travelers could eat, drink, and spend the night.

While such projects always have unforeseen circumstances, Elaine could never have foreseen the fact that Suzanne Rider was still acting as innkeeper. A practical woman, the former judge took a lot of convincing that her inn was haunted, but the overwhelming evidence was undeniable.

For example: When guests have forgotten their keys and have been locked out, they describe a woman in a white nightgown opening the door for them. That woman was not Elaine, and has never been identified. Camcorders have been set up in guest rooms to try to capture activity, and on one very hot night unseen hands removed the covers off an uncomfortable guest. When the hot water heater sprung a leak and threatened to set off sparks in the circuit box, a fireman who was spending the night just happened to wake up and sense trouble, and he went downstairs just in time to prevent a fire. And on several occasions when careless staff members emptied ashtrays that still contained smoldering cigarettes in the garbage, Elaine would be awakened just in time to avert a conflagration.

Every October, the inn hosts special Taleful Candlelit Dinners with ghost stories and an eighth-generation psychic, Jason, who believes this protective spirit is indeed Suzanne Rider. Jason feels that Suzanne had been poisoned, and that her spirit is still protecting the inn that her money paid for, and that she never had a chance to enjoy in life. When she appears to guests, she is only trying to be helpful, and when one hears the story of this unfortunate woman's demise, there is certainly nothing to fear.

This is an area rich in history, and Rider's Inn is a reflection of much of that history, for better and for worse. But guests should not allow Mr. Rider's bad behavior to taint their view of the place. Instead, one should celebrate the fact Suzanne, the ugly duckling who was so poorly used, has ultimately triumphed, as she is now the most popular girl in town!

## Recommendations

**Suzanne is harmless, and in fact is quite helpful, but if you just can't deal with the possibility of waking up in the middle of the night to find her standing next to your bed, you have the option of visiting the inn by dining in its restaurant. And as Elaine always tells customers, "If you clean your plate, I'll give you a tour." Elaine is a wealth of information about the area and the inn and her stories are very entertaining. If you can schedule your visit for October, be sure to attend one of their ghost story/psychic evenings. There are many special events throughout the year, and live entertainment Fridays and Saturdays.**

## Visitor Information

**Rider's Inn**
**792 Mentor Avenue**
**Painesville, OH 44077-2516**
**(440) 354-8200**
**www.ridersinn.com**

**Hours:**

**Restaurant: Lunch 11:30am – 4pm Monday to Friday. Dinner 4:30 – 9pm Sunday to Thursday, 4:30 – 11+pm Friday to Saturday. Sunday Brunch 10 – 3pm. The pub is open Monday to Sunday with live music on Friday and Saturday. There are special buffets and events on holidays. The inn and restaurant are closed on Christmas, Memorial Day, and Labor Day.**

**Taleful Candlelit Dinners with ghost stories and a guest psychic every October.**

**Directions:**

**From Cleveland: Take OH-2 East. Take the OH-640 E/Vine Street E exit toward Willoughby. Merge onto OH-640 E/Vine Street. Continue onto Mentor Avenue/US-20 E. Rider's Inn will be on the left.**

## The Bottom Line

**The History:** A stagecoach inn first built in 1810 by a man who had four wives and nineteen children. Also used for the Underground Railroad and as a speakeasy.

**The Haunting:** The murdered third wife appears and still protects the inn and its guests.

# Oklahoma

FORT GIBSON

FORT WASHITA

STONE LION INN

The Officer's Quarters at Fort Gibson in 1934. *Courtesy of The Library of Congress.*

# Fort Gibson

Imagine the morning of September 2, 1834, when representatives of the Kiowa, Choctaws, Cherokees, Creeks, Senecas, Osages, Delawares, Wichita, and Waco met for a grand council at the westernmost army fort on the frontier. The council was the result of the Dragoon Expedition led by General Leavenworth to gather members of local tribes and bring them to Fort Gibson to create peace treaties. What a scene it must have been!

Before getting too carried away with this quintessential Western moment, however, consider the fact that General Leavenworth and 150 other men died on the expedition, and peace amongst the tribes was important for the U.S. government because it would be easier for the army to exert their control. Still, who wouldn't want a time machine to be present at such an event?

Fort Gibson was established in Indian Territory in 1824 as part of a chain of forts that ran in a north-south line along the frontier. Many famous men passed through its gates, including Zachary Taylor, who would become President of the United States, and his future son-in-law, Jefferson Davis, who was the President of the Confederacy. Lieutenant Davis, who survived the ill-fated Dragoon Expedition, was afterward court marshaled for insubordination. Before a final judgment was rendered, he ended up resigning and leaving Fort Gibson, and moving to Kentucky to marry Taylor's daughter. The rest, as they say, is history. Other notable men at the fort included Robert E. Lee, J.E.B. Stuart, and a veritable "Who Would Be Who" of the impending Civil War.

It was a rugged life, to be sure, and conditions at the fort were quite unhealthy. Between 1824 and 1835, the deaths of 561 privates and 9 officers were recorded, many from yellow fever epidemics. These numbers earned the fort the nickname of the *Graveyard of the West*, and the charnel house of the army.

Then there was the sad plight of the Indian tribes of the southeast, such as the Cherokee, who were forced to relocate as the result of the Indian Removal Act. Thousands died along the "Trail of Tears" to Fort Gibson to await their assigned new lands. This was truly a dark period of American history, and one can only imagine the suffering they endured.

The fort was abandoned and reoccupied several times throughout its history. During the Civil War, the Confederates briefly manned the fort, and then Union forces took control (at which point it was called Fort Blunt). Fort Gibson was finally abandoned for good in 1890, and some of its structures were plundered for building materials for homes and other construction.

Fort Gibson Historical Site is now open to the public to explore original buildings from the 1840s-1870s, as well as a log reconstruction of the early fort. There is also a National Cemetery where over 19,000 soldiers, Native Americans, and their families were laid to rest. Although, not all of them may be resting in peace…

Arguably the most intriguing occupant of the cemetery is Vivia Thomas, and her story is surely one of the most unique in American history. She was born to a wealthy Boston family and fell in love with a lieutenant in the army after the Civil War. However, his love of adventure apparently outweighed his affection for her, and she was jilted so that he could go out west. Angry and humiliated, Vivia was not one to pine in solitude. Instead, she headed west to seek revenge.

The frontier was not a safe place for a woman traveling alone, so she cut her hair and dressed as a man. The disguise was so effective that when she arrived at Fort Gibson she was able to enlist as a soldier, and even her ex-fiancé didn't recognize her! Keeping a careful eye on the lieutenant, Vivia discovered that he was seeing a local Indian woman. That was the last straw, and one night as he was returning to the fort after being with the Indian girl, Vivia shot and killed him. People assumed that Indians had shot the lieutenant, and his body was buried in the cemetery.

Here is where the legend takes an even more bizarre twist. Vivia, her fury now spent, became racked with guilt and remorse. Each night she visited the grave of the man she'd murdered and cried in anguish. One evening in 1870 was particularly bitter cold, but Vivia still made her nightly pilgrimage. In the morning, her frozen body was found on top of the lieutenant's grave. Only after death did the army discover it had a woman in its ranks, and she was given a proper burial in the cemetery under her true identity.

From that day, people have claimed to see a young soldier standing in the cemetery, pacing back and forth by a grave, and they can hear the sounds of crying. It is believed that Vivia is not resting in peace because she is still bound to the earth by her guilt.

Despite the many difficulties and tragedies over the years, there is a sense of adventure at Fort Gibson. This was the starting point for expeditions of exploration and the opening of a new frontier, and just possibly even today, Vivia can be glimpsed standing on the edge of another frontier...

## The Bottom Line

**The History:** A remarkable site of Western frontier history, established in 1824. Many famous American soldiers were stationed here, including Zachary Taylor, Jefferson Davis, Robert E. Lee, and many future Civil War officers. Representatives from many Indian tribes met here for councils. This was the final destination along the infamous Trail of Tears that forcibly relocated southeastern tribes. The fort was called Fort Blunt when it was occupied by Union forces during the Civil War. It was permanently abandoned by the army in 1890.

**The Haunting:** Can you think of any other ghost stories involving a woman who dressed like a man and joined the army to exact revenge on the man who jilted her?

## Recommendations

Take the time to see the reconstructed fort and original buildings, then come back another time to enjoy one of their many special events (see below). This is one of those sites where you just need to shut off your cell phone and take some quiet moments to imagine what this place was like when it was a remote outpost in Indian Territory. Don't forget to visit the National Cemetery and pay your respects, and of course, keep an eye open for Vivia.

## Visitor Information

**Fort Gibson**
907 N. Garrison
Fort Gibson, OK 74434-0457
(918) 478-4088
www.okhistory.org

**Events:**
There are special events throughout the year. Call or check the website for details. Public Bake Day in March, Heritage Festival in April, Fourth at the Fort on the 4th of July weekend, Mexican War Fall Encampment in October, Fall Bake Day in November, and the 1848 Candlelight Tour in December.

**Hours:**
April 15 to October 14: Tuesday-Sunday 10am – 5pm. October 15 to April 14: Thursday-Sunday 10am – 5pm.

**Admission:**
Adults $3, Seniors (65+) $2.50, Students 6-18. $1, Children 5 and Under are free.

**Directions:**
From Tulsa: Take the US-64 E/OK-51 E ramp on the left to Broken Arrow. Keep left at the fork to continue toward OK-51 E/US-64 E and merge onto OK-51 E/US-64 E. Continue onto OK-51 E. Continue onto Muskogee Turnpike E. Continue onto OK-165 S. Exit onto East Shawnee Avenue/ US-62 E toward Ft. Gibson/Tahlequah. Continue to follow US-62 E. Turn left at North Georgetown Road/U.S. 62 Bus. Continue to follow U.S. 62 Bus. Turn left at East Street. Turn left at Garrison Avenue. The fort will be on the left.

The west barracks of Fort Washita.

# Fort Washita

Due to the Indian Removal Act, the Choctaw and Chickasaw Indians were forced to leave their ancestral lands and relocate to southern Oklahoma. This left them vulnerable to attacks from the Plains Indians, so Fort Washita was established in 1842 to try to keep the peace. The first commanding officer of the fort was General Zachary Taylor, who would go on to become the twelfth President of the United States just six years later. Other famous military figures would be stationed here, including George McClellan and Braxton Bragg.

During the Mexican War, which began in 1846, Fort Washita's proximity to Texas made it an active staging point, and its garrison swelled from 150 troops to 2,000. In the 1850s, as the frontier pushed westward and the region became more peaceful, the decision was made to abandon the fort in February of 1858. However, as hostilities with the Comanches escalated, the fort was reoccupied again in December. At the start of the Civil War, Union troops once again abandoned the fort, but it wasn't empty for long. On May 1, 1861, U.S. forces left, and on May 2, Confederate troops moved in. While no battles occurred here, Fort Washita became an important supply depot. Unfortunately, at war's end, the Confederates burned all of the fort's buildings.

Eventually, the land was returned to the Chickasaw Nation, and one of their prominent families, the Colberts, was given ownership. Charles Colbert began farming the old fort grounds, and the east and west barracks were turned into houses. As the 1960s approached, people began to get more of an appreciation of their local history, so the Oklahoma Historical Society bought the property from the Colberts in 1962. At the time there were eighty-six structures, fifty foundations, with only two structures still standing, and grant money helped the OHS to restore some of the buildings and open the site to the public. Today, it is a popular location for reenactors, and it's also a popular place for ghost stories.

There is an old story about Aunt Jane, a misty white figure of a woman in a long dress who happens to be missing her head. There are so many versions of how this unfortunate woman lost her head that it could fill a book of urban legends. There aren't any documented incidences of such a crime being committed at the fort, so all of these stories were no doubt created to try to explain what witnesses have been seeing, and there have been many witnesses to Aunt Jane over the years.

Part of the legend of Aunt Jane is that she hates other women for some reason, and may have been responsible for an incident with some female reenactors in the 1990s. Three women were staying in the Bonahan cabin and all reported feeling a strong presence, having terrible nightmares, and feeling as if they were being strangled as they tried to sleep.

Is Aunt Jane malicious, or simply trying to let other women know what happened to her? Another part of the legend says she was killed for the gold she allegedly hid somewhere on the grounds of the fort, and her frightening apparition still prevents people from searching for it. There's nothing like adding a buried treasure tale to a ghost story!

It was said that a woman who lived on the property after the Colberts, suffered a nervous breakdown from all the paranormal activity—including seeing a headless woman—and over the years some of this other activity has included seeing Civil War-era soldiers, hearing heavy footsteps hurrying up and down staircases, and the sounds of groups of soldiers talking and going about their business.

It's difficult to say where legends end and actual paranormal activity begins, but there have been so many reports of inexplicable sights and sounds at Fort Washita that the two may not be that far apart here!

## The Bottom Line

**The History:** A fort established in 1842 to keep peace among the Indians. Held during the Civil War by the Confederates, then burned and abandoned.

**The Haunting:** A headless woman and Civil War soldiers.

## Recommendations

To best experience the history, attend one of the reenactments. The biggest event is the annual 1840s Fur Trade Rendezvous, where, in addition to reenactors, you can test your skills with period weapons. If you are there for the ghosts, pick a quieter time to explore both the reconstructed buildings and the old ruins. The nearby soldiers' cemetery also includes Confederates and members of the Colbert family. In the past, the OHS has conducted ghost tours, so call for the latest schedule.

## Visitor Information

**Fort Washita**
3348 Oklahoma 199
Durant, OK 74701-8503
(580) 924-6502
www.okhistory.org/outreach/military/fortwashita.html

**Events:**
The annual 1840s Fur Trade Rendezvous is held in early April, and includes "Trappers, Traders and Mountain Men from the Fur Trade Era" with "Archery, Knife and Hawk, Smooth Bore, Rifle and Pistol competitions."

**Hours:**
Monday to Saturday 8am – 4:30pm, Sunday Noon – 4:30pm

**Admission:**
Free. The Fur Trade Rendezvous is $5 per car.

**Directions:**
From Oklahoma City: Take I-35 South. Take exit 29 to merge onto US-70 E toward Madill/Ardmore/US-70 W. Turn left at Clayton Road/US-70 E. Continue to follow US-70 E. Turn right at North 1st Street. Turn left at E. Main Street. Turn right to stay on E. Main Street. Take the 2nd right onto E. Main Street/OK-199 E. Continue to follow OK-199 E.

*Courtesy of the Stone Lion Inn*

# Stone Lion Inn

Imagine the tension in the air on the morning of April 22, 1889 when 10,000 people gathered to grab a share of 2 million acres of land. The cannons were fired at noon, signaling that the race was on. Six hours later, Guthrie, Oklahoma was born, and only six months later, there was a town of brick and stone buildings with municipal water and electricity. When Oklahoma was granted statehood in 1907, Guthrie became its capital.

Oklahoma City became the new capital in 1910—some say by having the state seal stolen in the middle of the night, but that's another story. In the long run, that may have been a blessing for Guthrie, as it was spared from the destructive urban development that often obliterates a town's earliest structures. The end result is that today, Guthrie's downtown is designated as a National Historic Monument, and its historic district is the largest in the country, containing 2,169 buildings, 1,400 acres and 400 city blocks.

One of the early residents of Guthrie was F.E. Houghton, who appeared to adhere to the principle that more is better. In addition to owning several stores, he was the founder of the Cotton Oil Company, and also owned Oklahoma's first car dealership. Applying that same principle to his personal life, he had twelve children. With that many Houghtons running around, he needed a place big enough to put them all, so he built an 8,000-square foot Greek Revival mansion.

Unfortunately, tragedy struck the family soon after moving in. Eight-year-old Irene contracted whooping cough and the maid administered the wrong medicine, inadvertently killing her. Death was to return again in the 1920s, but in a different form. The family had moved out and the mansion became a boarding house for a time, but then became the Smith Funeral Home.

When Becky Luker purchased the property in 1986 with the intent of someday opening a bed and breakfast, no one bothered to tell her that little fact. And the one piece of furniture that had been left behind was a large, heavy porcelain table in the kitchen that Becky found to be ideal for a baking table, and she would regularly roll out her cookie dough on it to make treats for her two boys. Then one day the boys' teacher told them that their house was a funeral home, and Becky's cookie table had been the embalming table! They quickly moved the table out of the kitchen and into the hall, where it now serves as a bar—pickling of another sort, as Becky so aptly puts it!

The first signs that the house was haunted came at night, between the hours of 10pm and midnight, when they would hear a child's footsteps come up the back stairs to the third floor, and then a door would open and close. Becky tried to explain to her sons that it was just the normal settling sounds of a wooden house.

Then there was the large old toy box in a closet on the third floor where one of Becky's boys would meticulously arrange his toys—the boy grew up to be a tax attorney, need we say more?—but in the morning he would find his toys spread out around the room. He suspected his brother was to blame, until Becky put a lock on the door, and still the toys would somehow leave the closet and end up all over the floor, as if a child had been playing with them.

If there were any doubts, they were dispelled the day Becky's 7-year-old son came downstairs and said, "You might as well fix me something to eat and I'll go back upstairs when she's done."

The embalming table. *Courtesy of the Stone Lion Inn.*

When questioned, the boy plainly stated that the ghost of a little girl was playing with his toys!

They didn't know the identity of this girl until some members of the Houghton family arrived one day. They told Becky about the tragic death of their sister, Irene. They also mentioned that after their parents went to bed about 10pm, Irene used to sneak up the back staircase to the third floor to her toy chest—the one that is still there today—and play with her toys spread out all across the floor. They had no doubt that Irene was still in the house, still playing as she did during her brief life.

Overnight guests of the inn have often mentioned feeling a small hand touch their faces at night. One woman felt someone playing with her hair. It was if a child was using a finger to twist lengths of her hair, then releasing it. But Irene is not the only ghostly occupant of the Stone Lion Inn. A man has been seen in the basement wearing a black suit and a top hat. A man has also been seen smoking a cigar, and cigar smoke can often be smelled and seen in certain rooms of the house, even though no one smokes. Perhaps some former customers of the funeral home never left?

Does Irene Houghton still climb the stairs at night to play with her toys? Are there other spirits from the days of the boarding house or funeral home? Would you ever actually eat any cookies made on an embalming table? Visit historic Guthrie and stay at the Stone Lion Inn, and decide for yourself.

## Recommendations

**If you are looking for hauntings and history in Oklahoma, you might as well go to a town with the country's largest historic district, and sleep and eat in one of its most haunted inns. And if real deaths are not enough for you, you can participate in one of their popular Murder Mystery weekends. If things do start going bump in the night and you are feeling a bit nervous, just fix yourself a relaxing drink from the embalming bar.**

## Visitor Information

**Stone Lion Inn**
**1016 W. Warner**
**Guthrie, Oklahoma 73044-2730**
**(405) 282-0012**
**StoneLionInn@aol.com**
**www.StoneLionInn.com**

**Events:**
**Call or visit the website for reservations and Murder Mystery details.**

**Directions:**
**From Route 33, turn north onto 9th Street. Go one block and turn left onto West Warner. The inn is the first house on your right.**

## The Bottom Line

**The History:** The town of Guthrie was formed after a land grab in April of 1889 when 10,000 people rushed to stake their claims. The town was the capital of Oklahoma from 1907-1910, and the downtown is now the largest historic district in the country. E.F. Houghton was a wealthy businessman and built the house for his twelve children, one of whom died tragically when a maid gave her the wrong medicine. The house became a funeral home in the 1920s.

**The Haunting:** The spirit of a little girl, thought to be Irene Houghton, has been seen, heard, and felt. A man in a black suit and top hat has also been seen. There are also wisps of cigar smoke and the smell of cigars, even though no one smokes.

Oregon
Springs
MCLOUGHLIN HOUSE
THE HEATHMAN HOTEL
HOT LAKE SPRINGS

The McLoughlin House in 1934. *Courtesy of The Library of Congress.*

# McLoughlin House

The "Father of Oregon," Dr. John McLoughlin, was born Jean-Baptiste McLoughlin in 1784 in Rivière-du-Loup, Quebec. He studied medicine and earned his medical license in 1803, and became the doctor at Fort William in Ontario. It was here that he learned about business, especially the fur trading business, which would serve him well in his future career.

In 1824, McLoughlin was named Chief Factor for the Hudson Bay Company's vast Columbia District (essentially the Oregon Country). The following year, McLoughlin established Fort Vancouver which became the primary northwest outpost due to the lucrative fur trade, especially for beaver pelts to be made into hats for Europeans. At its peak, McLoughlin managed over 34 outposts, 24 ports, and 600 employees.

McLoughlin had a keen business sense and generated huge profits for the company. He was known for being fair in all his dealings, but he had a major flaw in the company's eyes—he was occasionally too generous. When settlers arrived from the Oregon Trail in desperate need of supplies, he gave them what they needed. Most companies frown on their employees giving things away, and this eventually led to a forced retirement.

But McLoughlin wasn't finished giving things away, not by a long shot. He divided some land he had purchased into 300 parcels, and gave them to those settlers in most desperate need. He and his wife also became known for giving land for schools and churches, as well as loaning money and offering assistance to newcomers who needed a helping hand to get on their feet and start businesses. The McLoughlins could afford to do this because they owned many of their own businesses, including a general store that was at the end of the Oregon Trail.

In 1846, he built a mansion by Willamette Falls in Oregon City, which he had founded in 1829. McLoughlin became an American citizen in 1851, and was elected mayor of Oregon City by a vote of 44-22. He continued both his business and philanthropic pursuits until he passed away in his home in 1857.

The house was slated to be demolished in the early 1900s, but the McLoughlin Memorial Association was formed to rescue the structure and move it to higher ground in 1909. In 1941, the house/museum was designated as the West's first National Historic Site, and in 2003 it became part of the National Park System's Fort Vancouver National Historic Site. The park now contains several historic—and haunted—buildings.

For a man who devoted his life to this land, it should not be surprising that Dr. John McLoughlin is believed to still occupy his home. Staff members and volunteers have heard footsteps and voices, smelled tobacco smoke (McLoughlin loved to smoke, and smoking has been prohibited in the house for many years), and a former curator was even tapped on the shoulder. Several witnesses have seen a tall shadowy figure (McLoughlin was six-foot-four) moving down the hall and entering McLoughlin's former bedroom, which is also the room where he died.

The bedding is often found disturbed in a child's room, as if someone had slept there. A visitor saw a woman in an old-fashioned dress standing by the staircase, and assumed she was a member of the staff, until she disappeared. Some believe she was McLoughlin's wife. People passing by have seen figures standing by the windows on the second floor when the house is closed and locked. There is also a rocking chair that moves back and forth on its own.

In short, Dr. John McLoughlin and his family still keep an eye on the house they loved. Perhaps their spirits were disturbed when the house was moved, or maybe they are just delighted that people are still traveling to Oregon City after all these years!

## Recommendations

**The McLoughlin House is considered to be the most haunted place in Oregon City. They offer a variety of special events and demonstrations of Victorian-era women's handwork. The graves of McLoughlin and his wife, Marguerite, are next to the house. The park also includes the Barclay House, which is believed to be haunted by Dr. Forbes Barclay and his young son, and the pedestrian elevator is also thought to be haunted by a small boy. If you have the time, visit The End of the Oregon Trail Interpretive Center which is just 10 blocks north and the Museum of the Oregon Territory and Willamette Falls which are 10 blocks south.**

## The Bottom Line

**The History:** A home built in 1846 by Dr. John McLoughlin, the "Father of Oregon" and moved to its present location in 1909.

**The Haunting:** The former owner is seen and heard, as is a woman in an old- fashioned dress.

## Visitor Information

**McLoughlin House**
**713 Center Street**
**Oregon City, OR 97045-1948**
**(503) 656-5146**
**www.mcloughlinhouse.org**
**www.nps.gov/fova/historyculture/mcloughlin-house.htm**

**Hours:**
**Wednesday to Saturday 10am – 4pm, Sunday 1pm – 4pm. Tours begin next door at the Barclay House.**

**Admission:** Free

**Directions:**
From their website—**The McLoughlin House is located at 713 Center Street, between 7th and 8th Streets, in Oregon City, Oregon. It is less than four blocks east of U.S. Highway 99E and about nine blocks from I-205 (exit 9). Directional signs are located throughout Oregon City. The house stands in McLoughlin Park, next to the historic home of Dr. Forbes Barclay at 719 Center Street.**

# The Heathman Hotel

George Heathman claimed that when his new hotel was completed in Portland, it would not only have elegant accommodations, it would also have the city's finest restaurant. Heathman delivered on his promises when the ten-story Italian Renaissance-style hotel opened in 1927 to cater to the refined needs of wealthy timber barons, railroad owners, and society's elite.

The party to celebrate the completion of the building was quite an affair, as all 1,200 construction workers were invited. The mayor and governor gave speeches at the formal dedication, and the event was broadcast on a local radio station, which had a studio in the basement of the hotel. The hotel was also unique as it could boast the largest coffee shop in the northwest and the first 24-hour pharmacy. The Heathman was the place to stay whether seeing a show in one of Broadway's theaters, visiting on business, or just looking for an excellent dining experience.

Hard times began to hit Portland's downtown in the 1950s as people moved to the suburbs. Businesses continued to suffer throughout the 1960s, but revitalization efforts were soon underway. The Heathman Hotel went through its own revitalization when it underwent extensive renovations in the 1980s.

OR

More recently, the hotel "went green" in a major effort to become more environmentally friendly and energy efficient. But have no fear, this award-winning hotel has not sacrificed elegance or service—it has remained on the world's top hotel lists for over twenty-five years.

It has also remained on the list of historic haunts, and in this regard The Heathman is also quite unique. The most active room is 703, where towels, glasses, and furniture move as if someone had been staying in the room—even though key card logs prove that no one had entered. In 803, the figure of a man has been seen. Activity has also been reported in 303, 403, 503…well, you get the picture.

This may just be one of the country's only vertical hauntings, where all the rooms in a column going from 303 up to 1003 have some paranormal activity. What could possibly be the cause of this bizarre pattern? The theory is that a man committed suicide by jumping to his death, and subsequently all the rooms he passed on his way down are now haunted by his tormented spirit. What a fascinating and chilling possibility!

The motto of the Heathman Hotel is that this is a place "where service is still an art." Perhaps in lieu of this very innovative ghost, they should also add that it is a place where "haunting is still an art."

## The Bottom Line

**The History:** Built in 1927 as a hotel for Portland's elite and wealthy visitors.

**The Haunting:** All of the rooms in a vertical column from 303 to 1003 have paranormal activity, perhaps from a jumper?

## Recommendations

**The hotel's library has many autographed books from authors who have stayed at the hotel. Public spaces are decorated with over 250 works of art and seasonal exhibits are on display in the mezzanine. Above the Tea Court there is an antique chandelier that once hung in the U.S. Embassy in Czechoslovakia. Guests can request the "Go Green" package that includes the hotel planting a tree for each package sold. The Heathman Restaurant and Bar continues to win top awards, so don't expect your average hotel restaurant food. Request 703 for the spookiest room in the house, but any room ending in 03 will give you your best chance at a paranormal encounter!**

## Visitor Information

**The Heathman Hotel**
**1001 SW Broadway at Salmon**
**Portland, OR 97205-3004**
**(503) 241-4100**
**Reservations: (800) 551-0011**
**www.heathmanhotel.com**

**Directions:**

**From their website—From the North (via I-5): I-5 South to I-405 South. Take Burnside/Couch Street exit. Continue straight to Salmon Street. Turn left onto Salmon Street. Hotel is 8 blocks, at Broadway.**

**From the South (via I-5): On I-5 North, follow signs for Beaverton/City Center to I-405 North. Take Salmon Street exit, bear right onto Salmon Street. Go 8 blocks to Broadway.**

**From the East (via I-84): On I-84 West, follow signs to I-5 South. On I-5 South, follow signs for Beaverton/City Center to I-405 North. Take Salmon Street exit, bear right onto Salmon Street. Go 8 blocks to Broadway.**

**From the West (via US 26): Stay in the middle lane through the tunnel. Go straight on Market Street, and turn left on 12th Avenue. Turn right on Salmon Street. Go 5 blocks to Broadway.**

**From Portland International Airport: From Airport Way, take I-205 South to I-84 West, to I-5 South, to I-405 North. Take Salmon Street exit, bear right onto Salmon Street. Go 8 blocks to Broadway.**

Hot Lakes Hotel in 2009. Werewombat, Wikipedia, Creative Commons Attribution-Share Alike 3.0 Unported.

# Hot Lake Springs

Hot Lake Springs has been called many things in the past. For example, in the early twentieth century it was called the "Mayo Clinic of the West." However, more recently it was featured on a television show as one of the "Scariest Places on Earth." With a look at the long and colorful history of this place, we can see how the one title is clearly related to the other.

Native Americans had long enjoyed the hot springs in this area, but it wasn't until 1812 that white men discovered them. In the following decades, fur trappers, travelers along the Oregon Trail, and gold miners all sought out the soothing warm waters that were believed to have medicinal properties. (Of course, the waters weren't all soothing—you had to be careful to avoid the scalding 205-degree lakes where one slip meant a very painful death.)

The first buildings were constructed in 1864, and other covered buildings followed, such as a post office, barber shop, blacksmith, dance hall, bath houses, and other shops. This "Town Under One Roof" may have been the country's first shopping mall! In 1884, when the population of Hot Lake was fifteen people, the Union Pacific Railroad came through the property and suddenly it was a destination anyone could reach.

Big changes began in the early 1900s when the old buildings gave way to a modern wooden hotel and then a large brick building. In 1904, Dr. W.T. Phy became the director of the medical facility there, and went on to purchase the place in 1917. Phy was friends with the Mayo brothers who were frequent visitors to Hot Lake, thus helping the facility earn the hospital/resort its nickname.

Phy performed many surgeries there, as well as conducted tests and experimental treatments with x-rays and radiation. Depending upon your point of view, such treatments could either be considered creative and innovative or reckless and dangerous, and many people may have died as a result of these experiments.

However, customers and patients must have been pleased overall, as in 1910 when the typical room rate was $2.50 and meals were a quarter, the facility earned over $175,000! Business began to decline after Dr. Phy's death in 1931. He fell ill after falling into the icy waters of the Columbia River on a duck hunting trip with the Mayo brothers. His son, Dr. Mark Phy, took over for a couple of years, but he committed suicide in 1933. Then in 1934 a massive fire devastated the hotel and hospital.

With the passing of the Phys, the fire, and the financial hardships of the Depression, the glory years of the Hot Lakes Sanitarium were in the past. The third floor of the brick building continued to be used as a hospital, nurses were trained here during World War II, and the facility served as a nursing home for a time. However, without a substantial investment of someone's time and money, the demise of the once-popular resort was inevitable. By 1991, the place was abandoned and left to the elements—and the ghosts.

The dark history of Hot Lakes frightened away at least one potential investor, but the property was eventually purchased and after extensive renovations reopened to tourists once again. While the current owners don't advertise the haunted aspects of the hotel, local lore and word of mouth keep the stories of the restless dead alive.

OR

There was the nurse, who in the 1920s, fell into the near-boiling lake and died a horrible death—or was she pushed? There was the caretaker who committed suicide by stabbing himself in the head with a screwdriver, then slashed his own throat. There's the gardener who hung himself. Another caretaker survived, but talked of having suicidal thoughts while on the property. Is there some chemical in the air from the hot springs that turns people toward thoughts of suicide, or are the many wandering souls just trying to convince others to join them?

In addition to the misty apparitions, footsteps, screams (particularly from the former operating room area), there are doors that open and close, cold spots, and people have been touched and pushed. For many years, people also heard the eerie strains of a phantom piano. There was a grand piano at the resort in its early years, and it was supposedly once owned by Mrs. Robert E. Lee, and was reputedly a "haunted piano" that played on its own before it was ever brought to the resort. Even after it was removed, the piano music could still be heard.

Then there are the figures in the fog that appear on the road leading to the hotel. Stories abound about accidents that occurred because drivers swerved to try to avoid hitting a person that suddenly appeared in the road, but no could later be found. Some speculate that the souls of Chinese workers who built the railroad still wander throughout the area on foggy nights.

Between the suicides, possible murders, and numerous deaths at the medical facility, there is more than enough paranormal fodder for hauntings here. There has also been more than enough bizarre and inexplicable activity at the Hot Lake Springs to earn it the title as one of the scariest places on earth.

## The Bottom Line

**The History:** Hot springs that drew visitors in the 1800s, which became the site for a resort and hospital which was built in the early 1900s.

**The Haunting:** Misty apparitions, footsteps, screams, doors opening and closing.

## Recommendations

**At the time of this publication, the property had or planned to soon have museums, a bed and breakfast, an RV park, a restaurant, a spa, and a bronze casting foundry and studio, so there are a variety of ways to see and experience Hot Lake Springs. The ghosts are not limited to the buildings; they could be anywhere on the grounds, as well. There are special events planned throughout the year, call or check their website for the latest information.**

## Visitor Information

**Hot Lake Springs**
**66172 Highway 203**
**La Grande, OR 97850-5230**
**(541) 963-4685**
**www.hotlakesprings.com**

**Directions:**

**From I-84 E in Portland: Take exit 265 for OR-203 toward La Grande/Union. Turn right at Adams Avenue/La Grande-Baker Highway/OR-203 S. Continue to follow La Grande-Baker Highway/OR-203 S. Turn left at East Beakman Street. Continue onto E. Arch Street/Medical Springs Highway/OR-203 S. Continue to follow Medical Springs Highway/OR-203 S.**

# Pennsylvania

FORT NECESSITY NATIONAL BATTLEFIELD

EASTERN STATE PENITENTIARY

GETTYSBURG

A reenactment at Fort Necessity. *Courtesy of Fort Necessity.*

# Fort Necessity National Battlefield

It's difficult to imagine a time when George Washington did not look upon the 4th of July with fondness, but long before that date heralded our independence, it signified Washington's surrender.

The year was 1754, and a 22-year-old Washington was in Pennsylvania in command of Virginia men and British regulars from South Carolina. He was there to build a road, and confront the French, if necessary. Tensions had been rising between the French and the British as both sought to control and exploit the rich lands of America.

Washington chose to fortify an area called the Great Meadows, which he found to be a "charming" place for an encounter. A round palisade of logs was erected about eight feet high, forming a circle fifty-three-feet in diameter. Within this crudely constructed wall was a small 10x14-foot shed, and earthworks were built around the perimeter. It wasn't pretty, but it was a Fort of Necessity, as Washington so aptly put it.

On July 3, Washington's defenses and mettle would be tested, and he would come to learn that there was nothing charming about battle. About 600 French troops and 100 Indians attacked Fort Necessity and its 400 men. In addition to being outnumbered, even Mother Nature seemed to have stacked the cards against Washington, as pouring rains wet the gunpowder, and without the support of firearms the fort could not be held.

The French presented Washington with documents of surrender for him to sign. As part of the agreement, he and his men were allowed to march away after he placed the fort in French hands, which he did on July 4, 1754. It must indeed have been a bitter day, but fortunately for the future President of the United States of America, this was the only time Washington ever surrendered.

This battle was the first of the French and Indian War, also known as the Seven Years War, and while the combined forces of the French and the Indians had won the day, they ultimately lost the war, ending France's colonial aspirations. This led to total British control; perhaps a little too much British control for American's liking, but that's another George Washington story…

Today, the Fort Necessity National Battlefield allows visitors to get a sense of what it was like at this historic moment in time, when a green American commander engaged in a conflict that ultimately became a world war as it spread to every major power. Be sure to use all your senses here, especially your sixth sense, as some claim that remnants of that battle still linger in the air with the sounds of musket fire. There are also voices on the wind—some appear to be commands being shouted in English to troops who are long gone, others sound like French or Indian words. The visitor's center also has inexplicable sounds of footsteps—perhaps curious soldiers admiring exhibits that honor the struggles for which they gave their lives?

For a nation that prides itself on our ancestor's revolutionary struggles for independence, it is worth a look at what preceded that well-known period of history. Here in the Pennsylvania wilderness in 1754, French, British, Indian, and American forces met in a manner that would be completely different two decades later. There is much to contemplate here, and while you're thinking, consider this: What if that day a French musket ball had found its mark with the 22-year-old commander of Fort Necessity? Instead of the "Star Spangled Banner" before every baseball game, we might be singing God Save the Queen!

## The Bottom Line

**The History:** The site of the opening battle of the French and Indian War in 1754, and the only battle in which George Washington surrendered.

**The Haunting:** There are sounds of musket fire, voices in English, French, and Indian, and footsteps in the visitor's center.

## Recommendations

Take a look at the model of the 1932 reconstruction of the fort—it is wrong! Thanks to archaeological work conducted in the 1950s, the original location, shape, and size were able to be determined so the fort was re-reconstructed to look as it did in 1754. In addition to the section of the park that contains the visitor's center, fort, 1830s stagecoach stop, and Mount Washington Tavern, there is Braddock's grave (a British general who died nearby in 1755) and the Jumonville Glen, the site of an important skirmish between Washington's men and the French which preceded the battle of Fort Necessity.

## Visitor Information

**Fort Necessity National Battlefield**
1 Washington Parkway
Farmington, PA 15437
(724) 329-5512
www.nps.gov/fone/index.htm

**Hours:**

The park is open daily from sunrise to sunset, all year.

NOTE: All visitor facilities are closed: November 11, Thanksgiving Day, December 25, January 1, Birthday of Martin Luther King Jr., and George Washington's Birthday.

Fort Necessity/ National Road Interpretive and Education Center: Open All Year 9am – 5pm.

Mount Washington Tavern: Open April 15 to November 1. Check at Visitor Center for hours. The Mount Washington Tavern is closed for the winter months.

Jumonville Glen, Braddock's Grave parking area, and Picnic Area: Open during summer months only.

There are daily tours throughout the summer, and special weekend events throughout the year, which may include: British, French, and Indian encampments, artillery demonstrations, and French and Indian War seminars. Call or visit the website for dates and details.

**Admission:**

Adults $5 for a 7-day pass, Children 15 and under are free.

**Directions:**

From their website—From Downtown Pittsburgh: US 51 South to Uniontown, US 40 East, Park entrance is on right 11 miles east of Uniontown.

From The Pennsylvania Turnpike from eastern PA: Exit #9 – Donegal PA 711 south to US 381 Stay on US 381 south to US 40, Right on US 40, Park entrance is one mile on left.

From Western Maryland: I-68 west to US 40, US 40 west toward Uniontown, PA. Park entrance is on left one mile past Farmington, PA.

From Morgantown, WV: I-68 east over Cheat Lake to Highway 857 (There are two Highway 857 exits), Highway 857 north to PA 43, PA 43 north to US 40, US 40 east 12 miles. Park entrance is on the right.

The cell blocks radiate from the center of Eastern State Penitentiary like spokes of a wheel.

# Eastern State Penitentiary

Prior to the nineteenth century, jails were basically large open rooms where all of the prisoners (men, women, and even children) were held together. Generally, the prisoners would be kept there on more or less a temporary basis until they received some type of physical punishment, e.g., whipping, hanging, etc. However, some citizens who professed to be more enlightened felt that such cruel punishments should be stopped, and they sought a more compassionate way to deal with prisoners. In 1787, a group of influential men in Philadelphia met at the home of Benjamin Franklin to discuss plans for a new type of facility.

Calling themselves The Philadelphia Society for Alleviating the Miseries of Public Prisons, they proposed an innovative design—a prison where each man was to be kept in complete isolation in his own cell. By having absolutely no contact or communication with another living soul, the designers felt that the prisoner would have no choice but to reflect upon his crime, realize the error of his ways, and ultimately become penitent—hence the new term: penitentiary. It was an idea that sounded marvelous to the gentlemen who discussed it over cigars and brandy after dinner, but to the inmates who would spend years completely alone, it was a torture as cruel and insidious as any medieval device.

In 1829, the long awaited Eastern State Penitentiary began operations on open farmland about a mile from the city of Philadelphia. At the time, it was the most expensive building ever constructed in the United States, and it boasted features that not even the White House contained—flush toilets, central heating, and running water. This was truly the first modern building in the country, and tourists from across the United States and from around the world came to see this wonder of new thought and new design.

While many tourists sang the praises of this revolutionary penitentiary, one visitor saw it for what it really was—a place that drove inmates to the depth of despair and insanity. In 1842, author Charles Dickens wrote, "In its intention I am well convinced that it is kind, humane, and meant for reformation; but I am persuaded that those who designed this system of Prison Discipline, and those benevolent gentleman who carry it into execution, do not know what it is that they are doing...I hold this slow and daily tampering with the mysteries of the brain to be immeasurably worse than any torture of the body."

Prisoners had no contact with one another or with the outside world. They ate, worked, and exercised in their own cells. If they needed to be moved to another location, hoods were placed over their heads so that they could not even see the guards, or where they were going. Inmates endured years of this silent isolation. Death seemed to be a blessed escape from the madness that resulted from this allegedly compassionate path to penitence. And for those who broke the rules, terrible forms of torture were used to "correct" their behavior.

However, as powerful men continued to perceive this to be a brilliant system, over 300 penitentiaries were constructed around the world based upon Eastern State. The long blocks of private cells radiating from a central rotunda became the standard of prison design, and the Quaker-based concept of the Pennsylvania System of isolation and work spread across the globe.

Eventually, however, the Pennsylvania System slowly eroded. The need for more space led to placing more than one prisoner in a cell, and pressure from human rights advocates finally brought about the official demise of the system in 1913. Prisoners were allowed to speak to one another, have visitors, and basically be treated like human beings.

Yet, as cruel as this system had been, it can't be forgotten that the people who were incarcerated there were far from innocent. The inmates at Eastern State constituted the worst examples of mankind—murderers, rapists, and the criminally insane. Arguments still rage as to how to treat such people, with one side insisting that cable television in every cell is hardly punishment, and the other extreme claiming that no crime deserves anything as harsh as the death penalty. For Eastern State, the argument resolved itself in 1971, when the decaying prison was officially closed.

In the 1980s, the old penitentiary was slated to be demolished to make way for a new development, but several groups successfully petitioned for its preservation. In 1994, Eastern State reopened—this time strictly for tourists. Today the site is operated by a non-profit organization, and in addition to its regular tours, it hosts other special events. One of the most popular is a Halloween tour called Terror Behind the Walls, with great special effects and real people jumping out of dark corners to scare you.

Like the place needs real people to do that...

Reports of ghosts began soon after efforts got under way to preserve the structure and open it to the public. Workmen complained of strange sounds, shadowy figures, and unnerving feelings of being watched. One locksmith had a particularly bad encounter where he felt completely overwhelmed by an evil entity.

There isn't any part of the prison that hasn't had some sort of activity, from the cell blocks, to the hospital ward, to the yard, to the watchtowers, death row, and the warden's building. EMF readings abound in areas that haven't had any electricity in decades. Visitors have been touched and pushed. Icy cold spots can envelope you at any point. In short, this is one of the most haunted places in the country.

There may be a dozen tormented spirits still imprisoned at Eastern State, or there may be hundreds. Some may simply be wandering the corridors and courtyards finally seeking a way out, while others may be crouching in darkened corners, filled with the rage and thirst for blood they had in life, waiting for another innocent victim to come to them.

If you have the courage to enter the strong iron gates of the empty penitentiary, don't assume you will be alone, and don't assume you will be safe. Many generations of murderers, rapists, and gangsters, who never had any regard for human life, once lived and died there, and it is doubtful that death has changed their evil intent. It is ironic that an institution designed to isolate these criminals to protect society may now be one of the most dangerous places on earth—because now that they are dead, no bars can protect you!

## Recommendations

**This is the ideal location if you are part of a ghost hunting group, as private tours are available for groups of fifteen or more. If you aren't brave enough for an investigation at night, take one of the daylight tours when lots of other people are around. Don't miss Al Capone's cell by the central rotunda, the very creepy death row cells, and the site of the dreaded "Hole." Be prepared with your camera, camcorder, digital recorder, and EMF meter, as you never know what may happen!**



## Visitor Information

**Eastern State Penitentiary Historic Site, Inc.**
**2027 Fairmount Avenue**
**Philadelphia, PA 19130-2610**
**(215) 236-3300**
**www.easternstate.org**

**Hours:**
**Every day: 10am – 5pm (last entry 4pm). June through August: Wednesday evenings until 8pm, last entry: 7pm. Closed Thanksgiving, Christmas Eve, Christmas Day, and New Year's Day. Children under the age of 7 cannot be admitted. No reservations necessary, except for group or private tours.**

**Admission:**
**$12.00 Adults. $10.00 Senior Citizens. $8.00 Students. $8.00 Kids (Age 7 – 12).**

**Directions:**
**From their website—From the North or West: Take Interstate 76 (the Schuylkill Expressway) to Exit 344 (Old Exit 38), which is Interstate 676, also know as the Vine Street Expressway. On I-676 take the first exit, "Benjamin Franklin Parkway/ 23 Street." Take the first left onto 22nd Street. Pass the Philadelphia Museum of Art (on your left) and continue five blocks north, to Fairmount Avenue.**

**From the South or East: Take I-95 to Exit 22 (Old Exit 17) and follow Interstate 676 West. Get off at "Art Museum/Benjamin Franklin Parkway" Exit. At the top of the ramp, turn right onto 22nd street. Pass the Philadelphia Museum of Art (on your left) and continue five blocks north, to Fairmount Avenue.**

## The Bottom Line

**The History:** The first "penitentiary" built in 1829, which at the time was the most modern building in the country. Inmates were kept completely isolated from other people.

**The Haunting:** All manner of terrifying activity! This is one of the most haunted places in the country.

# Gettysburg

England is often referred to as the most haunted country in the world. However, even that ghost-filled island nation would be hard-pressed to find a single town that is more haunted than the small Pennsylvania community that was the site of one of the greatest human dramas in history. To fully appreciate what happened at Gettysburg, and what remains there today, you must walk its fields, spend the night in one of its old homes, and sit atop a hill and silently watch the sun set. Gettysburg is a place that must be experienced—as no words or pictures can ever accurately describe the feelings that sweep over you there.

If you had to choose only one war in which to study extraordinary courage, devotion, and self-sacrifice, as well as the depths of suffering and anguish, the Civil War would be an excellent choice. And if you could only choose one battle of the Civil War to study, Gettysburg would be the obvious choice. Due to its massive scale, the pivotal importance of the outcome, the staggering number of casualties, and the relationships and interactions of the combatants, this battle contained an intense concentration of human emotions that can still be sensed to this day. You cannot stand on Little Round Top, or walk across the field of Pickett's Charge, or look down the long rows of unknown soldiers in the National Cemetery without feeling that something is here.

Cemetery Hill.

There are countless reports of ghostly soldiers across the battlefield, in the streets of town, and in the old farmhouses that served as field hospitals. In addition to spirits directly linked to the battle, there are other stories involving townspeople—predominantly women and children—who for a variety of reasons are still seen at the sites of their deaths or some other tragic event. It is actually difficult to find a Civil War-era building or section of the battlefield that is not reputed to be haunted.

PA

## Visitor Information

**Gettysburg National Military Park Museum and Visitor Center**
1195 Baltimore Pike
Gettysburg, PA 17325
717-334-1124
www.nps.gov/gett/index.htm

**Hours:**

Park Grounds and Roads: The park is open daily from 6am – 10pm April 1 to October 31, and 6am – 7pm November 1 to March 31.

Museum and Visitor Center: Open daily throughout the year. The center is closed on Thanksgiving Day, Christmas Day, and New Years Day. Yearly Operating Hours: 8am – 5pm November 1 through March 31. 8am – 6pm April 1 to October 31.

**Admission:**

Admission to the park is free. Admission for the museum exhibits, film, and cyclorama: $10.50 per Adult, $9.50 per Seniors and Active Military (with proper ID), $6.50 per Youth (ages 6-18). Children under 6 years old admitted free.

**Directions:**

From their website—Gettysburg National Military Park museum and visitor center is located at 1195 Baltimore Pike (Route 97) with a back entrance from the Taneytown Road (State Route 134). From North or South, follow US 15 to Gettysburg and watch for signs to direct you to the National Park Service Visitor Center. The signs are near the exit at Route 97. Go north on Route 97 and look for the visitor center entrance, which will be on your left at the stoplight. From East or West, drive into Gettysburg on US Route 30, turn South on Baltimore Street (Route 97), and follow signs to the entrance of the visitor center, which will be on your right at the stoplight.

## The Bottom Line

**The History:** The most famous battle of the Civil War was fought here on July 1-3, 1863, resulting in over 50,000 casualties.

**The Haunting:** Soldiers can appear anywhere at any time, and the sounds of battle can be heard anywhere at any time. Probably the most haunted place in the country.

## Farnsworth House

People have spent their lives studying the battle and battlefields, so don't expect to see everything in one day. If you want to spend the night in one of the best historic haunts during your visit, the place to stay in Gettysburg is the Farnsworth House. Originally built in 1810, it has an ideal location in town. The Farnsworth still has several bullet holes from the battle in its brick walls, as Confederate sharpshooters used the top floor of the home to fire upon Union troops. It is believed that the stray shot that killed Jenny Wade—the only Gettysburg resident to be killed in the battle—was fired from the Farnsworth. (Yes, Jenny Wade's ghost has been seen at her home, too.)

The Farnsworth House.

Now a bed and breakfast and restaurant, the Farnsworth nonetheless still looks much as it did during the battle on July 1st, 2nd, and 3rd in 1863. There is a famous photograph taken in November of that year in which the Farnsworth can be seen in the background. The photo captured the official procession making its way to the dedication of the new National Cemetery, where Lincoln was to deliver his famous Gettysburg Address.

In addition to the wonderful history connected with this house, there appears to be other connections—those to the other world. As many as fourteen different ghosts have been seen and felt there, and the staff will be happy to tell you about all of them during one of the evening ghost story presentations which are held in the Farnsworth's spooky basement. If you want to have the chance to possibly experience their ghosts firsthand, stay in one of their guest rooms in the main part of the house.

As for the best place and time to experience ghostly activity in town or on the battlefields, the short answer is anywhere at any time. Particularly intense locations include the Triangular Field, Devil's Den, Spangler's Spring, the Wheatfield, and the fields near the Eternal Light. While many sights and sounds occur at night, solid apparitions have been seen in broad daylight, along with all the sounds of battle.

Perhaps no other place in the country offers such a vast expanse of haunted ground, and so many haunted buildings. Visit Gettysburg to experience the paranormal, where so many men "gave the last full measure of devotion."

## Recommendations

**The Battle of Gettysburg was fought over three bloody days across miles of ground, so the more you know about the people and events before you arrive, the more you will get out of your visit.**

**Start at the park's Visitor Center and after seeing the exhibits, get one of the free maps and take the self-guided auto tour, as this will allow you to go at your own pace, and will help you get your bearings on this vast battlefield. Just remember that in Gettysburg at any given time there are probably more people dressed in period clothing than modern attire, so don't think everyone in uniform or a long dress is one of the walking dead! Civil War Heritage Days is an annual two-week series of events held the last week of June and the first week in July and includes various living history events, battlefield walks, lectures, book signings, special tours, the Fireman's Carnival (with great fireworks!), and culminates in the annual reenactment which includes thousands of reenactors.**

**Make hotel reservations far in advance if you have any hopes of staying within an hour of town during the Heritage Days. Spring and fall are great times to visit as the weather is better and you won't have to fight the traffic and the crowds—there's been enough fighting here already...**

## Visitor Information

**Farnsworth House Inn**
**415 Baltimore Street**
**Gettysburg, PA 17325**
**(717) 334-8838**
**www.farnsworthhouseinn.com**

**Directions:**

**From I-83S in Harrisburg: Continue onto PA-581 W. Take exit 5B to merge onto US-15 S toward Gettysburg. Exit onto US-30 W/York Road. At the traffic circle, take the 3rd exit onto Baltimore Street. The Farnsworth will be on the right.**

**From Washington, D.C.: Take US-50 W. Continue onto I-66 W. Take the exit onto George Washington Memorial Parkway Entering Virginia. Take the exit onto I-495 N toward Maryland Entering Maryland. Slight left at I-270 Spur N. Merge onto I-270 N. Continue onto US-40 W. Continue onto US-15 N Entering Pennsylvania. Take the PA-97 exit toward Baltimore Street. Turn left at Baltimore Pike/PA-97 N. Continue to follow PA-97 N. Continue onto Baltimore Street. The Farnsworth will be on the left.**

# Rhode Island

FORT ADAMS

SPRAGUE MANSION

INN BLISS B&B

The Officer's Quarters in 1934. *Courtesy of The Library of Congress.*

RI

# Fort Adams

On the 4th of July in 1799, the first Fort Adams was established in Newport on a point jutting out into Narragansett Bay. The infamous Captain John Henry was the fort's first commander. In 1812, Henry was paid the princely sum of $50,000 by President Madison to turn over his letters showing how Canada and Great Britain hoped the northern states would break from the union and ally themselves with America's former enemies. The plot revealed, passions throughout the country were inflamed, and war was declared.

In the years following the War of 1812, it became clear that a larger fort was necessary. Construction on the new Fort Adams was begun in 1824, and it was planned by a French military designer who had served under Napoleon, so he obviously knew a thing or two about war and fortifications. Construction continued until 1853 and by the time it was completed, Fort Adams was the largest and most complex coastal fortification in the country. It remained an active army post until 1950, playing roles in every major war throughout that period.

It's somewhat remarkable that during its long history, the fort's soldiers never fired a shot at an enemy, but that doesn't mean there weren't casualties. In 1819, one soldier shot and killed another. When the systems of tunnels were being dug, several men died when the walls collapsed on them. A tragic artillery accident took the lives of about twenty men. Many others died from other accidents and diseases. Have any of these tragedies left a paranormal imprint on Fort Adams? Many visitors and reenactors would say, "Yes!"

There are inexplicable noises around the fort, including footsteps that can be heard echoing down the hallways. A couple of visitors heard these footsteps rapidly approaching as if to chase them out of the building, and they obliged by running outside!

Apparitions have been seen, but they don't look quite right. They seem to be figures of men, but somehow grotesquely distorted. Some have speculated that these could be the ghosts of the men who were mangled during the artillery accident. Others claim to have been touched, heard voices, or felt a presence that can only be described as unnerving. In short, one member of the staff described the general feeling at Fort Adams to be "eerie," especially at night.

Unlike many historic sites who won't even talk about their ghosts, paranormal research has actually been encouraged here, and the public is invited to participate during their annual "Fortress of Nightmares" events in October. Overnight stays are also available throughout the season for groups. Where else can you spend the night in an old fort, learn about its history, then delve into its ghostly phenomena?

Of course, if all this seems a bit too daunting to the armchair ghost hunter, a visit to Fort Adams on a beautiful, sunny summer's day with its sweeping views of the bay will help to dispel its spookier aspects. But then again, you never know when or where one of the ghosts of the old fort might tap you on the shoulder and introduce himself.

RI

## The Bottom Line

**The History:** A fort first established in 1799, with a new fort constructed on the site beginning in 1824 which became the country's largest coastal fortification.

**The Haunting:** Many sounds, footsteps, and voices. Apparitions of soldiers who appear disfigured.

## Recommendations

The fort really is an amazing piece of military architecture. The long tunnels are quite creepy, but when you've had enough of them you can go outside and soak in the spectacular views. There are a variety of special events including military reenactments, music festivals, and classic car shows. If you don't have a large enough group for one of the overnight events, don't miss the public paranormal investigations, but book well in advance as they are very popular.

## Visitor Information

**Fort Adams State Park**
Fort Adams Drive, Newport, RI 02840
(401) 841-0707 www.fortadams.org

**Hours:**

Guided tours are conducted daily, Memorial Day thru Columbus Day, every hour on the hour from 10am – 4pm.

**Admission:**

$10 General, $5 Youth (6 to 17), 5 and under Free, $25 Family Rate (Two adults and up to four youths). Overnight Rates: (Minimum of 10 people) Barracks Overnight $25 per person per night, includes guided tour. Tented Overnight $15 per person per night, guided tour $3 per person.

Fortress of Nightmares: Ticket sales begin at 6pm and end at 9pm each evening. Ghost Hunt $10, Tunnels of Terror $10, Combo Ticket $15.

Tours are weather dependant and sturdy footwear is recommended. Please call the Gift Shop at (401) 841-0707 if the weather is questionable.

**Directions:**

By Car: From Route 138 east over the Jamestown-Verrazanno Bridge, continue over the Newport Bridge ($2 toll). (You can see Fort Adams to your right as you are crossing over the Newport Bridge.) Take first exit off of the bridge and take a right onto Farewell Street at the end of the exit ramp. Proceed ¼ mile to a fork in the road and take the right hand fork onto America's Cup Avenue. Get in the right hand lane. Take a right onto Lower Thames Street. Go ½ mile and take a right onto Wellington Avenue to the next intersection and take a right. Follow the road to the next intersection and take a right. Proceed approximately ¼ mile and look for two large black anchors on your right. This is the entrance to Fort Adams State Park. Take a right. Follow the road to the top of the hill. Continue straight on the road until you enter a large parking lot. At the far end of the lot is a red brick building where the Gift Shop/Ticket office and rest rooms are located.

From Boston: Take Route 93 (AKA, the Southeast Expressway) South to Route 24. Take Route 24 South until it ends in Portsmouth, RI (approximately 55 miles). Take Route 114 South (or Route 138 South if you wind up on it) to the intersection of Valley Road in Middletown, Route 214. Take a left on Valley Road, go 2 miles until you are facing the Atlantic Beach Club. Take a right onto Memorial Boulevard then turn left on Bellevue Avenue. Continue until you see the sign for Fort Adams and take a right onto Ruggles Avenue. Continue following signs to Fort Adams, which will take you through 2 4-way stops until the road dead ends at Brenton Road. Turn left and continue to 3-way stop and proceed to bottom of hill to right turn at entrance to Fort Adams State Park. Follow park directions above.

By Ferry: The Jamestown and Newport Ferry provides passenger service between Jamestown Village, Rose Island, Fort Adams, Perrotti Park and Bowen's Landing at the foot of Market Square. Parking is included with your ticket from the Jamestown Village departure. Fort Adams departures are at the water taxi dock directly opposite the visitor's center.

An early depiction of the Sprague Mansion.

RI

# Sprague Mansion

Snow covered the streets and fields of Cranston on New Year's Eve in 1843, which made a factory worker's discovery even more gruesome—the bloody and battered body of a man lying face down by a bridge. The victim had been beaten so badly that no one recognized him at first.

The shocking truth was that it was none other than Amasa Sprague, the man who not only owned the print works factory, but most of the town as well, and he had been murdered in cold blood as he was taking his usual Sunday walk to look over his property.

The Spragues were not just any wealthy family; they were *the* wealthy family in Rhode Island. In fact, at one point, they were the wealthiest family in America. Their fortunes were made from the textile empire they created and their power was enhanced by not one, but two family members ascending to the office of Governor of the state. Life was indeed good for the Spragues, until their perfect little world was shattered by the murder.

Amasa's body was brought back to the large house that the family built in 1790, which was expanded into a twenty-two-room mansion in the 1860s. His body was laid out in the parlor, and family, friends, and employees came to pay their respects—which basically amounted to the entire population of Cranston. However, one family, the Gordons, was conspicuous by their absence. Suspicions had already fallen on the family, as Amasa Sprague had lobbied to have the liquor license revoked for Nicholas Gordon's pub to stop factory workers from drinking at lunch, and there were rumors that Nicholas had threatened revenge.

Amasa Sprague's original grave marker that states he was murdered.

One assumption led to another, and despite the lack of evidence, the entire Gordon family was soon arrested. Even the family dog was taken into custody, as Amasa's body had bite marks. Officials were unable to uncover definitive proof that a Gordon committed the terrible crime, but there was one thing that doomed the family—they were Irish. Immigrants from Ireland were looked upon with suspicion and contempt by the locals, and this prejudice went so far as to have the judge essentially caution the jury that whatever an Irishman said was a lie.

Details of the trial read like a bad novel, but the end result was all too real—on February 14, 1845, John Gordon was hung by the neck until dead for the crime of the murder of Amasa Sprague. John's last words before his execution were, "I forgive them. I forgive all my persecutors, because they did not know what they were doing. I hope all good Christians pray for me."

Enough outrage was stirred up over Gordon's hanging that capital punishment in Rhode island was abolished. But if they did hang an innocent man, then who was guilty? Some speculate that Amasa's own brother, William, had paid someone to commit the foul murder, as Amasa had stood in the way of William's plans to expand the family business. It is doubtful that anyone will ever know for sure, but what is certain is that the shadow of two tragic deaths hangs over the Sprague Mansion. But could there be more?

While the murder and execution are the most widely-known events, as with any house over 200 years old, there must be many trials and tribulations that took place within its walls. For example, William and Amasa's father had gotten a bone caught in his throat, and died in the house two days later from a subsequent infection. In more recent years, a resident committed suicide in the house. Have all these events left unearthly energies in the former Governor's mansion?

If you can believe your own eyes and ears, then the answer is yes. Many people have heard clear and unmistakable footsteps and doors opening and closing (including the very day this author visited!). There is a small room on the second floor where a very credible witness saw a white, misty apparition floating above the floor. People walking or driving by have seen a woman standing in the cupola.

In the old wine cellar, there is a strong presence that has physically touched people, and a séance revealed it to be the spirit of a butler named Charlie. There may also be a haunted mirror that holds the spirit of Kate Chase Sprague—once one of the most beautiful and richest women in the country, but in her later years she was reduced to poverty and had to sell eggs to make ends meet. Does she still gaze into that mirror and try to recapture the glorious days of her youth?

There are so many stories to tell in this house, who can say for sure where facts end and legends begin?

## The Bottom Line

**The History:** This is one of those locations that offer something for every historical taste, from the building of an industrial empire, to political power, military history, and the intrigue of a murder, trial, and execution that subsequently changed Rhode Island law.

**The Haunting:** From footsteps to full apparitions, and from Charlie the Butler to Kate who fell from grace, this is one very haunted mansion.

## Recommendations

The amazing story of the Sprague family involves the Civil War, the Industrial Revolution, politics, Rhode Island history, a glimpse into the life of wealth and privilege, and a fascinating murder mystery. The house and furnishings are beautiful, and there is an excellent family portrait collection. Look for the goose bones collection, which were used as some sort of barometer to predict the weather. Then there's the doll room, and if the dolls staring at you isn't creepy enough, think about the fact that this is where the misty apparition was seen. In the wine cellar, note the enormous slabs of rock that form the ceiling. The carriage house and stables have an impressive collection of antique carriages, sleighs, and a Model T milk truck.

## Visitor Information

**Governor Sprague Mansion**
1351 Cranston Street
Cranston, RI 02920
(401) 944-9226
www.cranstonhistoricalsociety.org/

**Events:**

There are special historical programs available, and in October they have a Charlie the Butler Halloween party.

The Sprague Mansion is available for weddings, showers, receptions, parties, and corporate functions. To make the Wedding March very special, they offer use of their rare 1880 Steinway Grand Centennial Concert Piano.

**Admission:**

Mansion tours are $10 for adults, $5 for children under 12. Please call for hours and an appointment. There is convenient ample off-street parking behind the mansion.

**Directions:**

From their website—From 95N or 95S: Take Exit 16 to Route 10 Cranston. If heading north, bear left while on the exit; if traveling south, bear right while on the exit. Proceed north approximately ¼ miles on Route 10 and take the Industrial Park/Cranston Street exit; Stay on your left on the exit, take a left at the light to Cranston Street. Then take a left onto Cranston Street. At the sixth light take a sharp right staying on Cranston Street. Look for a big white house and our sign on the right. Turn right at the traffic light on Dyer Avenue and then a quick turn right at the brick carriage house into our parking lot.

From 295N or 295S: Take Exit 4 to Route 14 Plainfield Pike; If heading north, bear right to the end of exit; if traveling south, bear left to the end of the exit; Go through three traffic lights; take a right onto Atwood Avenue; Continue through the first traffic light, move into left lane as you approach the second traffic light; At the second traffic light, take a left onto Randall Street; At the next traffic light, take a left onto Cranston Street; The Mansion is on the left just after the traffic light. Turn left at the light and then a quick turn right at the brick carriage house into our parking lot.

# Inn Bliss B&B

Pride in ownership is all too rare these days, but it is a key ingredient at Inn Bliss, which has consistently won awards as one of Newport's best bed and breakfasts. This pride is also evident in the kind old woman who likes to show people around her house—although she hasn't technically owned it since 1974, when she died.

In 1888, carpenter Isaac Gleason built a Victorian house on Bliss Road for his new wife. While Isaac continued to make houses in Newport, his wife made babies—two daughters, Nellie and Daisy. In 1897, Isaac died of pneumonia. When Daisy married, she moved to Massachusetts. Nellie remained at home with her mother, who didn't pass away until 1934.

Nellie remained in the house that she grew up in after her mother's death. For many years, she was a kindergarten teacher at the Potter School, and she also gave piano lessons in the living room. Many people who grew up in Newport had been taught by Nellie Gleason, either in school or at her home on Bliss Road.

Nellie finally passed away in 1974, and with no family of her own, she left her beloved home to her nephews. Unfortunately, they apparently didn't see the place in the same sentimental light as their aunt, and sold the house just six months later.

Today, Nellie's home still has a piano in the same corner where she gave lessons, and the house is once again owned and visited by people who love and care for it. And, it may still have Nellie, herself.

The first night one of the owners spent there, he had a strange and vivid dream. An old woman came to him and she took him on a tour of the house. He never forgot that dream, and he never told anyone else about it. Then one day a guest came down for breakfast and told the owner about a strange dream in which an old woman had given a tour of the house. Then another time another guest related the same dream. Then another, and another…

How could so many people with no prior knowledge of the place all have the same dream? Or is it something other than a dream? It is believed that when we sleep our minds are more open to the other world, so perhaps this is when Nellie takes the opportunity to show people around the home she lived in for eighty-five years.

It may be a difficult concept to fathom, but spend the night at Inn Bliss and sleep on it…

## Recommendations

**Inn Bliss consistently receives excellent reviews for its rooms, food, service, and location, so it is an ideal place to stay while exploring all of Newport's historic haunts, mansions, shops, and restaurants. There are ghost tours of the town, but if you are too tired to go out at night, just stay in your room and let Nellie take you on a tour!**

## Visitor Information

**Inn Bliss Bed and Breakfast**
**10 Bliss Road, Newport, RI 02840-1837**
**(401) 845-2547 www.innbliss.com**

**Directions:**

**From their website—From Providence/ Western Massachusetts/T. F. Green Airport: Take 295 South or 95 South to Route 4 (Exit will be on your left) Route 4 turns into Route 1. Take the Route 138/ Newport exit. Follow Route 138 over the Jamestown and Newport Bridges (Newport Bridge has a $2 toll or EZ Pass). Take the first exit ramp off the Newport Bridge. At the end of the ramp, take a right. At the first set of lights, take a left onto Van Zandt Avenue. Go straight until you hit Broadway. Take a right onto Broadway and then take your first left onto Bliss Road. (Bliss Grocer and Cafe and Newport Prescriptions is on the corner.) Look for parking now. Inn Bliss is located one block down on the left, up on a small knoll. On-street parking is available on Bliss and Bradford. Bliss Road is a one-way so be careful not to pass us.**

**From New York/ D.C./Maryland/New Jersey/ Pennsylvania/Connecticut: Take 95 North to Exit 3A Route 138 East. Follow Route 138 over the Jamestown and Newport Bridges (Newport Bridge has a $2 toll or EZ Pass). Take the first exit ramp off the Newport Bridge. At the end of the ramp, take a right. At the first set of lights, take a left onto Van Zandt Avenue., then following Directions: above.**

**From Boston/ Maine/Vermont/Canada/New Hampshire: Take 93 South to Route 24 South. (Be careful as Route 24 turns onto Route 195 West for 1 Exit and then you must take your first exit to continue on Route 24.) Route 24 South turns into Route 114 South. Follow Route 114 South through Portsmouth and Middletown. Route 114 South turns into Broadway at the Middletown/ Newport town line. Continue down Broadway but SLOW down when you pass Fowler Street and Gibbs Road on the left. The next left will be Bliss Road. (If you come to a stop light, you missed it! (Bliss Grocer and Cafe and Newport Prescriptions is on the corner of Bliss.) Turn left onto Bliss Road and follow Directions: above.**

## The Bottom Line

**The History:** A Victorian home built in 1888, now an award-winning B&B.
**The Haunting:** A woman who lived here for 85 years likes to show guests around her home.

# South Carolina



BOONE HALL PLANTATION

BATTERY CARRIAGE HOUSE INN

POOGAN'S PORCH RESTAURANT

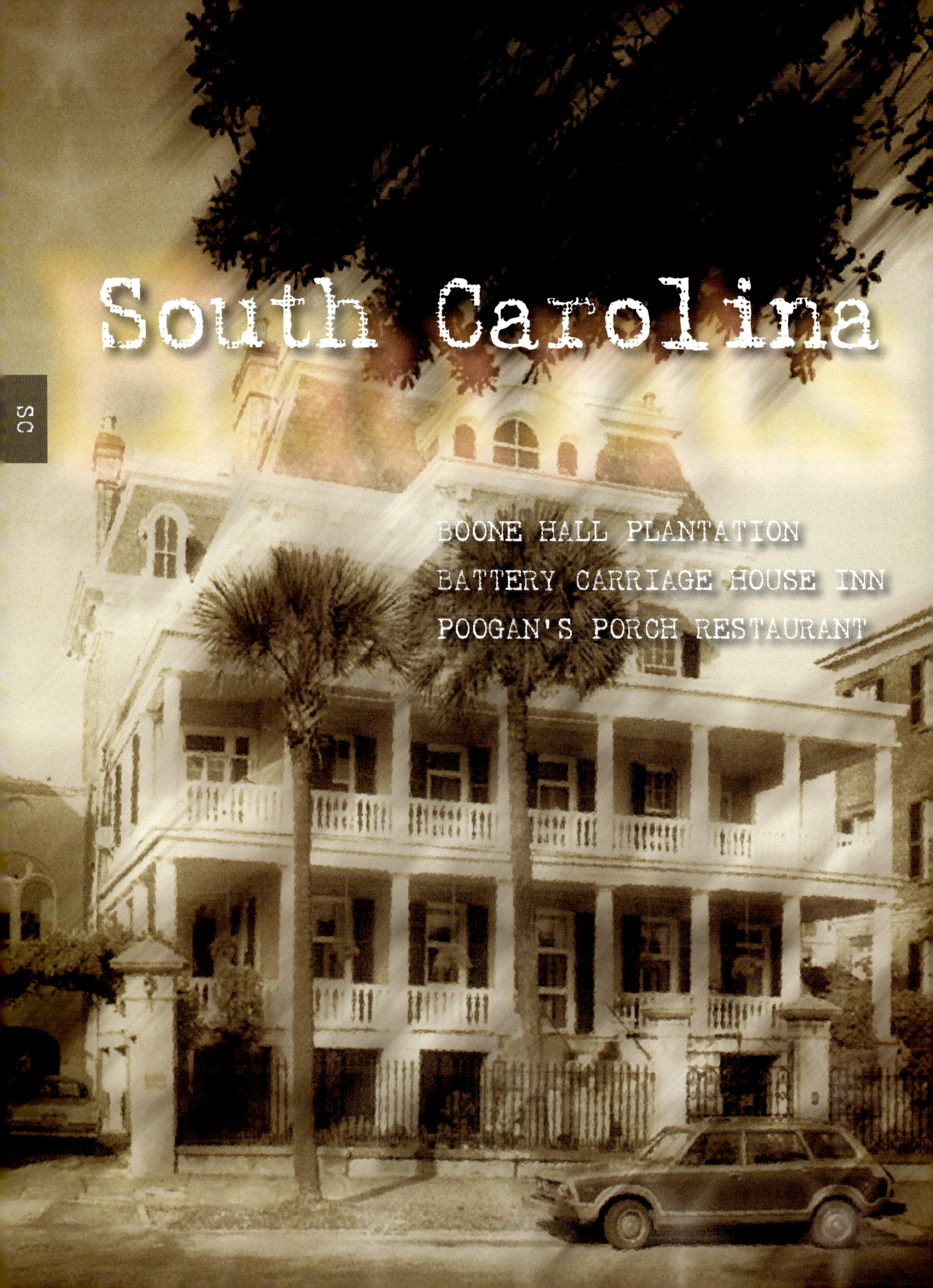

Boone Hall.

# Boone Hall Plantation

Traveling down the lovely three-quarter mile "Avenue of Oaks" to arrive at the brick mansion at Boone Hall Plantation may make you feel as if you're on the movie set of *Gone With the Wind.* The oaks were first planted in 1743, making a grand entrance to a cotton plantation which once stretched across 17,000 acres in Mount Pleasant.

Of course, all this elegance and genteel southern living came at a terrible price—the price paid by the slaves that worked in the fields and managed the household. Their tiny cabins are also still standing on the plantation grounds as a stark reminder of the antebellum south and all it stood for.

This land was granted to Major John Boone around 1680, and today Boone Hall is the oldest working, living plantation, as it is still growing a variety of fruits and vegetables after more than 300 years. Many of its buildings and walls were constructed from bricks made on the plantation. The mansion was only built in 1935 to replace the older home, but many early buildings still exist, such as the 1790-1810 slave quarters, the 1853 cotton gin, and a 1750 smokehouse. In addition, there are magnificent gardens that have rose bushes over 100 years old.

The house saw a variety of owners over the centuries that reflected the long history of this country. Then there was the owner in 1940 who didn't quite fit the model of the southern gentleman—Russian Prince Dimitri Djordjadze, a famous race car driver who married Clark Gable's ex-wife. In 1955, the property was purchased by current owners Harris and Nancy McRae, and they opened the plantation to the public in 1957. Thanks to their efforts, this iconic southern plantation lives on, and just in case it looks strangely familiar when you arrive, Boone Hill was one of the sites in the television miniseries *North and South*, and has also been used for several movies.

Boone Hall is a must-see place on any visit to the Charleston area, just be aware that if on your tour you happen to see a Civil War soldier trying to remove a bullet from a wounded comrade, this is not a scene from a movie or reenactors recreating a medical procedure for the benefit of visitors. For many years, this disturbing scene has played out over and over again before astonished witnesses, who are even more astonished when the two soldiers disappear! Is this just a static imprint of an event long ago, or are the ghosts of these soldiers doomed to remain here until that bullet is finally removed?

Who these soldiers were is not known, but they are surely not the only ghosts on this old plantation. What other spirits still linger on the grounds and in the buildings that have seen centuries of joy and despair, and the life and death of countless souls? Boone Hall may be the oldest working plantation, and it may also be the oldest haunted plantation.



## The Bottom Line

**The History:** The oldest working plantation, established on land granted around 1680.

**The Haunting:** A Civil War soldier tries to remove a bullet from another soldier.

## Recommendations

The plantation offers tours of the buildings, grounds, gardens, and exhibits, and if you think that's too much walking, have no fear—there is a trolley that takes you all around. There are many special events throughout the year to keep you coming back, such as the annual Oyster Roast in January (with 70,000 pounds of oysters!), the Strawberry Festival in the spring, the Boone Hall BBQ Championship and Bluegrass Festival on Labor Day weekend, the Scottish Games and Highland Gathering, Boone Hall Fright Nights for the Halloween season, Christmas festivals, concerts, food and wine festivals, and the reenactment of The Battle of Secessionville.

## Visitor Information

**Boone Hall Plantation**
1235 Long Point Road
Mt. Pleasant, SC 29464-9020
(843) 216-1032
www.boonehallplantation.com

**Hours:**

Labor Day to March 8: Monday to Saturday, 9am – 5pm; Sunday, 1pm – 4pm. March 9 to Labor Day: Monday to Saturday, 8:30am – 6:30pm; Sunday, 1pm – 5pm. Closed Thanksgiving Day and Christmas Day.

**Admission:**

Adults $17.50, Senior Citizens/Military/AAA $15, Children $7.50, Children 5 and under are Free.

**Directions:**

From Downtown Charleston: Take Highway 17 North towards Mt. Pleasant. Go approximately 7 miles and turn left onto Long Point Road. You will see signs for Boone Hall Plantation and Charles Pinckney NHS. Follow Long Point Road and the entrance to the site will be on the right.

From Myrtle Beach: Take Highway 17 South towards Charleston. Turn Right onto Long Point Road. You will see signs for Boone Hall Plantation and Charles Pinckney NHS. Follow Long Point Road and the entrance to the site will be on the right.

From I-26: Take I-526 East towards Mt. Pleasant. Take the Long Point Road exit. At bottom of exit turn Left. The entrance to Boone Hall will be 2 miles up on the left.

The Stevens-Lathers House, now the Battery Carriage Inn.
*Courtesy of The Library of Congress.*

SC

# Battery Carriage House Inn

In an area known for its history and elegant antebellum mansions, a stay at the Battery Carriage House Inn is the perfect way to experience the charm of Charleston, as well as to learn about the city's many trials and tribulations. The main house on the property was built in 1843 on land that was purchased by Samuel Stevens for the sum of $4,500. The original Neoclassical style of the house was later altered to the more elaborate Second Empire style, but given ensuing ravages of war, storms, and time, it's a wonder that the place was able to survive to the present day.

Charleston in the late 1850s was an affluent port city, but that prosperity was to come to an abrupt end during the Civil War. Battery Park was one of the sites of the Confederate artillery, and the residents nearby had to abandon their homes due to the heavy shelling from Union forces. The mansion sustained damage, but remained intact, while the city and its way of life seemed beyond repair.

The mansion—now known as the Stevens-Lathers House—was purchased in 1870 by Colonel Richard Lathers. He hired architect John Henry Devereaux and spent $10,000 renovating the structure. Lathers had hoped to revive the economy of Charleston through his many business and political connections. Although he was a South Carolina native, he had supported the Union during the war, so the Yankee Colonel didn't exactly receive a warm reception from the locals.

Realizing he was fighting a losing battle, he sold the property in 1874 to a banker, Andrew Simonds. He was the founder of the First National Bank of South Carolina, owned a fleet of ships, and also ran a successful fertilizer business. Unfortunately, wealth does not protect one from tragedy, and Simonds' son died in a sanatorium as a result of his dissolute lifestyle.

Another tragedy with one of the Simonds' children was narrowly—and perhaps miraculously—avoided. His young daughter decided to climb onto the roof of the ballroom, where she tried to walk on the glass skylight. The glass broke, and the girl would have plunged to her death, had she not fallen onto one of the large chandeliers, which was able to hold her weight until she could be rescued.

The family lived in the mansion until 1912, and the following decades witnessed a significant decline. In the 1920s, the place began its history as a lodging establishment, as one of the back buildings on the property became a "motor court" for tourists. While this may have not been the most dignified use of such an elegant property, it definitely went downhill from there. In the 1940s, the place was frequented by Navy sailors who spent their pay renting both rooms and women by the hour.

In the 1960s, it was converted to apartments for college students, and in the 1980s, it once again became a respectable hotel. While years of neglect had slowly taken their toll on the buildings, it took just hours for Hurricane Hugo in 1989 to really inflict major damage. The fate of the historic antebellum mansion looked bleak, but a direct descendant of Andrew Simonds came to the rescue.

Drayton Hastie and his wife, Katherine, lovingly restored his family's home to its former grandeur. While the mansion is their private residence, the carriage house in the garden has been converted into one of Charleston's finest inns. The Battery Carriage House Inn has become known for its romantic and intimate accommodations; it has also become a destination for those seeking another of Charleston's fascinating attributes—its ghosts.

Guests in room #3 reported witnessing glowing lights and several figures. Stranger still is what appears (and what doesn't appear) in room #8. Several guests have seen the figure of a "barrel-chested man," or at least part of him. Only the torso of the man is visible, and it is dressed in layers of rough clothing and a cape. Some speculate that the headless, partial figure was a Confederate soldier struck down by artillery. Others point to the fact that in the city's early days, dozens of captured pirates were hung in the trees of Battery Park. Regardless of whether this unique ghost was a soldier, a pirate, or some other unfortunate soul, he appears most often to men, and while unsettling to be sure, he is never threatening.

Then there is room #10, where the more refined "Gentleman Ghost" has made appearances. He has been described as being upwards of six feet tall, with a slight build, and of a pale, grayish hue. The prevailing belief is that this wandering spirit is the result of the self-inflicted demise of the son of an early twentieth-century owner. The young man was considered to be a "sensitive and cultivated college student," and for reasons he took to his grave, he ended his brief life by jumping off the roof.

While the Hasties have never experienced anything paranormal, they would certainly understand if something of the past can still be glimpsed here today. Charleston is all about preserving history and giving visitors a taste of a bygone era, and at the Battery Carriage House Inn, you have the rare opportunity to get in touch with the past in both tranquil and tantalizing ways.

SC

## Recommendation

**The inn is ideally located for exploring all the sites and events Charleston has to offer. And if you're just looking for a peaceful and romantic escape from your hectic lifestyle, the inn is also the perfect spot for a quiet retreat. Several packages are available, including the Ghost Adventure Package, and be sure to request rooms #8 or #10 for your best chance of a paranormal encounter.**

## Visitor Information

**The Battery Carriage House Inn**
20 South Battery
Charleston, SC 29401
(843) 727-3100
(800) 775-5575
www.batterycarriagehouse.com
batterych@bellsouth.net

**Directions:**

From I-26: Stay on I-26 until it ends and stay in the left lane. The road splits off toward Meeting Street (Exit 221B). Turn right onto Meeting Street and stay on it until the end, then turn right onto South Battery. The inn is the second house on the right.

From I-95 N to Highway 17 N: From I-95 N, take Exit 33 to Highway 17. After about 60 miles you will enter downtown Charleston by crossing the Ashley River. From the bridge, exit onto Lockwood Drive South. Lockwood Drive becomes Broad Street. Turn right at the Meeting Street intersection (look for the white church and post office). Take Meeting Street until it ends, then turn right onto South Battery. The inn is the second house on the right.

From Highway 17 S: Take 17 S across the Arthur Ravenel Bridge. Take the Meeting Street exit and turn left. Stay on Meeting Street until it ends, then turn right onto South Battery. The inn is the second house on the right.

## The Bottom Line

**The History:** From one of Charleston's most elegant mansions, to a stop for local sailors and prostitutes, this place has sustained damage from the Civil War, Hurricane Hugo, and neglect, but has persevered and returned back to a graceful historic mansion and inn.

**The Haunting:** Various experiences reported by guests. Most notably: glowing lights, the figure of the gentleman ghost, and the headless torso.

Poogan's Porch. Photo by Ben Williams. *Courtesy of Poogan's Porch Restaurant.*



# Poogan's Porch Restaurant

When Bobbie Ball, a state court reporter, decided to renovate a nineteenth century house in Charleston's historic district, she didn't realize there would be two additional residents. One was a scruffy stray dog named Poogan, who used to go from porch to porch in the neighborhood looking for food and some attention. He decided he liked Bobbie's house the best and Poogan became a fixture on the porch.

Poogan returned Bobbie's affection by becoming the guardian of the restaurant when it opened in 1976. He was there to greet the first guests, and remained a happy member of the staff until his death in 1979. The faithful companion was given a proper burial on the property with an engraved stone, and in his honor the restaurant bears his name and his favorite place to be.

According to some people, the porch of the restaurant is still where Poogan likes to be, as witnesses claim to have seen a dog on the porch. And for skeptics who may say it was just some other stray dog, Poogan has even been identified from his photo on the wall. Dogs truly are man's best friend, even after death.

The other unexpected resident is believed to be the ghost of Zoe St. Armand. There aren't any early records about the house, but in the late nineteenth century, Zoe and her sister, Elizabeth, were living here. They were school teacher-spinsters and kept each other company decade after decade. Then in 1945, Elizabeth died, and the ensuing loneliness slowly eroded Zoe's mind. Zoe didn't die in the house, but she has made her presence known on so many occasions in so many ways that Poogan's Porch was named by the Travel Channel as the 3rd Most Haunted Place in America.

You don't actually have to go inside to see Zoe—guests staying in the hotel across the street have often seen a woman in a black dress waving at them from a window. One witness called the police when she saw an old woman banging on the window as if she was trapped in the building. The police thoroughly searched the house, but found no one, and the security alarm had not been triggered.

People have also seen this old woman in a long black dress throughout the building. Apparently, Zoe likes to throw pots and pans in the kitchen, and knock items off of tables, right before the eyes of stunned staff and guests. While being mischievous, Zoe is harmless, although any encounter with even the most benign ghost can be frightening—as was evidenced by the poor woman who ran screaming from the ladies room. Perhaps Zoe was just trying to freshen up after being in her grave for half a century?



Bobbie had quite an experience one night, and believes it was Zoe up to her old tricks. The security system was giving her trouble and it simply wouldn't arm the alarm. As Bobbie struggled with it, two heavy wooden bar stools flipped over, and a very heavy door slammed open. No one else was in the building at the time.

The chef had his own encounter one day when he opened up. He was also alone, or so he thought, and he poured himself a cup of coffee. He placed the cup on the stairs while he brought in a delivery, and then couldn't find his coffee. Finally, he found the cup back by the coffee maker, and there was a faint smudge of lipstick on the rim!

No one can blame a lonely old spinster for having some fun now and then, and no one should be surprised that a faithful dog is still keeping watch over his restaurant. A trip to Poogan's Porch will undoubtedly reward you with fine southern cuisine, and it may also reward you with some colorful southern characters.

## The Bottom Line

**The History:** A nineteenth-century home in Charleston's historic district that was owned by two spinsters, then opened as a restaurant in 1976.

**The Haunting:** A faithful dog and a spinster are still seen.

## Recommendations

**In 1989, Hugh Grant's film *Champagne Charlie* was filmed here, and celebrities such as Jody Foster, Jim Carrey, James Brolin, and the late Paul Newman have frequented the restaurant. The food is outstanding, so you will probably have to visit more than once. Keep an eye out for Zoe and her tricks, and don't forget to pay your respects at Poogan's grave!**

## Visitor Information

**Poogan's Porch**
**72 Queen Street**
**Charleston, SC 29401-2220**
**843-577-2337**
**www.poogansporch.com**

**Hours:**

**Open 365 days a year, except the restaurant does close for one dinner seating on Super Bowl Sunday. Brunch: Saturday and Sunday 9 – 3pm. Lunch: Monday to Friday 11:30 – 2:30pm. Dinner: 5 – 9:30pm.**

**Directions:**

**From the I-526/Mark Clark Expressway, exit heading southeast on I-26 E. Take exit 221B on the left for Meeting Street toward Visitor Center. Turn right at Meeting Street. Turn right at Queen St. Poogan's Porch will be on the right.**

# South Dakota

FORT SISSETON STATE HISTORICAL PARK

SICA HOLLOW STATE PARK

BULLOCK HOTEL

The Commander's Quarters at Fort Sisseton. *Courtesy of The Library of Congress.*



# Fort Sisseton State Historical Park

It probably wasn't the best omen when Wisconsin and Minnesota volunteer soldiers tried to plant the flagpole while building the new Fort Wadsworth in 1864 and uncovered an Indian grave. It's possible the entire fort was constructed on an Indian burial ground which may account for the strange activity here. But first, some history…

The fort was established to protect settlers from attacks by the Sioux Indians, and it grew into an outpost of civilization for everyone traveling through the region. In 1876, the fort was renamed in honor of the friendly Sisseton tribe who was placed on a reservation next to the fort. Having outlived its usefulness to the U.S. Army, Fort Sisseton was given to the state in 1889. For decades after, the buildings deteriorated or were simply torn down, but during the 1930s the WPA began restoring the site. In 1959, Fort Sisseton was opened to the public as a historic park, and today visitors can get a sense of what it was like in the days when its soldiers protected the frontier.

The best way to experience those days is during the park's annual historical festival, which has been drawing thousands of visitors and reenactors since 1978. However, some might argue that the best way to really experience the past is to come into contact with one of the fort's many ghosts.

A sentry has been seen walking his post. Other soldiers have been seen throughout the grounds and buildings. A woman in a white dress carries a candle through one of the officer's quarters. There are phantom footsteps, voices, a strong presence, and one visitor even felt a hand on her neck!

The most common occurrence, however, is the strange lights. When the park is closed and empty, lights have been seen moving in and around the buildings, or simply emanating from various locations on the grounds. No explanations have ever been found for these lights, but perhaps they are connected with the soldiers and family members who died here (there is a cemetery), or with the old Indian burial ground.

Whatever is behind this activity, it is clear that this is a place that needs to be fully explored, both historically and paranormally. Come for the festival days or for a guided tour, then spend the night in a cabin or in the campground, and see for yourself what walks the grounds at night.

Is that the flashlight of a fellow camper, the candlelight of a ghost, or a spirit from an Indian grave?

## The Bottom Line

**The History:** A fort built in 1864 to protect settlers from attacks from the Sioux.

**The Haunting:** Ghosts of soldiers and a woman carrying a candle. Strange lights are seen throughout the fort.

# Sica Hollow State Park

The Dakota Sioux believed that the heavily wooded slopes and ravines of the Prairie Coteau Hills were haunted. They saw the swamp gases and glowing tree fungi as apparitions, and the red bog waters as blood and flesh of their ancestors. They named this land Sica (pronounced she-cha), meaning bad or evil.

Many Indian legends arose about this evil land of Sica Hollow. One speaks of a time when the people there were good and happy, until a strange man named Hand came to their village and turned the young boys into depraved killers. The people and their Medicine Man prayed to their god, called the Thunderer, to remove this evil from their land. The Thunderer sent flooding rains that washed everyone away, except for one innocent maiden named Fawn. Although Hand and his murdering braves were killed, their spirits remained in Sica Hollow to haunt the living.

Legends such as this persisted and grew over the centuries. The first white man, Robert Roi, ignored the legends and came to live in Sica Hollow in the 1840s. The local Indians thought he was crazy to stay in these haunted woods, as they refused to even enter them. When army soldiers visited Roi to gather information about the area, they also went away thinking he had to be crazy to live in such an unnerving place. Even today, visitors who know nothing of the legends describe Sica Hollow as "spooky," "creepy," and "eerie."

There is something otherworldly about the landscape here—the gurgling red waters by day and the glowing tree stumps at night. And it certainly doesn't help settle one's nerves hearing about the hikers that have disappeared here over the years!

Hikers, campers, and photographers have reported hearing voices, drumming, and all manner of bizarre

## Recommendations

The annual historical festival is held the first full weekend in June, and it covers all aspects of the daily lives of soldiers and civilians, and offers many activities and entertainment for all ages. Sica Hollow is only about twenty miles away, so you can spend a few days camping in both places, or at least visit both haunted historic parks.

## Visitor Information

**Fort Sisseton State Historical Park**
11907 434th Avenue
Lake City, SD 57247
(605) 448-5474
Reservations: (800) 710-2267
www.sdgfp.info/Parks/Regions/GlacialLakes/FortSisseton.htm

**Events:**
Camping. Cabins. Boating. Canoeing, rentals available. Fishing. Game/equipment checkout. Accessible hiking trail. Historic interest. Horse trail. Accessible picnic shelter with kitchenette. Snowshoe checkout. Guided walking tours of the fort available. Visitor center/museum/gift shop

**Hours:**
Weekend Before Memorial Day/Labor Day: Visitor Center, Museum, Gift Shop, Archives and Guided Tours: 7 Days a Week, 10am – 6pm. Campground and cabins open for reservations, special event rentals. All facilities are open.

September: Visitor Center, Museum; Monday-Friday, 8am – 4:30pm. Visitor Center, Museum, Gift Shop and Guided Tours; Saturday-Sunday, 10am – 6pm. All facilities are open.

October Mid-May: Building and Site Tours are by appointment only and facilities open and close due to weather conditions. Comfort station is closed. Campsites are first come first serve.

Year Round: Park Office Monday-Friday, 8am – 4:30pm. Cabin reservations.

**Admission:**
Park entrance license required: $6/day/vehicle or $28 for an annual pass. Camping and Fees: $10/non-electrical, $14/electrical. 14 campsites (10 electrical) Tent area with four sites. Showers. Water. Group rentals for special events available. Camping Cabins: Three rustic camping cabins, each sleeps six people. $40/night.

**Directions:**
Located 10 miles SW of Lake City off US Highway 10.

sounds. Many have experienced uncomfortable energies or a strong presence, and some have even seen the apparitions of Indian braves wandering through the forest. And if the ghost stories of Sica Hollow aren't enough to curl your hair by the campfire, there are the Big Foot legends of a large manlike creature living in the woods. It's all more than enough to keep you awake at night, listening for the sound of approaching footsteps.

Are the woods of Sica Hollow filled with ghosts and strange creatures? Walk some of the park's "Trail of The Spirits" and find out for yourself. Or better yet, spend a few nights camping there, but just be warned that you will not be alone…

*Courtesy of the Bullock Hotel.*

## Bullock Hotel

Storekeepers were usually easy prey for outlaws, but no thief in his right mind would have tried to rob the hardware store in Deadwood owned by Seth Bullock. Bullock was also the town's sheriff, and he was so tough that his grandson described him as being able to "outstare a mad cobra or a rogue elephant."

Bullock was born in Canada in 1849, and moved to Montana as a young man, where he also had a store, and became sheriff. As a member of the territorial legislature, he helped create Yellowstone National Park.

Bullock and his business partner, Sol Star, came to Deadwood in 1876 to open a store to capitalize on all the miners in the area who needed supplies. The day after arriving in town, the infamous shooting of Wild Bill Hickok occurred in one of the saloons, and his murderer went free. As lawlessness was running rampant in the area, the obvious choice for sheriff would be the one man who could stare down an elephant.

### Recommendations

The fall foliage is spectacular and attracts many visitors and photographers. You can walk or horseback ride on the trails, or cycle along the paved roads. There are some settlers' graves along the trails. The best way to experience the spooky side of the park is to spend the night in the campground.

### Visitor Information

**Sica Hollow State Park**
44950 Park Road
Sisseton, SD 57262
(605) 448-5701
www.sdgfp.info

**Events:**
Cross-country skiing, hiking, horse trails and camp, picnicking. Near a snowmobile trail.

**Hours:**
Open year round.

**Admission:**
Park entrance license required: $6/day/vehicle or $28 for an annual pass.

Camping and Fees: Horse camp: $10/site. 12 sites, all non-electrical. By reservation only. Water and vault toilets.

**Directions:**
Located 15 miles northwest of Sisseton, off S.D. Highway 10, within 35 miles of I-29.

### The Bottom Line

**The History:** The location of many ancient Indian legends of an evil land.

**The Haunting:** Strange sounds and the ghosts of Indian braves wandering through the woods.

Bullock did clean up the town, and eventually went on to become a U.S. Marshall under the administration of his lifelong friend, Teddy Roosevelt. Bullock and Star branched out into many other successful businesses, as well, so when their hardware store in Deadwood burned down in 1894, they decided not to rebuild it. Instead, they used the foundation to construct the town's first hotel, a sixty-three-room luxury establishment with chandeliers, velvet carpeting, a grand piano, and modern steam heat, and indoor plumbing. Guests could even order lobster and pheasant in the hotel's restaurant. The cost to build the hotel was $40,000, but it became *the* place to stay in Deadwood, and is still in operation today.

Bullock died in 1919, and depending upon the source, it is claimed that his death either occurred on his ranch or in the hotel. It really doesn't matter where he actually passed, because he is still keeping an eye on his namesake. Many people over the years have seen his tall figure throughout the hotel, or felt a strong male presence. Bullock seems to be particularly active whenever an employee is slacking off on the job. Then he might throw a glass, turn the lights or an appliance on and off, or even call the slacker by name. And if Sheriff Bullock calls you by name, you had better get back to work!

Bullock most likely is not the only ghost in the hotel. A cowboy has been seen in the cellar, misty or shadowy figures have been seen throughout the hotel, alarm clocks have gone off even when they are unplugged, and there are cold spots, footsteps, and voices.

You could stay somewhere that recreates the historic feel of Deadwood, or you could stay in the Bullock Hotel that *is* historic Deadwood. But don't even think of getting into any kind of trouble while you're there, because the sheriff just might appear and stare you down!

## Recommendations

**The hotel offers ghost tours throughout the year, so call for the latest schedule. When making reservations, ask for their most haunted rooms. If you are too chicken to spend the night, the hotel also has a restaurant, bar, and a 24-hour casino. There's a lot to see and do in and around Deadwood (including many other haunted places), so check for all the latest special events. And don't forget a visit to Bullock's grave in the Moriah Cemetery, where Wild Bill Hickok and Calamity Jane are also buried.**

## Visitor Information

**Bullock Hotel**
**633 Main Street**
**Deadwood, SD 57732-1123**
**(605) 578-1745**
**(800) 336-1876**
**www.historicbullock.com**

**Directions:**
**From I-90, Take exit 30 for South Dakota 34 E/S Dakota 79 N/U.S. 14A W/Lazelle Street toward Deadwood-Lead. Turn left at South Dakota 79 S/ Lazelle Street. Continue to follow South Dakota 79 S. Continue onto Boulder Canyon Road/US-14 Alt W. Continue to follow US-14 Alt W. Turn right at Lower Main Street. The Bullock Hotel will be on the left.**



## The Bottom Line

**The History:** A former hardware store built in 1876 by Sheriff Bullock. After it burned in 1894 it was rebuilt as a luxury hotel.

**The Haunting:** Sheriff Bullock is seen and felt throughout the hotel.

TN

# Tennessee

CHICKAMAUGA & CHATTANOOGA
*(see entry under Georgia)*

FORT DONELSON

MAGNOLIA MANOR

An 1887 lithograph of the Battle of Fort Donelson.



# Fort Donelson

When the calendar turned to 1862, the Confederacy was very optimistic. Buoyed by repeated victories over Union forces, citizens and soldiers of the south were beginning to feel that they were invincible.

General Ulysses S. Grant was of a differing opinion.

On February 6, Grant's army captured Fort Henry, which opened the Tennessee River to Union forces, and it was the first significant victory for the north. Grant then marched his army twelve miles to Fort Donelson on the Cumberland River. There were a few minor engagements on February 12 and 13; then on the 14th, Union gunboats began bombarding the fort from the river, but were repulsed. The Confederate troops cheered the retreat of the ships, but their celebration was short-lived as they knew they were surrounded.

An escape attempt was launched on February 15, and after hours of heavy fighting, it looked as though the Confederate forces had cleared a path through the Union lines, but they did not follow up on their initial success and retreated back to their entrenchments. Surrender was inevitable, and Confederate Generals Floyd and Pillow both made good their escapes and left General Simon Bolivar Buckner holding the bag. Perhaps they felt that Buckner would receive more generous surrender terms, as he and Grant had been friends before the war.

Once again, Grant was of a differing opinion. In a message that made Grant a household word in the north, he wrote the following to Buckner:

> Sir:
> Yours of this date proposing Armistice, and appointment of Commissioners, to settle terms of Capitulation is just received. No terms except unconditional and immediate surrender can be accepted.
> I propose to move immediately upon your works.
> I am Sir: very respectfully
> Your obt. sevt.
> U.S. Grant

Buckner had no choice, and he surrendered at his headquarters in the Dover Hotel. Union troops began to say that the U.S. in Grant's name stood for "unconditional surrender," and these back-to-back victories were a tremendous morale boost for soldiers and citizens alike. The fall of Fort Donelson gave control of the Cumberland River to the Union, and southern Kentucky and much of Tennessee slipped through the Confederacy's fingers.

**The total casualties for the battle were:** Union – 507 killed, 1,976 wounded, 208 captured/missing. Confederates – 327 killed, 1,127 wounded, 12,392 captured/missing. Such carnage left its imprint on the fort and many of the town's buildings that were turned into field hospitals. There is scarcely a place on the battlefield, in the National Cemetery, or in one of the former field hospitals that does not have at least some ghost stories. Figures of soldiers and doctors trying to tend to the wounded have frequently been seen, and all the sounds of battle have been heard, from gunshots and shouting to the famous rebel yell.

The Civil War would stretch on for three long years, and many battles would be far bloodier than this one, but the death and suffering of so many men here has left a strong paranormal residue. Regardless of whether your sympathies lie with the north or the south, the sacrifices made on both sides deserve our unconditional respect.



## The Bottom Line

**The History:** One of the first Union victories occurred here in February, 1862. General Grant's famous "unconditional surrender" letter was written to General Buckner.

**The Haunting:** Soldiers are seen throughout the battlefield and the original buildings. The sounds of battle can be heard.

## Recommendations

Begin your visit at the visitor center for a brief show about the battle and to get a self-guided auto tour and hiking trail map. The National Cemetery has 670 Union soldiers, 512 of whom were never identified, but the Confederates killed in the battle were put in a mass grave. The exact location isn't known, but it is somewhere near the Confederate Monument. The Surrender House/Dover Hotel still looks very much like it did in 1862. Apparitions and sounds of battle may occur anywhere at anytime. There are special events throughout the year, and living history events for the anniversary of the battle.

## Visitor Information

**Fort Donelson**
US Highway 79
Dover, TN 37058
(931)232-5706
www.nps.gov/fodo/index.htm

**Hours:**

Fort Donelson visitor center is open daily 8am – 4:30pm; closed Thanksgiving Day, Christmas, and New Year's Day.

Dover Hotel (Surrender House) is usually open from Memorial Day weekend until Labor Day, Noon – 4pm, depending upon staff availability.

Fort Donelson National Cemetery is open 8am – 5pm daily.

**Admission:** Free

**Directions:**

From their website—From Nashville: Take I-24W to Clarksville (Exit 4). Take a left on Wilma Rudolph Boulevard, until you reach 101st Airborne Division Parkway/Highway 374. Take a right at this intersection. Follow Highway 374, until you reach Highway 79. Turn right on Highway. 79 South. Follow signs to Dover (approximately 30 miles). The visitor center is one mile west of the town.

From Paducah, KY: Take Interstate 24 East to exit 31, and go south on Highway 453 to Land Between the Lakes (LBL). Follow this road through LBL to US Highway 79. Take a left on US Highway 79; the park visitor center is approximately 1.3 miles.

From Murray, KY: Take 641S to Highway 121. Drive approximately 30 miles on Highway 121, until you reach Highway 79 at Paris Landing. Take a left on Highway 79, and follow signs to the park (approximately 13 miles).

*Courtesy of Magnolia Manor.*

# Magnolia Manor

Imagine Tennessee without the city of Memphis.

The Constitution of the State of Mississippi names attorney Austin Miller as being responsible for establishing the northern border of the state. Why that was particularly important to Tennessee is that Miller placed Memphis in Tennessee, not Mississippi, and the rest, as they say, is history.

In 1849, Judge Austin Miller built a Georgian Colonial house in Bolivar, Tennessee, and three generations of the family would live there until the 1970s. Actually, slaves built the house with bricks they made on site. The thirteen-inch thick walls have withstood the elements for over a century and a half, and the house even withstood a Yankee occupation.

It is believed that Union Generals Logan, McPherson, Sherman, and Grant used the house as a headquarters in 1862, and it was here that they planned the Battle of Shiloh. According to family tradition, Mrs. Miller established the rules of this occupation by telling the generals they were allowed to "only use half of the house" as she was "a delicate woman." Her delicate sensibilities were further tested when she overheard General Sherman say that "all southern men, women, and children should be exterminated."

Upon hearing this, Mrs. Miller ran to the porch and burst into tears. When General Grant asked what was wrong, she told him of Sherman's remark. Grant then ordered Sherman to apologize, and Sherman was so angered by this that he slashed the banister of the staircase with his sword, and the mark is still there to this day.

Whether this is true, or just a colorful family legend to explain damage to the woodwork, it certainly makes for a great story! And there are other great stories at Magnolia Manor, stories of the ghostly variety, that is. One of the wandering spirits is described as being a rather heavy, short old woman in an apron. It is believed that she is Annie Miller, who died in the house in 1979 at the age of 84. She is harmless, as is the ghost of her white cat, and the two may just be going about her house as they always did, no doubt as curious about the living as they are of these shades of the past.

There is another female ghost, and this one is much better dressed and better looking. This beautiful spirit wears a Victorian-era dress and seems to enjoy pulling off bed covers and tugging on guests' clothing in the 1849 Room. One male guest scoffed at the idea of ghosts and stated without hesitation that he did not believe in such nonsense—until the Victorian lady walked over to his bed, pulled his sleeve, then disappeared on the spot. He ran from his room and refused to even return to get his bags!

Another female spirit is said to like to sit and hum a tune in the rocking chair in the C.A. Miller suite. She has also been seen throughout the house carrying a candle, so she may be from the earliest days of the house, well before electricity was installed.

There is also the figure of a soldier that is seen on the property, and cold spots, lights going on and off, being touched by an unseen hand, doors opening and closing, voices, laughter, and all the other classic signs of a good, old-fashioned haunting.

Since 1985, the house has been a bed and breakfast run by owner Elaine Nichols. She has taken great care of the judge's former home, and guests can immerse themselves in the beautiful surroundings and gracious hospitality. And if during your stay one of the ethereal residents happens to appear or give your sleeve a tug during the night, don't be afraid, just consider the experience a bonus. At Magnolia Manor, they don't charge extra for the ghosts.



## The Bottom Line

**The History:** A home built in 1849 by the attorney who helped decide the state border which made Memphis part of Tennessee. Union generals may have planned the Battle of Shiloh here.

**The Haunting:** Several female ghosts and a soldier have been seen. Clothes are tugged, voices, cold spots, and doors open and close.

## Recommendations

**The house is filled with beautiful antiques—including a massive wooden bed valued at over $35,000! (It's in the room where General Grant slept.) When making reservations, ask for the room that has had the most recent paranormal activity. Bolivar is only forty-five minutes from the Shiloh battlefield and less than an hour from Memphis, so you can get your history and barbeque fix in the same day. Magnolia Manor was featured on HGTV's** *If Walls Could Talk.* **Don't forget to look for the sword cut on the banister.**

## Visitor Information

**Magnolia Manor**
**418 North Main Street**
**Bolivar, TN 38008-2014**
**(731) 658-6700**
**www.magnoliamanorbolivartn.com/**

**Directions:**

**From Memphis, take I-40E toward Nashville. Take exit 47 for Dancyville Road/TN-179 toward Stanton. Turn right at Dancyville Road/TN-179 E. Continue onto Dancyville Eurekaton Road. Slight right at Fayette Corners Road. Turn left at Fayette Corners Drive. Turn right at Chapel-Whiteville Road/TN-179 E/Whiteville Road. Continue to follow TN-179 E. Turn left at West Main Street/ TN-15 E/US-64 BUS E. Turn left at TN-100 E/US-64 E. Continue to follow US-64 E. Turn right at TN-15 E/US-64 E. Turn left at North Main Street. Magnolia Manor will be on the right.**

# Texas

THE ALAMO

MENGER HOTEL

FORT PHANTOM HILL

The Alamo in 1936. *Courtesy of The Library of Congress.*

TX

# The Alamo

"Remember the Alamo!" is one of the most famous phrases in American history, and indeed, this small Spanish mission has not been forgotten. Today, over 2.5 million visitors come to see where Jim Bowie, Davy Crockett, and William Travis lost their lives in the fight for the independence of Texas.

The Mission San Antonio de Valero was established in 1724 as a place to teach Native Americans who had been converted to Christianity. There were five missions in San Antonio that were officially secularized in 1793 and their lands were given to the Indians. Ten years later, this former mission was occupied and fortified by Mexican soldiers, and it was probably then that it became known as the Alamo.

As American immigrants began to settle in Texas, tensions rose with the ruling Mexican government. By 1835, the Americans felt that President General Antonio López de Santa Anna was becoming too much of a dictator and they were determined to expel all Mexican soldiers. Initially, they were successful, but Santa Anna was equally determined to crush the rebellion, and he would not be taking any prisoners.

Beginning February 23, 1836, Mexican forces laid siege to the Alamo. Though the siege lasted 13 days, the outcome was never really in doubt—roughly 200 Texans were defending against as many as 4,000 Mexican troops. The Texans sent desperate appeals to Sam Houston for more men and supplies, but they were on their own on the morning of March 6 when the Mexican soldiers breached the Alamo defenses. In bloody hand-to-hand fighting, the Texans fell one by one. Those few who did try to surrender were also killed. Even after every Texan man lay dead or dying, the Mexican soldiers continued to shoot and bayonet the bodies. Their bodies were then stacked up and burned.

Casualties were also high for the Mexicans, with estimates of the killed ranging from 500-1500, with hundreds more wounded. Whatever the actual number was, it was clearly a very costly victory and spoke to the tenacity of the Texans. One of Santa Anna's aides put it best when he wrote, "One more such glorious victory and we are finished."

The Texan women and children were allowed to leave, and Santa Anna believed that their stories would convince the rest of the rebels to lay down their arms and give up the fight. He couldn't have been more wrong. As word spread of the gallant defense of the Alamo and the brutal treatment by the Mexicans, Texans flocked to the cause of their independence and the formation of the Republic of Texas, and they would not have long to wait for that freedom.

At the Battle of San Jacinto on April 21, 1836, the Texas army of only about 900 men under General Sam Houston—who shouted, "Remember the Alamo"—soundly defeated the Mexicans in just 18 minutes, killing over 600 and capturing over 700. The Texan casualties were just 9 killed at 30 wounded. The next day, Santa Anna was taken prisoner, and after a few weeks of captivity he signed a peace treaty.

There are so many stories about the deeds of bravery at the Alamo, from Jim Bowie who was too ill to stand, but still fought from his bed, to Davy Crockett taking down more than a dozen Mexicans in hand-to-hand fighting before he was struck down. What is the truth and what are exaggerations will never be known for sure, but there are some stories that keep repeating themselves to this day—the stories of all the ghosts.

Legend has it that the first sighting occurred just a couple of weeks after the battle. Santa Anna had ordered the remaining Mexican troops to burn the Alamo to the ground. As the soldiers approached the mission building with torches, the angry spirits of six slain Texans frightened them away. When the commanding general heard the story, he refused to believe a word of such obvious nonsense and ordered another group of soldiers to burn the barracks. Once again as the soldiers approached, the ghost of a Texan appeared on the roof of the barracks and the terrified Mexicans at first fell to their knees, then got up and ran for their lives, and the Alamo's buildings were spared.

The Alamo was eventually used as a police headquarters and jail for the city of San Antonio, and in the late 1800s newspapers reported about all the ghostly activity both the police and prisoners were experiencing. There was the unearthly moaning, the footsteps, and the figures of the old Texan defenders still standing at their posts, particularly on the rooftops.

Over a century later, the paranormal activity continues. Staff and visitors still see men on the roof, looking out of windows, or walking through the walls. There is a man in buckskins (Crockett?), a Mexican officer, a little blond boy, a woman, an Indian, and countless other figures roaming the Alamo both day and night. And for those who don't actually see an apparition, there are the cold spots and intense feelings of a presence—or many presences. In short, you are never alone there.

If human emotions, death, and historic events leave paranormal imprints on a place, then the Alamo is surely a prime location to experience the past in a very unique way. Visit this place where so many men bravely fought and died, and open your heart and mind to the possibility that many of them still stand watch here. And if you do experience something from the other world, then you, too, will always "Remember the Alamo."

## Recommendations

**Quite simply, the Alamo is high atop the short list of America's "Must See" historic haunts. There are special events throughout the year, so call or check the website to see what's happening. You will get a lot more out of your visit if you take the guided audio tour. Some of the staff may be willing to talk about their ghostly encounters, but please be discrete and respectful of the history. And while admission is free, funding comes solely from gift shop sales and donations, so make sure to exercise your wallet!**

## Visitor Information

**The Alamo**
**300 Alamo Plaza**
**San Antonio, TX 78205-2606**
**(210) 225-1391**
**www.thealamo.org**

**Hours:**
**Monday to Saturday 9am – 5:30pm. Sunday 10am – 5:30pm. Fridays and Saturdays until 7pm in June, July, and August. Closed Christmas Eve and Christmas Day.**

**Admission:**
**Free. Guided audio tour is $7.**

**Directions:**
**From their website—To Reach the Alamo from U.S. 281/Interstate 37 southbound, exit at Houston Street, turn right, and proceed three blocks to Avenue E, turn left and continue to the intersection of Houston and Alamo Plaza. From Interstate 37 northbound, exit at Commerce Street, turn left on Commerce and proceed ten blocks to Alamo Plaza, turn right and continue on one and one half blocks. Parking is available at several pay lots in the vicinity of the Alamo.**



## The Bottom Line

**The History:** One of the country's most iconic buildings, the Alamo was the site of a bloody battle in 1836 as part of Texas' struggle for independence.

**The Haunting:** Within weeks of the battle, the ghosts of the Texan defenders began appearing. Many other figures are seen and heard in this very haunted location.

The Menger Hotel in 1865.

# Menger Hotel

TX

William Menger came from Germany to San Antonio in the 1840s and opened a brewery adjacent to the Alamo. As the years passed, he realized he could make even more money by building a hotel to accommodate all those visitors who weren't exactly in any shape to travel after spending some time sampling the products of his brewery.

Construction began in 1857, and on February 1, 1859, the Menger Hotel welcomed its first guest. Since then, the hotel has undergone several expansions and it became the place to be, as is evidenced by the many famous people who have enjoyed Menger's fine accommodations. The long list includes Sam Houston, Robert E. Lee, U.S. Grant, and Presidents McKinley, Taft, Roosevelt, and Eisenhower. Teddy Roosevelt recruited his Rough Riders in the hotel's bar, which brings up another long list.

The Menger Hotel is said to have at least thirty-two ghosts, one of whom is Teddy Roosevelt, who has been seen drinking at the bar. Perhaps he is still looking to recruit a few good men for new adventures? Another recognizable spirit is that of Captain Richard King, the wealthy founder of the King Ranch. When doctors informed King that his death was near, he chose to spend his final days in his suite in the hotel. His figure is still seen walking down the hall and through the wall into his suite. Research showed that in King's time, the doorway to his suite was actually in that location. Looks like old habits are hard to break!

Then there's the sad story of Sallie White. In 1876 she was a maid and her figure has been seen in a long skirt and bandana, carrying a stack of clean towels. Sallie may still be at work out of gratitude to the hotel, because they paid the $32 for her funeral.

Sallie had an argument with her husband and he threatened to kill her. Fearing for her life, she sought the safety of the hotel and spent the night there. Unfortunately, her husband was determined to get Sallie. He tracked her down and attacked the defenseless woman in the hotel, and she died two days later of the terrible wounds. The Mengers then felt that the least they could do for the poor woman was to pay for a decent burial.

There's another woman who is seen, although no one knows her story. She sits in the lobby wearing an old-fashioned blue dress, a beret with a tassel, and small metal glasses. She needs the glasses as she is always working on her knitting. When a member of the staff asked the woman if there was anything she needed, she rudely said, "No," and then disappeared. Apparently, she doesn't like to be disturbed while she's working.

There's also a man wearing buckskins who appears in one of the rooms. One day, a startled guest stepped out of the shower to see the man standing there arguing with someone who wasn't visible. Three times the man in buckskins asked, "Are you gonna stay or are you gonna go?" Then he disappeared.

Could this man have died at the Alamo? It is suspected that at least some of the thirty-two ghosts are connected with that battle. And on an interesting note, some of the rooms at the Menger have a view of the Alamo, and guests have actually looked out their windows and have seen ghostly sentries and other figures around the old mission building. Talk about a room with a view!

Of course, your best chance of seeing a ghost at the hotel is to look inside your room, or the hallways, lobby, bar, etc. In 1976, the hotel was added to the National Register of Historic Places, and today the Menger Hotel is one of Texas' oldest hotels, and certainly one of its best historic haunts. With a huge roster of at least thirty-two ghosts, it simply proves that in Texas, even the spirits like to do things bigger and better.

### The Bottom Line

**The History:** Built in 1859, one of the oldest hotels in Texas, many famous people have been guests.

**The Haunting:** At least thirty-two ghosts haunt this hotel!

### Recommendations

**During your stay, the hotel suggests speaking with the Director of Public Relations, who will share some ghost stories about the Menger that will "curl your hair." The rich, cherry wood bar room was built in 1887 as a replica of the House of Lords Pub in London, at a staggering cost of $60,000. After a long day of sightseeing, relax in the outdoor pool and dine in the beautiful Colonial Room (open for breakfast, brunch, lunch, dinner, and buffets). In addition to the Alamo, the hotel is next to the Rivercenter Mall, the IMAX Theater, and River Walk, and two blocks from the Henry B. Gonzales Convention Center. There are several ghost tours of San Antonio. Staying here and visiting the Alamo makes this the perfect historic haunted trip!**

### Visitor Information

**Menger Hotel**
**204 Alamo Plaza**
**San Antonio, TX 78205**
**(210) 223-4361**
**www.mengerhotel.com**

**Directions:**
**Follow the directions for the Alamo. The hotel is on its south side.**



## Fort Phantom Hill

Things didn't bode well for the army's "Post on the Clear Fork of the Brazos" when it was mistakenly established in the wrong location in November of 1851. This resulted in a post that had no trees for lumber to build with, and at best, an unreliable water supply that often meant transporting barrels of fresh water from miles away.

Then there was the snowstorm that greeted Lieutenant Colonel John J. Abercrombie and his five companies of men that November. The storm killed a teamster, and froze to death twenty horses, mules, and oxen. The miserable conditions at the post prompted another lieutenant to write to his wife that he could not imagine "that God ever intended white man to occupy such a barren waste."

The soldiers tried to make the best of a bad situation until November of 1853, when orders were happily received to abandon the fort. As the soldiers marched away, they noticed smoke rising from the vicinity of the post. Indians were blamed for setting fire to all the wooden structures, but some suspected it was soldiers who torched the place they had grown to hate.

However, despite the location's shortcomings, in 1858 the burned and abandoned buildings were repaired to become a station for the Southern Overland (Butterfield) Mail Stagecoach Line. A few years later during the Civil War, some Confederate troops occupied the site, then in 1871, the fort became a subpost for Fort Griffin. After the threat of Indian attacks subsided, a small town was established here in 1876 for commerce in buffalo hides. By 1880, there were 545 residents of the town. However, by the 1890s, Phantom Hill Fort had become a virtual ghost town, with someone describing it as having only "one hotel, one saloon, one general store, one blacksmith shop, and 10,000 prairie dogs."

Which brings up the very interesting name of this place.

There are a couple of different theories about the name. One involves the topography and the hill that can be seen in the distance, but seems to disappear up close. The other theory is of far more interest—the theory that one day a soldier on sentry duty started firing at an Indian near the fort. The troops were called to action but couldn't find any Indians, or any indication that anyone was nearby. Had the sentry fallen asleep and dreamed the Indian, or had it been a phantom?

For generations there have been reports of the figures of Indian warriors in and around the ruins of Phantom Hill Fort—Indians who appear real and solid, then disappear. Then there is a man who was supposedly hanged at the fort, although he was innocent. Does he wander the remains of the old post looking for justice? Others have seen army officers who also look real and alive, until they vanish into thin air.

One of the area's most mysterious apparitions haunts the nearby Lake Fort Phantom Hill. The "Lady of the Lake" as she is now called, has been seen for at least 150 years, which is almost a century before this lake existed. There are numerous theories about the origin of the lady, but all agree that she appears to be wearing a long white gown or robe, and she is either floating above the surface of the water or walking along its shores. Did something happen to this woman on this site, and are her remains now covered by the lake, or is she searching for someone or something that was once here?

There could be many reasons why these ghosts walk the Phantom Hill region, but the bottom line is that this area provides an opportunity for a most unique experience. The old fort consists of twenty-two acres of a somewhat surreal landscape with chimneys of long-gone buildings seemingly growing out of the ground. There is also a stone powder magazine, a stone guardhouse, and most of the old commissary to explore.

These desolate ruins may not have the tourist appeal of sites with reconstructed buildings and snack bars, but if you are in search of a pristine location where a site remains as it was left, then this is worth a visit. And after all, how can any fan of historic haunts resist a place called Phantom Hill?



## Recommendations

**There are no facilities here so be sure to bring plenty of water. Restrooms are available at Seabee Park and Johnson Park at the lake. Informational pamphlets are available on site and major structures are marked. If you have plenty of time and are looking for a long drive, Fort Phantom Hill is part of the 650-mile-long Texas Forts Trail. With 22 acres of haunted ground, there's plenty of room to set up your ghost hunting equipment and explore; just remember it's only open during daylight hours, and you are not allowed to remove anything from the site.**

## Visitor Information

**Fort Phantom Hill**
**Farm to Market Road 600**
**Fort Phantom Foundation**
**P. O. Box 58**
**Abilene, TX 79604**
**(325) 677-1309**
**www.fortphantom.org**

**Hours:**
**Open during daylight hours.**

**Admission:**
**Free**

**Directions:**
**From the Fort Phantom Foundation website—Fort Phantom Hill is conveniently located a few miles north of Abilene, Texas. Near the geographic center of Texas, Abilene is easily accessible by four major highways: Interstate 20 and Highway 84 East-West, and Highways 83 and 277 North-South. To get to Fort Phantom Hill from Abilene, exit Interstate 20 at FM Road 600 and go 11 miles north. The main portion of the fort is located on the east side of FM 600, 11 miles north of the interstate highway in present-day Jones County. You can also access the fort on the Texas Forts Trail on FM2833.**

## The Bottom Line

**The History:** A fort established in 1851, abandoned and reoccupied several times.

**The Haunting:** Indians, army officers, and other apparitions.

# Utah

MOUNTAIN MEADOWS

UNION STATION

BEN LOMOND HOTEL

UT

An 1877 lithograph of the wagon train entering Mountain Meadows. Note the Indians hiding in the rocks to the right.

## Mountain Meadows

In 1857, the Fancher-Baker wagon train of 800 head of cattle and about 140 men, women, and children left Arkansas to undertake the arduous and perilous journey to California, but no one ever made it to their destination. Was it the weather, disease, or bandits that stopped them? No, it was the Mormons, who slaughtered the emigrants in one of America's worst massacres—the first 9/11 tragedy.

Tensions were running high in Utah at the time, as the Mormons were at odds with the Federal Government in what became known as the Utah War. While the exact reasons for the massacre will never be known—and can never be justified—paranoia was certainly rampant in September when the wagon train stopped to rest at Mountain Meadows.

Whether due to greed, politics, or religion, the local Mormon militia hatched a plot to attack the wagon train. They disguised themselves as Indians, and also enlisted the aid of some local Pauite Indians. The attack turned into a siege as the members of the wagon train hastily formed defensive positions. For five days the emigrants fought off their "Indian" attackers, and their ammunition and supplies ran low. Finally, on September 11, several Mormons, who had removed their Indian disguises, approached the wagon train under a white flag.

They assured the emigrants that if they would put down their arms and leave everything—which amounted to over $300,000 worth of cattle, equipment, and personal belongings—they would personally guarantee safe passage to Cedar City. Knowing they would eventually be overrun, the emigrants agreed, dropped their weapons and began to walk out.

The Mormons knew that these people had seen through the disguises, and realized they would tell authorities about the attack, so the commander of the militia, Colonel William Dame, gave the "extermination" order. As soon as all the emigrants were all out in the open, the command was shouted to "Do your duty," and the Mormons and Indians opened fire, killing 120 unarmed men, women, and children. Only 17 lives were spared—all children deemed to be too young to be able to report what had happened. Most of the bodies were left to rot or be scavenged by animals, and the emigrants belongings were auctioned off at the Latter Day Saint's tithing office in Cedar City.

These innocent victims of the Utah War were never fully avenged for these crimes against humanity, as only one man, John Lee, was eventually brought to trial. Convicted, he was fittingly executed by firing squad at Mountain Meadows in 1877. The rest of the Mormons were granted a full presidential pardon to defuse the tensions between the group and the government.

Is it any wonder then, that people visiting the Mountain Meadows Massacre site have reported an

An 1859 depiction in Harper's Weekly showing the skeletons of the victims.

overwhelming feeling of sadness? Such emotions seem to sweep over and engulf people, as if spirits from the past are surrounding them and trying to tell their tragic tale. Many witnesses have also clearly heard voices crying out, but no one can ever be found.

Today, the massacre site is a mass burial site with just a plaque and a rock cairn to mark the final resting place of 120 victims. But make no mistake, these souls are not resting in peace…

## The Bottom Line

**The History:** The site of one of the worst massacres in American history, where Mormons slaughtered 120 unarmed men, women, and children on 9/11, 1857.

**The Haunting:** Overwhelming feelings of sadness, many voices crying out.

## Recommendations

There is much to learn about the people and events surrounding the massacre, so some extra research will make your visit more meaningful. The US Army later gathered as many bones as they could find and buried them, so as this site is essentially a mass grave, please treat the area with respect. Use your sixth sense and a good digital recorder for evidence of the paranormal.

## Visitor Information

**Mountain Meadows**
Highway 18
Veyo, UT 84782

**Directions:**

From St. George, in the Southwest corner of Utah, go north on state Highway 18 about 30 miles. Look for the signs indicating the parking lot on Dan Sill Hill on the right side of the road.

From Cedar City, north of St. George on Highway 15, go west on State Highway 56 about 35 miles to the intersection of state highways 56 and 18. Turn south on 18 and go about 11 miles to Enterprise. Continue south approximately 5 more miles to Mountain Meadows. The monuments are on the south end of the valley.

Just before you go up a small rise into the main parking lot for the 1990 monument, there is a road on the left that leads to the old monument in the valley.

Photo by Lee Witten, Utah State Railroad Museum.

# Union Station

Today, people across America may never have heard of Ogden, Utah, but there was a time when there was a saying that, "You can't go anywhere without coming to Ogden!" That was because it was an important railroad hub, being the junction of the Union Pacific and Central Pacific Railroads.

UT

In 1869, the Transcontinental Railroad had reached the Ogden area and after considering several towns, Ogden was chosen for the junction. The first depot was a simple two-story wooden building. Then in 1889, an impressive Romanesque brick and stone building with a clock tower was constructed. Unfortunately, in 1923, an unattended iron started a fire on an ironing board on the second floor, and the spreading flames devastated the old station.

Soldiers at the station during WWII. Utah State Railroad Museum.

The current Spanish Colonial Revival-style station building with its large grand hall was of a very different design than its predecessor, but it used the old depot's foundation. From the onset, the new Union Station was a busy place, but during WWII, service skyrocketed as over 100 troop, freight, and passenger trains per day came and went around the clock. LeRoy Johnson, who worked as a Red Cap at the station for over forty years, remembers that, "At one time, during World War II, sixty-two passenger trains left the depot every day—streamliners from all over the nation carrying presidents, kings, ambassadors, movie stars, doctors, lawyers, authors, poets—and just people—thousands of them, every day, from all walks of life."

As the era of traveling in the family car took hold after the war, and airlines began offering viable alternatives to trains, rail service steadily declined. One by one the famous passenger railroads that had moved America ceased operations, and by 1971, Amtrak became the nation's only passenger carrier. Once bustling stations across the country went dark or were demolished. Fortunately, Union Station—which saw its last passenger service in 1997 with the cessation of the Amtrak Pioneer—was preserved and converted into a museum.

Railroad buffs can now see a Union Pacific steam switch engine that used to work in the yards, and cabooses from Union Pacific, Southern Pacific, and Rio Grande. The Eccles Rail Center features the Union Pacific number 833, one of the fastest steam-powered passenger locomotives, and the turbine-powered locomotive number 26. There's also a restored WWII hospital car and a Union Pacific Railway Post Office car. If your timing is right, you might even get to see a former railroad employee on your visit—but this isn't part of any historical presentation.

Utah State Railroad Museum. *Photo by Lee Witten.*

There are many spooky stories of apparitions and paranormal activity at Union Station, but one of the oldest ghost stories involves the Romanesque train station fire in 1923. There was some consideration as to restoring the burned structure, but while decisions were being made, business had to go on as usual as the trains kept on running. One clerk was dutifully sitting at his desk beneath the burned old clock tower when a large stone came loose. It plummeted down onto his head, killing him instantly. Much of the activity here is attributed to this unfortunate clerk, but by all accounts he is a happy ghost who likes to play pranks and tap people on the shoulder—especially when they are alone at night.

Some believe the paranormal activity may be connected with the victims of a 1944 train collision. On the morning of December 31, an express train crashed into the rear of a passenger train, the Pacific Limited from Ogden. The collision occurred seventeen miles away at the town of Bagley, killing forty-eight and injuring seventy-nine. Rescue trains brought the casualties to Union Station, and this terrible tragedy may have left its imprint on the building.

Whether you come to the historic district of Ogden for the shopping, restaurants, or entertainment, a visit to the old Union Station should be first on your list of things to do. There's just something about trains that brings out the kid in all of us, and the railroad museum and collection of train cars here provide the perfect opportunity to step back in time to when the railroad was king. Just remember, if on your visit someone taps you on the shoulder, you might want to think twice about turning around!

## Recommendations

There is so much to see and do here, as in addition to the Utah State Railroad Museum and the Eccles Rail Center, there is the John M. Browning Firearms Museum, the Browning-Kimball Classic Car Museum, one of the state's top-rated restaurants, the Union Grill, a model train store, and the forest service operates an information center on outdoor activities. If you are staying in Salt Lake City, a cool way to visit is to ride Utah's new commuter rail, the Front Runner, which stops just north of Union Station. You can go inside both the WWII hospital and post office train cars. A model train festival is held every year during the first weekend of March and draws upwards of 8,000 visitors, and an annual Art Festival (check website for dates) includes the station and historic 25th Street which runs directly east of the station to downtown Ogden. Visitors are welcome to research in the railroad museum's library and archive which houses thousands of historic photographs, books, and documents. Ghost hunting groups have been allowed to conduct investigations in the station.

## Visitor Information

**Utah State Railroad Museum at Union Station**
2501 Wall Avenue
Ogden, UT 84401
(801) 393-9886
http://theunionstation.org/index.html

**Hours:**
Monday-Saturday 10am – 5pm.

**Admission:**
$5 Adults, $4 seniors, $3 Children. For all 3 museums: Family One Day Pass $12 (2 adults and up to 4 kids 2-12), Annual Family Membership $40.

**Directions:**
From Salt Lake City: Take I-15 N to the UT-79 E/31st Street exit, EXIT 341. Merge onto 31st Street/UT-79 E toward Weber State University/ Hospital. Turn LEFT onto Wall Avenue/UT-204, the station is on the left.

UT

## The Bottom Line

**The History:** The Union Pacific came to Ogden in 1869, and the current station was built in 1923 and was a vital hub during WWII.

**The Haunting:** A clerk killed in the station taps people on the shoulder, and spirits from a train collision may still wander the building.

# Ben Lomond Hotel

Historic 25th Street in Ogden was notorious for its bars, brothels, and opium dens, made possible by the steady stream of customers who arrived night and day at the Union Train Station. However, there was a clientele that preferred a more refined experience, and for them the Bigelow Hotel was built in 1927. The Bigelow replaced another hotel on the site, the five-story Reed Hotel built in 1891, and the goal was to create the largest, grandest, most modern hotel in town. They succeeded, and in 1990 the beautiful old hotel was placed on the National Register of Historic Places.

Built at a cost of $1,250,000, the eleven-story (actually thirteen if you count the two levels below ground) Italian Renaissance Revival-style hotel was typical for the time, except in Utah. As impressive as the ornate terra cotta exterior was, however, it's the interior where the designers really excelled. There was the Arabic-style coffee shop, Florentine Palace ballroom, Spanish meeting room, and the remarkable Shakespeare Room lined with murals. While the hotel became the talk of the town, it also became the talk of the nation when it hosted the 1927 Western Democrats convention. The Democrats were campaigning for Alfred E. Smith for president, but he lost the 1928 election to Herbert Hoover.

Utah banker Marriner Eccles bought the hotel in 1933 and renamed it the Ben Lomond, in honor of the mountains he loved. Eccles had already made his first million by the age of 22, and he would go on to serve as the Chairman of the Federal Reserve. The hotel would change hands, and functions, several times and was finally purchased and restored by Radisson in 1980. It is currently a hotel with both short-stay rooms and long-stay suites. And speaking of long stays, there just may be a few guests who have never checked out.

During Prohibition, the hotel may have been used by bootleggers and some other unsavory characters, which may have left both some active spirits and residual energy throughout the building. The most concentrated energy, however, can be found in rooms 1102 and 1101. Supposedly, a woman drowned in her tub in room 1102 on her wedding night, and strange things have been occurring with that tub ever since. Some guests have even felt as though they were being pushed in this room. Is this some indication that the woman's death was not an accident?

Some time later this woman's son came to retrieve her belongings, and he stayed next door in room 1101. That night he became so upset over his mother's tragic death that he committed suicide to be with her! In that regard, at least, he was successful, because the mother and son have both been seen and heard on numerous occasions.

Staff has also reported that the elevator seems to operate by itself, taking unseen passengers to different floors. The front desk receives calls from rooms that are unoccupied. Many other inexplicable things happen to the staff and guests, and it's all chalked up to the wandering spirits who, for various reasons, still feel the need to try to interact with the living.

If you plan to check into the Ben Lomond Hotel, ask for a room on the 11th floor. You can tell reservations that you want to stay there for the view—the view into the paranormal realm, that is.

## Recommendations

**The hotel is located in the historic district and is ideally located near many restaurants and shops, and it's a short walk to Union Station. Ask for the 11th floor for the best chance at a paranormal experience, and watch those elevators! This is a beautiful hotel, and harkens back to the days when things were done in a much grander style.**

## Visitor Information

**Ben Lomond Historic Suites**
**2510 Washington Boulevard**
**Ogden UT 84401**
**(877) 627-1900**
**www.benlomondsuites.com**

**Directions:**

**From Salt Lake City: Take I-15N. Slight right at US-89 N (signs for US-89 N/I-84 E/So. Ogden). Turn right at E. 2500 S./25th Street. Take the first right onto Ogden Avenue. The hotel will be on the right.**

## The Bottom Line

**The History:** One of three "grand hotels" in Ogden, built in 1927.

**The Haunting:** A mother and son are seen and heard, the elevator operates on its own.

# Vermont

HILDENE

GREEN MOUNTAIN INN

MAPLEWOOD INN

Hildene, the home of Robert Todd Lincoln. *Photo by Rolf Müller, Wikipedia, GNU Free Documentation License, Version 1.2.*

# Hildene

VT

The father of the builder of the Hildene mansion was born in a log cabin, so this stately home was a far cry from the family's humble beginnings. But then, his father did also have a chance to live in a rather nice mansion—the White House, in Washington, D.C.

Robert Todd Lincoln will forever be known as Abraham Lincoln's son, but he found his own success in the military, politics, and business. He was born in 1843, the eldest of four boys, but the only one to survive to adulthood. Captain Lincoln served on General Grant's staff at the end of the Civil War, and was present when Lee surrendered at Appomattox. Lincoln served as Secretary of War from 1881-85, and Ambassador to England 1889-93. He then went to work for George Pullman (as in Pullman sleeping cars for trains) and went on to become Chairman of the Board for the company.

Robert Lincoln first visited Manchester, Vermont during the summer of 1863, with his mother, Mary, and brother, Tad, who stayed at the nearby Equinox Hotel. He fell in love with the area, but it wasn't until the early 1900s that he bought 500 acres overlooking the Battenkill Valley and built Hildene as a summer home. It was completed in 1905, and became his permanent home until his death there in 1926. Lincoln's descendants continued to live at Hildene until 1975.

Today, thanks to ongoing restoration efforts, the magnificent mansion and gardens are open to the public to enjoy. The ghost of Robert Lincoln may still be enjoying Hildene, as well…or is he? Witnesses have seen a distinguished man with a beard, dressed in an old-fashioned business suit pacing back and forth in front of the house. He looks like Robert Lincoln, but he doesn't look like he is enjoying the other side, as he appears to be quite melancholy. Do all the tragedies he witnessed still weigh heavily upon him, not allowing him to rest in peace?

Robert had been invited to Ford's Theater the night his father was assassinated, but had been too tired to attend. He was awakened after the shooting and was at his father's bedside when he died. Robert was present when both Presidents Garfield and McKinley were assassinated, and came to believe he was some sort of presidential jinx. Is the ghost of Robert Todd Lincoln still haunted by all these deaths?

Perhaps he still feels guilty about not being at Ford's Theater that night, where he might have been able to prevent John Wilkes Booth from killing his father. Perhaps he is also contemplating the bizarre twist of fate that had occurred several months earlier when he began to fall under a moving train, and was saved from certain death by Edwin Booth—John's brother!

Then again, Robert Todd Lincoln may remain at Hildene simply because it was his beloved family home, and he just wants to keep an eye on it to make sure it is being kept properly. Whatever the reason, it is a beautiful place to visit, and gives one the opportunity to tread where Lincolns walked, and at least one still does.

## The Bottom Line

**The History:** The home of Robert Todd Lincoln, completed in 1905 and remaining in the family until 1975.

**The Haunting:** Robert Todd Lincoln is seen pacing with a melancholy expression.

## Recommendations

Hildene is particularly beautiful when the 1,000 peonies are in bloom, but it is also stunning in winter when decorated for the holidays and during Vermont's legendary fall foliage. Check out the pipe organ that was installed in 1908 for a whopping $11,500. The mansion contains much of the original family furniture and personal objects. There are a great number and variety of special events, including craft festivals, art shows, concerts, and farm fairs, so call or check the website for the latest schedule. While visiting Hildene, consider staying at the historic Equinox Hotel, where the ghosts of Mary and Tad Lincoln have been seen.

## Visitor Information

**Hildene**
1005 Hildene Road
Manchester, VT 05254
(802) 362-1788
www.hildene.org

**Hours:**

Open Daily 9:30am – 4:30pm. Guided Tours are offered at noon each day, by appointment at other times. Please allow about 2 to 3 hours.

Mid-December to Mid-March: Cross-Country Skiing and Snowshoeing, Weather Permitting, 9:30am – 4pm.

Closed Thanksgiving, Christmas (December 24, 25, and 26) and Easter.

**Admission:**

Tickets: $12.50/Adults, $5/Youth, Children under 6 and Members/Free. Grounds Pass: $5/Adults, $3/Youth, Children under 6 and Members/Free. Summer Weekend Wagon Rides: $2 Adults, $1 Children.

**Directions:**

Hildene is located off of Vermont 7A/Main Street, just south of downtown Manchester.

*Courtesy of the Green Mountain Inn.*

# Green Mountain Inn

There are ghosts that are the result of tragic love affairs, crimes, suicides, and those who simply linger because they don't seem to know to move on. There are ghosts that open doors, throw things, play the piano, shout, cry, and do just about anything a living person can do. However, the Green Mountain Inn located in Stowe may be unique in the country—perhaps even the world—because its ghost tap dances!

The original inn began as a private home built in 1833 by Peter Lovejoy. He later traded his home to Stillman Churchill for his 350-acre farm. Churchill had plans to convert the house into a hotel, and added two brick wings and a dance hall, calling it Mansfield House. Perhaps Churchill was too ambitious, as he lost the property in a foreclosure. A subsequent owner renamed the place the Brick Hotel.

In 1893, Mark Lovejoy bought the hotel, returning the property back to the family. The current inn, owned by the Gameroff Trust, now includes several historic buildings, including the depot for the electric train, and Sanborn House, which was a blacksmith shop and livery, both built in 1897. The original inn and depot are listed as number 13 and 14 on the National Register of Historic Places, and the Sanborn House is number 105. Other historic notes: Lowell Thomas used to broadcast from the inn, President Ford visited here when he was a student on a modeling assignment for *Look* magazine, and President Chester A. Arthur actually performed here in a theatrical production!

That's the historic side of this historic haunt, now for the haunting part.

In 1840, a chambermaid and the inn's horseman became the parents of a son, who was born in room 302. Their last name was Berry, and their son would later take on the nickname "Boots," after he learned to tap dance while in jail in New Orleans, but first things first. When Boots was in his twenties, he succeeded his father as the horseman responsible for providing fresh horses for the stagecoach that stopped here.

One day a team of horses took off with the coach, threatening the lives of all the passengers. Boots risked his own life to stop the horses and was declared a hero—and that was the point where his life began to spin out of control. The story of his courage spread far and wide and as a local newspaper stated, "Boots's popularity was such that there wasn't a place in the county where he could pay for his own drinks." Apparently, Boots took full advantage of the free drinks, and the adoring women. He ended up losing his job, leaving Vermont, and somehow managed to land in a jail in New Orleans.

Boots Berry did return to Stowe in 1902, but he was a broken man. However, fate gave him one more chance for a moment in the sun—and it came during a terrible snowstorm. For some reason, a little girl got stranded on the roof of the inn, and no one knew how to rescue her. As Boots was born and raised there, he knew how to get to the girl and he carefully handed her down to safety. But as fate would have it, just as he was about to become the local hero for the second time, he slipped on the ice, fell off the roof and was killed. Ironically, the roof from which he fell to his death was over room 302, the room in which he was born!

From that day, people claimed to hear Boots Berry tap dancing on the roof, particularly during snowstorms. Some may think that fate cruelly used Boots Berry, but he was the one who chose to use his fame to his disadvantage, rather than to help him along in life. And, how many people are given a second opportunity, the opportunity for redemption?

If you stay at the Green Mountain Inn as the snow is falling, and you hear Boots tapping above you, don't think of it as a dance of death. Think of him as a man who made some wrong choices, but when other people's lives were at stake he was a hero, twice. And after all, he did die with his boots on.

## The Bottom Line

**The History:** A private home built in 1833 converted to a stagecoach inn.

**The Haunting:** Boots Berry is still dancing on the roof.

## Recommendations

The inn has grown to encompass a variety of buildings containing a total of 107 rooms, luxury suites, and village townhouses, so there's something for everyone's taste. Of course, if you want Boots' room, request 302 in the main inn. The inn also contains two restaurants and several shops. Vermont is beautiful any time of year, but it is absolutely spectacular during fall foliage, but you must book well in advance to reserve for the peak foliage time.

## Visitor Information

**The Green Mountain Inn**
18 Main Street
Stowe, VT 05672-5071
(800) 253-7302
(802) 253-7301
www.greenmountaininn.com

**Directions:**

From their website—Stowe is a convenient drive from Interstate 89. Take exit 10 and follow Route 100 ten miles north to Stowe. The Inn is located on Main Street (Route 100) at the intersection of Route 108 (also called "The Mountain Road"), on the right after the blinking light when you approach the center of town. Ample parking is available behind the Inn.

*Courtesy of the Maplewood Inn.*

# Maplewood Inn

VT

When this beautiful Greek Revival home was built in 1843, there was a tavern across the street that was already almost half a century old. Farmer Asahel Kidder owned the property, and when it came time to expand the house in 1880, his family used good New England sense. Rather than undertake new construction, the 1795 tavern building was picked up, moved, and joined to the house to make the structure you see today.

At this time, Kidder's son-in-law, Isaac Wood, established a successful dairy farm and creamery at this location, and his descendants continued to operate the Maplewood Dairy until 1979. The old barns and creamery buildings were torn down in 1981, but fortunately the house was left standing. In 1986, the restored farm house was opened as a bed and breakfast, and it is now listed on both the State and National Registers of Historic Places.

It is always intriguing when two buildings are joined, both from a historical perspective, as well as a more other-worldly view—if you move a building, do you also move its ghosts? In this case at least, the answer may be yes. Over the last two decades, guests and staff have witnessed some unusual things. Some may be attributable to the family that occupied the home for over a century, but some sound more likely to be the result of the old tavern.

For example, one night several women saw three people dressed in 1800s-style clothing. One witness described the experience:

"A young couple with a little girl walked from the bedroom entrance into the living room of the suite where we were all seated, continued to quietly walk through the living room, then headed down the stairs as if going to the first floor. It was extremely vivid. The man was wearing a black suit and was carrying a carpet bag. The woman was wearing a long blue dress, with a shawl and was carrying her hat in one hand. She was holding her little girl's hand in her other hand."

Had this family been traveling and stopped at the tavern to rest 200 years ago, and for some reason never left? Or had they been visitors to the old farm house? We may never know, but we do know such appearances continue to this day. The very morning the author called for information about the inn, a woman had announced to the other guests at breakfast that she had been awakened at 4am and there at the foot of her bed stood a woman and child who simply faded from sight!

Even though no smoking is allowed in the inn, for years people have detected the rather strong odor of cigar smoke. Perhaps an old dairy farmer is just relaxing after a long day with a phantom cigar? There are also footsteps and creaking floorboards, the sound of a child's ball bouncing, cold spots, and a white, misty form was once seen in the Oak Suite.

Do former patrons of the tavern or family members from the old farm still occasionally walk the halls of the historic Maplewood Inn? If they do, they appear to be just as curious about the guests in their house as the living are with these shadows of the past.

## The Bottom Line

**The History:** A 1795 tavern was joined to an 1843 Greek Revival home and a successful dairy farm was operated on the site for a hundred years.

**The Haunting:** A family from the 1800s and a woman and a little girl have been seen. There is the smell of cigar smoke, a bouncing ball, footsteps, and cold spots.

## Recommendations

If you're looking for a recommendation for the best time of year to go to the Maplewood Inn, you're out of luck, because every season in Vermont is beautiful. Summer in the Green Mountains offers all manner of outdoor activities, winter skiing is within half an hour, and there is no more spectacular fall foliage place on earth. Then there's the shopping and restaurants, and the inn is also convenient to both Green Mountain College and Castleton State.

## Visitor Information

**Maplewood Inn Bed and Breakfast**
1108 South Main Street (Route 22A South)
Fair Haven, VT 05743-9163
(800) 253-7729, (802) 265-8039
www.maplewoodinn.com

**Directions:**

From the east and west: From Routes 4 and 4A, turn south on Main Street to #1108 on South Main.

From north and south on Routes 87 and 7: Take Route 4 and follow Directions: above.

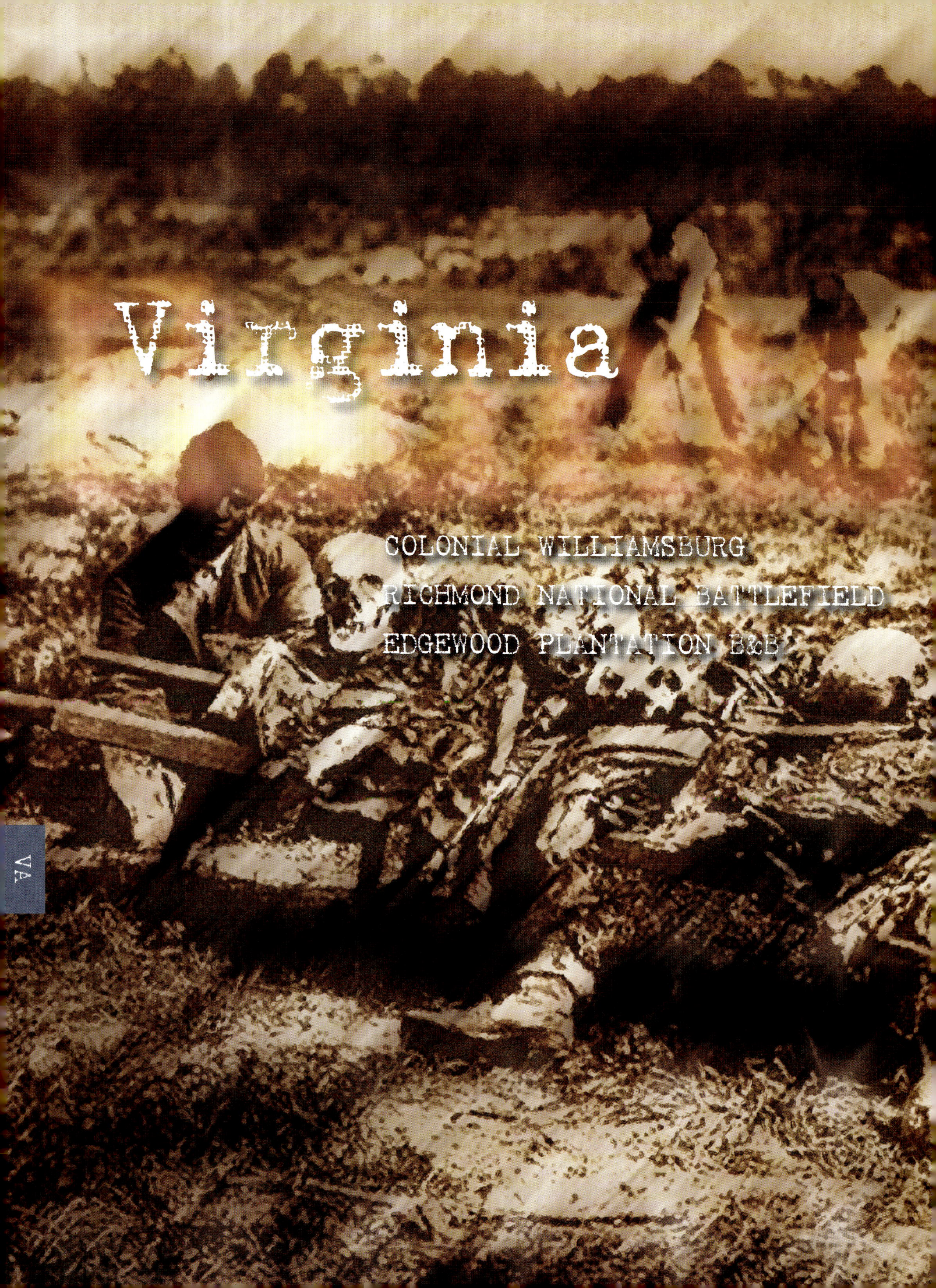

# Virginia

COLONIAL WILLIAMSBURG
RICHMOND NATIONAL BATTLEFIELD
EDGEWOOD PLANTATION B&B

The Wythe House at Colonial Williamsburg. *Photo by Francis Benjamin Johnston, Courtesy of The Library of Congress.*

# Colonial Williamsburg

There is simply no other place like Colonial Williamsburg. It is the largest living history museum in the world and its historic district covers 301 acres with 88 original eighteenth-century structures. In addition, there are hundreds of other buildings that have been reconstructed on their original foundations. At Colonial Williamsburg you can totally immerse yourself in another time by visiting period homes and shops, and dining and spending the night in period taverns, restaurants, inns, and B&Bs.

This unique town has its roots way back in 1632 when Middle Plantation was established as a fortified settlement. In 1693, the College of William and Mary opened its doors to students, and is now the second oldest university in the country. In 1698, it became the capital of the Virginia Colony (previously it was Jamestown) and was renamed Williamsburg.

Williamsburg was a center of political, intellectual, and cultural life in the colonies, and the list of America's founding fathers who walked these streets reads like a Who's Who, such as George Washington, Thomas Jefferson, and Patrick Henry. In 1780, during the Revolutionary War, it was Governor Thomas Jefferson who dealt a blow to the city when he moved the capital to Richmond, as he feared Williamsburg's location made it an easier target for the British.

The greatest impact on Williamsburg, however, came during the Civil War. At the start, the College of William and Mary lost so many students to the army they decided to close until the war was over. Battles were fought nearby during the Peninsula Campaign. On May 6, 1862, Union troops occupied the town, and the soldiers caused considerable damage to many of Williamsburg's buildings, including burning the College Building. While the area was economically revitalized in 1881 when the railroad finally came to Williamsburg, for the most part progress passed it by—which turned out to be a very good thing from a historical perspective, and it all began with a single church.

In 1907, the Reverend Dr. W.A.R. Goodwin restored his historic Williamsburg church building for the 300th anniversary of the founding of the Episcopal Church in Virginia. He then worked in New York until 1923, but when he returned to Williamsburg he recognized the incredible opportunity this colonial city presented. It was a very ambitious concept: If all of the hundreds of historic buildings could be restored or reconstructed, Williamsburg would become a living museum city. There's nothing like thinking big!

Of course, big thoughts require big cash, but with his faith, elbow grease, and the wealth of John D. Rockefeller, Jr. behind him, the dream of Colonial

Williamsburg became a reality. Thanks to their efforts, and countless craftsmen, historians, and volunteers, visitors can escape the twenty-first century and experience the people, places, and events of the eighteenth century. In fact, quite literally, throughout the town you can experience the eighteenth century people, not just the costumed interpreters and actors. To be completely accurate, of course, these are not living, breathing centuries-old people, just their ghosts.

There are several ghost tours of Colonial Williamsburg that can orient you to the many wandering spirits and their stories, and as there are just so many ghosts in so many places, a tour or two is a good place to start. The following are just a sampling of some of the ghost stories.

## Peyton Randolph House

One of the oldest and most haunted buildings is the Peyton Randolph House, built in 1715 by William Robertson. Sir John Randolph purchased part of the house in 1721, and willed it to his son, Peyton. In 1824, the house was purchased by Mrs. Mary Monroe Peachy. The Marquis de Lafayette was a guest of Mrs. Peachy in October of that year. Unfortunately, many tragedies were to befall the Peachy family, as several children died of illness, and one died from a fall. A relative committed suicide in the drawing room. A Civil War soldier was staying with the family after the war while he attended William and Mary College, but he became sick and died. With so much death, is it any wonder that ghost stories have been told about the Peyton Randolph House for over 200 years?

The most common occurrence is footsteps; very heavy footsteps in boots. There's also the sound of breaking glass. Apparitions include a young man in colonial clothing who appears to be real, until he vanishes. Another male spirit is also seen, but he is decidedly ghostly, as he appears to be a misty, white, almost shining figure.

One of the most interactive ghosts is that of a very thin old lady in a nightgown. In a second-floor bedroom, she would softly speak the name of whoever was sleeping there. Once this person was awake, the old lady would wring her hands and appear to be very upset. Could this be Mrs. Peachy, still grieving the loss of all those who were dear to her?

## George Wythe House

The two-story brick George Wythe House (pronounced "with") is often considered the most attractive house in town. It was built in the mid-1750s as a wedding gift from his father-in-law. George Wythe was a law professor and patriot leader, and Virginia's first signer of the Declaration of Independence. Thomas Jefferson (one of Wythe's students) was a guest in the house in 1776, and General George Washington and French General Rochambeau both used the Wythe house as their headquarters at different times during the war.

As for the haunted activity, a woman in colonial attire has been seen throughout the house. She is believed to be Lady Ann Skipwith who was a frequent guest in the house and died in childbirth in 1779. Lady Ann has been seen brushing her hair by a mirror, coming out of her closet wearing a satin gown and red shoes, and standing at the top of the stairs in a beautiful evening dress. On one occasion by the stairs, she appeared so real that a custodian walked over to speak to her, thinking she was a guide, but the lady just vanished before his eyes!

## Still More Ghosts

You can even sleep with ghosts at Colonial Williamsburg in one of their many haunted accommodations. For example, there's the Brick House Tavern where an unseen presence walks through one of the rooms. At the Orrell House, the ghost there is far more mischievous, and you can never be sure what it might do. The college is also said to have several ghosts, and even the streets of Williamsburg have wandering spirits.

While the focus at Colonial Williamsburg is obviously on the history, there's no denying that this is one of the most haunted sites in the country, in terms of both the sheer size of the place and the number of ghost stories. And what would the Reverend Dr. Goodwin have said about all the ghost stories being connected with his beloved town? You may be surprised to learn what he told the famous newspaper columnist Ernie Pyle on his visit to Williamsburg in 1936: "I wouldn't give a hoot for anybody who doesn't believe in ghosts."

If anyone would have known about the spiritual side of Colonial Williamsburg, it would have been Dr. Goodwin. So, if you do give a hoot about historic haunts, treat yourself to one of the world's largest, finest, and most fascinating!

## The Bottom Line

**The History:** What first began as Middle Plantation in 1632, became Williamsburg, the capital of the Virginia Colony, and is now the largest living museum in the world.

**The Haunting:** Ghosts are everywhere! You can visit haunted houses, stay in haunted lodging, and dine in haunted taverns. If that's not enough, take one of the several ghost tours.

## Recommendations

**If you were to try to compose the definition of a historic haunt, you would only need two words: Colonial Williamsburg. There is just so much to learn, see, and experience here with the architecture, crafts, stories of the historic people, stories of historic events, food, lodging, special events and reenactments, and ghost stories—it's simply amazing, and admittedly a bit overwhelming, so don't even think you can appreciate it all in a single day. Go to:**

**www.history.org/visit/whatToSeeAndDo/historicArea/itineraries.cfm**

**...to print a First Visit Itinerary or the one focusing on Colonial Trades to help plan your visit. Some houses are private residences, so look for a flag at a building's entrance, which indicates that the site is open. Book a ghost tour for some spooky fun, and if you plan on spending the night, ask for one of the haunted accommodations.**

## Visitor Information

**Colonial Williamsburg**
**101A Visitor Center Drive**
**Williamsburg, VA 23185-4565**
**(757) 229-1000**
**www.history.org**

**Hours:**
**Open 365 days a year. Call or check the website for the latest seasonal hours.**

**Admission:**
**Basic 1 Day Pass: $36 adult, $18 youth (6-17), 5 and under free, 1 Day Plus Pass, includes Governor's Mansion and a second consecutive day: $46 and $23, Annual Pass $58 and $29.**

**Directions:**
**From their website—Williamsburg is midway between Richmond and Norfolk on I-64 (exit 238). After exiting, look for the America's Historic Triangle directional signs (blue with red-and-white "ribbon"), where you'll notice the Colonial Williamsburg logo. The signs will direct you to the Visitor Center (address: 101A Visitor Center Drive (Highway 132Y)). Once you purchase your Admission: pass, you can either take the complimentary shuttle bus or walk to Colonial Williamsburg's Historic Area.**

# Richmond National Battlefield

During the Civil War, Richmond was the capital of the Confederacy and a bustling center of political, military, and civilian activity. It would be difficult to overestimate the city's importance to both sides in the conflict, and one only needs to see the long list of battles fought in an attempt to take Richmond to understand its preeminent position in the scheme of things.

## Cold Harbor Battlefield

To try to encapsulate four years of war and thirty battles in the Richmond area would be futile in a single location, which is why the Richmond National Battlefield Park encompasses more than 1,900 acres in thirteen separate locations. All of the sites have amazing stories to tell, and one would be hard pressed to find a site that didn't also have ghostly tales, as well, so it is worth visiting all the sites to learn about and experience all this incredible park has to offer. For the purposes of this book, however, the focus will be placed where the history and haunts are arguably the most intense, Cold Harbor.

During the Civil War, General Ulysses S. Grant had managed to accomplish something most Union generals could not—victories. He also knew that the ultimate victory would come at a very high price in lives, but he was determined to fight this bloody battle of attrition to

A burial party at Cold Harbor in April of 1865

war's end. However, what happened at Cold Harbor in June of 1864 made even Grant lament his actions. As he would later write in his memoirs.

"I have always regretted that the last assault at Cold Harbor was ever made. At Cold Harbor no advantage whatever was gained to compensate for the heavy loss we sustained."

That heavy loss totaled a staggering 13,000 Union casualties (killed, wounded, and captured) over several days of fighting, with almost half of those coming on just the morning of June 3. One soldier later wrote, "We felt it was murder, not war, or at best a very serious mistake had been made."

That mistake was something Union troops had been repeating for years—thinking they could successfully attack entrenched Confederate forces. The best way to illustrate the lopsided nature of the results of such a foolish strategy is to look at the total number of those killed at Cold Harbor: 1,844 for the Union, as opposed to only 83 for Confederate General Robert E. Lee's men!

Even if Grant didn't recognize the futility of the series of assaults he ordered at Cold Harbor, his soldiers did. Before the fateful attack on the morning of June 3, an officer came upon a group of men writing something on slips of paper. When asked what they were doing, one soldier calmly replied that none of them expected to survive, so they were writing their names on paper so their bodies could be identified. Perhaps the most poignant example of this sad sentiment was in a bloodstained diary later found on the battlefield. The final entry simply read, "June 3, 1864. Cold Harbor. I was killed."

These were not the only deaths that occurred on the Cold Harbor Battlefield. On June 27, 1862 during the Seven Days Battles, this ground was also the site of the Battle of Gaines' Mill. The soldiers' sense of doom was most likely accentuated in 1864, when, while digging their entrenchments, they unearthed the skeletons of the men who died there two years earlier!

The results of the battle, beyond the scope of the casualties, was one of shock and horror in the north, with some labeling Grant an incompetent butcher and calling for the war to end. For General Lee it was a victory, but it would actually be the last victory for his command. While Confederate deaths were relatively low, there were about 4,500 wounded, captured, or missing, and these were losses Lee knew his army could not afford.

So, what effect has all this death had on the Cold Harbor Battlefield? For generations, visitors and local residents have heard gunfire, footsteps, voices, shouting, and moaning. They have felt awful feelings of dread when walking along the Union lines where men wrote their names on papers before marching to their deaths. They have felt sharp pains where men were killed and wounded, and sensed the fear and suffering of countless souls.

Apparitions appear here in all forms, from misty shapes, to solid black forms, to soldiers who look so real they are mistaken for reenactors. There is also the strange blue fog that engulfs part of the battlefield almost every night. Some claim the fog is nothing more than the result of the weather, others claim it is a concentration of paranormal energy.

Suffice to say, the human toll at Cold Harbor has left a deep paranormal imprint, one you can clearly feel as you walk along the battlefield. Such can also be said for the other sites in the park, as men fought, suffered, and died all too often and in too many places in and around Richmond. They say for some people in the south, the War Between the States has never ended. Sadly, for many of those who actually fought in that war, it has obviously not ended for them, either.

## The Bottom Line

**The History:** Richmond was the capital of the Confederacy and many Civil War battles were fought throughout the area. The Richmond National Battlefield Park preserves 1,900 acres at 13 different sites.

**The Haunting:** The full range of apparitions, sounds, cold spots, feelings, etc., throughout the battlefields, particularly Cold Harbor.

## Recommendations

With so many sites to explore, don't expect to see everything in a single day. The park recommends beginning at the Visitor Center at Tredegar Iron Works where Rangers will help plan your tour. From the park's website you can download podcasts of battlefield tours and maps which will greatly enhance your visit. The more you understand about the Civil War, its battles, and its officers and men, the more you will appreciate the sites. But even if you know very little, the park offers a treasure trove of historic haunts not to be missed.

## Visitor Information

**Richmond National Battlefield Park**
Visitor Center at Tredegar Iron Works
470 Tredegar Street
Richmond, VA 23219-4328
(804) 226-1981
www.nps.gov/archive/rich/home.htm

**Hours:**

Park battlefields are open sunrise to sunset. Visitor centers at Tredegar Iron Works, Chimborazo, and Cold Harbor are open daily 9am – 5pm. Visitor centers at Glendale and Fort Harrison are open daily June-August, 9am – 5pm. The park is closed Thanksgiving, December 25, and January 1.

**Admission:**

There are no entrance fees to Richmond National Battlefield Park sites. However, there is a parking fee for the American Civil War Center at Tredegar Iron Works. Free parking is available nearby.

**Directions:**

From their website—We recommend that you start your visit to our park at the Civil War Visitor Center at Tredegar Iron Works located at 470 Tredegar Street. Park Rangers will provide maps for touring the battlefields. The following directions will get you there.

Traveling north on I-95: Take exit 74C, which merges onto 17th Street. Take 17th Street to Broad Street (4 blocks). Turn right on Broad Street and stay on it to 14th Street (3 blocks). Turn left on 14th Street and stay on it to Canal Street. Turn right and stay on Canal Street to 5th Street (9 blocks). Turn left on 5th Street and stay on it to Tredegar Street (2 blocks). Turn right on Tredegar Street and then turn right again into the parking lot for the American Civil War Center and Richmond National Battlefield Park's Civil War Visitor Center.

Traveling South on I-95: Use exit 75 (3rd Street) for Civil War Visitor Center. The off ramp will merge onto 3rd Street. Stay on 3rd Street to Cary Street (9 blocks). Turn left onto Cary Street. Stay on Cary Street to 5th Street (2 blocks). Turn right onto 5th Street and stay on it until Tredegar Street (about 2 blocks). Turn right on Tredegar Street and then turn right again into the parking lot for the American Civil War Center and Richmond National Battlefield Park's Civil War Visitor Center.

Traveling east on I-64: Follow to intersection with I-95 south through the city of Richmond. Follow the above directions for I-95 south.

Traveling west on I-64: Use the 5th Street (downtown) exit for the Richmond National Battlefield Park Civil War Visitor Center at Tredegar Iron Works. Take 5th Street to its end (12 blocks), turn right onto Tredegar Street, then right into the parking lot. (Note: Due to construction downtown, 5th Street is sometimes blocked at Broad Street. In this event, turn left onto Broad Street and drive three blocks to 8th Street. Turn right on 8th Street and continue on it to Canal Street. Turn right on Canal Street and drive three blocks to 5th Street. Turn left onto 5th Street and take it to its end at Tredegar Street. Turn right onto Tredegar Street and then right again into the parking lot.)

**The following are the GPS addresses for all the battlefield sites:**

**Beaver Dam Creek Battlefield**
7423 Cold Harbor Rd.
Mechanicsville, VA 23111

**Chickahominy Bluff Battlefield**
4300 Mechanicsville Turnpike
Richmond, VA 23223

**Chimborazo Medical Museum**
3215 East Broad St.
Richmond, VA 23223

**Civil War Visitor Center**
470 Tredegar St.
Richmond, VA 23219

**Cold Harbor Battlefield and Visitor Center**
5515 Anderson-Wright Dr.
Mechanicsville, VA 23111

**Drewry's Bluff (Fort Darling) Battlefield**
7600 Fort Darling Rd.
Richmond, VA 23237

**Fort Harrison Battlefield and Visitor Center**
8621 Battlefield Park Rd.
Richmond, VA 23231

**Gaines' Mill Battlefield**
6283 Watt House Road
Mechanicsville, VA 23111

**Glendale Battlefield Visitor Center**
(Inside Glendale National Cemetery)
8301 Willis Church Road
Richmond, VA 23231

**Malvern Hill Battlefield**
9175 Willis Church Rd.
Richmond, VA 23231

**Park Headquarters**
3215 East Broad St.
Richmond, VA 23223

**Parker's Battery**
*1801 Ware Bottom Spring*
*Chester, VA 23831*

**Tredegar Iron Works**
470 Tredegar St.
Richmond, VA 23219

# Edgewood Plantation B&B

Edgewood Plantation exists today because it escaped the fate of so many other southern homes that were burned to the ground during the Civil War, as it was used as a field hospital for wounded Union soldiers. The grounds were once part of the famous Berkeley Plantation, and still contain the 1725 grist mill used by both Union and Confederate troops during the Civil War, and visited by Benedict Arnold during the Revolutionary War.

The house was built for Richard Rowland around 1849 in a Gothic Revival style, and is the only one of its kind along the James River. In addition to housing wounded soldiers during the Civil War, the house served as a Confederate lookout post. On June 15, 1862, General J.E.B. Stuart stopped at Edgewood for coffee on his way to Richmond to report to General Lee about the Union troop strength. Another claim to fame for Edgewood was during the 1900s when it was converted into The Blue Tea Pot, which was Charles County's first restaurant.

One of the main claims to fame today, however, are the ghosts, or at least one in particular, that of Elizabeth "Lizzie" Rowland. Lizzie's fiancé joined the Confederate army and went off to war. Lizzie patiently sat by her bedroom window looking for him to return, and etched her name in the window pane as she waited. And waited. And waited.

Her beloved fiancé never returned, and legend has it she died of a broken heart. For many generations, people passing by have seen Lizzie still sitting looking out that window. People inside the house have also seen the sad figure of the grieving woman, who is bound to this place by a love that hasn't died.

Lizzie is not alone at Edgewood, however, as guests staying in the former slave quarters have also reported seeing Civil War soldiers. One woman even had a soldier tell her his name, which later checked out to be the name of a soldier who most likely had been here during the war.

Edgewood Plantation is definitely a place steeped in both history and hauntings, and it the perfect place to connect to a time gone by—except for a few souls for whom time is standing still.



## Recommendations

**It's possible that during the time wounded soldiers stayed here that many died, so there could be more than a few spirits wandering around in addition to Lizzie. Ask for Lizzie's room, or at least ask to see her name etched in the window, if that room is already booked. Edgewood hosts both history and ghost tours, Victorian teas, and other events. This is a great place to stay to explore the rich history of this region of Virginia.**

## Visitor Information

**Edgewood Bed and Breakfast**
**4800 John Tyler Memorial Highway**
**Charles City, VA 23030-3300**
**(804) 829-2962**
**www.edgewoodplantation.com**

**Directions:**
**From Richmond, take VA-5 E which becomes John Tyler Memorial Highway.**

## The Bottom Line

**The History:** A plantation established around 1849 that was a field hospital during the Civil War, and is now a bed and breakfast.

**The Haunting:** A woman still awaits the return of her fiancé and soldiers are seen on the grounds.

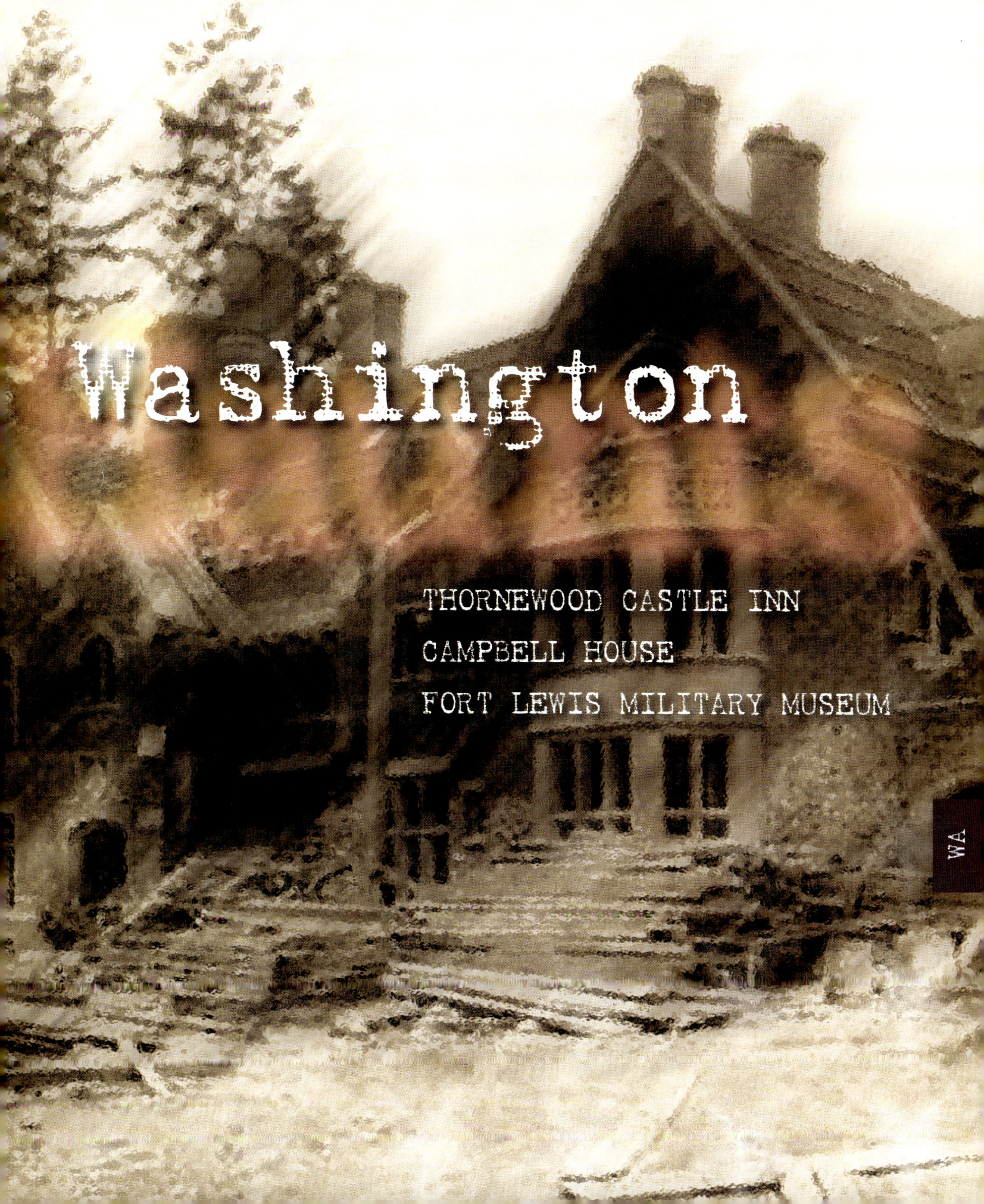

# Washington

THORNEWOOD CASTLE INN

CAMPBELL HOUSE

FORT LEWIS MILITARY MUSEUM

Thornewood Castle under construction in 1910.

# Thornewood Castle Inn

Have you ever read a Stephen King novel about some extraordinary haunted location and said to yourself, "I want to stay in a place like that!" If so, then Thornewood Castle in Lakewood is made for you, as it was the setting for Stephen King's mini-series *Rose Red*.

Actually, this stunning 27,000-square-foot Tudor/Gothic mansion was made for Chester Thorne between 1908-11, and included 54 rooms with 28 bedrooms and 22 bathrooms. Many of the materials used in construction—such as medieval stained glass and oak paneling—were transported from England from a fifteenth-century manor house that was completely dismantled. The red bricks for the exterior were imported from Wales, and the walls are three-feet thick. Everywhere it is evident that this place was built to last at least a few more centuries!

The estate also contains the magnificent "Secret Garden," a sunken, half-acre English garden designed by the Olmsted brothers, whose family is responsible for many of the country's famous gardens and parks. The original 100 acres (there are now only 4 acres) had an additional 37 acres of formal English gardens. Thornewood's gardens were so extensive that they required a full-time staff of 28 gardeners. The house staff needed 40 servants to attend to Thorne, his wife, Anna, their daughter Anita, and perhaps an occasional President such as Theodore Roosevelt and William Howard Taft. Not a bad servant-to-master ratio!

Thorne was born in Thornedale, New York, in 1863 to a family of financiers, and he graduated from Yale in 1884 with an engineering degree. He worked for the railroad for several years, then moved to Tacoma in 1890. Three years later he became President of the National Bank of Commerce at the age of only 30. His continued success in a variety of businesses allowed him to construct his dream home, or dream castle to be more accurate, and the house remained in the family until 1959.

*Rose Red* was filmed at Thornewood in 2000, and the story involved a team of psychics investigating paranormal activity in an old manor house in Seattle. It seemed to be written just for Thornewood, although the fictional ghosts were a bit over the top. However, the nonfictional ghost sightings here over the years still makes for a very good story.

The primary spirit is, fittingly, that of the former lord of the manor, Chester Thorne. He seemed to be a bit peeved by some renovations and showed his displeasure by smashing glasses and unscrewing light bulbs. Chester has also been seen on the grounds and in the house wearing a brown riding outfit, and his presence is very strong in his bedroom. On one occasion he even asked a woman what she was doing, and then vanished. Perhaps he is a little confused as to why all these people are in his home.

His wife, Anna, has also been seen in her bedroom (now the bridal suite). Often she is seen looking out the window at the garden. One of Anna's mirrors is in that room, and people have seen the reflection of a woman wearing old-fashioned clothing behind them, but when they turn to see who it is, no one is there.

There is nothing threatening about the ghosts of Chester and Anna, they simply loved this house and still enjoy being here. In fact, many people enjoy being here—really enjoy it to the point where there seems to be some sort of intense positive spiritual energy throughout the house that causes visitors to experience visions and actual sightings of loved ones who have passed. There are also many reports of other bizarre, but positive, paranormal experiences, possibly the result of residual energies attached to the original English building that was taken apart to build Thornewood. Or, maybe there's something about the land itself.

There is one sad note about a spirit seen here. A past owner's granddaughter drowned in the lake, and witnesses have seen a small child standing next to the water's edge. Concerned for her safety they run outside, but the child is nowhere to be found. Whether you love architecture, history, ghost stories, Stephen King novels, or you just feel like living like a king (or at least a duke) for a few days, Thornewood Castle offers an unparalleled experience. There are few American castles, and fewer still that allow you to spend the night.

Life is short, so treat yourself to a regal historic haunt and add your own experiences to the paranormal chronicles of Thornewood Castle.

### The Bottom Line

**The History:** A fifteenth-century English manor house that was dismantled and used to build a fifty-four-room mansion.

**The Haunting:** The original owner and his wife are seen, along with a small child by the lake.

### Recommendations

Thornewood is truly a place that seems to step right out of fiction, both for its magnificent design and furnishings, and its strange energy has a profound effect on some people. Ask for Chester's or Anna's room for the best chance at a paranormal encounter, but things can occur anywhere on the property. There may be less expensive historic haunts you can stay in, but this is truly a one-of-a-kind location that deserves the highest recommendations.

### Visitor Information

**Thornewood Castle Inn and Gardens**
8601 N. Thorne Lane S.W.
Lakewood, WA 98498
(253) 584-4393
www.thornewoodcastle.com

**Directions:**
From their website—Take I-5 to the Thorne Lane exit (Exit #123 ) just south of Tacoma, Washington. Turn west on Thorne Lane. Go three-tenths of a mile. Watch 25 mile speed limit. Turn right on the first street to the right (Thorne Lane). Immediately after turning right off Thorne Lane (3/10 mile from I-5) you will see the gate into Thornewood Estates. Drive up to the entry phone on the left. Please do not come without an appointment or reservation (unless you are on the invited guest list to a scheduled function).

## Campbell House

Amasa B. Campbell was born in Ohio in 1845. In 1867, he left his home state for a unique opportunity—working for the Union Pacific Railroad as it stretched westward to meet the Central Pacific. That meeting took place at Promontory Summit in the Utah Territory in 1869, completing the first transcontinental railroad.

Campbell then turned his attention to mining in Utah, a career choice that would ultimately prove to be very lucrative. In 1887, he came to Spokane Falls, as it was initially called, and with his partner John Finch, invested in the Coeur d'Alene mining district of Idaho. The enterprising duo also opened mines in British Columbia. Campbell further invested in timber, water power, banks, a railroad, and other business ventures, and it seemed that everything he touched turned to gold.

In 1897, Campbell was a millionaire in need of a suitable mansion. He hired Kirtland K. Cutter to design a beautiful English Tudor Revival style home in the exclusive millionaires' neighborhood known as Browne's Addition. The mansion was built with nineteen rooms and nine fireplaces, and designed for both entertaining guests and as a place for Amasa to conduct business. The lady of this new manor house was Campbell's wife, Grace, a former school teacher in Youngsville, Ohio. From schoolhouse to mansion, Grace took her rightful place in Spokane's elegant social scene, welcoming guests in the formal gilded French reception room. As for their daughter, Helen, she was able to enjoy everything the modern world had to offer a young woman of wealth.

Amasa Campbell died in 1912, and Grace survived him for another twelve years. Helen, who had married W.W. Powell, decided to give the family mansion to the Eastern Washington State Historical Society in memory of her mother. The house became a museum, and today, as part of the Northwest Museum of Arts and Culture, it is a stunning example of how Spokane's elite lived during the "Age of Elegance" around the turn of the twentieth century.

One of the most popular times to visit the Campbell House is during the Christmas season when costumed volunteers cook holiday favorites and the house is decked with vintage decorations and children's toys. Visitors might even get the opportunity to glimpse some vintage children—or at least their ghosts.

There are many unfounded stories relating to these ghost, but the fact remains that over the years staff and guests have seen and heard little children in the house, particularly a little girl who sometimes appears very real and solid. Were these the children who were once happy here, and are just trying to recapture the good times of their short lives? Or, were their spirits brought to this house, attached to some historic object?

Certainly not every sound or strange feeling here is caused by a ghost, but enough has happened to warrant paying extra attention on your visit. Why this house is haunted may never be known, but if you're going to be a ghost, you might as well pick a lovely mansion like the Campbell House as your historic haunt.

## The Bottom Line

**The History:** An English Tudor Revival-style mansion built in 1897 for Amasa Campbell who had made his fortune in mining.

**The Haunting:** Who are the children that are seen and heard playing in the house?

WA

## Recommendations

A guided tour of the house is nice any time of the year, but this place is extra special during the Christmas holiday season. The forty-five-minute guided tour includes the carriage house, where an exhibit introduces the Campbell household and community issues. MAC hosts a variety of events for the whole family, including living history, so check their website or call for the latest schedule.

## Visitor Information

**Campbell House**
2316 West 1st Avenue
Spokane, WA 99201-5906
(509) 456-3931
www.northwestmuseum.org

**Hours:**
Wednesday to Saturday: 10am – 6pm. (The first Friday of each month, open until 8pm.) Sunday to Tuesday closed. Closed Thanksgiving Day, Christmas Day, Easter, Memorial Day, 4th of July, Labor Day and Veterans Day. (The Museum is open on New Year's Day as part of "First Day Spokane.")

**Admission:**
Adults: $7, Seniors: $5 (62 and over), Students: $5 (Valid School ID required for students over 18), Children (5 year of age and under): Free. MAC Museum Members: Free.

**Directions:**
From their website—From Seattle (and other points west of Spokane): East on I-90 to Maple Street (Interstate Exit 280). Turn left (north) onto Walnut and continue for three blocks, moving to left lane. Turn left (west) onto Second Avenue and immediately move to the right lane. Continue straight ahead on Second Avenue for six blocks. Turn right (north) onto Hemlock Street and continue for two blocks. Turn left (west) onto First Avenue and then immediately turn right into the Museum parking lot. Free parking on all levels. Admissions, Exhibits, Store, and Cafe are in first building next to parking. Administration and Archive Library are in next building, Cheney Cowles Center.

From Coeur d'Alene (and other points east of Spokane): West on I-90 to Maple Street. (Interstate Exit 280). Turn right at the stop light at end of exit. Immediately move to the left lane as you will be turning left after 2 blocks. Turn left (west) onto Second Avenue and immediately move to the right lane, then follow directions above.

From Colville (and other points north of Spokane): South on I-395 or Highway 2 (both merge onto Division Street going south). Continue into downtown Spokane, staying left to continue south to 2nd Avenue. Turn right (west) onto 2nd Avenue and proceed approximately 1.6 mi. through downtown, and into Browne's Addition Neighborhood, (stay right on 2nd, do not curve left with arterial). Turn right (north) onto Hemlock Street and continue for two blocks. Turn left (west) onto First Avenue and then immediately turn right into the Museum parking lot.

From Pullman (and other points south of Spokane): North on I-195. East on I-90 to Maple Street (Interstate Exit 280), then follow Directions: above for East I-90.

Panoramic view of Camp Lewis on September 28, 1917.

# Fort Lewis Military Museum

Today, Joint Base Lewis-McChord is one of the country's leading military bases, but it had more modest beginnings as simply Camp Lewis, named after Meriwether Lewis, of the famous Lewis and Clark Expedition. In 1918, the Salvation Army built a 150-room hotel for soldiers at the camp and their families, called the Red Shield Inn.

After World War I, the soldier population declined sharply and the inn was no longer needed. While the Salvation Army had spent $107,000 in its construction, in 1921 they sold it to the army for just $1. The hotel was used as apartments for a time, then became the Fort Lewis Inn in 1927.

Most of the camp's original buildings were demolished, but the old Red Shield Inn was saved in 1972 to be used as a museum. The Fort Lewis Military Museum is now on the National Register of Historic Places and is the only certified U.S. Army Museum on the West Coast. Its mission is to "collect, preserve, exhibit, and interpret the history of Fort Lewis, the units which served there, and the story of the US Army in the Pacific Northwest." However, the property may also be preserving other things from the past.

There have been many reports of strange cloaked figures and the ghosts of Native American warriors in the woods of the old fort. Inside the buildings, doors open and close and lights turn on and off by themselves. Footsteps are often heard, as are the sounds of men marching. Objects move on their own, and many other inexplicable events have occurred over the years.

Are restless spirits of Native Americans solely responsible for the activity here, or are they joined by soldiers and energies connected with all the weapons on display in the museum? War always leaves a deep imprint on the lives of those who experience it, and perhaps it leaves an imprint in the afterlife, as well.

## The Bottom Line

**The History:** A military museum housed in a former hotel for soldiers, built by the Salvation Army in 1918.

**The Haunting:** Native Americans and cloaked figures are seen in the woods. Inside the buildings there are all manner of sights, sounds, and objects moving.

## Recommendations

**The website states: "Visitors without a current military vehicle registration decal and federal ID card must first obtain a Visitor Pass at the Main Gate Visitors Center by presenting a driver's license, vehicle insurance and registration." The Museum has an extensive collection of original uniforms, weapons, and equipment, and the Vehicle Park has tanks, cannons, missiles, and various vehicles and hardware associated with the history of Fort Lewis. The Cannon Shop has merchandise representing the heritage of the Army and Fort Lewis.**

## Visitor Information

**Fort Lewis Military Museum**
**Fort Lewis, WA 98433**
**(253) 967-4523**
**www.fortlewismuseum.com**

**Hours:**
**12pm – 4pm Wednesday to Sunday, special tours by arrangement.**

**Admission:**
**Free**

**Directions:**
**The visitors center is located at exit 120 of I-5 between Tacoma and Olympia.**

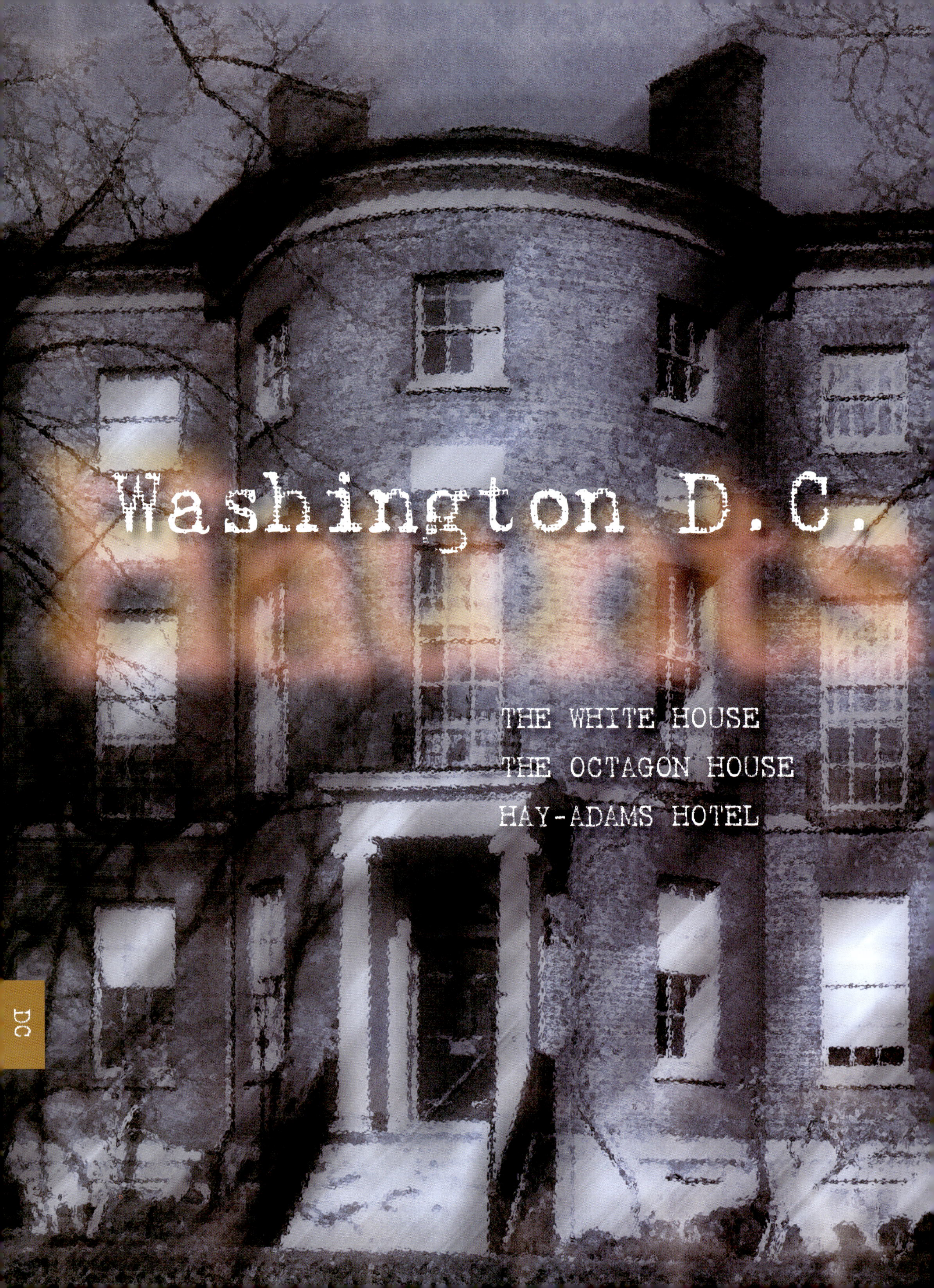
Washington D.C.
THE WHITE HOUSE
THE OCTAGON HOUSE
HAY-ADAMS HOTEL
DC

Early 1900s view of the White House. *Courtesy of The Library of Congress.*

# The White House

Although construction was begun on the most famous house in America in 1792, it wasn't until 1800 that the White House had its first presidential occupant, John Adams. Unfortunately, nothing of the original interior structure remains, as in 1814 the British set fire to the place, leaving only the stone walls standing. During Truman's administration (1948-52) the interior was in danger of collapsing, so the building was once again gutted, albeit intentionally this time, and rebuilt. So other than the outside walls, the oldest things at the White House may be its spirits…

The first identifiable ghost in the house was that of First Lady Abigail Adams. During her husband's presidency, she used the East Room to hang her laundry, and her spirit has been seen hurrying to that room with her arms in front of her as if she was carrying a load of clothing. Fortunately, she does not appear to be doomed to just doing laundry throughout all eternity, as she has also been seen in other parts of the White House, wearing her distinctive lace shawl and white cap.

Perhaps the most famous and frequently seen spirit is that of Abraham Lincoln. He was first encountered in the 1920s when President Coolidge's wife, Grace, saw him standing in the Oval Office looking out a window. Lincoln was seen on many occasions during FDR's administration, perhaps drawn by the troubling times the country once again faced during those years. Eleanor Roosevelt claimed to feel Lincoln's presence, as did Lyndon Johnson's wife, Lady Bird.

Perhaps the most distinguished eyewitness was Queen Wilhelmina of the Netherlands. One night when she was staying in the Lincoln Room she was awakened by someone knocking on her door. When she opened the door, there was Abraham Lincoln wearing his trademark stovepipe hat. The Queen promptly fainted, and by the time she regained consciousness, the ex-President had gone.

Abraham is not the only member of the Lincoln family to be seen in the White House. His son Willie, who died in 1862 at the age of 11, was allegedly seen during Grant's administration. In fact, not only did a staff member claim to see the boy, but she spoke with him, as well.

Another former President has also made his presence known, and in a very colorful manner, befitting his character in life. Andrew Jackson has been heard swearing and walking around in his former bedroom, the Rose Room, by many witnesses, including Mary Lincoln

One of the most famous First Ladies in history, Dolley Madison, has made an appearance on the White House grounds. Mrs. Woodrow Wilson had plans to remove Dolley's rose garden. However, the gardeners claimed that when they went to start digging up the roses, Dolley's angry spirit scared them away. The story either indicates a very determined former First Lady, or very lazy, but imaginative, gardeners.

There are many other accounts of paranormal activity in the White House, which given its numerous spirits, could be considered one of the most haunted houses in America. While there's no guarantee a former President or First Lady will make an appearance on your tour of our nation's most famous residence, keep an open mind and a sharp eye—if you feel as if you're being watched, it could be more than just security cameras. And if you turn the corner at come face-to-face with a tall man in a stovepipe hat, just make sure you find a soft spot to faint.

## The Bottom Line

**The History:** This is the most historic and recognizable house in America. Decisions that affect the entire world are made here, and the most powerful and influential people in history have passed through its doors. For 200 years it has been the quintessential symbol of democracy.

**The Haunting:** Can you name any other place in America where a queen has seen the ghost of a President, or where former First Ladies still attend to their duties? This place has been the focal point of so much tragedy, emotion, and earthshaking events, it's no wonder that unusual energies—and entities—abound here.

## Recommendations

Everyone visiting our nation's capitol should take the time to visit its most famous (haunted) home. Tickets are free; however, you have to plan in advance, as tickets must be obtained through your local Member of Congress (see below). Plan your visit so you will have time for the Visitor's Center, and don't be shy about asking the staff questions on your self-guided tour—remember, you're a taxpayer so it's your house, too!

This is a very popular tourist destination, so be prepared for it to be very busy from the spring through the fall. Off-season will give you your best chance at tickets on the day you want them.

## Visitor Information

**The White House**
1600 Pennsylvania Avenue
Washington, D.C. 20500

**White House Visitor Center**
Southeast corner of 15th and E Streets

**Special Note:** There are all kinds of rules and prohibited items, so it's best to check the White House website or call the 24-hour line to make your visit go smoothly: www.whitehouse.gov/about/tours_and_events/. For the most current tour information: (202) 456-7041.

**Hours and Admission:**

Here's the Visitor's Center and tour information from their web site: Requests must be submitted through one's Member of Congress and are accepted up to six months in advance. These self-guided tours are available from 7:30am – 11am. Tuesday through Thursday, 7:30am – 12pm. Fridays, and 7:30am – 1pm Saturdays (excluding federal holidays). Tour Hours: will be extended when possible based on the official White House schedule. Tours are scheduled on a first come, first served basis. Requests can be submitted up to six months in advance and no less than 30 days in advance. You are encouraged to submit your request as early as possible since a limited number of tours are available. All White House tours are free of charge. Please note that White House tours may be subject to last minute cancellation.

All tours are significantly enhanced if visitors stop by the White House Visitor Center located at the southeast corner of 15th and E Streets, before or after their tour. The Center is open seven days a week from 7:30am until 4pm and features many aspects of the White House, including its architecture, furnishings, first families, social events, and relations with the press and world leaders, as well as a thirty-minute video. Allow between 20 minutes to one hour to explore the exhibits. The White House Historical Association also sponsors a sales area. Please note that restrooms are available, but food service is not.

**Directions:**

From their web site—The closest Metro-rail stations to the White House are Federal Triangle (blue and orange lines), Metro Center (blue, orange, and red lines) and McPherson Square (blue and orange lines). On-street parking is not available near the White House, and use of public transportation is strongly encouraged.

In other words, unless you take a taxi, be prepared to walk or use the Metro—which is sound advice regardless of where you are going in Washington, D.C.

The Octagon House. *Courtesy of The Library of Congress.*

# The Octagon House

The Octagon House is full of mysteries, not the least of which is its name, as it only has six sides! The building is also rich in history, and was designed by Dr. William Thornton, who was one of those remarkable early Americans who seemed to be able do everything. In addition to being an architect, he was a physician, painter, and inventor. For all his varied achievements, Thornton's greatest claim to fame is architectural, as it was his design that won the competition for another local building, none other than the U.S. Capitol, one of the world's most iconic structures.

The Octagon House was built between 1799-1801 for Colonel John Tayloe III, a plantation owner who loved the political scene, which is why he chose a site just two blocks from the White House. At the time of construction, the surrounding streets were no more than wooded paths, and the Potomac River was only two blocks away (today, it is ten blocks to the river). This was the first private home in the area, and it must have created quite a stir for both its location and unique design.

It's also one of the oldest buildings in the area, as the British put the others to the torch when they burned the White House in 1814. The Octagon House was only spared because the French Ambassador was staying there at the time, and he claimed that the building was the embassy. It may not have really been an embassy, but it did become a temporary White House of sorts.

As the real White House had burned, President Madison and his wife, Dolley, occupied the Octagon House for about six months. In a bedroom converted to Madison's office, important national business was conducted, including the signing of the Treaty of Ghent, which ended the War of 1812. Many years later, it was also in the Octagon House that plans were drawn up for the site of the Lincoln Memorial and the clearing of the Mall. During WWII, the building housed the O.S.S., the organization that was to become the C.I.A.

With so much history it's easy to overlook Colonel Tayloe's family. However, having raised fifteen children in the house, I'm sure it was impossible to ever ignore the many little Tayloe's for more than about two minutes. While the comings and goings of the family members may not have the same historic importance as the presidential events, they are crucial to the haunted history of the house.

According to legend, one of Tayloe's daughters fell in love with a British officer and wanted to marry him. Clearly this would not have been a popular choice, what with the British having torched the neighborhood. As Tayloe argued with his daughter, she slipped and fell down the stairs to her death.

Another daughter also met the same unfortunate fate, although she didn't ask permission to marry, no doubt given what happened to her sister. Instead, she eloped, then returned to tell her father and ask his forgiveness. Different tactic, same result, as during their argument she also fell from the stairs to her death. Coincidence? You be the judge.

The result of these two suspicious deaths is that Tayloe was never charged with any crimes, but the atmosphere of the Octagon House was certainly charged with the paranormal energies of the tragic events. Witnesses have claimed to see a woman on the stairs followed by screams, then heard the sickening sound of a body falling to the floor. Others have seen phantom candlelight moving up the stairs.

There may be other spirits as well, if the many other legends are to be believed. A gambler was said to have been killed when he was caught cheating. As he was dying he grabbed the bell chain, and ever after the sound of a bell could be heard echoing through the house in the dark of night.

Others claim to have seen Dolley Madison, although there doesn't appear to be any good reason why she would haunt the Octagon House. Still, witnesses say that when this ghost makes an appearance, the scent of lilacs fills the air, and Dolley's favorite scent was lilacs.

One man saw a soldier dressed in an early nineteenth-century uniform. Some believe the house was used as a hospital during the Civil War, and the spirits of soldiers who died there still can be heard moaning and crying out. And there are many other stories of strange sights, sounds and smells. Can all of these accounts be merely fanciful stories or the result of over-active imaginations?

The best way to find out is to visit the Octagon House and judge for yourself if the legends could be true. The building is currently owned by the American Architectural Foundation, and has been open to the public since the 1970s as a museum of architecture and design.

Special Note: At the time of the writing of this book, the museum was temporarily closed for some renovations, so there is no official word as to how the organization regards the ghost stories. As always, use your discretion when visiting and respect the fact that it is a museum.



## Recommendations

As they are only two blocks apart and closely related in history, plan on visiting the Octagon House and White House on the same day. As you enjoy the quiet of the exhibit spaces, imagine fifteen little Tayloes running around the house, or the hustle and bustle of the presidential staff.

## Visitor Information

**The Octagon Museum**
1799 New York Avenue NW
Washington, D.C. 20006
(202) 638-3221
www.archfoundation.org/octagon/index.htm

**Hours and Admission:**
As the museum was temporarily closed for renovations at the time of the writing of this book, please check their web site or call for hours and fees.

**Directions:**
The Octagon House is located downtown at 18th Street and New York Avenue NW, just two blocks west of the White House. The closest Metro stop is Farragut West.

## The Bottom Line

**The History:** One of the earliest and most distinctive private homes in Washington, D.C., built between 1799-1801 for Colonel John Tayloe III. Occupied by President Madison after the White House was burned in 1814. Madison signed the Treaty of Ghent here. The O.S.S. worked out of the Octagon House during WWII.

**The Haunting:** Did two of Tayloe's daughters "accidentally" fall from the staircase, and do they still haunt the scene of their tragic deaths? Many figures are seen throughout the house, and there are all sorts of unnerving sounds and smells.

Photo by Theodor Horydczak, Theodor Horydczak Collection *Courtesy of The Library of Congress.*

# Hay-Adams Hotel

Since its opening in 1928, the Hay-Adams Hotel has hosted the rich, famous, and powerful. Such was also the case when the property was the site of the side-by-side mansions of John Hay and Henry Adams, who entertained prominent politicians, artists, and writers.

Hay and Adams purchased the adjoining properties in 1884, and the prominent architect Henry Hobson Richardson designed the two Romanesque mansions that were to see so many of society's elite pass through their elegant doors. Imagine having sculptor August Saint-Gaudens over for tea, or dinner with Mark Twain or Teddy Roosevelt?

Unfortunately, while the best and brightest discussed art, science, and the news of the day, all was not well behind closed doors at the Adams residence. Henry Adams' wife, Marian Hooper Adams, nicknamed Clover, was an accomplished photographer, but she suffered from depression which only deepened when her father died. Soon after, in 1885, Clover committed suicide by drinking chemicals used to develop her photos.

This is the official story of Clover Adams, but the case is not closed on her life, or her death. There were rumors that Henry Adams had a mistress, which may have led to Clover's depression. There were whispers that it wasn't a suicide, that it had been murder. After her death, Henry burned all of Clover's letters, diaries, and photographs, and when he wrote his autobiography, he didn't even mention her! This was unusual behavior and there were suspicious circumstances to be sure, but no proof exists that any crime was committed.

Whatever actually did occur, there are lingering effects of the tragedy in the form of a restless spirit in the Hay-Adams Hotel, which many believe to be Clover. Even though both mansions were demolished in 1927 so the hotel could be built, it appears as though the new structure inherited Clover's ghost. She took her own life on the fourth floor of her mansion, and it is on the fourth floor of the hotel where staff and guests have heard a woman crying, witnessed locked doors suddenly open and close on their own, and watched as clock radios turned on and off when no one was near them. Others have heard a woman calling them by name, and some have even felt an unseen form give them a hug!

Today, the 138-room Italian Renaissance-style apartment hotel is one of Washington, D.C.'s finest hotels, and its location is ideal for exploring the city, as it is just a stone's throw from the White House. Admittedly, this place may be beyond the average traveler's budget, but if you are looking for one of the most elegant haunted places in the heart of one of America's most historic cities, this is it!

## The Bottom Line

**The History:** The site of two elegant mansions owned by John Hay and Henry Adams, who entertained many famous people. Clover Adams committed suicide in her house in 1885. In 1927, the mansions where demolished and the current hotel was built. Many twentieth-century celebrities, artists, and politicians have stayed here.

**The Haunting:** The ghost of Clover Adams is thought to haunt the fourth floor of the hotel. People have heard voices and a woman crying, doors open and close on their own, and some have even felt a phantom embrace.

## Recommendations

The Hay-Adams is a wonderful place to stay any time of year, but if you want your best shot at encountering Clover, make your reservations for some time during the first two weeks of December. That appears to be the time Clover is most active, which may be because it is the time of year when she died. The White House is very close (there are great unobstructed views from the hotel), so you can easily walk there, and to the Octagon House, as well.

## Visitor Information

**The Hay-Adams Hotel**
800 16th Street N.W. (16th and H Streets)
Washington, D.C. 20006
(202) 638-6600
www.hayadams.com

**Directions:**

From their web site—From New York, Baltimore and Baltimore-Washington Airport: Take I-95 South toward Washington, D.C. to 495 West at Silver Spring, MD. Exit onto Connecticut Avenue. South (No. 33). Take Connecticut Avenue. South approximately 7 miles. Stay in the center lane and continue under Dupont Circle for approximately 7 blocks to H Street. Turn left on H Street, to 16th Street. Turn left on 16th Street. The hotel is on the left.

From Richmond, VA: Take I-95 North to 395 North, the 14th Street Bridge. Exit onto 14th Street Bridge, Route 395 North. Stay in the two left lanes to exit on to Route 1 which will become 14th Street, continue to I Street. Turn left on I Street to 16th Street. Turn left on 16th Street. The hotel is on the right.

# West Virginia

HARPERS FERRY NATIONAL HISTORIC PARK

TRANS ALLEGHENY LUNATIC ASYLUM

JACKSON ROSE B&B

Harpers Ferry in 1865.

# Harpers Ferry National Historic Park

In the 1700s, there was a point of land commonly referred to as "The Hole," where the Shenandoah and Potomac Rivers met. The name would suggest an ugly, unpleasant place, but nothing could be farther from the truth. In fact The Hole, now known as Harpers Ferry, is a scenic wonder of wild, natural beauty. It is also a town brimming over with history and ghosts.

It was 1747 when Robert Harper decided to purchase land here, much to the chagrin of his wife, Rachel, who found this place to be too wild for her liking. Harper built a mill and took over the ferry service. When their original cabin was destroyed in a flood, Harper began building a bigger and better house, but he died before construction was complete. Rachel died soon after when she fell from a ladder trying to finish the house.

Robert's grave is in the Harper Cemetery, where Revolutionary War soldiers who died of cholera while stationed there are also buried. In 1785, George Washington visited Harpers Ferry on business, and it was on his recommendation in 1794 that a federal arsenal and armory was built at the location.

During the Civil War, Harpers Ferry changed hands between Union and Confederate forces eight times, and suffered greatly as a result. During the Battle of Harpers Ferry in September of 1862, General Stonewall Jackson surrounded the federal forces, bringing about the largest surrender of U.S. troops until Bataan during WWII. However, despite all of these momentous events, arguably the most famous conflict occurred just prior to the Civil War during abolitionist John Brown's Raid.

To say that John Brown fiercely opposed slavery is an understatement, as he and his men were willing to kill to achieve their goal, which was nothing less than to form an army to free all the slaves. On October 16, 1859, Brown and 21 men (he had hoped for an army of 4,500) seized the armory at Harpers Ferry, along with several other buildings. They also took hostages, including Colonel Lewis Washington, the great-grandnephew of our first president.

On October 18, U.S. Marines had surrounded Brown's men inside of the engine house. In a curious twist of fate, the Marines were commanded by Colonel Robert E. Lee, and Lieutenant J.E.B. Stuart was also among the U.S. forces. Of course, both of these men would go on to fight against the United States during the Civil War.

Brown was captured, as were all of his men that weren't killed, and he was hanged for his crimes in December. While his plans far exceeded his results, John Brown did light an abolitionist fire in the hearts and minds of many Americans, and as he predicted, the crime of slavery "of this guilty land will never be purged away but with blood."

Today, much of the old town is preserved in the Harpers Ferry National Historic Park, and you can walk in the footsteps of the likes of Washington, Brown, and Lee. If you're lucky, you can also walk in the phantom footsteps of some of the town's many ghosts.

At the Harper House, people have seen Rachel gazing out an upstairs window. It is believed that when Robert was dying, he told his wife to bury their gold for safekeeping. With Rachel's sudden death, the secret of the treasure went with her to the grave, but she is still keeping an eye on it.

Then there is the sound of the Revolutionary War soldiers on parade through the streets playing their instruments. They have been heard many times, but have never been seen.

John Brown's ghost has also been witnessed on many occasions walking through the streets. He appears so lifelike that many tourists believe he is a costumed look-alike hired by the park—until he disappears in front of the engine house. Many have tried to photograph this man, but no one ever appears in the pictures.

There is the flaming apparition of Jenny, whose dress caught fire and she was killed by a train when she ran onto the tracks in her panicked attempt to get help. There is also the ghost of a priest and a Civil War soldier who died in his church. An ex-slave named Dangerfield Newby is also seen wandering the streets. Newby had joined John Brown in hopes of freeing his family and was killed during the raid. His body was mutilated and thrown to the hogs.

In short, Harpers Ferry is a beautiful, fascinating, and spooky concentration of history and hauntings—the perfect destination!

## The Bottom Line

**The History:** A ferry crossing town founded in the 1700s. The site of John Brown's Raid and the largest surrender of Federal troops during the Civil War.

**The Haunting:** Many ghosts walk the streets and inhabit the houses, including John Brown himself.

## Recommendations

**You must park at the visitors center and then take a shuttle into the park. There is much to see and do, so allow plenty of time. You can walk to restaurants and shops in the town. The guided tours are very informative, and special events, lectures, and concerts are offered. There are ghost tours and walks available from independent operators. Harper's Ferry is really a special place, so take the time to appreciate its natural beauty, impressive history, and its many ghosts.**

## Visitor Information

**Harpers Ferry National Historic Park Visitor Center**
**171 Shoreline Drive**
**Harpers Ferry, WV 25425**
**(304) 535-6029**
**www.nps.gov/hafe/index.htm**

**Hours:**
**The park is open daily from 8am – 5pm and closed Thanksgiving Day, Christmas Day, and New Year's Day.**

**Admission:**
**Vehicle Pass: $6 per private vehicle. Individual Pass: $4 per person arriving on foot or bicycle. Passes are valid for 3 consecutive days.**

**Directions:**
**From their website—From Northern Virginia: From Interstate 495 West take the left exit (EXIT 45) and merge onto VA-267 West, the Dulles Toll Road (stay in local lanes, not express airport traffic lanes)/Dulles Greenway toward Leesburg (Portions toll). Follow to Exit 1, VA-7 W on the left toward Leesburg/Warrenton. Take the VA-9 exit toward Hillsboro/Charles Town, WV merging to the right onto Charles Town Pike / VA-9. After approximately 10 miles on VA-9 you will come to a light where you will bear right onto VA-671 N/Harpers Ferry Road. Follow this road until it ends at the lighted intersection of US 340/ Jefferson Pike. Turn left onto 340. Follow US-340 N to the four way intersection in Harpers Ferry (approximately 2.5 miles), staying in the left lane. Turn left at the light (you will see a large sign for the Park) and continue through to the entrance station.**

**From Baltimore-Washington Intl. (BWI) Airport: Take I-695 (Baltimore Beltway) west toward Catonsville/Towson. Exit onto I-70 west toward Frederick, Maryland. Continue west on I-70 past Frederick for about 1 mile. Take Exit #52 onto U.S. Route 340 (Charles Town and Leesburg exit). Continue south/west on U.S. Route 340 to Harpers Ferry (22 miles). Cross the Potomac and Shenandoah rivers. After crossing second bridge (Shenandoah River) proceed to stoplight at top of hill. Turn left into the main entrance of the park.**

*Photo by Tim Kiser, Wikipedia, the Creative Commons Attribution-Share Alike 2.5 Generic.*

# Trans Allegheny Lunatic Asylum

It was a novel concept in the nineteenth century to actually attempt to treat the mentally ill. For the most part, those who were deemed to be insane were usually chained to the walls of a dark prison cell, or kept locked in an attic or basement for the rest of their lives. The mentally ill were to be removed from society, not helped to get well and return to society.

Dorothea Dix and Dr. Thomas Story Kirkbride urged a more "moral treatment" and recommended the construction of mental asylums with long wings that allowed for plenty of sunshine and fresh air, and grounds that were "tastefully ornamented." Kirkbride believed that such pleasant surroundings would have a therapeutic effect and act as "a special apparatus for lunacy." The Kirkbride plan led to the building of the Trans-Allegheny Lunatic Asylum in Weston, and 300 other institutions like it across North America.

Construction on the 242,000-square-foot asylum began in 1858, but was interrupted by the Civil War. Union soldiers occupied the grounds and the unfinished building. Camp Tyler became an important military post, and in both 1862 and 1863, Confederate forces successfully—although temporarily—drove the Union soldiers out. In 1864, another Confederate raid resulted in the confiscation of all the food and clothing that had been intended for the asylum's first patients.

Despite the trials and tribulations of these early years, the asylum was completed and remained in operation for 130 years. It is the largest hand-cut stone masonry building in North America, and second in the world next to the Kremlin. It was designed to accommodate 250 patients, but became seriously overcrowded. By the 1950s, over 2,400 patients were packed into the asylum and conditions correspondingly deteriorated and violent incidents became all too frequent. The building was also deteriorating, and as treatment of the mentally ill shifted toward de-institutionalization, the asylum closed its doors in 1994.

Today, the old psychiatric hospital once again welcomes people, only now they are tourists, not patients. Although, some may argue that you have to be at least a little bit crazy to choose to visit a place where so many lost spirits wander...

In short, the Trans-Allegheny Lunatic Asylum is considered to be the most haunted hospital in the country. Thousands of patients died and were buried here, and by all accounts, they never left. Apparitions of all shapes, sizes, and consistency have been witnessed, including Civil War soldiers, patients, and doctors. Footsteps, voices, screams, laughter, and whispers have been heard. There are many cold spots, unnerving feelings of strong presences, and mixtures of emotions that can flood over visitors.

While paranormal activity can be experienced anywhere, the most active locations are on the fourth floor and in the Civil War wing. And unlike some places that are only open to the public for brief tours, this former asylum allows you to spend the night, if you are brave—and crazy—enough to be locked into one of the most haunted places in America!

## The Bottom Line

**The History:** A former lunatic asylum that began construction in 1858 and closed in 1994.

**The Haunting:** You name it, they have it. Full-bodied apparitions, voices, cold spots, footsteps, screams, EVPs.

# Jackson Rose B&B

"I have a nice, green yard, and if you were only here how much we could enjoy it together! But do not attempt to come as before you could get here I might be ordered elsewhere. My chamber is on the second story and the roses climb even to that height, and come into my window, so that I have to push them out, when I want to lower it. I wish you could see with me the beautiful roses in the yard and garden, and upon the wall of the house here; but my sweet little sunny face is what I want to see most of all!"

Few would guess that such tender sentiments of love and talk of roses would have been written by one of the most brilliant and ruthless generals of the Civil War, Thomas "Stonewall" Jackson. But these words were indeed written by Jackson (actually before he earned the nickname Stonewall) in a house in Harpers Ferry he used as his headquarters from April to June of 1861. That same pink rose bush is still growing in the yard, and it came to be called the Jackson Rose because of the Confederate officer's letter.

The house was built around 1795 by the Lee family—relatives of Robert E.—and is listed on the National Register of Historic Places. In its long history, the house has had a variety of owners and functions,

## Recommendations

For the faint of heart, you can take a daylight historic tour, or attend one of a variety of special events such as concerts, festivals, and expos. Photography tours are offered on a regular basis. For those with a somewhat stronger constitution, you can participate in a two-hour guided ghost tour. The very brave can immerse themselves in an overnight independent ghost hunt where you are free to investigate with your equipment and test your psychic abilities. Best of all, your group can rent the entire asylum for the night.

## Visitor Information

**Trans-Allegheny Lunatic Asylum**
71 Asylum Drive
Weston, WV 26452
(304) 269-5070
www.trans-alleghenylunaticasylum.com

**Hours:**

Historic tours offered March – October. Monday: by appointment only. Tuesday to Friday and Sunday 12pm – 6pm. Saturday 10am – 6pm. Off-season by appointment only.

2-hour Ghost Tours and 8-hour Ghost Hunts are offered throughout the year. Please call or check the website for the current schedule.

**Admission:**

Historic tours: First Floor $10, all 4 floors $30. Ghost Tours $40, Ghost Hunts $100, private hunts $150 per person, 10 person minimum.

**Directions:**

From Charleston, WV: On I-79 North, take exit 91 for US-19 toward Roanoke. Turn right at US-19 N. Turn left at Middle Run Road. Sharp right at Olive Street/Terrace Avenue. Continue onto Arch Street. Turn left at S. River Avenue. The Asylum will be on the left.

From Pittsburgh, PA: On I-376 W, take exit 64A to merge onto I-79 S toward Washington. Take exit 21 to merge onto I-79 S toward Morgantown. Entering West Virginia. Take exit 105 for County Road 7 toward Jane Lew. Turn right at Co Road 7/Co Road 8/Hackers Creek Road. Turn left at Main Street/US-19 S. Turn right at N. Main Street. Turn right at the 1st cross street onto 2nd Street. Take the 3rd left onto S. River Avenue. The Asylum will be on the right.

including a funeral home (the bodies were kept in the basement which has been converted into a pub) and as an antique store. The ghost stories go back at least as far as when it was an antique store in the 1960s and 70s, as is evidenced by the following story.

Two elderly ladies were browsing through the store and after a while approached the owner on the first floor. They were both very angry and insisted on knowing why he had left a baby all alone in a cradle on the second floor. The poor baby was crying and it was unthinkable that he would leave this child all alone. The owner had no idea what the women were talking about, as he didn't have a baby. Had someone snuck into his store and abandoned the child?

Rushing upstairs, he went to the room that had the antique cradle for sale, but it was empty. After a thorough search, no babies were found in the house, but the two women were certain of what they had seen and heard. Some time later while researching the history of the house, the owner discovered that just after the Civil War, a baby had died in that very room!

The bulk of the sightings here are more recent and come from guests spending the night. One female guest was in bed reading one morning when a lady in a hoop skirt and full Civil War-era clothing entered her room—without knocking—and said, "You had better come downstairs now." The guest was both intrigued and a little taken aback. Obviously something interesting was going on involving this costumed lady, but she wasn't thrilled about the lady entering unannounced, and then essentially ordering her to go downstairs. However, before the guest could ask for an explanation, the lady in the hoop skirt simply vanished!

Several guests have felt a strong presence in their rooms, sometimes accompanied by a feeling of pressure and the smell of whiskey. Could these be the somewhat inebriated spirits of Civil War soldiers? One psychic held a séance in the house, and had "a long conversation" with a slave named Jenny who had lived on the top floor with the two children she had with the owner of the house.

While the current owners have not yet had any experiences of their own, they are fascinated by the stories their guests tell them. And like all of the owners before them, they will care for this beautiful old house and its famous rose bush, and preserve and pass down both the history and the haunts for future generations to enjoy.

## Recommendations

**If you are visiting the very haunted town of Harpers Ferry, you ought to stay in one of its most historic and haunted B&Bs. Civil War buffs should request Stonewall Jackson's room. And of course, you must take the time to stop and smell the flowers—the famous pink Jackson Rose, that is!**

## Visitor Information

**The Jackson Rose Bed and Breakfast**
**1167 W. Washington Street**
**Harpers Ferry, WV 25425**
**(304) 535-1528**
**www.thejacksonrose.com/**

**Directions:**

**From their website—From Washington/Northern Virginia/Suburban Maryland: Head North on I-270 to Frederick, MD. At Frederick watch for signs for Charles Town, West Virginia, and Route 340 West, you'll get on I-70 briefly and get off at Exit 52. Get on Route 340 West heading for Charles Town. Stay on Route 340 until you come into West Virginia; you will pass over the Potomac and Shenandoah Rivers on 2 separate bridges (after approximately 20 miles). After the 2nd bridge, continue one mile to the traffic light. Turn right at the light; this is Washington Street. The B&B is one mile down on the right hand side.**

**From the North-Heading South on Interstate 81: Once you are in West Virginia, take the 12E exit to get on Route 9 heading East. You will be taking a left turn onto Route 9 off the exit ramp. Continue straight on Route 9 for approximately 13 miles. Take the Charles Town/Harpers Ferry exit to get on Route 340 North. You will take a left turn off the exit ramp to head North on 340. Proceed on 340 for approximately 6 miles. At a traffic light near the Welcome Center turn left towards Harpers Ferry. The B&B is approximately 1 mile on this street on the right hand side.**

## The Bottom Line

**The History:** A home built by the Lee family around 1795. Stonewall Jackson used the house as his headquarters in 1861, and wrote to his wife about the beautiful rose bush, which is still growing.

**The Haunting:** A woman in a Civil War-era dress, a baby, and a former slave.

# Wisconsin

TALIESIN

GRAND OPERA HOUSE

THE KEWAUNEE INN

Hillside Home School at Taliesin. Photo by Jeff Dean.

# Taliesin

Frank Lloyd Wright (1867-1959) was Wisconsin-born of Welsh descent, and became one of America's greatest architects. His innovative homes were known for their tranquility and harmony with nature. However, at Taliesin, the personal home he began building in Spring Glen in 1911, events proved anything but tranquil and harmonious. In fact, the worst mass murder in the state's history occurred there.

To set the stage, Wright had fallen in love with a client's wife, Mrs. Cheney, and left his wife and six children to go to Europe with her for a year. This created a great scandal, but criticism did not deter the couple. Mrs. Cheney had moved into Taliesin, and in August of 1914, she was dining with her children, acquaintances, and some staff while Wright was in Chicago on business.

In Wright's employ at the house was a 30-year-old servant from Barbados, named Julian Carlton, who suddenly became homicidal. Perhaps Mrs. Cheney had fired him, as she often did with many other servants, or perhaps it was for personal reasons Carlton took to his grave. Whatever the reason, Carlton doused the place with gasoline, ignited it, then attacked the panicked people with a hatchet. The following report of what ensued appeared in *The Weekly Home News*, August 20, 1914.

**MURDERER OF SEVEN:** Sets Fire to Country Home of Frank Lloyd Wright Near Spring Green

While the members of the household were at dinner, last Saturday, Julian Carlton, a Negro servant, fired Frank Lloyd Wright's bungalow, murdered seven and seriously wounded one with a hatchet and another received injuries in jumping from a window.

**The dead are:**

Mrs. Mamah Borthwick (Cheney), their son and daughter, John and Martha Cheney, aged 11 and 9 respectively; Emil Brodelle, aged 30, an architectural draftsman; Thomas Brunker, of Ridgeway, hostler; Ernest Weston, 13-year-old son of Mr. And Mrs. Wm. Weston of Spring Green; and David Lindblom, gardener.

**The wounded are:**

William H. Weston of Spring Green, foreman of the bungalow activities, and Herbert Fritz of Chicago. The latter escaped the Negro's wrath but received a broken arm and glass cuts in making his escape through a window. He was also slightly burned.

Mr. Wright was in Chicago, where business had called him several days before and he escaped the murderer's hatchet.

When authorities arrived, Carlton was found hiding by the furnace. In a suicide attempt, he had swallowed acid, but survived. He also survived the crowd's desire to hang him on the spot. However, he did die in prison seven weeks later and the families were spared having to endure a trial.

When Wright and Mr. Cheney arrived after the murders, Wright described what they saw in the burned house as a "devastating scene of horror." Personally devastated by the tragedy, Wright fulfilled his promise to rebuild the home in memory of the woman he loved. Today, Taliesin—which Wright named after a Welsh poet—is one of the most-visited of Wright's creations, and it is said to also be visited by the unfortunate victims of the hatchet murders.

The ghost of Mrs. Cheney, dressed in a long, white gown, has made the most appearances. The bodies of the dead and dying had been taken to the Tan-Y-Deri Cottage on the property, and it is in and near this cottage that Mrs. Cheney is most often seen. Other strange things also occur in this cottage, such as lights going on and off and doors opening and closing.

It only takes one death to bring about a haunting, so it isn't surprising that the brutal hatchet murder of seven men, women, and children would leave its imprint. But perhaps Mrs. Cheney and the others stay at Taliesin because of the tranquility, harmony, and beauty of the place. Visit for yourself, and see whether or not Frank Lloyd Wright's home is a place worth spending eternity.

## The Bottom Line

**The History:** One of Frank Lloyd Wright's homes that was the scene of a mass murder in 1914.

**The Haunting:** The ghosts of the murder victims still make their presence known, and Mrs. Cheney is seen in a long, white, gown.

## Recommendations

There are several different tours depending upon your time and budget, so you can see all of the buildings and grounds in 4 hours, or just get a taste of Taliesin in one hour. The Riverview Terrace Café is in the visitor center and has windows that span the entire length of the building and spectacular views of Wisconsin River. Check the website's calendar for the latest special events. There is a beautiful shop with books and Wright-inspired furnishing and decorative objects. You can visit Mrs. Cheney's grave in the nearby Unity Chapel.

## Visitor Information

**Taliesin**
5607 Cty. Road C
Spring Green, WI 53588
(608) 588-7900 or toll free (877) 588-7900
www.taliesinpreservation.org

**Hours:**

May 1 to October 31, 5 types of guided tours are offered at different times throughout the day, and last between 1 and 4 hours. April and November, there is one tour twice a day on the weekends, as well as the day after Thanksgiving.

All tours begin at the Frank Lloyd Wright Visitor Center, which is open 9am – 5:30pm, 7 days a week during the tour season, May 1 to October 31.

Riverview Terrace Café: May 1 to October 31, 9am – 4pm, lunch served between 10:30am and 3pm.

**Admission:**

Depending upon the type of tour, tickets range from $14 to $80.

**Directions:**

From their website—From Madison, WI: Take Highways 12/18 West. Follow Highways 12/18 W to Highway 14 W (exit 251). Follow Highway 14 W for 45 minutes through a series of small towns, the last of which is Arena. Four miles (6.5km) outside of Arena, turn left onto County Road C. The Frank Lloyd Wright Visitor Center is approximately 3 miles (5 km) down this road on the left hand side, near the intersection of Highway 23 and County Road C.

# Grand Opera House

Oshkosh is famous for hosting the world's largest air show every summer, and for the children's clothing made here since 1895. However, long before there were planes filling its skies and even before little overalls were being manufactured, Oshkosh had an opera house.

It was in 1882 that the Oshkosh Business Men's Association proposed building "a more metropolitan place of entertainment" for the growing upper classes. So construction was begun on the brick edifice to refined taste, the Grand Opera House. The popular opera, *The Bohemian Girl*, was performed on opening night on August 9, 1883.

Initially, grand opera reigned supreme, but tastes gradually changed and the theater began playing host to traveling road shows. Those shows transitioned into classic vaudeville acts, which then gave way to the true king of twentieth-century entertainment, motion pictures. But even that era lost its luster when in the 1970s, the once grand opera house had degenerated into an X-rated movie house.

In the late 1880s and early 1900s, the feet of many famous people trod upon this stage, such as those of Susan B. Anthony during her fight for women's rights, Mark Twain with his unique wit, opera great Enrico Caruso, magician Houdini, and comic geniuses Charlie Chaplin and the Marx Brothers. This place had seen an amazing cross section of American life, and was recognized in 1974 by being placed on the National Register of Historic Places.

Age and neglect had taken their toll, however, but fortunately government and private funding came to the rescue and the restored Grand Opera House reopened in 1986 for theater productions. And almost immediately, the actors and stage hands realized they were not alone.

There were clear footsteps, cold spots, lights going on and off, objects moving, and doors opening and closing. Solid-looking apparitions who then disappeared were seen in the orchestra pit and underground passageway. In the dressing room, a man in nineteenth-century clothing was seen holding a playbill from an 1895 production. Then there was the man with the distinctive round glasses who stood in the balcony, and was also seen from the street looking out a window. Can any of these ghosts of the Grand Opera House be identified? In the case of the man with the glasses, yes.

## Recommendations

**Theaters are unique haunts, and obviously you can't set up your equipment in the aisle, but you can get to a performance early and linger a bit after the curtain to see what your sixth sense is telling you. Ask the staff about their experiences, and if you see a man in old-style clothes and round glasses, tell him he is still doing a good job!**

## Visitor Information

**Grand Opera House**
**100 High Avenue**
**Oshkosh, WI 54901-4809**
**(920) 424-2350**
**www.grandoperahouse.org**

**Hours and Admission:**
**Call or check the website for the current schedule of performances and ticket prices.**

**Directions:**
**From Milwaukee: Take US-45 N toward Fond Du Lac. Continue onto US-41 N. Take exit 116 for South Park Avenue/WI-44/WI-91 toward Ripon Road. Keep right at the fork, follow signs for U.S. 41 W/County Road K/Wittman Aviation Center/ EAA Aviation Center/WI-44 N and merge onto West South Park Avenue/WI-44 N. Turn left at Ohio Street. Continue onto Wisconsin Street. Turn right at High Avenue, the opera house will be on the left.**

He is believed to be Percy Keene, the stage manager here from 1895 until his death in 1967. Obviously, spending seventy-two years in the theater he loved has created a bond between spirit and building that has endured.

It is not uncommon for old theaters to be haunted. To the actors, directors, managers, and production staff, the theater is more than just a job, it is a life's work. And in the case of the Grand Opera House, it also appears to be an afterlife's work!

## The Bottom Line

**The History:** Wisconsin's oldest operating theatre building, which opened in 1883.

**The Haunting:** A former stage manager is seen, along with several other apparitions.

# The Kewaunee Inn

The land upon which this inn was built was purchased from the government in 1835 for the sum of $8.95. In 1858, The Steamboat House hotel was constructed here and became a popular spot for businessmen and travelers on Lake Michigan, and its ballroom even served as a courtroom until 1873. During the Civil War in 1862, this ballroom was a meeting place where the Kewaunee Rifles Company A, 27th Infantry was formed.

The hotel changed hands several times and in 1911 it was purchased by William Karsten, a larger-than-life character both figuratively and literally. At 375 pounds, he was once known as America's largest mayor. He was born in Germany and at the age of 14 ran away for an exciting life at sea, which provided many stories in his later years. He had come to Kewaunee to establish a local Pabst Brewing Company and no doubt had high hopes for his hotel.

Unfortunately, on Valentine's Day in 1912, a kitchen fire spread throughout the building and the historic structure burned to the ground in just three hours. Determined that the Hotel Karsten would rise from the ashes and be bigger and better, plans were drawn up to spend $30,000 on a luxurious new hotel. Exactly one year and $55,000 later, there was the grand opening of the fifty-five-room hotel with its bar and dining room that could serve ninety people.

Karsten lived in the hotel (rooms 205-210) and loved sitting in the lobby chatting with guests—and telling them of his many seafaring adventures. He was greatly saddened by the loss of his beloved wife in 1928, but his own death in 1940 spared him another painful loss. The apple of his eye was his grandson, Billy Karsten III, and just weeks after his grandfather's death, the boy fell seriously ill and died at the age of only 5.

William Karsten, Jr. died in 1964, and the hotel was closed for two years before a series of owners poured substantial time and money into restoring the place. Again closing in 2007, it reopened in 2008 as the Kewaunee Inn at Hamachek Village. William Karsten, Sr. would be proud of the place now…in fact, he probably is as he regularly makes his presence known throughout the inn in a variety of ways, most often in his former rooms. Though generally good natured, he has been known to give off an unpleasant odor and move furniture when he's in a bad mood.

Karsten's grandson is also with him. The energetic boy has often been heard running down the second floor hallway to his grandfather's rooms. Children have even reported playing with a little boy, and later identifying Billy from his photograph!

Then there's the sad story of Agatha, who was the housekeeper from 1925-1937, and stayed in room 310. She suffered a life of tragedies, and she can still be heard weeping. Her white, misty form has been seen in her room, and one member of the staff even clearly saw Agatha in her 1930s maid uniform.

There may be other spirits here as well; those who are drawn to this place by both happy and sad memories. Whoever is here at The Kewaunee Inn may be mischievous, they may surprise you with their appearance or sounds, but they are never threatening. People have come and gone and had good times here since 1858, and there's still plenty of room at the inn for both the living, and those who still think they are.

## Recommendations

**There's a journal in each room so you can read about other guest's experiences. The dining room offers German or Classic American cuisine. The inn is within walking distance of the beach, marina, and shops. Ask for any of the rooms 205-210 for your best chance to encounter big William Karstens, 310 for Agatha's room.**

## Visitor Information

**The Kewaunee Inn**
**122 Ellis Street**
**Kewaunee, WI 54216-1004**
**(920) 388-0800**
**www.kewauneeinn.com**

**Hours:**
**Kitchen open daily 11am – 2pm, 5pm – 9pm (closed Tuesdays), Sunday Brunch 10:30 – 2:30. Tavern open daily 11am – 2pm, 5pm – close (closed Tuesdays).**

**Directions:**
**From Green Bay: Take Main Street/US-141 S. At the traffic circle, take the 2nd exit onto Main Street/US-141 S/WI-29 E/WI-29 Trunk E. Turn left at Kewaunee Road/WI-29 E/WI-29 Trunk E. Continue to follow WI-29 E/WI-29 Trunk E. Continue onto Ellis Street. The inn will be on the right.**

## The Bottom Line

**The History:** The site of a hotel since 1858, the original building burned and a larger structure was built in 1912-13.

**The Haunting:** A former owner and his grandson make their presence known in a variety of ways, as does a former housekeeper.

# Wyoming

WYOMING TERRITORIAL PRISON

WYOMING FRONTIER PRISON

THE VIRGINIAN HOTEL

Wyoming Territorial Penitentiary, North side. Historic American Buildings Survey. *Courtesy of The Library of Congress.*

# Wyoming Territorial Prison

Prisons are usually known for the notorious criminals they have held. In the case of the Wyoming Territorial Prison in Laramie, it has the unique distinction of being the only prison to ever hold one of America's most famous outlaws, Robert LeRoy Parker, better known as Butch Cassidy. However, in a facility that tried to rehabilitate its inmates through education and skill training, it's obvious that Cassidy wasn't paying much attention to his lessons during his eighteen months there, as after his release in 1896 he became the leader of the Wild Bunch gang. The rest, as they say, is history.

The history of the prison began when its construction was completed in 1872. There were only a total of forty-two cells on three levels, and overcrowding often resulted in two inmates per tiny six-foot-square cell. In addition to the lack of room, the physical conditions were quite harsh, as the temperature inside the prison would barely rise above the frigid outdoor winter temperatures.

In its thirty-one years as a federal and state prison, 1,068 men and a dozen women were incarcerated in this facility that was "dedicated to evil doers of all classes and kinds." However, no one convicted of capital offenses was held here, and there were no executions. In fact, despite the number of inmates over the years, only two deaths were recorded within the prison walls. But before you think this was due to the high level of care, it was really a matter of economics—the prison didn't want to pay for burials, so anyone who was dying was pardoned and sent home so relatives could provide the funeral.

Of those two deaths, one was an inmate killed during an escape attempt, and the other was a man named Julius Greenwald, who died as the result of a heart attack. Greenwald was a cigar maker who ended up in prison under unique circumstances. He had a habit of visiting bordellos, even after he was married. One day when he entered his favorite bordello, he discovered that his wife Jennie was working there! Enraged at her choice of a part-time job, he drew his gun and shot her on the spot. Guilty of murder and double standards, Greenwald was sentenced to life in prison, where he continued making cigars until his death in 1901—but that may not be the end of his story.

In 1903, a larger prison was built in Rawlins (see entry on Wyoming Frontier Prison) and the Territorial Prison became a stock farm for the University of Wyoming. In 1989, the structure was renovated and became a museum. During that renovation, Greenwald's cell was removed to make a doorway, and it was the result of this disturbance that some speculate Greenwald's spirit became active.

Numerous people have smelled cigar smoke, and in 1991, two visitors saw a man wearing prison clothes. The figure vanished, but not before the two got a good look at him. Later, when they were looking through photos of former inmates, they both recognized Julius Greenwald as the man they had seen! There are other reports of locked doors opening, cold spots, and a figure seen standing in the doorway where Greenwald's cell had been.

Considering the unsavory characters that were incarcerated in this prison, these are all quite benign occurrences. But then, apart from the brief wife-shooting episode, Greenwald didn't appear to be a very violent man and just wanted to be left in peace to continue practicing his cigar-making skills. Does this man still appear to visitors of the Wyoming Territorial Prison, where he took his last breath? Take the tour and keep your eyes—and nostrils—open for a fleeting figure or whiff of phantom cigar smoke.

## The Bottom Line

**The History:** Opened in 1872, the prison held some of Wyoming's most notorious criminals, including Butch Cassidy. For most of the twentieth century, the University of Wyoming used the property for a stock farm. In 1989, the prison was restored and became a museum.

**The Haunting:** Cigar-maker Julius Greenwald shot his wife and died in the prison. People have reported smelling cigar smoke and seeing his figure standing where his cell used to be.

## Recommendations

You can just tour the prison, or bring a picnic lunch and spend some time enjoying all the sites on the 190-acres. Book early if you want to go on their Ghost Tours of Laramie City during the Halloween season.

## Visitor Information

**Wyoming Territorial Prison**
975 Snowy Range Road
Laramie, WY 82070
(307) 745-6161

**Events:**

There is a self-guided tour of the prison, and the 190-acre site also features a Ranchland Exhibit, the recreated Frontier Town, the historic Horse Barn, the Warden's House, the broom factory, and a gift shop.

Every Halloween season, the Wyoming Territorial Park State Historic Site hosts the popular Ghost Tours of Laramie City, which includes a hayride through historic old Laramie and a candlelight tour of the prison.

**Hours:**

9am – 6pm daily, call for winter hours. Grounds open year round. Frontier Town open weekends only; prison and exhibit hall open May through September.

**Admission:**

$5 for adults and $2.50 for teens 12-17, children under 11 get in free.

*Courtesy of the Wyoming Frontier Prison.*

## Wyoming Frontier Prison

There is the romanticized Hollywood version of western outlaws, and then there is the reality—there were a lot of brutal and vicious men (and women) who needed to be securely locked away forever. Some were so bad they needed to be executed.

Protecting law-abiding citizens from these criminals was what gave rise to the fortress-like Wyoming Frontier Prison, which was designed by the same architects who created Alcatraz. Land was purchased for the prison in the town of Rawlins in 1888, but due to budget problems, the facility didn't open its barred doors to inmates until 1901. For the next 80 years, the prison would see the deaths of over 200 inmates and guards, and be the scene of 14 executions by the gallows and gas chamber.

Almost immediately overcrowded, officials were forced to add another thirty-four cells to the prison in 1904. In 1906, the Dungeon House was built to try to deal with the worst offenders. Even though conditions were most unpleasant in the Dungeon, none of the other 104 cells would have qualified for country club status—they were all cramped and poorly heated with no electricity and no hot water. Two prisoners actually died from the cold. This was hard time for hardened criminals, and for many, death must have seemed like a blessed escape.

Unfortunately, while the stone walls of the main prison building gave the impression of security, chaos was often the order of the day, especially in the early years. Remarkably, while women were incarcerated there, they were not kept separated from the male population, and one doesn't need much of an imagination to envision what kind of trouble that caused! Reason finally prevailed and the last female inmates were transferred to other facilities in 1909.

The first escape occurred in 1903, and subsequent attempts cost several guards, and at least one local resident, their lives. The worst breach took place in 1912 when an astounding thirty prisoners broke out through the wooden stockades. As walls were fortified and security tightened over the years, the number of escapes declined, but clever inmates still found ways to break out.

Of course, for those who were sentenced to death, there was great incentive to try to escape, particularly considering the form of execution that was in use before the gas chamber was introduced in 1936. An architect from Cheyenne, Wyoming, James Julien, decided that it was unfair to subject executioners to the guilt of having to pull the handle of the gallows and send men to their death. He therefore devised an insidious device that in effect forced the prisoner to execute himself.

After the noose was placed around the condemned man's neck, he had to step onto the trapdoor of the Julien Gallows. His weight would activate a switch that would begin draining water from a bucket perched on a lever. The prisoner would have to stand there for as long as two full minutes listening to the streaming water, knowing full well that when the bucket became light enough it would rise and the lever would open the trapdoor. As if the agony of anticipation wasn't enough, the Julien Gallows was not designed to let the prisoner drop far enough to break his neck, so he had to swing in the air until he was slowly strangled to death. Nine men met their fate on these gallows at the Wyoming Frontier Prison.

While the gas chamber may be viewed as being an equally horrific way to go, it was at least a faster end—theoretically at least. The last man to die in the prison's gas chamber was Andrew Pixley in 1965. He reportedly withstood the poisonous cyanide gas at least twice as long as any other man before finally succumbing. But no one need feel any sympathy for Pixley, as he may have been the most evil criminal in Wyoming history, having been found guilty of raping and murdering (and possibly cannibalizing!) two young girls.

Does such evil leave a lasting impression? Perhaps, as it is Pixley and his execution that may be behind two of the prison's ghostly legends. The prison closed in 1981, but was restored and now operates as a historical museum. Members of the staff and visitors taking the tour have commented about the creepy feelings of a presence in Pixley's cell, as if he is still there with them.

The other potential spirit involved with the Pixley case is of a much more unusual nature. Before every execution, the gas chamber would be tested on a pig. However, with no pigs readily available in this instance, a poor stray black cat was used instead. To this day, some of the staff claims to have witnessed a black cat darting through the hallways, only to disappear into thin air.

Many other strange things take place throughout the prison, such as the sound of footsteps and voices, and the overwhelming feeling of anxiety or an angry presence in the Death House, the showers, and the isolation cells. In addition to the unfortunate black cat, human forms have also been seen, including a man in a brimmed hat standing by the gas chamber.

For the most part, the experiences seem to be those of a residual type of haunting—memories and perhaps energies left over from eighty years of criminals and their infamous deeds. A tour of the prison today cannot help but leave a lasting impression in many ways, as one takes a step back into darker times of Wyoming's history. In modern times where prisoners may feel abused if they don't have televisions in their cells, a walk through the Wyoming Frontier Prison will be a stark reminder of what crime and punishment was like not all that long ago.

## Recommendation

**For those interested in a unique part of Wyoming history or who have a fascination for true crime, the guided tour provides a wonderfully unsettling and realistic look at prison life. On the weekend before Halloween and Halloween night, there is a special "Haunted Prison" event. Call for times and Admission:.**

## Visitor Information

**Wyoming Frontier Prison Museum**
**500 W. Walnut Street**
**Rawlins, WY 82301**
**(307) 324-4422**
**www.wyomingfrontierprison.org**

**Hours:**
**The prison museum is open from Memorial Day to Labor Day, 7 days a week from 8:30am – 5:30pm, with 9 tours each day. Tours are available in the off season by appointment.**

**Admission:**
**Guided tours are $7 for adults, $6 for children and seniors, or $30 per family.**

**Directions:**
**On I-80 take exit 211. Turn east onto Spruce Street and drive 1.5 miles. Turn left onto 5th Street. It's two blocks to Walnut Street and the prison will be straight ahead.**

## The Bottom Line

**The History:** The "Old Pen," as it is now called, was opened in 1901 and for eighty years held some of Wyoming's most notorious criminals. Over the years there were many escapes, over 200 deaths, and 14 executions. After the prison closed, the facility was renovated and now offers fascinating guided tours, as well as the Wyoming Peace Officers Association Museum. In 1987, the movie *Prison* was filmed here.

**The Haunting:** Voices and footsteps are heard, figures of various men and a cat have been witnessed, and the strong feelings of a presence have been experienced in many parts of the prison.

*Courtesy of The Virginian.*

# The Virginian Hotel

Owen Wister's 1902 novel, *The Virginian*, is considered to be the book that started the classic cowboy genre. Set in Medicine Bow, Wyoming, the book spawned several movies and a popular television show which ran from 1962 to 1971. It also inspired the name of a historic hotel in the town of Medicine Bow. Opening its doors on 1911, The Virginian hotel offers a genuine experience of the Old West. It may also offer the spirit of a genuine old cowboy. But first, the history.

It was the railroad that gave birth to the town, and it soon became a primary location for shipping cattle. Rough and rowdy as these cattlemen were, however, it was the lumber men who literally rode the logs down the river who were the wildest bunch. Then there were the gamblers, drifters, and all other manner of unsavory characters who rode into town—and they all stayed at The Virginian.

Medicine Bow's first mayor, August Grimm, built the hotel and to assure its future success he went on a special trip. Grimm went to Chicago to make sure the new coast-to-coast Lincoln Highway would pass through his town, thereby providing a steady stream of customers for years to come.

Grimm also went out of his way to make his hotel a very special place, installing the town's first electricity and plumbing. Unfortunately, such ambitions were expensive, and Grimm ran out of money. In order to complete the hotel, he sold shares to local residents, so the town literally banked on The Virginian's success.

Another thing that made the hotel special is now a hidden mystery. Murals of western scenes had been painted on the original walls. Unfortunately, over the years these murals were covered up by layers of wallpaper, and the current owners don't know the locations of these large paintings. Whoever was responsible for putting up the wallpaper made a very costly mistake, because the artist of these murals was none other than Charles Russell, the premier artist of western scenes, whose paintings now fetch millions at auction. Perhaps some day this mystery will be solved and the paintings will be uncovered and restored to their former glory.

There are some interesting features of the hotel's past that are still visible—the bullet holes in the saloon! When an argument erupted over a poker game, the two gamblers drew their guns. Only one of the gamblers walked away alive, and the bullet holes from that fatal shoot out speak volumes about what life was like in this place not all that long ago.

Does an unlucky gunslinger still walk the halls of the old hotel? While it isn't certain who may be walking the halls, staff members do know that someone is sitting on the freshly made beds, and they know his name—

because he told them! For years the staff complained that they would make a bed, carefully smooth out the covers, only to turn their backs for a second and then discover a wrinkled depression on the bed as if a man had just sat down.

One day a frustrated maid, seeing her work once again disturbed, wondered who could possibly be causing all this mischief. Suddenly she heard a male voice saying, "My name is Henry, but I like to be called Hank." To this day, whenever the phantom imprint of someone appears on a bed, the staff will say out loud, "Cut it out, Hank!"

Other people have reported various cold spots, and some claim to have heard the strains of old music. Is all of this activity the result of Hank, or does he have company? No one knows for sure, but clearly some part of the hotel's colorful past can still be encountered here. And even if you are the only one who sits on your bed, The Virginian offers a true western experience that will take you back to a time when cowboys and gamblers made this place their temporary home, before they rode off into the sunset.

## The Bottom Line

**The History:** A 100-year-old hotel that has seen all of the good, the bad, and the ugly that the old west had to offer. There are Charles Russell murals somewhere under the wallpaper, and there are bullet holes in the saloon.

**The Haunting:** Hank likes to tease the staff by sitting in the freshly made beds. There are also reports of cold spots and phantom music.

## Recommendations

Since the hotel is halfway between Laramie and Rawlins, it's the perfect spot to stay on your Wyoming ghost tour. And there's no need to try to rustle up some grub at the nearest chuck wagon, because the hotel also has the Eating House restaurant that serves breakfast, lunch, and dinner. If you're thirsty, there's the hotel's Shilo Saloon, which is proud to say it's just the same as it was a hundred years ago, bullet holes and all! Once you've rested, eaten, and wet your whistle, you can also kick up your heels at one of the dances held in the Back 40. Short of cattle driving, could you get a more complete western experience?

## Visitor Information

**The Virginian Hotel**
404 Lincoln Highway
Medicine Bow, WY 82329
(307) 379-2377
www.medicinebow.org/virginian/
virginianhotel@yahoo.com

**Directions:**

From Laramie and the east: Take 287/US 30 and drive about 53 miles to Medicine Bow.

From Rawlins and the west: From I-80 E/US-287 S/US-30 E, take exit 235 for WY-130/US-30 toward Walcott/Saratoga. Turn left at US-287/US-30/WY-130 and continue to follow US-287/US-30 into Medicine Bow.

# Conclusion

From the smallest B&B, to vast battlefields, this country offers historic sites in all varieties and sizes, but don't let size fool you when it comes to ghosts. That charming, cozy inn on the coast may offer more intense paranormal experiences than the deck of a battleship—even more so if you plan to spend the night!

When planning your historic haunts tour, be sure to keep an open mind and chose a variety of locations. Also, if you limit yourself to crowded ghost tours at peak tourist season, you limit your chances of a true brush with the spirit world. And remember, ghosts do not appear on demand, so be patient, and if time permits visit a site on more than one occasion.

It would help to keep a journal of your travels and encounters, and don't be afraid to share your experiences with the staff and owners of these places. Your insights just might provide the piece of the ghostly puzzle that could solve the mystery of the haunting.

Above all, please be respectful of every haunted location! Many sites have closed their doors to ghost hunters due to their irresponsible behavior, so always conduct yourself in a manner that shows you aren't just a regular tourist—you are an intrepid explorer of America's Historic Haunts...

# Places Index